THE
DIGITAL FILMMAKING
HANDBOOK

THIRD EDITION

THE
DIGITAL FILMMAKING
HANDBOOK

THIRD EDITION

BEN LONG

AND

SONJA SCHENK

CHARLES RIVER MEDIA, INC.

Hingham, Massachusetts

Cover Design: Tyler Creative

CHARLES RIVER MEDIA, INC.
10 Downer Avenue
Hingham, Massachusetts 02043
781-740-0400
781-740-8816 (FAX)
info@charlesriver.com
www.charlesriver.com

This book is printed on acid-free paper.

Ben Long and Sonja Schenk. *The Digital Filmmaking Handbook, Third Edition*.
ISBN: 1-58450-438-2

Library of Congress Cataloging-in-Publication Data

Long, Ben, 1967-
   The digital filmmaking handbook / Ben Long and Sonja Schenk.— 3rd ed.
      p. cm.
   Includes index.
   ISBN 1-58450-438-2 (alk. paper)
  1. Digital cinematography—Handbooks, manuals, etc. 2. Digital video—Handbooks, manuals, etc. 3. Video recording—Data processing—Handbooks, manuals, etc. I. Schenk, Sonja, 1965- II. Title.
   TR860.L64 2005
   778.5'3—dc22

               2005027102

Printed in Canada
05 7 6 5 4 3 2 First Edition

CHARLES RIVER MEDIA titles are available for site license or bulk purchase by institutions, user groups, corporations, etc. For additional information, please contact the Special Sales Department at 781-740-0400.

Requests for replacement of a defective DVD-ROM must be accompanied by the original disc, your mailing address, telephone number, date of purchase and purchase price. Please state the nature of the problem, and send the information to CHARLES RIVER MEDIA, INC., 10 Downer Avenue, Hingham, Massachusetts 02043. CRM's sole obligation to the purchaser is to replace the disc, based on defective materials or faulty workmanship, but not on the operation or functionality of the product.

CONTENTS

CHAPTER 14   EDITING   345

INTRODUCTION

In This Chapter

- Digital Video and the Independent Filmmaker
- What Type of Equipment Do I Need?
- What Is Digital Video?
- Why Digital Video?
- What This Book Covers
- Exercise

In the late 1980s and early 1990s, the term "desktop publishing" was used to indicate graphic design and publishing work that was done using a desktop computer instead of traditional paste-up and photolithography tools. Today, for the most part, people do not differentiate between desktop publishing and "real" publishing because all publishing is now a digital process that is driven by computers.

Digital filmmaking is following a similar course. When we wrote the first edition of this book six years ago, there was "filmmaking," which was performed by "professionals" with lots of money and expensive gear, and there was "digital filmmaking," which was the only alternative for those who couldn't afford the "real thing." Today, that is no longer the case. Increasingly, digital video is seen as a "peer" technology that is often better or more appropriate than film.

Whether it is George Lucas shooting his last two *Star Wars* movies digitally to improve his post-production workflow, or Steven Soderberg and Spike Lee choosing digital video for its exceptional portability, digital video technology is now a respected part of the filmmaker's total potential arsenal.

This doesn't mean that digital video and film yield the same type of results. Film and digital video have very different visual qualities, but both can yield beautiful, professional results. Digital video has come into its own and is no longer the "ugly stepchild" of filmmaking, but there are still some huge differences between the two technologies, the most important being cost.

Digital filmmaking has indeed come into its own. Today all filmmaking is digital to some degree. In fact, there is often no "film" involved in digital filmmaking. Lack of film is the whole appeal of using digital video (DV) technology to make movies. While film, film cameras, and film processing are very expensive, high-quality digital videotape and cameras cost but a fraction, and when you throw in the editing and effects power of a DV-equipped desktop computer, then digital filmmaking becomes substantially more affordable than its celluloid-based alternatives.

For the independent filmmaker, DV technology presents an entirely new model for getting a film made. (See Figure 1.1.)

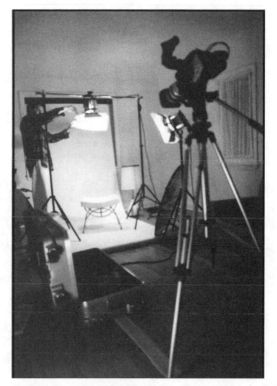

FIGURE 1.1   Photo of a DV production. Using a smaller, digital video crew doesn't mean you have to sacrifice quality. Modern digital video equipment can deliver results that are a good substitute to expensive analog video, high-end digital video, or film.

DIGITAL VIDEO AND THE INDEPENDENT FILMMAKER

"Indie" films are nothing new, but the number of independent productions has increased dramatically since the 1970s and 1980s when people like John Cassavettes, John Sayles, and Spike Lee scraped together shoestring budgets and begged and borrowed equipment and talent to produce their films. In 1998, more than 1000 films were submitted to the famed Sundance Film Festival, and four of 1997's Best Picture Oscar nominees were independent productions. Although independent filmmaking is cheap by Hollywood standards, the independent filmmaker still has to come up with tens or hundreds of thousands of dollars to pay for sets, actors, locations, and, most of all, equipment. In the past, cameras, lights, film stock, editing facilities, special effects, and post-production were the most expensive items in an indie film budget. The indie producer had to cover those costs, just to get the film made at all, with no guarantee that it would be picked up for distribution (meaning no guarantee of a return on the investment).

With digital video, though, those core expenses are much lower. With digital video, it is possible to get a polished, edited feature "in the can" for substantially less than if you were shooting on film. Once your feature is finished, you can use your final, edited digital videotape to shop around for a distributor who will pay for a transfer to film. In other words, you can "back-end" what used to be the most expensive part of indie filmmaking.

Digital Video in the Home and Office

Even if you're not interested in becoming a movie mogul, you might find yourself facing increasing demand for video production. Thanks to Web-based streaming technologies and faster desktop computers, more and more businesses are finding corporate and industrial applications for high-quality video production tools. Whether it's live Webcasting or producing a CD-ROM-based annual report, you might have recently found yourself needing to wear the video producer hat.

Or, it might just be that you want to make a movie simply because it's really fun. The fact is that the collaboration, imagination, and work involved in crafting even a short film is extremely enjoyable. Digital video technology actually makes it possible to be a *hobbiest* filmmaker—something that has never before been possible. And, with Web-based film festivals and distribution, you no longer have to be a hobbyist filmmaker with no audience. You can actually present your finished work to an audience for practically zero cost.

This book will teach you everything you need to know, whether your aim is to create a feature-length production with the hope of a theatrical release, an industrial or corporate production, or a short film or music video simply for your own enjoyment.

This book is meant to be both a start-to-finish production guide and a reference for learning more about particular tasks. For more experienced users, we've included details on the latest technologies, tips and guidelines for transitioning from older video or film technology, and suggestions and strategies for using digital equipment and digital workflow to reduce your production costs. From sophisticated titles to complex compositing, *The Digital Filmmaking Handbook* will show you how to create shots and effects that are rarely associated with low-budget productions.

Full-blown video production is a huge affair that involves many different arts, crafts, and sciences. No single volume can address the tremendous amount of training and expertise that is required to master all of these disciplines. However, we have tried to fill you in on the questions you need to ask and the major problems and issues you will have to solve at each stage of your production. So even though this book doesn't cover, for example, 3D animation, our post-production chapters should at least bring you up to speed on the issues you can expect to face when trying to pull off an effects shoot. These questions should help you better interface with the artisans and craftspeople who *do* have the skills for these various disciplines and point you in the direction of further self-education if that's your intention.

New to this version are updated technical details on the latest hardware and software, including coverage of the latest high-definition digital video formats and technologies such as HDV and HD. In addition, the book has been slightly reorganized so that it more closely matches the workflow of a typical digital filmmaking production.

Whether your goal is an industrial project, a short subject for your Web site, or a feature-length movie for a film festival, *The Digital Filmmaking Handbook, 3rd Edition*, contains everything you need to know to get your project in the can.

WHAT TYPE OF EQUIPMENT DO I NEED?

This book assumes you will be using a Macintosh or Windows-compatible computer. Some familiarity with your operating system of choice is required, as well as a video camera of some kind. Guidelines for selecting equipment are provided throughout the book (see Figure 1.2).

FIGURE 1.2   Typical desktop editing setup showing a Macintosh computer.

We also assume that you are familiar with some basic computer terms—RAM, kilobytes, megabytes, clock speeds, and so forth. A glossary is included in the back of the book.

Finally, although we assume no formal training in video or film production, we might—on occasion—use film and video production-related terms. These are also included in the glossary. You might be surprised to learn how much you already know about video production. Watching movies is the best way to learn the visual literacy required of a good filmmaker, and most people have seen plenty of movies.

WHAT IS DIGITAL VIDEO?

The phrase *digital video* is very confusing because there are many things that are, technically, "digital video." A QuickTime movie downloaded from the Web is digital video, as is an animation generated by a computer graphics program. A video hobbiest might use an inexpensive digital video camera to pour video from her home video camera into her computer, while a big film studio might use special scanners to transfer 35mm motion-picture film into high-end graphics workstations. The results are all "digital video."

Things get even more complicated when you consider that some people use the phrase *digital video* to refer to very specific pieces of equipment (a "DV camera," for example), while others use "digital video" as a broader term that encompasses any type of digitized video or film.

Your computer salesperson might have said something like "with this FireWire interface, this computer is a great 'digital video' machine." What does this really mean? Can you plug any old camera into it? Is the machine ready to create a great new digital video feature-length movie? Unfortunately, the answer to both of those questions is no. However, such a computer can be used as one component of a system that can take video from a video source, edit it, add special effects and graphics, and then output the results to a video or film recorder. In some cases, your source video will be a special digital video camera or tape deck. In other instances, it might be a traditional analog camera or deck. The main difference between a digital and an analog camera is that a digital camera digitizes video *while* you shoot, and stores it on tape in a digital format or even a hard disk, while an analog camera stores video and audio on tape as analog waves.

For the most part, when we say "digital video," we're referring to the broadest definition: a process wherein your source video is "digitized" at some point so that it can be manipulated and edited on the computer.

What Is Digitizing?

A digital video camera is a lot like a flatbed scanner, in that both devices "digitize" an image. A flatbed scanner, for example, divides a page into a grid of tiny pixels and then *samples* each pixel. Each sample is analyzed and assigned a numeric value—a digit, or series of digits—that represents the pixel's color.

A frame of video can be digitized using the same process. However, since one video frame is comprised of an average of 720 × 480 pixels (or 345,600 pixels), and each second of video requires 30 frames, you need a fast computer with a lot of storage to handle even a small amount of video.

A digital video camera has built-in digitizing hardware that digitizes while you shoot and then stores the resulting numbers onto a tape. Consequently, if you use a FireWire connection to transfer video from a DV camera into your computer, you don't technically "digitize" the video, because the camera has already done that for you. Rather, you simply copy the numbers (which represent the digitized images) from the tape into your computer, a process called "capturing."

If you have an analog video camera, then you will need special digitizing hardware in your computer that can change the analog video signal from your camera into digital information and store it on your computer's hard drive. Like a DV camera, these "video capture boards" also compress the video before storing it and decompress it when you're ready for playback. Video capture boards run the gamut from inexpensive, low-quality capturing to very expensive, uncompressed capturing (Figure 1.3). High-end digital video editing (such as HD) also requires special video capture cards.

We'll discuss the details and merits of both systems later in this book.

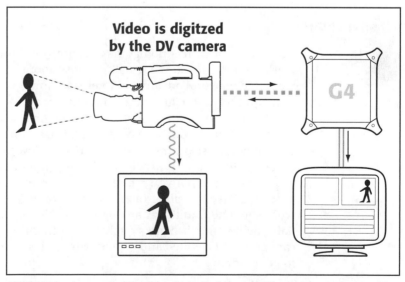

FIGURE 1.3A   In a typical FireWire-based editing workflow, video is digitized by the camera and the resulting digital file is sent to the computer. When editing, the computer transmits a compressed digital signal back to the camera, where it is decoded for playback on an NTSC monitor.

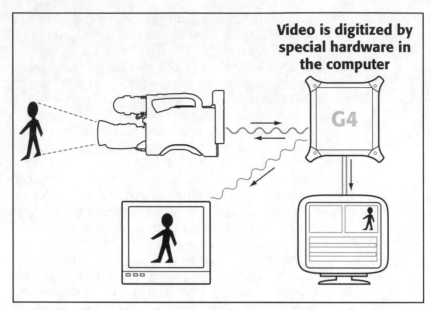

FIGURE 1.3B   If your editing system uses a video capture card, then video is sent to the computer's capture card where it is transferred for editing and converted back for final output to tape. The computer also takes care of sending a signal to a video monitor for playback.

WHY DIGITAL VIDEO?

Obviously, video technology has been around for a while and has been working just fine, so what's all the fuss about? Digital video technology has three potential advantages over traditional video editing and production equipment: quality, function, and price.

Although *inexpensive* might not be the first word you'd use to describe the thousands of dollars you'll need for a computer and digital video equipment, trust us, it's much cheaper than what you'd spend on traditional video or film. With digital video, you don't have the film stock and processing costs that you'd face if you were shooting film, and your computer can take the place of entire racks of equipment you'd need if you were shooting traditional analog video. Digital video formats can potentially deliver much higher quality than traditional analog video formats can, and can be edited and copied with no loss in quality from generation to generation.

PRICE CHECK

How much will it really cost to get your digital video production up and running? The following chart shows two rough price comparisons (circa June, 2005): a medium-budget situation—digital video production using a high-quality DVCAM camera—and a low-budget production—digital video production using a single-chip DV camera. It's noteworthy that the cost of both systems has decreased by about $3000 since the second edition of this book, three years ago. Naturally, the details of your production might vary. If you're shooting on film and transferring the negative to digital videotape, you'll need to consider the added costs of film stock, negative processing, and transfer to video.

DIGITAL VIDEO HARDWARE COSTS

	Medium-Budget	**Low-Budget**
Computer	$1,299[1]	$799[2]
Storage	$979[3]	$169[4]
Camera	$6,000[5]	$2,500[6]
Video deck	$2,700[7]	$500[8]
Speakers, video monitor, cables	$3,500[9]	$500[10]
Editing software	$1,000[11]	$1,000[11]
Tape stock	$1,800[12]	$400[13]
Total:	$17,278	$5868

[1]Macintosh 1.8 GHz G5 iMac with 512MB of RAM, 160GB hard drive, 17" screen, CD burner, 56K modem, two built-in FireWire ports.

[2] Macintosh eMac with 256 MB of RAM, 80 GB hard drive, 17" screen, CD burner, 56K modem, two built-in FireWire ports.

[3]1 Terabyte drive for storage of 80 hours of DV-compressed video, audio and graphics using a single LaCie 1 Terabyte external FireWire drive with Firewire 800 interface.

[4]250GB drive for storage of 15 hours of DV-compressed video, audio, and graphics using external FireWire 400 drive.

[5]Sony DSR-500, rented for four weeks at $1500/week.

[6]Purchased Canon XL2.

[7]Purchased Sony DSR11 DVCAM deck.

[8]Purchased cheap DV camera to use as deck.

[9]Professional video monitor, 8-channel Mackie mixer, self-powered speakers, miscellaneous cables.

[10]Consumer TV set, consumer stereo w/speakers, no mixer.

[11]Both using Apple Final Cut Pro.

[12]Fifty 60-minute DVCAM tapes @ $30 each + 10 90-minute DVCAM tapes for editing.

[13] Fifty 60-minute miniDV tapes @ $10 each + 10 90-minute miniDV tapes for editing.

In addition to being less expensive than film or analog video, your desktop computer can perform functions that are normally not possible using traditional technology (or only possible with very expensive dedicated equipment and teams of skilled craftsmen). The difference between digital and analog video production is as profound as the difference between using a typewriter and using a word processor.

Finally, with digital video, you no longer have to think in terms of pre- and post-production. With laptop computer-based editing systems, for example, you can edit as you shoot, trying out rough edits on-set, which makes it easier to ensure that you've shot what you need.

LINEAR VERSUS NON-LINEAR

The non-linear editing that computers make possible is a great boon, but don't get confused by the linear and non-linear nature of different media. The digital media that you "digitize" or "capture" into your computer is non-linear, which means you have random access to any part of it. Digital *videotape* is a different story; because it's on a piece of tape, it's linear. To access a given point in your digital videotape, you have to roll forward or backward through the tape, just as you do on analog tape.

WHAT THIS BOOK COVERS

This book follows the traditional filmmaking stages of pre-production, production, and post-production. Throughout the book, we'll show you how to throw out the traditional approach and begin to mix and match the different stages of production to take advantage of digital filmmaking technologies.

Part I: Pre-Production

Chapters 2 through 5 cover the traditional stage of "pre-production," the part of the process during which you make all the decisions necessary to start shooting: writing, technology basics, planning, scheduling, storyboarding, set design, and choosing a camera.

Part II: Production

Chapters 6 through 9 cover the traditional stage of "production," the principal shoot of your project: lighting, using the camera, shooting and recording production sound, including tips for special shooting situations such as blue-screen photography.

Part III: Post-Production

Chapters 10 through 19 cover the traditional stage of "post-production": building a workstation, editing room equipment, preparing to edit, advanced editing techniques, sound design, color correction, titles, special effects, and delivery of the finished product—everything from streaming video for the Web to getting your 35mm release print.

EXERCISE

If you're seriously thinking of embarking on a digital filmmaking production, you're about to begin a very complicated process. The more you know before you start, the more smoothly things will go for you. Before you dive in, you should know the answers to these questions:

- What is your final product? Projected 35mm film? Home video? Broadcast television? DVD? Live Webcast? CD-ROM? Foreign release? Corporate/educational use? (Chapters 3 and 19 can help you understand the technical specifications for these different formats.)
- What peripheral products will you be creating? Work-in-progress DVD copies, trailers, press kits? Outputting different formats requires more planning than a project that sticks to one type of output does.
- What equipment do you already own or have access to that you can use to produce your project? Consider this question carefully, as some older equipment—especially computer equipment—might be more of a hindrance than a help.
- How much time and money do you want to spend in post-production?

If you take the time to make some hard decisions before you shoot, you'll save time and money throughout the process. You may not know all the answers, but you should at least know all the questions.

2 WRITING AND SCHEDULING

In This Chapter

- Writing for Digital Video
- Scheduling
- Exercises
- Summary

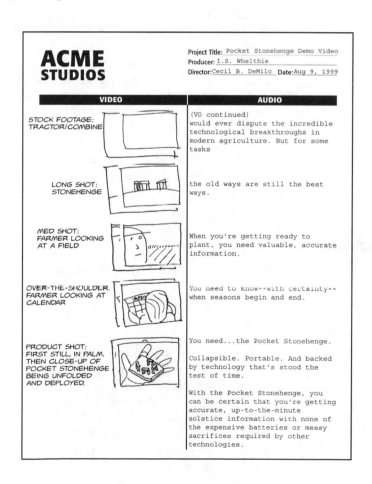

All successful video productions begin, of course, with a well-written script and a lot of planning. Planning can involve everything from budgeting and scheduling, to pre-visualizing your shots using storyboards or animation software. Because pre-production is where you'll determine much of the look and quality of your project, good planning weighs heavily on your production and post-production success.

If you're eager to start shooting, then it can be tempting to skimp on planning, but foregoing any part of the planning stage can lead directly to increased expenses and headaches. Bear in mind that planning is probably the *last* time in your production cycle where your project is still truly under your control, so you might as well enjoy it! Once production starts, you'll have to start facing the reality of things going wrong, so revel in the joy of imagining and planning for how you'd *like* things to go.

In this chapter, we're going to thoroughly discuss the writing and scheduling of your project. Due to space limitations, we won't be covering budgeting or financing in this book. However, there are voluminous budgeting and scheduling articles that you can download for free from *www.dvhandbook.com/budgeting*.

Pre-production is a very dynamic process. For example, your schedule is often affected by the size of your budget, and troubles with scheduling can often impact your finances, which might shrink your budget, which could result in the need for rescheduling. Both schedule and budget are, of course, guided by the nature of your script. Because these processes all affect each other, it's important to realize that pre-production is not necessarily a linear, step-by-step process. Keep that in mind while reading this chapter.

WRITING FOR DIGITAL VIDEO

No doubt, at some point in your life you've read a book that's been made into a movie. And, no doubt, you've probably walked out of the movie adaptation thinking "why did they change that part?" or "why did they leave that other part out?" It's easy to simply think that the screenwriter did a bad job and, certainly, moviemakers don't always share your own take on the emotional tone of a particular book.

More often than not, though, movie adaptations are very different from their source books because cinema and prose are simply very different art forms. To think that a book can be directly translated into a movie shows an ignorance of the particular narrative, pacing, and content differences that exist between these two forms. Someone once said "trying to talk about music is like trying to dance about architecture." Trying to make a straight translation from written text to moving images is almost as difficult.

The point is: screenwriting is a very particular type of writing and, as such, it demands a good amount of study and practice. No amount of production can save a poorly written script, so it's important to spend the time building a sturdy screenplay.

No matter what type of project you're shooting—feature film, documentary, corporate training video—you still need to understand the basic concepts of good storytelling and strong screenwriting.

Finding a Story

We're going to spend a lot of time talking about "story," so let's get some basic concepts out of the way. Consider the following:

> Mary had decided to go for a walk, so she called her dog, Spot, got his leash, and went outside. She walked down the sidewalk and crossed the street in front of the small, neighborhood grocery store. She liked the store and was always happy to see the "regulars" buying their food. She kept walking until she got to the park. As always, the park was filled with dogs that were running, and jumping, and catching Frisbees. Both she and Spot really liked it in the park.

Not much of a story, huh? In fact, Mary's story isn't really a "story" at all, it's just a series of events. That series of events could continue for pages and pages, covering all of the events that happened during Mary's day. In the end, we would simply have a much longer, boring description of a bunch of events.

"Maybe Mary is just a boring person," you might be thinking. Certainly, subject matter has a lot to do with making a story interesting. If Mary was an international super-spy instead of a woman walking her dog, the story might automatically be more interesting. However, even with the seemingly boring events of Mary's life, it is possible to tell a more compelling story:

> Mary was going stir crazy. She'd been stuck in the house all day long and it was starting to get to her. She called her dog, Spot, put on his leash, and went outside. She crossed the street in front of her neighborhood grocery store. She liked the store and always felt comfortable there. But now, when she looked in and saw the lines of people loaded down with heaps of cans and boxes, she just felt more stir crazy. She walked on until she finally reached the park, and there, at last, she was able to relax.

This story might not be Shakespeare, but it does feel more like a story than a simple chain of events. However, both stories contain exactly the same series of events. Nothing new happens in the second story—it's still just a tale of a woman going for a walk with her dog—but in the second story Mary has a goal: she's stir crazy and she needs to relax. This goal is stated in the very first sentence.

The simple addition of a goal provides a structure and direction to the tale, transforming it from a chain of events into a story. Why does this difference matter? Because the goal we created is not just for Mary. By stating it, we've also given the reader a goal—something to find out, a reason to continue listening.

 No matter what type of production you're planning, your first writing task is to decide what your story is about. Industrial and corporate presentations, music videos, documentaries, marketing or advertising pieces—they all need to have clear, well-defined stories even if the story is as simple as the one about Mary and her dog.

Structure

In the preceding example, we took a pretty boring chain of events and turned them into a story by giving our main character a goal. However, we did something else as well: we gave the story a structure. If you look at the second story, you'll see that it has a very definite beginning, middle, and end.

In the beginning, we learn that Mary has a problem: she's stir crazy. In the middle, we see her go to a store, which is normally comforting, but this doesn't solve her problem. Perhaps her problem is worse than she realized. In the end, she finally finds a comfortable place to be and is no longer stir crazy.

Learning this simple structure will do more than anything else to help you tell better stories and make better movies. Not only will you be able to create movies that are more interesting to your audience, but by following this structure, you'll have an easier time finding your way through the writing, shooting, and editing of your movie.

This beginning/middle/end structure is commonly referred to as *3-act structure,* and it is the basis for all Hollywood movies. If "beginning, middle, and end" is too abstract, think of the three sections as *setup, complication,* and *payoff.* In our story about Mary, the setup was that she was stir crazy, the complication was that her usual way of calming down didn't work, and the payoff was that she finally found peace.

Failure to deliver on any of these parts results in very predictable audience reactions. Projects that have a weak first act (the setup) are usually perceived as boring; projects with a weak second act (the complication) are usually seen to be lacking in substance; and projects with a weak third act (the payoff) are typically regarded as pointless.

This beginning/middle/end structure can be applied to any type of production. Even if you're doing a simple corporate training video that is nothing more than a talking head, what that head says should have a discernible structure. Remember, 3-act structure is designed to keep your audience engaged and compelled.

Treatments

If you've worked out the details and structure of your story, you might want to consider writing a "treatment" before you begin writing the script. A treatment is the telling of your story in prose. Sometimes your treatment will have some dialog, at other times it will simply be a description of what's happening in the story. Treatments help you organize your thoughts, get any initial images and dialog down on paper, and serve as a way to present your story to other people. If you have a producer or investor who's interested in your story idea, showing him a treatment might help you secure some funding.

Hollywood Structure

Hollywood movies use a very well-defined, *3-act structure*. In fact, it's so well defined, you can usually set your watch to it.

> **Act I: The beginning.** Wherein the main character is introduced, along with his or her nemesis, and the supporting cast. The main character's "problem" is also introduced. This section usually takes 20 to 30 minutes.
> **Act II: The middle.** The main thing that happens in Act II is that the character's problem is complicated. This is the bulk of the movie, and any subplots are usually introduced and solved here. Very rarely are new characters introduced in this act. Halfway through the act—that is, in the exact middle of the movie—the main character's luck will change, and things will start working out in his or her favor. By the end of the second act, the solution to the problem will be clear. This act is usually 40 to 50 minutes long.
> **Act III: The end.** In this act, the main character's problem is solved. This usually takes about 20 minutes.

Yet another way to define this structure is: Act I: Introduce the hero; Act II: Torture the hero; Act III: Save the hero.

Unlike a stage play, there is never a clear separation of acts presented in a movie. The actual change might be a simple cut from one scene to another, or the scene might just barrel on ahead into the new act. It's not important that the audience *knows* where the act breaks are, but that doesn't mean that they aren't there.

You don't have to follow this structure, and many movies don't. However, it is a fairly simple, effective way of ensuring a compelling story that "moves."

RAIDERS OF THE LOST ARK

Raiders of the Lost Ark follows the typical Hollywood structure very closely, and so provides a good example of how 3-act structure works (if you haven't seen the movie, you'll need to in order for this explanation to work).

Act I ends right after the fight in Marion's bar. We have all of our main characters, and we have our problem—find the Ark before the Nazis do.

Act II ends when the Nazis show up to take the Ark off the ship. More specifically, it ends when Indy swims to the Nazi sub and climbs aboard. With Indy, the Nazis, the girl, and the Ark all on board, we're ready for the final confrontation.

Act III ends with the end of the movie. He got the Ark (never mind that it was taken away from him by the good guys, he still did what he was supposed to do).

More about Structure

For more about feature film structure, check out www.dvhandbook.com/structure. *This essay provides a much more detailed analysis of the structure of* Raiders.

Writing Visually

Most beginning screenwriters make a very simple mistake: they forget that movies are made up of *pictures*. Yes, there's dialog and talking and music and all that other stuff, but first and foremost: movies are a *visual* form of storytelling.

Let's go back to *Raiders of the Lost Ark* for a moment. Consider the beginning of the movie. In *Raiders*, you have to go two minutes into the movie before you encounter the first line of dialog, the line "the Hovitos are near." In other words, the first two minutes are told completely in pictures. Sure, there's music and sound effects, but you can turn the sound down and the scene still makes sense.

In screenwriting "show, don't tell" should be your constant mantra. To understand more about writing visually, check out the essay Writing Visually.pdf located at *www.dvhandbook.com/writing*.

Write Silents

One of the best ways to practice writing visually is to deny yourself dialog. Writing silent shorts and scenes is a great way to learn how to explain things without talking. An example of a silent short script entitled Consumer Electronics is included in the Chapter 2>Tutorials folder of the companion DVD.

Script Format

Traditional movie screenplays have a very specific format that has been designed and refined to convey much more than just dialog and scene descriptions. Screenplay format makes it easy to quickly judge budget and scheduling concerns in a script. No matter what type of project you're working on, writing screenplays in this format will make your production job much easier.

Screenplay Format

One of the biggest advantages of screenplay format is that it makes it easier to determine the length and pacing of your script. If you follow standard screenplay margins and layouts, your script will average one minute of screen time per page. In reality, there is a lot of variation, of course. A one-page description of an epic sea battle might actually take five minutes of screen time, while a page of witty banter might fly by in 20 seconds. On average, the one-page-per-minute rule is a good guideline to follow.

If you follow traditional screenplay format, your script will be divided into scenes delineated by *sluglines*. A slug tells whether the following scene is INTerior or EXTerior, the location of the scene, and whether the scene takes place during the day or night. For example:

```
INT. MAD SCIENTIST'S PANTRY—NIGHT
```

Sluglines make it easy to count and reorder your scenes, and make it simple for a producer to quickly arrive at an approximation of cost. If your script has a lot of EXT scenes at NIGHT, then it's going to be more expensive (lights, location shots, and overtime add up quickly). Similarly, if your slugs all run along the lines of:

```
EXT. UPPER ATMOSPHERE OF MARS—NIGHT
```

then it's pretty obvious that your script is effects-heavy and, therefore, expensive.

Standard screenplays are always typed in 12-point Courier with the margins shown in Figure 2.1.

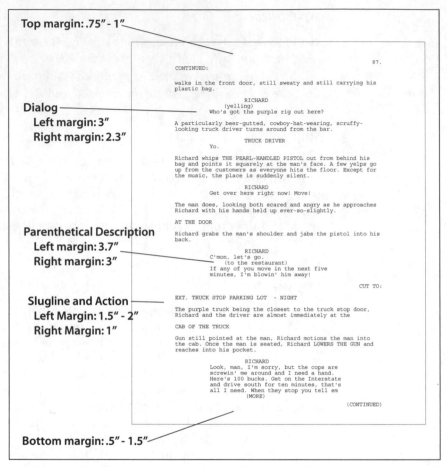

Top margin: .75″ - 1″

Dialog
  Left margin: 3″
  Right margin: 2.3″

Parenthetical Description
  Left margin: 3.7″
  Right margin: 3″

Slugline and Action
  Left Margin: 1.5″ - 2″
  Right Margin: 1″

Bottom margin: .5″ - 1.5″

FIGURE 2.1 Although measurements can vary, if you use the margins shown here you'll have a script formatted in "standard" screenplay format.

Standard screenplay format has a number of other conventions as well. For example, if a scene continues from one page to the next, then "CONTINUED" is placed at the bottom of the first page. Similarly, if a character's dialog jumps to another page, then "MORE" is placed below the flowing dialog. Through the years, screenplay conventions have been refined and standardized as a way of making script breakdown, budgeting, and scheduling much simpler. It's safe to say that if your screenplay is not formatted according to standard conventions, no one in the film industry will read it. A poorly formatted screenplay is an instant indication of a very "green" screenwriter.

A Sample Screenplay

In the Chapter 2>Tutorials folder of the companion DVD is a copy of a scene from Richard III (Richard III.pdf) presented in standard screenplay format. This document will let you see what a normal screenplay should look like. We'll be using this script for many examples later in the book. The Richard III Cut.pdf is an alternate version of the scene that we'll be looking at later.

Two-Column Formats

If you're writing a script for a news, industrial, corporate presentation, or advertising production, then you'll most likely want to use a two-column, A/V script format. Much simpler than screenplay format, A/V formats are ideal for planning and scripting live broadcasts, short subjects, and other multi-camera, multi-source shoots (Figure 2.2).

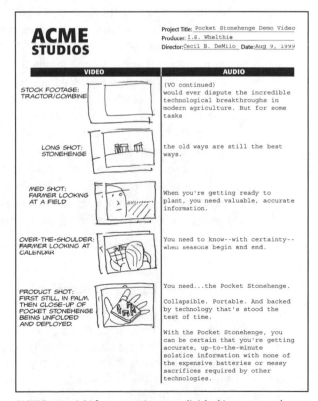

FIGURE 2.2   A/V format scripts are divided into two columns, one for the spoken text (either live talent or voice-over), and another showing simple sketches of any accompanying visuals. Because of its simple format, the same A/V script can be used by on-camera talent, directors, and editors.

Sides

Sometimes it is useful to create "sides" for your talent, especially when recording dialog or voice-over narration. "Sides" usually consist of one or two relevant pages pulled out of your script. Often they only contain the actors' lines, making it easier to read and giving the actor(s) more freedom to uniquely interpret the dialog by removing stage directions that would otherwise dictate the performance.

SCREENWRITING SOFTWARE

A whole range of writing software exists that not only makes it easy to render your scripts in standard screenplay format, but also provides some valuable tools for editing and restructuring your script.

For standard screenplay formats, programs such as BC Software's *Final Draft* and *Final Draft A/V* format your scripts as you write (Figure 2.3). Anyone who has tried to add all the MOREs and CONTINUEDs manually will find this one feature worth the investment. In addition to formatting, *Final Draft* provides a lot of automation. Character names can be entered by simply typing the first few letters of a name, and the program does a very good job of anticipating what the next character's name will be, making it simple to type back-and-forth dialog. *Final Draft* provides other utilities, including a Scene Navigator that lets you see your scenes as a series of index cards that can be easily rearranged (Figure 2.4). Before you make a final choice as to which program to use, consider that some packages work in tandem with other software to automate your budgeting and scheduling tasks. If you can afford it, it's worth considering packages that work together to create a complete pre-production toolbox.

Writing for Corporate and Industrial Productions

For the most part, when you write for any type of "industrial" project—be it a training video, marketing piece, or presentation video—you face the same issues and concerns as when you write a fictional short or feature. You still have a story to tell, that story needs to have a structure, and you must tell that story visually. So, just as you need to apply a goal and structure to a fictional script, corporate and industrial scripts also need to have the same type of beginning/middle/end narrative drive to them. Corporate and industrial scripts are usually heavily based on interviews, or on voice-over narration with additional video footage or graphics to illustrate concepts. Even though these types of video do not always

FIGURE 2.3 *Final Draft* provides a complete, automated screenplay-writing environment. Character names, scene locations, and other repeating elements can be automatically entered by the program. Most importantly, *Final Draft* automatically indents and paginates your screenplay according to standard, accepted specifications.

FIGURE 2.4 Like many screenwriting programs, *Final Draft* includes a special Scene Navigator mode that lets you view your script as a series of index cards, one per scene. In this mode, you can simply rearrange cards to restructure your script.

have "dramatic" real-world scenes in them, they still benefit from a sturdy 3-act structure.

Before you commit any words to paper, try to get a clear idea of the "problem" that will be solved. Introducing and explaining the problem will constitute your first act. Next, you'll want to explain why this problem is difficult to solve and perhaps delve into why others have failed. This will serve as your second act, the complication. Then, you present the solution to the problem.

In a fictional project, the second act is usually the longest. In a corporate production, however, the third act is usually the longest, as you'll want to spend a long time dealing with the details of the solution you're proposing.

Corporate productions have an additional wrinkle, though. Before you begin writing you need to give thought to who you believe the audience is for your particular production. A production aimed at a management team will probably have a very different message from one aimed at a board of directors. If your audience already has a deep understanding of the problem you're going to present, then you'll want to make a shorter first act, and devote the time to beefing up the areas that they'll be less familiar with. You don't want to bore your audience with information they already have, so an understanding of who your intended audience is, what they already know, and what they need to know, is essential.

Corporate script writing often involves several levels of approval, and this type of writing by committee can quickly become a frustrating "too many cooks in the kitchen" kind of situation. Because you don't want to invest a lot of time writing a detailed script, only to have it ripped asunder by your boss or client, it's often best to write your first few script passes in the form of simple treatments. Treatments are easier to write, and allow you to quickly present a concept that can then be re-worked and adjusted before you start writing the actual shooting script.

Writing for Documentaries

Documentary "writing" is a little different from the other forms of script writing that we've discussed because it's usually more of a "journalistic" type of writing. There are two approaches to documentary production:

- Inductive, where you spend as much time as you need, (or can afford) shooting your subject, and then cut that source footage into a finished product.
- Deductive, where you write a scripted piece and then go out and shoot the footage you need to support that script.

In an inductive documentary, the shooting and editing is, in a sense, the writing process. During shooting, you'll capture all of the raw material that you will then pare down and organize into a finished edited piece. In a deductive documentary, the production process is more akin that of scripted projects.

There's no right or wrong way to work, though there are advantages and pitfalls to each approach. An inductive process is usually better for covering an event, person, or place. You'll want to keep an open mind and not have any preconceived notions about your subject, lest you blind yourself to good footage or important events. But even if you're committed to being open-minded, you'll still benefit from planning and anticipating the problems and challenges of your shoot by creating a shot list. Later, when you get back to the editing room, you'll look at your footage and try to see what kind of story is there. Often, you'll be surprised to find out that the final story is very different than what you thought it was going to be.

In the deductive process, you'll do your research and learning at your writing desk. Once you've finished writing, you'll then try to find footage that illustrates your text. Though shooting will occasionally lead you to revise your script and make changes on the fly, in general your final project will probably end up fairly close to what you scripted.

Finishing Up

Eventually, after many rewrites, you'll have a "finished" script. (The script won't really be finished because you'll make loads of changes in production and post-production, but you'll at least have something you can use to start shooting.) Presumably you've already gotten some feedback at this point, either from friends, former friends, colleagues, or relatives. Now you're ready to start preparing for your shoot.

The Pitch

Unfortunately, you can't expect your script to speak for itself. Most potential backers and crewmembers won't have the time or patience to read an entire script, so you'll have to win them over with a good pitch. For more on pitches, check out www.dvhandbook.com/pitching.

SCHEDULING

The first step in taking a story from the page to the screen is to create a schedule for the production. To make a realistic *shooting schedule*, you'll need to determine the resources you need for each scene, the number of script pages you'll try to shoot each day, and the order in which you want to shoot the scenes. There are many variables involved in every production—actors, crewmembers, props, locations, available daylight and weather conditions, equipment rental limitations, and so on. The organization of these elements can be complicated and difficult, and variables can change at any time. In addition to managing resources, a good schedule also helps you conform to a specified budget while allowing for the creative needs of the production.

There's an adage in Hollywood that a film can be any two of the following three things: good, fast, or cheap. Assuming you want your project to be good (we hope!), then your production will probably be either slow or expensive. Are you going to choose to shoot slowly, working around actors' and crewmembers' day jobs? Or are you going to throw all the money you can at the production and get it over with quickly? There are advantages and disadvantages to both choices. A fast shoot means that the cast and crew are fully dedicated to the project. A long shoot might lack focus, but can provide the time for editing scenes as you go, allowing you to identify and reshoot things that don't seem to work.

As you might have guessed, scheduling is intimately tied to budgeting. Often, the same person who creates the schedule also creates the budget. You can create a realistic schedule without a budget, but you do need to have a general idea about how much money you can afford to spend on the principal shoot, whether it's $2,000 or $200,000. A $2,000 budget for a feature-length project will be dependent on getting most things for free—especially locations, props, and talent—so scheduling a day of shooting in the ballroom of the most expensive hotel downtown is probably not going to be an option. With $200,000, however, the ballroom is something you can realistically consider. Keeping your budgetary limitations in mind is the key to creating a realistic schedule.

Breaking Down a Script

The first step in creating a shooting schedule is to analyze your script to determine exactly what you'll need in terms of cast, crew, locations, props, and other resources. Fill out a breakdown sheet for every scene in your movie, using a form like the one shown in Figure 2.5. Script breakdown marks the first time that you'll need to translate your vision of each scene into a list of tangible things. Be meticulous as you make these lists, so that you don't leave out anything important. It's also a good idea to consult with your director of photography, art director, costume designer, and so forth during this process.

Choosing a Shooting Order

Once you've determined the resources you'll need for each scene, you can start to organize your shoot accordingly. You might organize the shoot in terms of your locations, shooting all of the scenes in the main character's house first, then all of the scenes at his job, and so on. Or, you

SCRIPT BREAKDOWN

SCENE #	SCENE NAME		BREAKDOWN PAGE #
DESCRIPTION			INT. OR EXT.
SCRIPT PAGE			DAY OR NIGHT

CAST	EXTRAS	EXTRAS/ATMOSPHERE
PROPS	**WARDROBE**	**MAKE-UP/HAIR**
VEHICLES	**SPECIAL EQUIPMENT**	**SOUND FX/MUSIC**

FIGURE 2.5   A sample breakdown sheet. To begin scheduling, you need to fill out such a sheet for each scene in your script (a template for this breakdown sheet, breakdown.pdf, is included in the Chapter 2 folder on the companion DVD).

ON THE DVD

might organize the shoot based on the availability of cast members, or the need for special shooting conditions, such as a blue-screen stage or a rain-storm. Or, you might want to schedule the biggest, most expensive, most complicated scene first to guarantee that it gets shot before you run out of money, or last to make sure that you don't blow your entire budget on a single expensive scene.

If you organize the shoot in one of these ways, you'll be shooting *out of sequence*. It's very common to shoot out of sequence, but many people prefer to shoot as close to the script order as is reasonably possible to get better performances from the actors. Just imagine if you were an actor and had to shoot a scene where you celebrate your first wedding anniversary one day, and then shoot the scene where you first meet her on the next day. On the other hand, if your movie includes a subplot about a terrorist who never interacts with the main characters until the final scene, you can easily shoot all those subplot scenes out of order without making things difficult for the actors.

CHAOS THEORY

Why is good scheduling important? Consider the following production schedule scenario for a medium-budget DV production with a union cast and crew:

You're shooting a Western on location in Arizona. Everything's good to go, you have a bunch of extras, four actors, and a union crew. After getting everyone from the airport to the location—which counts as a day of paid labor plus per diem money for cast and crew—you awaken at your desert location the next day to a giant thunderstorm. It's short-lived, but now the dusty town isn't very dusty. Luckily, you've prepared for just such an event by scheduling alternate "cover sets" throughout your shoot. Therefore, you move everyone into the saloon to shoot the gambling scene. Unfortunately, you don't need your lead actress for this scene, but you'll have to pay her anyway, since anything less than a 10-day break is considered a "holding" day in a SAG (Screen Actor's Guild) agreement. To "hold" her, you'll have to pay her.

Because of the delays due to changing locations, you're only going to shoot one page of script instead of the three that you were aiming for that day. Moreover, you have a very early, 3:00 A.M. call tomorrow for some crew members, and you have to give them 10 hours of "turnaround"—the time between the "wrap" of one day's shoot and the "call" of the next day's shoot. This means that your lighting crew and art department must leave the set at 5:00 P.M., to have enough turnaround time before you need them at 3:00 the next morning. It's hectic, and you're patting yourself on the back for having it all under control, when your lead actor takes you aside and explains that shooting the gambling scene out of sequence is a big problem for him, motivation-wise, so he'd prefer to shoot the scene in the barn where he has a heart-to-heart talk with his horse. Unfortunately, the horses don't arrive until tomorrow.

How Much Can You Shoot in a Day?

Traditionally, most film productions aim to shoot a certain number of pages each day. Studio films often shoot about two pages per day, whereas many independent filmmakers must opt for a less luxurious schedule, often shooting upwards of four pages per day. Of course, this all depends on what you are shooting. Typically, a page of dialogue requires much less time to shoot than a page of action does. A page that includes special effects will require even more time.

Production Boards

Shooting schedules for feature films use a tool developed long before the advent of computers: the *production board*. Production boards provide a method for tracking a very large amount of information in a way that's modifiable and portable. Using the information that's entered in the breakdown sheets (refer back to Figure 2.5), you create a production strip for each scene in the film. Each production strip contains the duration of the scene (in script pages), the slugline of the scene, and a one-line description of the scene. The production strips are placed in a set of production boards. The result is a spreadsheet with rows of cast member names and other important elements, and columns for each scene in the movie (Figure 2.6). At the intersections of the rows and columns, you can see which cast members are involved in a scene, and when those scenes will be shot. In addition to cast members, you can list special props and equipment. The final set of production boards is a hard-backed folder that is taken onto the set for easy reference. Because each scene is on a separate, removable strip, you can easily rearrange the scene order on the fly if, for example, an actor gets sick or the location is rained out. Production boards allow for the type of thinking on your feet that's always necessary during a shoot. You can buy traditional production boards and strips at a film stationery supplier.

USING *MOVIE MAGIC SCHEDULING* SOFTWARE

No matter what your project, film production scheduling software such as Screenplay Systems' *Movie Magic Scheduling* can be invaluable. *Movie Magic Scheduling* can import properly formatted screenplays and automatically create breakdown sheets (Figure 2.5) and production strips (Figure 2.6). Screenplay Systems also makes production boards and paper for printing production strips that you can put in special plastic sleeves for placement on the production board.

Sheet Number:	1	2	3	4	— End Of Day 1 — 7/22/99 — 12 7/8 pgs.	13	39	16	11	12	14	— End Of Day 2 — 7/23/99 — 138 3/8 pgs.	5
Page Count:	2 3/8	2 5/8	3 1/8	4 6/8		14 4/8	37 6/8	38 3/8	10 5/8	13 5/8	23 4/8		6 3/8
Shoot Day:	1	1	1	1		2	2	2	2	2	2		3
	EXT - Intersection - Cole/Carl - Night Scs. 1, 2	EXT - Top of stairs outside X's building - Ni Scs. 6	INT - Leo's apartment building - Night Scs. 4	INT - Leo's Room - Night Scs. 5		INT - Leo's Room - Day Scs. 15	INT - Leo's Room - Day Scs. 39	INT - Leo's Room - Day Scs. 44	INT - Leo's Room - Night Scs. 12	INT - Bathroom in Leo's apartment - Night Scs. 14	INT - Leo's Room - Night Scs. 24		INT - Leo's Room - Day Scs.

Rush

Director: B Long
Producer: B Baker
Asst. Director:
Script Dated: July 1, 1999

Character	No.	1	2	3	4		13	39	16	11	12	14		5
Leo	1	1	1	1	1		1	1	1	1	1	1		1
Annie	2							2	2					
Grandfather	3													
John	4													
Satij	5													
Wayne Houston	6													
Dan Tuttle	7													7
Vince	8			8	8									
Bill	9													
Bus Dev 1	10													
Bus Dev 2	11													

Extras:

| | Leo Arrives in town and gets off the MUNI | Leo arrives at his front door for the first time | Leo arrives inside his apartment for the first time | Leo sees his room for the first time | | Leo wakes up for his first day on the job | Leo shows Annie his project for the first time | Leo calls Annie for the first time | Leo sits by his window and sketches | Leo brushes his teeth and finds his mail | Leo arrives home after his first day on the job | | Leo wakes up and calls Dan Tuttle on the phone |

FIGURE 2.6 Screenplay Systems' *Movie Magic Scheduling* can automatically import text from your screenwriting software and generate production strips and boards.

Pick-Ups

After you're done with your principal shoot, you might find that you need to reshoot or add new scenes. These "pick-ups" are usually shot after a first rough cut has been finished. Maybe there was a video drop-out in the only good take of a key scene, or maybe you decided that the way an actor played a scene doesn't work. Most projects schedule a few days or a week for pick-ups to reduce the likelihood of cast and crew availability problems.

Scheduling for Documentaries

While scheduling for a feature or industrial project can be complicated, you at least know what your end product is going to be and so can account for all of the shots that you might need to get. With a documentary project, or any form of "journalistic" project, where you're covering a person or event with no set goal or list of particular shots or scenes, your scheduling tasks will be a little different.

They're called "documentaries" for a reason; your goal when shooting one is to document your subject as thoroughly as possible so that you'll have plenty of footage to work with once you're back in the editing room. In general, you'll probably shoot 20 to 30 times more footage than you'll actually use, and in some cases this ratio may go even higher.

Obviously, if you're covering a particular event, your scheduling chores center around the duration of that event. If it's a complex event that involves several crews of shooters, then you'll need to map out a shooting strategy and schedule ahead of time. Similarly, if you only have one camera rig but it's a very long event, then you'll need to schedule your crew in shifts for continuous shooting.

Most of your other shooting tasks will probably involve interviews or trips to other locations to gather supporting material. Scheduling these is usually just a simple process of sorting out which interview subjects or locations are available at particular times and scheduling accordingly.

Though documentary scheduling is nowhere near as complex as feature film scheduling, you still need to give it some serious thought during your pre-production cycle.

EXERCISES

1. If you're finding yourself a little short on ideas for scripts and stories, why not give yourself a predefined structure of some kind. That's what we did for the *Consumer Electronics* script that's included on the DVD in the Chapter2>Tutorials folder. We wanted to write a short, and we wanted it to be something we could shoot easily, so we decided to try to think of a story that could be shot in a house, and that featured a single item that one might find in a typical home. To make the exercise a good lesson in visual storytelling, we also delineated that it had to be a dialog-free scene. We'll be using this script throughout our production examples. If you'd like to follow along with your own project, try writing a simple story using the same guidelines.

ON THE DVD

2. One of the hardest tasks that a writer faces is cutting his script, but it's very easy to write things that are too long. Usually, any "fat" in your script becomes obvious once you start shooting. Sometimes, though, you might have a good, tight script, but still be bound by time or money. That was our problem when we decided to shoot a scene from *Richard III*. Take a look at the Richard III.pdf file in the Chapter 2>Tutorials folder. This is the complete Shakespeare scene and it runs over 10 minutes when read by the actors. We wanted it to come in

ON THE DVD

around 5 minutes. See if you can cut it down to that length. (To see our cutting, with some explanations of why we chose the cuts we did, check out the Richard.rft file will use in Chapter 14.)

3. A simple writing warm-up. Although it might not always feel like it, your brain constantly makes things up and tells stories. Very often, though, this storytelling part of your brain is tripped up by the rational, sensical part of your brain. Try this simple yet difficult exercise: Get a piece of paper and a pen and start writing a story while counting backward, out loud, from 100. Count at a consistent, regular pace and don't stop writing. The idea is that the counting will tie up that sense-obsessed part of your brain, freeing the content-creating part to write. Lean too far in either direction and you'll stop counting or stop writing. When you do it right, you'll usually find that you get stories that are very dream-like. Just as you need to warm up before exercising, or playing a musical instrument, performing writing warm-ups before you start can often greatly ease your real writing work.

4. Because it's a rhythm, 3-act structure is something you can actually start to feel after a while, once you start learning to pay attention to it. Being able to recognize the rhythms in the movies you watch will help you better understand and control the structure and rhythmic beats in your own script. Start watching movies with an eye toward picking out the act breaks and other rhythmic elements. Can you feel where Act I is? Where the midpoint is? When Act III begins? See if you agree. Be warned, though: once you start watching movies with an eye or feeling toward these structural devices, it can change the way you experience some stories. Suspense stories, in particular, become much less suspenseful when you're able to realize things like "this must be a false ending, because they haven't actually solved the problem yet." However, such a reading also makes you realize that the enjoyment of these types of movies usually derives much more from the telling, than from the actual narrative points.

5. Feeling stuck on a script? Though you can follow all sorts of structural guidelines, and pound your head against your desk, often the answer to your script problems lies not with you, but with your characters. They're often the ones that have the information you need to figure out what happens next. The problem is that you usually only hear what your characters have to say from the scenes they're in. If you're stuck, and not writing scenes, then you'll quickly get out of touch with your characters. In these instances, it's often a good idea to find *other* ways of getting your characters to talk to you. Try conducting interviews with them for various publications. See what they say to the editor of your local newspaper, to a tabloid magazine, to a news weekly, or an entertainment news program. Or, write a scene

where they're all on a daytime talk show arguing about their issues. Sure, they might start throwing chairs at each other, but this kind of unbridled talk just might give you some insights into their wants and desires that will feed you lots of ideas.

6. Now a breakdown exercise. Read the text of the scene from Shakespeare's *Richard III*, which is on the DVD in standard screenplay format (RichardIII.pdf in the Chapter 2 folder), and determine how you want to interpret the scene. Will you create a period piece set during the actual reign of Richard III? Will you transpose the scene to the modern-day White House? Or maybe an inner-city gangster drama? Use your creativity and come up with something you'd enjoy directing. Then, print out the script breakdown sheet on the DVD (Chapter 2>Resources>BreakdownSheet.pdf) and start filling it out. Who are the cast members? Will there be extras? What props do you need? Where is the location?

ON THE DVD

SUMMARY

Writing a script, treatment, or outline is the first crucial step in filmmaking—whether for a narrative or documentary project. Once you've completed a script, breaking it down helps you determine the needs of your production so that you can create a schedule. Once you've completed these tasks (and the writing process might take awhile!), you're ready to learn some basic concepts about video technology that will help you understand the subjects covered in the rest of this book.

3

VIDEO TECHNOLOGY BASICS

In This Chapter

- What Is Video?
- Digital Video Primer
- Video Broadcast Standards
- Audio Basics
- High-Definition Video (HD)
- Choosing a Format
- Quality Isn't Everything
- Exercise: Look at Some Video Quality Examples
- Summary

Y ou hear a lot of talk these days about how digital video technology has brought video production "to the masses" both by making production more affordable, and technically easier. No doubt about it, if you want to shoot some footage of your family and then do a little editing to take out the boring parts, FireWire-based DV technology will prove to be much easier than conventional analog editing systems. However, if you're envisioning a more complex project—something longer, with sophisticated production values, and high-quality images and sound—then you're going to have to "get your hands dirty" and spend some time learning a little more about how video technology works—both analog and digital.

In this chapter, we're going to introduce you to the fundamentals of video technology. Consider this chapter a reference for the terms and concepts you will encounter on a day-to-day basis during your production process, as well as throughout the rest of this book. By the end of this chapter you should be able to make an informed decision about which video format best suits the needs of your project.

WHAT IS VIDEO?

The answer to that question has become a lot more complex in recent years, but at the simplest level, video is a collection of electronic signals recorded by a camera onto a piece of magnetic media, usually videotape. But what about video for the Web, or video that's computer generated, or DVDs? Although it's true that within the next ten years videotape is likely to become obsolete, as the technology required to record directly to disk improves, at present most video footage—whether digital or analog—is still acquired through a camera that records onto videotape.

If you have any desire to deliver a project outside of your computer—using a video projector, television display, or by transferring to film and projecting in a theater—then you have to understand some fundamentals about videotape. Note that many of the terms and concepts in this chapter apply to any recorded media, whether direct-to-hard-drive recorders or optical disks such as DVDs.

Tracks

A video camera takes audio and visual information from the real world and turns it into electronic data that can be stored on a piece of magnetic tape. Videotape works by manipulating magnetic particles that are suspended in a medium applied to a thin piece of celluloid. During playback, the tape is pulled out of the tape cassette and wrapped partway around a spinning metal housing, called a *capstan*. The tape is pulled across *heads* that record and play back information to and from the tape.

Whether analog or digital, the data stored on a videotape is laid down in separate *tracks* along the tape. A track (sometimes called a *channel* or a *stream*) is a linear piece of information recorded along the tape. Wider tape has more physical space to store data, and so can yield better image quality. To maximize the space provided by any type of tape, video frames are recorded diagonally across the width of the tape, rather than straight across. This diagonal orientation yields more physical space, and so allows engineers to eke out a little more quality from the same tape width (Figure 3.1).

Usually, four tracks are recorded onto the videotape: the video track, two audio tracks, and the *control track*. Some types of videotape recorders can record four tracks of audio, usually at a lower quality level so that they take up the same physical space on the tape as two tracks. The control track is the equivalent of sprocket holes on a piece of film. It contains sync pulses that define where each frame of video starts and ends, which is crucial for stable playback. If you encounter a videotape that has an image that rolls across the monitor, the trouble is probably due to a damaged control track. Sometimes this can be fixed by dubbing the footage to a new videotape.

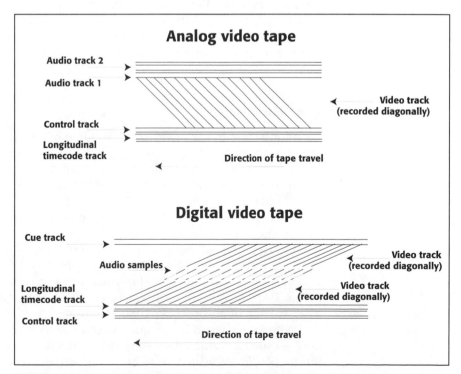

FIGURE 3.1 These two diagrams show how information is typically stored on analog and digital videotape.

Digital video files such as QuickTime movies also contain "tracks" of video, audio, timecode, and other elements. Manipulating, and sometimes even replacing, these individual tracks will be a regular part of your editing process.

Frames

The video track on a piece of videotape consists of a series of still images, or *frames*, that, when played in sequence, appear to be moving. When motion picture film was invented, it originally ran at a *frame rate* of 18 frames per second (fps). With the advent of sound, the frame rate had to be increased to 24 frames per second to get audio that sounded right. The frame rates of video vary, depending on where you live (see the following section "Video Broadcast Standards" and Table 3.3). Frames of video are similar to frames of film, except that you can't see them by holding them up to the light. Instead, you need a videotape player to decode the electronic information that constitutes each frame, and display it on a video monitor.

The frame rate of analog video in the United States is 29.97 frames per second. The frame rate of video in most of the rest of the world is 25 frames per second. Frame rate issues can get pretty complicated when you start to talk about HD and transferring footage between different formats. We discuss frame rates for HD later in this chapter and we discuss pull-down and other frame rate transfer issues in Chapter 13, "Preparing to Edit."

Video Resolution

Each individual frame of video is composed of a series of horizontal lines that are drawn across the screen. The number of horizontal lines that fit on the screen is known as the *vertical resolution*. The vertical resolution is one of the characteristics of video that is determined by the video broadcast standards listed in Table 3.3. Some of the horizontal lines in each video frame are used to convey information that isn't part of the visible image, such as the *vertical blanking interval*—something you don't really need to worry about. For example, the vertical resolution of analog video in the United States (a.k.a. NTSC) is 525 lines, of which 480 are visible. The vertical resolution of analog video in most of the rest of the world (a.k.a. PAL) is 625 lines, of which 575 are visible. HD 1080 consists of 1125 vertical lines, of which 1080 are visible.

When it comes to image quality, you hear a lot of talk about "resolution"—especially when discussing video cameras. When speaking of resolution, people are usually referring to the *horizontal resolution*—that is, how many individual pixels (or dots) there are in each one of those horizontal lines. The vertical resolution mentioned earlier is fixed, but the horizontal resolution is variable.

Due to the way in which the human eye works, a set of alternating black and white lines, like those in Figure 3.2, will look like gray mush if the lines are small enough. Horizontal line resolution measures how many alternating black and white lines can fit in a video image before turning into an indistinct gray mass. Due to its subjective nature, horizontal line resolution is not a hard-and-fast figure: it varies according to such factors as the monitor or TV, the camera hardware, how bright the room where the monitor is, how far you are from the monitor, and how good your vision is. Some cameras, lenses, and monitors have a greater capacity for displaying distinct vertical lines, and these devices are considered to have better "resolution."

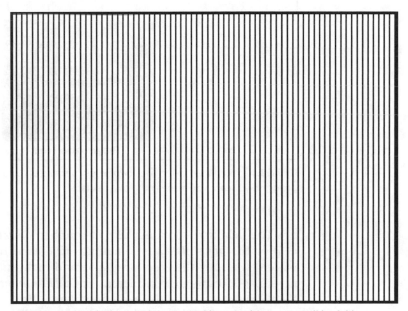

FIGURE 3.2   The black and white vertical lines in this image will look like a mass of gray if you hold the book far enough away from you.

Scanning Methods

We already mentioned that each frame of video consists of hundreds of horizontal lines. What we didn't mention is that the way that these lines are scanned across a monitor can vary: they can be *progressively scanned (p)* or *interlaced (i)*.

All of the current, analog video broadcast standards (NTSC, PAL, and SECAM) are *interlaced*. For each frame of video, your TV first displays all of the even-numbered scan lines—from top to bottom—and then goes back and fills in all the odd-numbered scan lines (Figure 3.3). Each pass across the monitor is called a *field*, and each frame of interlaced video consists of two fields. The order in which the fields are drawn can change, depending on how a videotape is recorded.

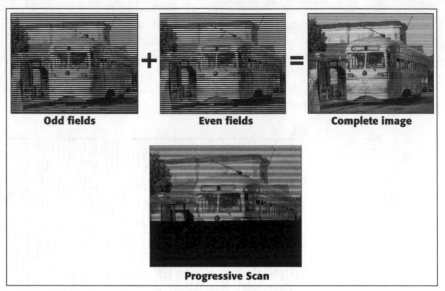

FIGURE 3.3   Interlaced video uses two fields to make up a complete frame of video; progressive scan video does not have fields.

The field that contains the odd-numbered scan lines is called the *odd field* or the *upper field* (or sometimes *field one*). If this field comes first, which is usually the case for analog and high-end digital videotape formats, the recording is considered *odd field dominant* or *upper field dominant*. If the field containing the even lines comes first, it's considered *even field dominant* or *lower field dominant* (or more rarely *field two dominant*) which is the case for the DV formats.

Know Your Field Dominance

When outputting video from rotoscoping, compositing, effects, or animation programs, you'll usually need to know which field to specify as dominant. If you're shooting with one of the DV-based formats, your footage is field two dominant.

Your computer monitor and some of the new digital television broadcast standards use *progressive scanning* to display the video image on the screen. They draw each line, in order, from top to bottom, in a single pass. Progressively scanned video has frames but no fields; the result is a cleaner-looking image. Many digital video cameras offer a progressive scan shooting mode, which we discuss in Chapter 4, "Choosing a Camera." Digital video cameras that shoot "24p" record 24 frames per second using progressive scanning.

Digital television standards are named according to the number of lines of vertical resolution and whether they are interlaced (i) or progressively scanned (p). 1080/60i has 1080 lines of vertical resolution and uses interlaced scanning. 720/60p has 720 lines and is progressively scanned.

Native Aspect Ratio

The ratio of the width of an image to its height is called the *aspect ratio* (Figure 3.4). Television displays and most computer monitors have a native aspect ratio of 4:3, or 1.33:1. In addition, analog video, most digital video, 16mm, 8mm, and Super8 film all have a native aspect ration of 4:3. High-definition (HD) video (both 1080 and 720) and 35mm film formats have a much wider native aspect ratio, 1.78:1 (a.k.a. 16:9) for HD video and 1.85:1 for most 35mm film. Formats with wide native aspect ratios are also called *widescreen*. Typically, wider is considered more "cinematic." Shooting in a wider format lets you put more information across the screen and is a truer representation of the way our field of vision works.

FIGURE 3.4   The larger rectangle has a 16:9 aspect ratio, while the smaller rectangle has a 4:3 aspect ratio. HD formats have a 16:9 aspect ratio, most other formats only provide a 4:3 aspect ratio.

Video and film formats that have a native aspect ratio of 4:3 can be manipulated by using special anamorphic lenses to record the image differently and then stretch it out to widescreen. It can also be manipulated by digitally cropping, or *letterboxing*, the image which makes the image look like widescreen even though it isn't *true 16:9*. We'll talk more about anamorphic lenses in Chapter 4,"Choosing a Camera," and letterboxing in Chapter 19, "Output."

Because the 1.78:1 aspect ratio of widescreen video is close to the 1.85:1 aspect ratio of 35mm film, choose an HD format with a native 1.78:1 aspect ratio or use anamorphic lenses to get a 1.78:1 aspect ratio if you're shooting video and plan to do a final transfer to 35mm film.

An Aspect Ratio by Any Other Name . . .

The 4:3 aspect ratio of television and most computer screens is sometimes referred to as a 1.33:1 ratio. This is to allow for easier comparison to other aspect ratios (Table 3.1). Similarly, 16:9 is also called 1.78:1.

TABLE 3.1 Film and Video Aspect Ratios

Video		Film	
Format	**Aspect Ratio**	**Format**	**Aspect Ratio**
Analog TV (NTSC, PAL or SECAM)	1.33:1	8mm	1.33:1
		Super 8mm	1.33:1
Computer screen (640 x 480 pixels)	1.33:1	16mm	18:13 (approx. 1.33:1)
DV	1.33:1	Super 16mm	5:3
DVCPro	1.33:1	35mm (projected)	1.85:1
DVCAM	1.33:1		
Betacam SP	1.33:1	35mm (full)	1.33:1
Digital Betacam	1.33:1		
D1	1.33:1	Vistavision	3:2
HDV	1.78:1	65mm	16:7
DVCPro-HD	1.78:1	IMAX	6:5
HDCAM	1.78:1	70mm	2.19:1
D9 (Digital S)	1.78:1	Techniscope	2.35:1
D5	1.78:1		
HDTV	1.78:1		

Physical Characteristics of Videotape

Videotapes themselves are limited by their physical characteristics, which include tape lengths (or run times), recording speeds, and cassette sizes.

Each videotape format has its own set of available tape lengths, although not all tape formats have tapes that are longer than 90 minutes. If your final project is going to be more than 90 minutes, you might need to use two tapes for your master. Generally, shorter tapes are used for shooting, and longer tapes are reserved for mastering (if needed).

Just as a VHS deck supports different recording speeds to trade quality for longer recording times, many formats allow for SP or LP recording modes. For digital filmmaking purposes, always record at the highest quality mode, which is SP. Most professional cameras and decks only offer a single, high-quality recording speed.

Traditionally, professional video formats have different cassette sizes—large (therefore longer) sizes for mastering, and smaller (shorter) ones for shooting. In fact, the miniDV-size cassette is the cause of much confusion these days. All of the DV-based formats (DVCPro, DVCAM, DV, and HDV) use the small miniDV cassettes for shooting and editing. Some of these formats (DVCPro, DVCPro-HD, DVCAM, and HDCAM) also use larger tapes for shooting and editing. The consumer-oriented DV format equipment cannot use the larger-size cassettes. As a result, many people who are only familiar with the miniDV cassettes mistakenly think that "miniDV" is the tape format, when it's actually just the cassette size.

DIGITAL VIDEO PRIMER

All of the information we've discussed so far holds true for both analog and digital video. However, digital video is a little more complicated than analog video. As analog video starts to fade away with the advent of newer and better digital video formats, it's important to understand the unique technical attributes of digital video.

Color Sampling

In grade school, you might have learned about the primary colors that can be mixed together to create all other colors. What they probably never explained in school was that those are the primary *subtractive* colors, or the primary colors of ink. When you talk about the color of *light*, things work a bit differently.

Red, green, and blue are the three primary colors of light—you can create any other color of light by mixing those primaries together. However, whereas mixing primary colors of ink together results in a darker color, mixing light creates a lighter color. Mix enough ink and you eventually get black, but if you mix enough light, you eventually get white.

Video cameras and televisions create color by mixing the three primary colors of light. In addition to red (R), green (G), and blue (B), the video signal has another element, which is lightness, or *luminance* (Y). The camera sees each of these four elements as separate, continuous analog waves.

While analog cameras store an analog representation of these waves on videotape, digital cameras first convert the waves into numbers, through a process called *sampling*. Each wave is broken into a series of bits that can be stored on the digital tape as 0s and 1s. The denser the samples, the better the perceived quality of the image (Figure 3.5).

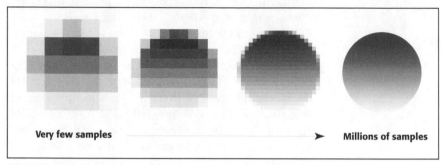

FIGURE 3.5   As the number of samples increases from left to right, the image becomes clearer.

When a digital camera samples an image, the degree to which it samples each primary color is called the *color sampling ratio*. A fully uncompressed video signal—also known as RGB color—has a color sampling ratio of 4:4:4. The first number stands for the luminance, or *luma*, signal (abbreviated y'), and the next two numbers stand for the color difference components (Cb and Cr), which together add up to the full chroma signal. 4:4:4 means that for every pixel, four samples each are taken for the luma signal and the two chroma signals.

To make the resulting data smaller, and therefore more manageable, about half of the color information is discarded. The highest quality digital video formats throw out half of the color information. These formats have a color sampling ratio of 4:2:2, which means that for every four luma samples, there are two color difference complete samples. The human eye is more sensitive to differences in light and dark (luminance) than to differences in color (chrominance). In theory, the discarded color information is detail that the human eye cannot perceive, so it's worth throwing it out for the sake of saving storage space.

The color sampling ratio of most HD formats is 4:2:2. Some HD formats, like HDV, use 4:2:0 color sampling which reduces the color information of 4:2:2 by 25 percent. Digital PAL formats also use 4:2:0 color sampling. DV formats use 4:1:1 color sampling, half the color of 4:2:2, which is an amount of color reduction that is considered visible to the viewer.

Compression

To fit more data onto a tape and to better facilitate digital post-production, most digital video formats use some type of data compression. This compression process can greatly affect the quality of your image. Uncompressed video has a compression ratio of 1:1, while compressed video can range anywhere from 1.6:1 to 10:1. Video compressed at a 10:1 ratio has 10 percent of its original data. Although throwing out 90 percent of your image data might sound a little scary, rest assured that modern compression schemes can deliver excellent results, even with very high compression ratios. In fact, video DVDs use a fairly extreme level of MPEG-2 compression, showing that heavily compressed video can still be commercially viable.

As explained earlier, a video format with a 4:2:2 color sampling ratio compresses the video signal by discarding half of the color information. However, this discarded information is not visible to the human eye, so this compression is considered *lossless*.

When the color sampling rate dips to 4:1:1 or 4:2:0, the information that has been discarded *is* visible to the eye, so this compression is considered *lossy*. However, the image quality of 4:1:1 and 4:2:0 video, such as DVCAM, DVCPro, and HDV, is still considered excellent.

Compression can also occur when you capture media through a video card (whether it was originally shot with an analog or digital camera) and when you render or output digital video files on your computer.

Bit Depth

Digital video usually has a bit depth of either 10 or 12 bits. Digital devices speak in ones and zeros (two "digits," hence the term "digital"). A single one or zero is called a *bit*, and a group of bits can be grouped together to represent a single number. When it comes time to assign a numeric value to the color of a particular pixel, then the number of bits that are used to make up that number becomes something of an issue. With more bits, you can record a greater range of numbers, which means you can represent more colors. This *bit depth* of a particular format refers to how many bits are used to represent the color of each pixel.

Basically, it's just the same as boxes of crayons. If you only have eight crayons, the pictures you draw don't have nearly as much color detail and variation as if you have a box of 64 crayons. Similarly, if you only have 8 bits available for representing the color of each pixel, you don't have nearly as much color detail and variation to work with as if you have 10 or 12 bits per pixel.

Bit depth will probably never be a make-or-break factor in your format choice, but it's still worth noting it when comparing specs. For blue screen work, or other compositing tasks, or for projects where you really want to be able to manipulate the color of your final image, a format that uses a higher-bit depth will allow higher-quality, cleaner adjustments.

CODECs

Video and audio data must be compressed before they can be played and stored by your computer (unless you have special hardware for playing uncompressed video). The software that handles this task is called a *CODEC*, short for COmpressor/DECompressor. CODECs are built into the hardware in a digital video camera or video card. In your computer they are usually software-based and managed by the video architecture—QuickTime, Windows Media, RealMedia, and so forth—or by the digital video editing application that you are using (Figure 3.6).

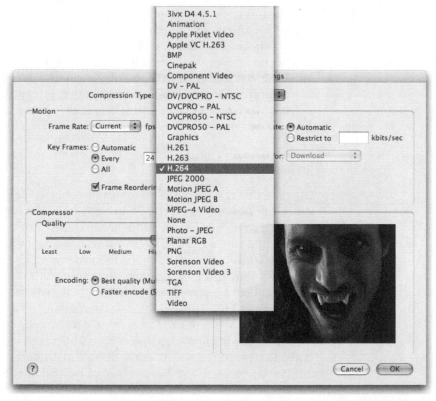

FIGURE 3.6   The standard QuickTime Export dialog presents a choice of many different CODECs, allowing you to precisely control how your video will be compressed.

If you have ever created a QuickTime movie on your computer, you have probably been presented with a choice of the different compression options that QuickTime provides. Video, Sorenson, Animation, Cinepak, MPEG-4, H.264, and many others are all CODECs that are used to compress video for storage, and then to decompress it for playback.

Different CODECs are used for different purposes. You'll use high-compression/lower-quality CODECs for Web or CD-ROM delivery, and low-compression/higher-quality CODECs for higher-quality playback. Other CODECs are used if you are using special video hardware. With newer compression technologies such as H.264 and MPEG-4, the compression/quality ratio has greatly improved. Highly-compressed Web video is increasingly indistinguishable from lower compression, high data rate video.

CODECs can be either lossy or lossless; that is, they either degrade the image quality or leave it unaffected. Many CODECs take longer to compress than they do to decompress (these are called *asymmetrical*). Most of the CODECs that ship with QuickTime are asymmetrical. For example, although it might take hours to compress a QuickTime movie using Sorenson or MPEG, the computer can decompress it and play it back in real-time. When you compress a piece of video, QuickTime hands the video stream to your chosen CODEC, which performs the compression calculations, and then writes out the compressed information to a file. Similarly, when you are ready to play back, QuickTime reads the compressed data and hands it to the appropriate CODEC, which decompresses it into video that the computer can display.

There are many different CODECs. Here are some that are important to digital filmmakers (some of which are shown in Figure 3.7):

DV-based editing applications and video boards designed to work with FireWire-based DV video (Digital8, DV, DVCAM, or DVCPro) use the hardware DV CODEC in the camera or video deck to compress and decompress the video on a videotape. After you transfer that media to your computer and use it in an editing application, a software DV CODEC is used to decompress the video for playback and to compress it when you're ready to record onto videotape. Some applications offer a proprietary software DV CODEC that offers more control and extra features than the stock DV CODEC used by your operating system.

DCT-based compression is a hardware CODEC used in some professional quality digital video cameras and digital video decks (with the exception of the DV formats mentioned earlier). Digital Betacam uses DCT-based compression. DCT-based compression is a hardware-only CODEC, so it isn't used in any editing applications.

MJPEG (Motion-JPEG) is a CODEC that provides several quality levels, ranging from very lossy to not noticeably compressed. Most high-quality video boards that offer digital and analog component I/O, such as Avid Meridien use MJPEG CODECs.

MPEG-2 is a CODEC that was originally developed for full-frame broadcast-quality video. DV video boards that offer analog composite I/O usually use MPEG-2 to compress and decompress analog video. MPEG-2 is also used for DVDs and to broadcast certain types of Digital Television (DTV). Newer digital video formats, such as D-VHS, MPEG-IMX and HDV, use MPEG-2 encoding. As DVD is now a standard delivery format, you'll probably spend a fair amount of time compressing videos as MPEG-2.

Uncompressed digital video still involves a CODEC, even though it's technically not compressed. That's because 4:2:2 digital video is still compressed down from 4:4:4 video; however, since this compression is invisible to the human eye, or "lossless," it's considered "uncompressed."

HD (High Definition) video is "uncompressed" (see above) but the files are so large that they are cumbersome to work with in post-production. As a result, many companies that make HD editing systems have special HD CODECs that make file sizes more manageable when working in HD. Avid's DNxHD is an example of one of these special proprietary HD CODECs.

HDV is the new "consumer" HD format. With its 25 Mb/sec data rate, HDV is poised to become the DV of the high-def world video. However, at the time of this writing, not all editing programs support HDV, though major applications such as Apple's Final Cut Pro HD and iMovie have been updated to work with HDV. Some applications, though, still depend on an intermediary CODEC. By the time you read this, all this might have changed. Because this is a new format, it's important to investigate your entire production workflow, to make sure that the necessary CODECs are available for your chosen software.

H.264 is just beginning to develop a presence. An extremely high-quality CODEC that has been chosen as the CODEC for HD-DVD and BluRay (the two specifications competing to become the replacement for the current DVD standard), H.264 has strong support from Apple in the form of a high-quality QuickTime implementation. For Web or final delivery, H.264 may prove to be your CODEC of choice in the near future.

Web-oriented CODECs such as *Sorenson, RealVideo 10, WMV9 (Windows media), Spark, MPEG-1,* and *MPEG-4* are designed to create very small file sizes for better distribution over the Web. For the most part, they aren't used in cameras and aren't always native to the non-linear editing systems discussed in this book. We discuss outputting video for the Web in Chapter 19, "Output."

FIGURE 3.7   The same image compressed with, from left to right, DV compression, Sorenson compression, and Cinepak compression. As you can see, image quality varies a lot between different compression algorithms.

Data Rate

When a digital video camera records an image, the amount of information that is stored for each second of video is determined by the video format's *data rate*. For example, the DV format has a data rate of 25 megabits per second (Mbps). This means that 25 Mbps of information are stored for each second of video. (If you factor in audio, timecode information, and the other "housekeeping" data that needs to be stored, DV actually takes up about 36 Mbps.) DVCPro50, on the other hand, stores about 50 Mbps of information for each second of video. As one would expect, more information means a better picture, and the 50 Mbps data rate is one of the reasons that DVCPro50 has higher quality than DV. If you hear people talking about the "25 Mbps formats" or the "50 Mbps formats," they're simply referring to these two different categories of formats.

Pixel Shape

While your computer screen and a frame of video might have the same 4:3 aspect ratio, they won't necessarily have the same pixel dimensions because, unfortunately, not all video formats use pixels of the same shape. Yes, in addition to all of the other concerns and complications, you also have to think about the shape of the individual pixels! Pixel shape is primarily a concern when dealing with graphics and special effects in post-production.

Computer displays—as well as many video formats—use square pixels. This means that a screen with a resolution of 640 × 480 pixels will have an aspect ratio of 4:3. DV, DVCAM, and DVCPRO all use rectangular pixels and require pixel dimensions of 720 × 480 pixels to achieve the same 4:3 aspect ratio. But wait, there's more—the two most popular HD formats, 720 and 1080, use square pixels to create images with an aspect ratio of 16:9.

The trouble with the difference in pixel shapes is that images will become distorted when you move from a rectangular-pixel format to the square-pixel format of your computer screen (Figures 3.8a through d).

Most software applications let you specify the pixel shape of your source media. If you're planning on a lot of graphics or special effects, pixel shape can become more of a hassle. If you've already created a bunch of graphics at 640 × 480 on your computer screen and don't want them horizontally distorted when you go out to tape, you might want to pick a format with square pixels. In Chapter 17, "Titling and Simple Compositing," we discuss how to handle differing pixel shapes when working with titles and other graphic elements.

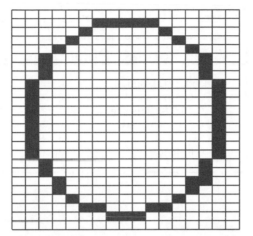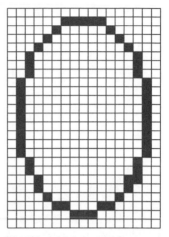

FIGURE 3.8   (a) Converting a circle built with rectangular pixels into square pixels. . .
(b) results in an ellipse.

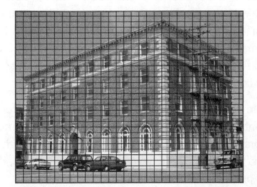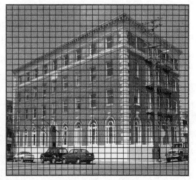

FIGURE 3.8   (c) Therefore, images shot with rectangular pixel cameras... **(d)** can look
distorted and squished when displayed on your square-pixel computer monitor.

Incidentally, *pixel dimensions* are another way that some people describe
the resolution of an image. Instead of saying the image has 480 lines, they
say it has 640 × 480 pixels. (Each line of horizontal or vertical resolution
has a width of one pixel.) Table 3.2 lists the pixel dimensions of various
types of media.

TABLE 3.2   Pixel Dimensions Chart

Video Format	Pixel Dimensions
Analog NTSC (square)	640 x 480
NTSC DV (rectangular)	720 x 480
NTSC 16:9 (unsqueezed)	854 x 480
PAL DV (rectangular)	720 x 576
720 HD (square)	1280 x 720
1080 HD (square)	1920 x 1080

ANALOG COLOR AND CONNECTORS

Even though your video hardware might be digital, many digital formats use analog connections to connect to monitors and often to other types of decks or your computer. There are three types of analog video connections, and each treats color differently. (See Chapter 12, "Editing Hardware," for more on cables and connectors.) Luckily, they are easily identified by the hardware associated with each type of analog signal. In ascending order of quality, the three types of analog video connectors are:

Composite video bundles all of the luminance and chrominance information into one signal (i.e., a composite signal). Composite video connectors typically attach to a deck or monitor through one RCA or BNC connector. If you own a typical consumer VHS deck, the connectors on it are probably composite.

S-video (a.k.a. Y/C video) breaks the video signal into two parts: luminance and chrominance. S-video yields a signal quality that is better than composite, but not as good as component video. S-video connects using a proprietary connector. Many laptops come with an S-video output to allow display on a TV monitor.

Component video divides the video signal into four different parts— YRGB—where Y = Luminance; R = Red; G = Green; and B = Blue. This results in a higher quality signal than composite or Y/C video. Component video typically connects using three separate BNC connectors.

If you are using an HD monitor or TV set you will use special digital cables to connect your video hardware to your digital monitor. There are several different types of digital cables but all of them are comparable to the analog component video described in the sidebar, "Analog Color and Connectors." This is why you will sometimes hear digital video described as "component"—it simply means high-quality.

Types of Digital Video Files

When you pull digital video media off a piece of videotape and onto your computer, the media is stored in a file on your hard drive. The type of file depends on the type of hardware you are using to capture the video. FireWire-based video is usually saved as QuickTime files, while many turnkey systems save the video as M-JPEG files, and Windows-based systems often save as AVI or WMV9 files.

If you're capturing from a FireWire-based DV camera, then your video will already be compressed using whatever CODEC your video format uses. So, if you're capturing from a DV camera or deck, then the resulting file on your computer will be DV-compressed—the camera will have performed this compression when you shot the footage.

If you're capturing using a digitizing board in your computer, then your resulting files will be compressed using whatever CODEC your digitizing hardware uses, usually Motion JPEG or MPEG-2. Although files can be converted from one format and one compressor to another (a process called *transcoding*), you must be very careful not to add extra compression during these conversions.

VIDEO BROADCAST STANDARDS

Videotape recording was invented in the late 1950s as a way of keeping archived copies of broadcast TV shows. (Prior to that, television was "live" and simply sent straight from the studio camera into the airwaves, much like radio.) As a result, the technology of video recording is intrinsically tied to the technology of television broadcasting and this link is still evident fifty years later, even though video has diversified far beyond broadcast television.

TV broadcasting and video recording developed differently in different parts of the world. Each of the three areas that were early adopters of television—North America, France, and the rest of western Europe— came to have a different set of rules that defined the qualities of a broadcast television signal. These *video broadcast standards* were designed to regulate and standardize the quality of a television broadcast. Other parts of the globe soon took on one of the three broadcast video standards based on which area they were politically, culturally, or geographically aligned with at the time. The different video standards have different frame rates, color characteristics, aspect ratios, and image resolutions, among other things (Table 3.3).

Fifty years ago, everything was analog, including the technology described by each of the three video standards. The analog broadcast standard in North America and Japan is called *NTSC* and has a frame rate of 29.97 fps. The analog broadcast standard in most of Europe, South America, and Asia is called *PAL* and has a frame rate of 25 fps. The rest of the world, which includes France, Russia, parts of Asia, Africa, and the Middle East uses a standard called *SECAM*, which also has a frame rate of 25 fps. Recently, a digital standard has been added to the list, DTV (Digital Television). DTV is meant to eventually replace NTSC, PAL, and SECAM.

Just as digital media is more flexible than analog media, the DTV standard is much more flexible than the three analog standards. There are eighteen variations of the DTV standard and they fall into three subcategories based on resolution:

- **480** (a.k.a. Standard Definition Television or SDTV) is the digital upgrade of the analog NTSC standard.
- **720** is true High Definition Television (HDTV) standards, offering very high-quality digital signals.
- **1080** is also true HDTV, offering higher image resolution than 720.

Just to make things a little more complicated, each subset of the DTV standard has several different possible frame rates (Table 3.3). (Unlike the analog video broadcast standards, which each have only one frame rate.) These multiple frame rates allow the DTV standard to encompass both analog NTSC video and analog PAL video and allow for better playback of film (which has a native frame rate of 24 fps). We'll talk in depth about these different HD standards and their frame rates in the HD section later in this chapter.

Video standards are intrinsically tied to television and the type of TV sets (or video monitors) that are sold in a particular country. Computer monitors are not limited by the same technical constraints and can handle any of the standards listed in Table 3.3. If you have, for example, a PAL project and you want a distributor in New York City to watch it, you can make a DVD (avoiding any regional encoding) and they'll be able to watch it on their computer.

35mm film has an aspect ratio of 1.85:1 when projected.

TABLE 3.3   Changing Your Video Standard

Standard	NTSC	PAL/SECAM	480 SD	720 HD	1080 HD	Film
Frame rate(s)	29.97	25	23.976/24 25 29.97/30	23.976/24 25 29.97/30 59.97/60	23.976/24 25 29.97/30	24
Fields	2	2	0 or 2	0 or 2	0 or 2	0
Vertical res.	480	576	480	720	1080	n/a
Scanning	Interlaced	Interlaced	Interlaced or Progressive	Interlaced or Progressive	Interlaced or Progressive	n/a
Aspect ratio	1.33:1	1.33:1	1.33:1	1.78:1	1.78:1	1.85:1

It is possible to convert from one standard to another through expensive tape-to-tape conversions, cheap but shoddy-looking tape-to-tape conversions, or time-consuming software-based conversions. In other words, it's something you'll wish to avoid.

Why should you care about standards? It used to be that you would simply choose the standard that's right for the geographic region in which you live. But now you need to choose between the analog standard for your geographic region and DTV. DTV is a better choice if you are shooting on video and plan to later transfer your footage to film.

24p is used when shooting video footage that will eventually be transferred to film. It is also used when transferring projects shot on film to HD for broadcast. Some argue that shooting 24p results in more film-like footage even if it is never transferred to film. Before the advent of 24p, the PAL standard (at 25 frames per second) was a popular choice for video footage that would eventually be transferred to film.

AUDIO BASICS

There's a saying that sound is 50 percent of a movie. Luckily, it's not nearly as complicated as video.

Mono, Stereo, and Surround Sound

Mono sound consists of one channel (or track) of audio. Almost all production sound is mono. If you record a line from a microphone into a MiniDisc recorder, you are recording mono sound because most microphones are not stereo microphones. Even if you record onto both channels of the MiniDisc recorder, you're still not recording separate left and right channels. Instead, you're simply recording the same mono signal on the recorder's two channels.

If you patch a lavalier mic into channel one and let the camera's built-in mic record to channel two, you are still recording in mono. Granted, you are creating two different mono recordings of the same thing, but the two different channels will sound very different due to the quality of the microphones, and their positioning. In no way do they add up to a stereo recording.

Stereo sound consists of two channels of audio mixed together in a special way: one channel is balanced somewhat to the left, and the other is balanced somewhat to the right. When added together, stereo tracks give a more three-dimensional feeling to the recording.

The only type of production sound that is typically recorded in stereo is music. Stereo sound is usually reserved for the final mix of a soundtrack for a film or TV show. The built-in microphones on most camcorders are stereo, but these mics are usually not suitable for serious production work. You can, of course, buy or rent stereo mics to attach to your camera, and these units will record separate left and right channels directly to tape, however this is not necessary if you are primarily recording dialog.

For theatrical release films, DVDs, and HD television, surround sound mixes are the norm. Surround sound mixes generally consist of 5.1 or 7.1 channels of sound that correspond to the position of speakers in the theatre. They give an even more intense three-dimensional feeling to the environment than do stereo mixes. Mixes and surround sound are discussed more thoroughly in Chapter 15, "Sound Editing" and also in Chapter 19, "Output."

Audio Sampling

Just as waves of light are sampled to create digital video, waves of sound are sampled to create digital audio (Figure 3.9). The rate at which the audio is sampled can vary, and, as with a video or still image, the higher the sampling rate, the better. Professional digital audio is sampled at either 44.1 kHz (CD quality) or 48 kHz (DAT quality), although there is little appreciable quality difference to the listener. Many lower-end cameras offer the option to record audio at 32 kHz, which sometimes allows you to record four channels of sound instead of two. However, if you're serious about your production, it's better to have two good channels of audio than four mediocre channels. As a rule, never record at less than 44.1 kHz—audio files aren't that big so you won't save much space by skimping during production. If you're working with one of the digital video formats, including DV, stick to the native 48 kHz sampling rate.

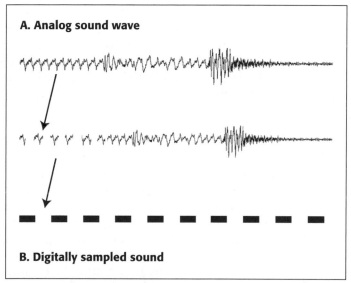

FIGURE 3.9   An analog sound wave (a) is broken into small samples, resulting in a digital audio file (b).

Types of Digital Audio Files

Once you capture audio onto your computer's hard drive, it is stored in a file. Audio is usually stored in one of several standard formats: *WAV, AIFF,* or *SDII.* These are all uncompressed formats, and all fall under the category of *PCM* audio. (You might not ever encounter the term PCM, but if you do, just think "uncompressed, high-quality audio.")

Most likely, when you're working with digital audio on your computer, you'll be using WAV files (for Windows computers) or AIFF files (for Macs). As long as you maintain the same sampling rate, conversions between different PCM audio file types are lossless. *MP3* is a highly compressed audio format that offers very small file sizes and good sound quality, despite the compression. When compressed at 192K or better, MP3 files are indistinguishable from CD audio. *MP4* (sometimes called *MPEG-4* because both MP3 and MP4 are part of the MPEG video specification) is a successor to MP3 that offers better compression without degrading quality. A 128K MP4 file delivers 160K MP3 quality in a much smaller space. AAC format (which you might have encountered in downloads from the iTunes Music Store) is just an MP4 audio file with a special digital-rights-management (DRM) "wrapper." (For more information about editing with MP3 and MP4 files, see Chapter 13, "Preparing to Edit.")

Dolby AC-3 audio consists of 5.1 channels of Dolby Digital Surround Sound. Typically, the 5.1 channels are designed to create a surround environment in a movie theater, so the channels are laid out as left, center, right, left surround, right surround, and the .1 channel is an optional subwoofer track for low-frequency sounds. HD video formats offer AC-3 5.1 sound. *DTS* and *SDDS* audio are other forms of surround sound used for feature films.

HIGH-DEFINITION (HD) VIDEO

HD, or *high-definition video* is the talk of the digital filmmaking world these days. But what exactly, is it? We've mentioned HD and related topics, such as DTV, in other parts of this chapter, and we also talk about HD later in this book in terms of editing and post-production, but we thought we'd put a basic explanation of HD together for you in one place as a reference. Be aware that you'll need to understand all of the content of this chapter so far to fully understand the technical aspects of HD.

HD is a tricky thing to discuss because the term itself does not actually reference any particular format. There are loads of formats that can sport the HD moniker because, in the end, anything with higher-resolution than standard definition PAL video can be considered HD. Therefore, HD runs the gamut from affordable systems that record to inexpensive miniDV tapes to extremely expensive systems that record directly to hard drives.

However, when digital filmmakers talk about shooting HD, they're talking about one of the two DTV subsets: *720* and *1080*.

- **720** has a resolution of 1280 × 720 (Figure 3.10) and is always scanned progressively. It supports the following frame rates: 23.976p, 24p, 25p, 29.97p, 30p, 59.94p, and 60p. It has a native aspect ratio of 16:9 or 1.78:1.
- **1080** has a resolution of 1920 × 1080 (Figure 3.10) and can be scanned progressively or interlaced. It supports the following frame rates: 23.976p, 24p, 29.97p, 30p, 50i, 59.94i, and 60i. It has a native aspect ratio of 16:9 or 1.78:1.

720 and 1080 both have advantages and disadvantages. Each frame of 1080 is more than double the size of a frame of 720. However 720 offers the option of 60 frames per second, which doubles the information of the highest 1080 frame rate, 60 fields per second (or 30 fps).

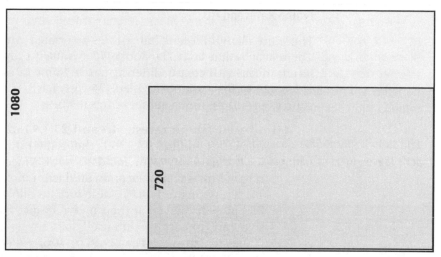

FIGURE 3.10   A frame of 1080 HD video is almost twice as big as a frame of 720 HD video.

HD TERMINOLOGY

The idea of HD has been around for a long time—since the 1960s—but it has only become a viable, practical, medium in recent years. As a result, the terminology is quite new and still in the process of refinement. Here is a guide to the way people are talking about HD.

The various types of HD video are usually described by three things: their resolution, whether they are interlaced or progressively scanned, and their frame rate. *720/24p* (or sometimes *720p24*) is HD video with a resolution of 1280 x 720 and a frame rate of 24 progressively scanned frames per second. *1080/60i* (or *1080i60*) is HD with a vertical resolution of 1920 x 1080 and a frame rate of 60 interlaced fields per second. Because 1080/60i is probably the most widely used of the 1080 HD configurations, it is often simply called *1080i*. Similarly, 720/60p is often referred to as *720p*. In this book, we use the full description (1080/60i) in order to avoid confusion. We use *720* and *1080* to refer to the entire range of frame rates sharing those resolutions respectively.

With HD video, interlaced video is described by the number of fields instead of frames. 1080/60i has 60 *fields per second*. Since two interlaced fields of video add up to one frame of video, the frame rate is still 30 frames per second—60i is just a different way of describing the same thing and letting you know that it's interlaced.

Frame Rates and HD

There are many different frame rates associated with 720 and 1080 HD. The reason is that both 720 and 1080 are able to support a variety of different media with greatly differing native frame rates: film (24 fps), NTSC video (29.97 fps), and PAL video (25 fps). Each of these three potential sources for HD defines a subset of frame rates:

Film-based frame rates: 24p and 23.3.976p. 24 fps is the native frame rate of film. 23.976 is the frame rate of film compensated for compatibility with standard NTSC video. (This translation is referred to as *pull-down* and you'll learn more about it in Chapter 13, "Preparing to Edit.") These formats allow for the broadcast of film projects played at their native frame rate. Both are progressive scan (p) because film itself does not have fields.

NTSC-based frame rates: 29.97p, 30p, 59.94i, 60i, 59.94p, and 60p. 29.97 fps is the native frame rate of NTSC video. With native HD video, the NTSC frame rate can be rounded up to an even 30 fps. As a result, there are three pairs of frame rates: 29.97p and 30p are the progressively scanned versions of standard NTSC and 59.94i and 60i are the interlaced versions. 59.94p and 60p provide higher-quality video by doubling the number of frames in a second of video. They are only available in 720 HD.

PAL-based frame rates: 25p and 50i. The native frame rate of PAL is 25 frames per second. 25p is the progressively scanned HD frame rate for PAL material and 50i is the interlaced version.

 Why 29.97? When NTSC video was first standardized, all television was black and white (or more correctly, monochrome, a "black and white" TV can display far more tones than just black or white) and had a frame rate of 30 fps. When color technology was added, broadcasters and the FCC needed to figure out a way to differentiate color video from black and white. The solution? Slow the frame rate of color video down by 1/1000th of a percent (.001). That way, existing monochrome TV sets could continue to pick up the monochrome 30 fps signal and new color TV sets could pick up the 29.97 fps color signal.

HD Pros and Cons

A frame of HD video contains more pixels than a frame of analog video. As a result it requires more disk space, as well as hard drives and cabling that are capable of handling very high data rates (sometimes over 1000 Mbps), and lots of computer processing power. In addition, to view true HD footage, you need an HD display, which can cost several thousand dollars. Computer monitors (CRT or LCD) can substitute for a real HD monitor but they don't have the same color space, so what you see won't necessarily be what you get.

Due to resource-heavy requirements for editing in HD, many people choose to transfer their HD footage to SD work tapes and edit in SD, a process known as *downconverting*. Either way, there are extra costs and hassles.

But for some projects, HD is definitely worth it: you should consider shooting on HD if image quality is of paramount concern, if you plan on doing any blue screen special effects work, if you know you will be delivering using an HD distribution such as DTV, or if you simply want the greatest number of output and finishing options.

Finally, thanks to its high-resolution, native widescreen aspect ratio and capacity for 24 fps, HD is an optimal choice if you're shooting video for an eventual transfer to 35mm film.

When it comes to HD, HDV is the exception to the rules. HDV is much more compressed than the other HD formats, resulting in a lower quality image. As a result, it also has a low bit-rate (about 25 Mbps) which means it can be transferred or captured via FireWire. HDV uses the same color space as SD video (ITU-R BT.601), as opposed to the color space of the other HD formats (ITU-R BT.709).

CHOOSING A FORMAT

Now that you're informed about video and audio technology, it's time to decide on a videotape *format* for your project.

The way in which the signal is recorded on a piece of video can vary greatly, and each of these variations is called a *format*. VHS is a consumer-grade videotape format, as are DV and Digital8. Professional videotape formats include DVCAM, DVCPro, Betacam SP, Digital Betacam, MPEG-IMX, and the HD (high-definition) formats: HDV, HDCAM, DVCPro-HD, D5-HD, and D9-HD.

Formats exist independently of the broadcast standards mentioned earlier; in other words, you can shoot PAL DVCAM or NTSC DVCAM. However, only HD format cameras can shoot 1080 or 720 DTV. The difference between the formats lies in the hardware in the camera (or video deck), and the videotape stock. HD cameras typically shoot 1080 or 720 but not both. In addition, they may not offer all the possible frame rates defined by the DTV specs for 720 and 1080. For a detailed list of the different existing videotape formats and their technical specifications, see

ON THE DVD   videotape formats.pdf in the Chapter 3 folder on the companion DVD.

The digital video world has become increasingly complicated over the last few years as more and more hardware companies have released more and more formats (Figure 3.11). Luckily, manufacturers often make the new formats backward compatible with the older formats that they are based on: MPEG-IMX is a newer digital version of Betacam SP that is backward compatible with both Betacam SP and Digital Betacam. You can expect the number of formats to continue to grow as digital video technology continues to improve. Although the selection might be confusing, the great variety of formats provides an advantage to the digital filmmaker: As you balance costs against image quality, you're likely to find that you have several format options that are appropriate for your project.

FIGURE 3.11   A quick look at the Sony family of tape stock gives you a good idea about the number of different recording formats on the market today.

DIRECT-TO-DISC RECORDING WITH P2

In addition to all of these tape formats, Panasonic's P2 tapeless, direct-to-disc format is beginning to get some traction. Though tape is relatively inexpensive, easy to find, and portable, it's also fairly fragile and is somewhat inconvenient to work with—you must digitize or capture all of your tape before you can start editing. P2 is a variant of Panasonic's DVCPro specification that records directly to tiny hard drives that can be inserted in P2-compatible cameras (Figure 3.12), similar to the flash media cards that are used with digital still cameras. With P2, you don't have to hassle with capturing and because hard drives are a little more weather-resistant than tapes, you don't have to worry as much about shooting in extreme conditions.

Like DVCPro, P2 is primarily aimed at electronic newsgathering, where production deadlines are tight and having to digitize or capture footage is not always possible. Such short deadlines are usually not an issue with feature film production, but if you've decided to shoot DVCPro format for quality or compatibility reasons, then P2 might be a convenient option to consider.

FIGURE 3.12   The Panasonic AJ-SPX800 camcorder records directly to a P2 disk.

If you already own—or have access to—equipment that you plan to use for your production, then your format choice has been made by default. However, it's still important to understand the workings of each format so that you're aware of any limitations. Also, just because you've decided to shoot on one format, doesn't mean you won't use other formats during production. From creating VHS copies for test screenings and promotion, to dubbing high-end HD camera masters to lower-end DVCAM worktapes, you may end up using two or three formats before your final project is completed.

Delivery Is Everything

The delivery medium is one of the most important considerations when choosing a format for shooting. Before you decide on a format, it's crucial to know what your end product is going to be. A projected feature film? A corporate presentation on videotape? A Webcast? Choosing the right format now can save you time and lots of money in tape stock and transfers later on.

Web/Multimedia

The compressed video that is used for Web and multimedia projects may be of lesser quality, but this doesn't mean that you should just get that old

VHS camcorder out of the closet and start shooting. These days, Web video is good enough to reveal many of the artifacts that low-quality formats like VHS suffer from. Similarly, if you're planning on night shoots or special effects such as blue-screen compositing, you will need a higher-quality format. And, shooting better quality affords you the option of repurposing your footage later. Even though the low-quality of streaming Web video means you could get away with consumer VHS or Hi8, go ahead and spend a little extra money and shoot DV. The higher quality will yield a better image and provide more shooting and effects flexibility, while the camera's FireWire interface will make for an easier post-production workflow.

Video

If you're planning a "straight-to-video" release such as a corporate presentation, trade show video, or home movie then your project will eventually end up on either VHS or DVD (or both). There's a substantial quality difference between VHS and DVD but even low-quality VHS is capable of displaying good-looking video if it was shot on a high-quality format. Think about how movies you've rented on VHS that were shot on film still look pretty good, especially when compared to something that was shot on a poor-quality format like home movies or surveillance footage. Today, there's really no good reason today to shoot on any format with lower quality than DV. DV cameras can be very cheap to purchase or rent and since most have FireWire interfaces, your editing workflow will be simpler than if you use an analog format and analog capture hardware.

Broadcast Television

Almost any of today's digital formats pass the muster for being broadcast, though broadcasters all have different criteria for what they will accept. In general, if you ultimately want your project to be suitable for broadcast television then you should aim to shoot at the highest quality that you can afford. Also, you'll have to master your final project according to very exacting specifications. We'll talk more about this process in Chapter 19, "Output."

Shooting for broadcast now means making the decision between an SD (Standard Definition) shoot, and an HD (High Definition) shoot. A few years ago, this was a very simple decision: if you didn't have tons of money, you were shooting SD (i.e., DV, DVCAM, DVCPro, Digital Beta-cam). Nowadays, thanks to inexpensive formats like HDV, it's possible for even low-budget producers to consider HD. At present in the United States CBS and NBC broadcast 1080 DTV while ABC broadcasts 720 DTV.

Projection

Any format can be used for projection, but there is one important thing to keep in mind: People will be seeing your video footage at 10 to 50 times the size of a video monitor. Noise and digital compression artifacts can be enlarged to the size of someone's head. Consequently, you should try to work at the highest quality possible.

If you ultimately want your project to be projected on 35mm film—in a movie theater, ideally—your final video will have to be transferred to film. In theory, you can shoot any video format for eventual film transfer. However, if quality is your primary concern, you should choose a higher-end digital format or shoot on film itself.

HD projection has come a long way in the last couple years. Although only a few theatres use digital projection, it's common to see digital projection—or even just a normal, high-quality video projector—in film festivals for projects that haven't been transferred to film.

Videotape Formats

In the following list, we've summarized the pros and cons of many different video formats. This should provide an idea of how you can use each format. Some of the higher-end formats may require cameras that are more expensive than you can afford. However, because these cameras are readily available for rental, and because such formats are required for very high-quality work, we've chosen to include them. It's important to be aware that the cameras designed for lower-end formats do not have the same set of features that the higher-end format cameras offer. If you're planning a complicated shoot that requires precise control of the camera, you may need a higher-end format for your shoot.

Analog consumer formats. Most people are familiar with VHS, S-VHS, Betamax, 8mm, and Hi8, all of which were developed for home video. These formats are very inexpensive, but their lack of image quality should deter most serious video producers. In addition, because they require a separate digitizing step, your post-production workflow will be more complex, and more expensive. With DV cameras so inexpensive, there's really no reason to consider these formats. If you plan on using lots of archival and found footage that's stored on these formats, then you'll need to choose between buying and renting the requisite hardware to digitize your old footage or transferring the old footage to DV tape. For new material, though, stick with a digital format.

Digital 8. Digital 8 is an 8mm consumer format intended to replace analog Hi8. It can use Hi8 or its own Digital 8 tapes. It has a 25 Mbps data rate, a 4:1:1 color sampling ratio, and 5:1 DV-based compression, but is slightly lower-resolution than DV. Again, this format is really only useful if you need to access older material.

DV. Intended as a digital replacement for the home video formats mentioned previously, DV has far surpassed the manufacturers' expectations. It has a 25 Mbps data rate, a 4:1:1 color sampling ratio, and a 5:1 compression ratio. The image quality is frequently rated higher than Betacam SP and has the advantage of being less subject to generation-loss.

DVCAM. DVCAM by Sony offers a higher tape speed than DV, but not quite as high as DVCPro, and it uses the same metal tapes as DV. The resulting higher-quality image is aimed at industrial users, but appears to be quickly becoming the low-end format of choice for broadcast.

DVCPro. With a faster tape speed than DV and DVCAM JVC's DVCPro sports a more stable image that is less prone to drop-outs but is otherwise similar to DVCAM.

The Right Format for the Job

All of the 25 Mbps formats—Digital 8, DV, DVCPro, and DVCAM—use the same CODEC. Therefore, any differences in image quality are hardware dependent; i.e., due to camera technology, lenses, tape transport speed, etc. The reason DVCPro and DVCAM are considered superior formats is due to their reliability in editing-intensive applications such as newsgathering, and due to the higher quality cameras and lenses available for these formats and also the availability of larger (and more durable) cassettes.

Betacam SP (BetaSP). Developed by Sony in the 1980s, Betacam SP was once the most popular format for broadcast television.

Digital Betacam (DigiBeta). Sony introduced Digital Betacam in 1993 as a digital upgrade of Betacam SP. Its extremely high quality has made it the broadcast mastering format of choice. Digital Betacam decks can also play (but not record) analog Betacam SP tapes.

MPEG-IMX. A 4:2:2 component, digital 50 Mbps format that uses MPEG-2 encoding and is backward compatible with Digital Betacam and Betacam SP.

D-VHS. Using the same tape shell as standard VHS, D-VHS offers digital MPEG-2 encoded video. D-VHS tapes are not compatible with standard VHS players and there are no D-VHS cameras. Rather, D-VHS is mostly intended for recording high-quality video from satellite or digital television. They are also frequently used to output viewing copies of HD projects before the final output.

D1. The first digital mastering format, D1 has until recently set the standard for high-quality digital video. The specifications that define D1 are known as ITU-R BT. 601, which consists of 4:2:2 color and a 4:3 aspect ratio. D1 has been superceded by the HD formats but it still used as a quality reference for non-HD video formats.

HDV. Newest on this list is the HDV format, which records HD footage on miniDV tapes. The low data rata (about 19 Mbps for 720 and 25 Mbps for 1080) allows for data transfer using FireWire technology. Interframe MPEG-2 compression keeps the data strcam small but requires special CODECs for editing.

HDCAM. Perhaps the most popular of the HD acquisition formats, Sony's HDCAM offers a resolution of 1080.

D5-HD. Panasonic's D5-HD format can handle both 720 and 1080 DTV resolutions.

DVCPro-HD (D7-HD). Panasonic's other popular HD format, DVCPro-HD uses the same large-size DV tapes as DVCAM and DVCPro. It supports both 720 and 1080 DTV formats.

D9-HD. JVC's D9-HD is a high-end HD format based on their Digital S format. It supports both 720 and 1080 resolutions.

Film. This may be the *digital* filmmaking handbook, but that doesn't mean that there isn't a place for film in your production workflow. Even though they may be editing and posting digitally, many filmmakers still choose to shoot on actual film. In addition to the quality, unique look and flexibility of film, if you already own film gear, or are experienced and comfortable with shooting film (and assuming you have the budget) then shooting in traditional 16mm or 35mm might be the best way to go. Super8 film is a popular choice for music videos and other projects that don't require synchronized sound. Obviously, choosing to shoot film completely changes the discussion of what gear you need, and we won't be covering those issues. However, if you're an experienccd film shooter, but are new to digital workflow, then you need to know that shooting film will introduce some new wrinkles into the post-production workflow. You'll have to pay for transfers of your film to video, and plan for a more complex editing workflow that involves matching back to film.

Finally, there are other parameters that might affect your format decision. Perhaps you've got access to free, or loaner gear—if you've got a friend with a nice DVCAM setup, there's no reason to invest in new gear. Or, maybe you have very particular output needs. Many film transfer houses prefer video shot in 24 frame-per-second progressive scan, while some "film look" software is designed for 30 frame-per-second interlaced video. These issues might constrain your format decision.

Choose Carefully

The movie The Cruise *was shot on NTSC using a Sony VX1000 DV format camera, but the director was so unhappy with the frame rate issues that resulted from the transfer to film that he ended up going back to his sources and remastering onto a Sony uncompressed HD format and then going to film. The process of changing from one digital video format to another is called "transcoding." It is not a lossless process and can be expensive so it should be avoided, if possible.*

QUALITY ISN'T EVERYTHING

In the 1980s, video artists scrambled to buy Fisher-Price Pixelvision cameras that were intended as toys for children. These cameras recorded video onto standard audio cassettes, and the resulting extremely grainy, low-resolution, black-and-white images were (and still are) considered fascinating in ways that perfectly clear HD video could never be. You don't need 4:2:2 video to make an interesting project. If the content is compelling, no one is going to complain about the compression artifacts dancing around in the darker parts of your image. However, you do need to decide early on what's right for your project and your intended workflow, as that decision will influence your equipment choices and have a profound effect on how you shoot.

EXERCISE: LOOK AT SOME VIDEO QUALITY EXAMPLES

In this chapter, you read about many of the technical concerns that affect video quality. Although it's very easy to debate the finer points of different compression ratios or CODECs, in the end, such debate might not tell you much about how good (or bad) a particular format looks. The only way to really determine if a particular video format is good enough for your needs is to see some examples.

The best way to get examples is to buy, rent, or borrow some equipment and shoot some samples under the conditions in which you expect to be working. While this might be practical for inexpensive DV gear, for more expensive DVCAM, or Digital Betacam, such expense might not be feasible. Fortunately, with so many movies being shot digitally now, you can find a number of examples of digital movies at your local video store. Check out the following movies for real-world examples of particular video formats:

Collateral: This big budget film was shot primarily on HD in order to take advantage of high-end digital video's ability to capture lots of detail in extremely low light situations. Although an experienced filmmaker might notice the appearance of *noise* on the big screen (as opposed to *film grain)* a difference in quality isn't noticeable to the average viewer.

***Buena Vista Social Club*:** This documentary about the now-famous Cuban music "club" was shot using a combination of Digital Betacam and DV (using a Sony VX-1000). It's a fine example of the excellent level of quality that can be achieved with high-end gear. It's also an interesting opportunity to compare DigiBeta and DV side by side.

***The Celebration*:** Shot entirely with a Sony DCR-PC7, an under-$1,000, single-chip DV camera, this intense film is a good example of what can be achieved with a cheap camera and ambient lighting.

***Hands on a Hard Body*:** This excellent, hilarious documentary was shot on Hi-8 under very difficult lighting conditions. A good sample of analog video quality, and excellent proof that no matter how "inferior" your gear might be, if you've got a good story, and you know how to tell it well, everything will be fine.

***Bamboozled*:** Spike Lee's second digital video feature (after the concert movie *The Original Kings of Comedy*) was shot using several Sony VX-1000s. This movie is a good example of "playing to the strengths" of DV. Rather than trying to mimic the look of a film camera, the filmmakers accepted the "video" look and used it to their advantage. Because the movie is about the TV industry, the DV quality supported their story.

Nadja: This cult-favorite vampire film set in New York City was shot partially with a Fisher-Price Pixelvision camera. The resulting grainy, black and white footage gives the film a mysterious quality reminiscent of the famous silent vampire film, *Nosferatu.*

Note that all of these features underwent a transfer to film at some point, so these are not examples of the type of quality that you get straight out of the camera. If your ultimate goal is a feature release, though, these movies show the range of quality that is possible.

SUMMARY

The information in this chapter is designed to provide a strong technical foundation before delving into the specifics of shooting, editing, sound, and special effects. You might not retain this information until you find use for it in the real world, during the production or post-production of your project. However, when you get to that stage, you'll be able to refer back to this chapter as a technical reference. Now it's time to put some of it to practical use in the next chapter, "Choosing a Camera."

4

CHOOSING A CAMERA

In This Chapter

- Evaluating a Camera
- Camera Features
- Progressive Scan
- Accessorizing
- What You Should Choose
- Summary

When you hear people talk about the "DV Revolution," they're really referring to three different pieces of technology: high-performance desktop computers with sophisticated editing software; high-speed digital interfaces such as FireWire that allow for video capture without expensive add-on digitizing hardware; and high-quality cameras that allow the capture of broadcast-quality digital video. These three technologies work together to make it possible to produce high-quality finished output using far less gear (and money) than ever before.

The digital filmmaker can now buy an affordable camera that rivals professional cameras of just a few years ago. Understanding the features and trade-offs of different cameras is essential to selecting a camera and using it to its full potential.

In this chapter, we'll explain the various features and functions of digital video camera, with details of how these features work, and guidelines for evaluating and selecting the right camera for your project.

Choosing a camera is a process of weighing three factors: image quality, price, and features. Feature filmmakers should be most concerned about image quality, particularly if planning on digital projection or a video-to-film transfer.

Choosing a camera also means making a decision about which tape format to shoot on. Because there are so many digital formats available, it's worth taking some time to consider your choice of format. This choice can have many ramifications for your production process because not all cameras have the same features. Cameras that record high-quality formats, such as the various HD formats, tend to have high-end features whereas cameras that record consumer-oriented formats, such as DV, can range from surprisingly high-end feature sets to the video equivalent of "point and shoot."

EVALUATING A CAMERA

Once you've selected a format, you're ready to choose a camera that can shoot that format. Unlike many high-tech industries, the digital video world is surprisingly stable. Computers may be rendered obsolete every year, but digital video cameras tend to have a longer shelf life. Though we will mention a few cameras by name at the end of this chapter, the goal of this section is to give you the information and techniques you need to evaluate a camera on your own.

Whether you're buying or renting, if you consider the questions raised here, you should be well prepared to make a shrewd camera choice.

Image Quality

Portability and cool features are nice, but if that lightweight camera with the cool special effects produces images with lousy color and distracting artifacts, the audience is going to be less inclined to pay attention to your story.

The format you choose has a lot to do with image quality, of course—HDV is going to look much better than VHS—but within a particular format, you will be able to choose from among many different cameras. Film shooters have an advantage over video shooters in that image quality is heavily dependent on lenses and the film stock they stick in their camera. It's not so simple with video: in addition to the usual concerns about lens quality and camera features, you also have to worry about how good a job the camera does at actually capturing, processing, and storing an image.

Two factors contribute the most to your camera's image quality (or lack thereof): the camera's lens and the number of chips the camera uses to create an image. Your first choice, then, will be to decide between single-chip and three-chip models.

CCD

In the old days, video cameras used vacuum tubes for capturing images. Today, video cameras use special imaging chips called *CCDs*, or *charge-coupled devices*. Just as their tube-based predecessors used either one or three tubes to capture an image, CCD-based cameras use either a single CCD to capture a full-color image, or three separate CCD sensors to capture separate red, green, and blue data, which is then assembled into a color image (Figure 4.1).

FIGURE 4.1   An Olympus CCD image sensor.

A CCD looks like a normal computer chip, but with a sort of light-sensitive "window" on the top. The imaging window is divided into a grid; the finer the grid, the higher the resolution of the CCD. The circuitry controlling the CCD can determine the amount of light striking each cell of the grid, and that data is used by the camera to build an image.

Single-chip cameras have red, green, and blue filters arranged over clusters of cells in the CCD. These filter the light coming through the lens and allow the camera to record color images. In a three-chip camera, a series of prisms splits the incoming light into separate red, green, and blue components, and directs each of these components onto a separate CCD. Because the camera is dedicating an entire sensor to each color, color fidelity and image detail are much improved over single-chip cameras (Figures 4.2 and 4.3).

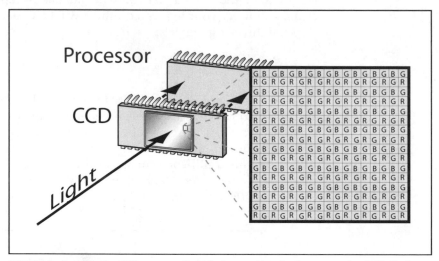

FIGURE 4.2 In a single-CCD camera, light is focused by the lens onto the CCD. Red, green, and blue filters placed over alternating cells of the CCD enable the camera to calculate color. The resulting data is passed on to the camera's processor. (Notice that there are far more green cells to accommodate your eyes' high sensitivity to green.)

When compared to a three-chip camera, a single-chip image might show strange color artifacts or bleeding, smeary colors as well as a softer, lower-resolution image.

The image data gathered by the CCD(s) is passed to an on-board computer that processes the data and writes it to tape. How the computer processes the data can have a lot to do with how images differ from camera to camera. Some cameras tend to produce warmer images, with stronger reds and magentas while others might produce cooler, less-saturated images with stronger blues. One approach is not better than the other, but

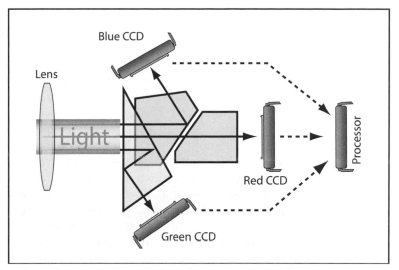

FIGURE 4.3   In a three-CCD camera, light is focused by the lens onto a series of prisms that split the light into red, green, and blue. Each component is directed toward its own CCD.

you may find that you have a personal preference, or that one is better-suited to the tone of your project.

Evaluating a CCD

You shouldn't have any trouble determining if a camera is a single or three-chip device, as vendors tend to clearly tout their extra chips in writing on the side of the camera. Typically, three-chip cameras start at around $1,500.

Three-chip cameras are definitely better than single-chip units are but the difference is not as extreme as it used to be. If a single-chip camera is all you can afford, don't worry, there are plenty of good single-chip units out there. As an example, Thomas Vinterberg shot *The Celebration*—which went on to a wide theatrical release and a special jury prize at the Cannes Festival—using a Sony PC7, a $1,000 single-chip camera that has long since been replaced by newer models.

CCDs come in different sizes, usually ranging from 1/8" to 1/3". Though you won't be basing your buying decision on CCD size, if you're aiming for extremely high image quality, you might want to limit your search to camera's with larger sensors. A 1/3" CCD will yield a noticeably better image than a 1/4" CCD.

When evaluating a camera, first look at its color reproduction. If you're a stickler for accuracy, you'll want to see if the camera can create an image with colors that are true to their originals. Even if you're not concerned with color accuracy, look for color casts or odd shifts in color.

It's also important to pay attention to *noise*. Noise comes in two flavors, *luminance noise* which appears as monochromatic speckly patterns in your image, and *chrominance noise*, which shows up as colored blotches, usually red, green, or magenta. Though you ideally want an image without noise, this isn't always possible, especially when shooting in low light. However, when evaluating noise response, you'll find luminance noise less annoying, since it tends to look a lot like film grain. Chrominance noise, however, is never attractive, and is extremely difficult to minimize in post-production.

You'll also want to check the camera's response to different lighting situations. Unfortunately, your average electronics store is not the best place for testing a camera. However, if you can manage to point the camera out a window, or into the dark recesses of a shelf or cabinet, you should be able to get an idea of the CCD's color response under different lighting. In addition to color consistency, and casts or shifts in color, keep an eye out for noise.

CCD-based cameras can have a tendency to create vertical white bands when exposed to bright elements in a scene. Different cameras employ different techniques to deal with this problem, and some are better than others. When evaluating a camera, point it at a bright light (but never at the sun!) and then quickly tilt the camera down. Look for vertical banding and smearing during the camera move. Vertical banding is not a reason to reject a camera, since you can always work around it, but it is important to know if your camera has this tendency.

Stay Sharp

Many cameras try to improve image detail by applying sharpening filters to each frame of video, just as you might apply a sharpen filter to an image in Photoshop. While these features are great for improving fine detail in a shot, they are often too much of a good thing. Apply too much sharpening, and diagonal or curved lines will appear jagged, or *aliased*.

Oversharpening is easiest to spot on moving objects or during camera movements. Areas of high-contrast—a car in front of a brightly-lit wall, for example—are also prone to oversharpening artifacts. When testing a camera, pan it about and look at objects that have very high-contrast edges. Look for "moving," jagged edges. Next, point the camera at an object with a thin, high-contrast horizontal line across it. Look to see if the line is stable or if it flashes on and off. Tilt the camera off-axis and watch how much the edge of the horizontal line changes and whether or not aliasing increases (Figure 4.4).

FIGURE 4.4 Oversharpening can create annoying artifacts that jump and slide around your image. In the upper image, (shot with a Sony DCR-PC1) notice the strong aliasing around the top of the glasses. The bottom image (shot with a Canon GL-1) lacks the aliasing around the glasses.

Sharpening can also be a *good* thing, so as you are watching for aliasing, also pay attention to how sharp the camera renders fine detail. If you are testing in an electronics store, objects with buttons, switches, and LEDs make great subjects for camera tests.

Higher-end cameras often have a sharpening control. If the camera in question has such a control, play with it and see if you can use it to resolve oversharpening problems. Pay attention to how fine detail changes as you adjust the sharpening. Also, look for any color shifts or changes as you adjust sharpening controls (Figure 4.5).

FIGURE 4.5   If your camera has a manual sharpness control, you can decide how much sharpening is appropriate for your image.

Blue Screen Troubles

If you're planning on doing any chroma key work (which will be discussed in detail in Chapter 17, "Tilting and Simple Compositing," then you'll definitely want a camera with a sharpening control. See Chapter 17 for more details.

White Balance

To accurately represent color, your camera needs to know what objects in your image are white. Once the camera is calibrated for white, it can more accurately reproduce other colors. Most cameras can automatically adjust their *white balance* once they've been told what kind of light is being used to light the location. We'll discuss white balance in Chapter 16, "Color Corrections." When evaluating a camera, though, see what white balance options are included. At the least, a camera should provide separate settings for indoor or outdoor. Better are cameras that provide presets for specific kinds of lights. The ideal white balance control is a fully manual control that takes a white balance reading off a white object that you hold in front of the camera.

Image Tweaking

While most cameras offer simple color balance controls, experienced shooters will want more advanced controls that allow them to perform exacting adjustments to the camera's image quality. High-end HD cameras are typically accompanied by a special on-set video technician whose job it is to make sure that the video signal is properly recorded using special instruments. Video engineering is way beyond the scope of this book, and if you're not going to be running the camera yourself, it's not something you need to concern yourself with. However, if you're planning on using an experienced director of photography, and you want the best image quality possible, you'll want a camera that can afford corrections such as custom gamma settings and pedestal or black level adjustments.

Lenses

Just as a film camera works by using a lens to focus light onto a piece of film, a digital video camera uses a lens to focus light onto the imaging window of a CCD (or group of CCDs). Moreover, just as the quality of lens on a film camera can mean the difference between good or bad footage, the quality of the lens on your video camera can mean the difference between sharp images with good color, and soft images with muddy color.

At the high-end consumer level, most DV cameras have fixed, zoom lenses; that is, you can't change the camera's lens as you might do on your 35mm SLR camera. At the higher end, DV cameras have interchangeable lenses that let you select from a variety of zoom ranges, wide angles, and telephoto options.

Lens Quality

When evaluating lens quality, look for changes in brightness across the image. Does the lens produce images that are brighter in the middle than at the edges, also known as *vignetting*? As you zoom the lens in and out, does the image get darker as the lens goes more telephoto?

Look for distortion around the edge of the image, particularly at wide angles. Does the image bow in or out as you zoom the lens back and forth? Similarly, look for changes in sharpness and detail throughout the lens's zoom range.

Chromatic aberration occurs when the lens does not equally focus all wavelengths of light. This problem is usually worse in single-chip cameras, though three-chip cameras with lower-quality lenses can also suffer from chromatic aberration. You can spot chromatic aberration by looking for fringes of red or green in high-contrast areas or around dark lines.

Lens Flares are those weird circles that appear when the lens is pointed into a bright light. Though lens flares have their uses—you'll see them a lot in "hot burning desert" scenes, or around flying logos—you want to be sure that flares only happen when you *want* them to happen. A lower-quality lens will flare very easily, and most lenses will have trouble with flares when shooting bright light sources at very wide angles. When evaluating a camera, zoom the lens to its widest angle outside during the day and see how easily it flares when you pan it around.

Lens Features

Depending on the quality of their controls, some lenses are easier to use than others. To make sure your lens provides controls that let you get the kind of camera movements and effects that you want, consider the following:

Zoom control. Is the zoom control well-positioned? How long does it take to zoom from full wide to full telephoto at the slowest speed? Ideally, this should be about 30 seconds. How quickly can it zoom its full length? You'll want this to be fairly quick to allow for quick framing of shots. How well does the zoom control work? Can you zoom at a constant speed? Can you make smooth zooming accelerations and decelerations? Is there a knob that allows for very fast zooms, or *snap zooms*?

Manual focus. If your camera has manual focus, where is the control? Whether electronic or mechanical, test the camera's manual focus for ease of use and reliability. Also be sure it holds focus when set. If the lens in question has a focusing *ring* (like what you'd find on a 35mm SLR camera), check to see if it has distances marked on it.

Aperture. As with focus rings, some higher-end lenses have manual rings for controlling the lens aperture (apertures are discussed later in the chapter). Check for f-stop markings, ease-of-use, and accuracy.

Minimum objective distance. How closely can the lens focus? For shooting small objects or getting extreme close-ups for cutaways, this can be important.

Lower-end cameras tend to have lenses built right in to the camera's body but this doesn't mean that they're necessarily low-quality lenses. Canon and Sony both include very high-quality lenses on cameras priced all the way down to $1,200. We'll discuss manual camera operation in more detail later in this chapter.

Never Mind the Reasons, How Does It Look?

At some point, you need to take a step back and look at the images produced by the cameras you are considering. You may find that you like one image better than another, and you may have no idea why. That's okay. If you prefer one image over another, but can't find a technical reason for your preference, don't worry about it. In the end, your subjective opinion is more important than any technical benchmarks or specifications.

DIGITAL ZOOM

Most consumer video cameras include a digital zoom feature. When digital zoom is activated, the camera will begin to digitally enlarge the image after you have zoomed to the optical limit of the lens. The results of these "fake zooms" are usually terrible. At extreme zooms, shapes become blobby mosaics of muddy color, and even a minor amount of digital zoom can introduce noise and ugly artifacts. Unless you are intentionally going for a grungy look, digital zoom is a useless feature—turn it off and leave it off! (If you are going for a grungy look, shoot non-grungy footage and grunge it up in post-production. You'll have much more flexibility, and can always repurpose the footage for non-grungy uses if you need to.)

CAMERA FEATURES

Once you've narrowed down your choices to a few camera models that offer the quality and lens features that you want, you can begin assessing other camera features to try to narrow your choice further. As a film-maker, your feature requirements are different from the casual home user, so examine each camera's features carefully.

Ergonomics

Currently, DV cameras range in size from a portable MP3 player all the way up to large, shoulder-mounted units. Choosing a particular camera body involves balancing features and shooting style with cost.

Smaller cameras typically lack high-end inputs such as XLR audio jacks (more about audio jacks in Chapters 9, "Production Sound," and 12, "Editing Hardware." They also usually don't have as many manual features and practically never include such niceties as lenses with aperture and focus markings, sharpening controls, and refined image quality adjustments.

On the other hand, small size makes a camera easier to carry, and ideal for surreptitious shooting. For documentaries, a low-profile camera might help you to get candid footage (nothing shuts up an interview subject faster than sticking a big lens in his or her face) or to shoot clandestinely in locations that wouldn't normally allow a camera (Figure 4.6).

A

B

FIGURE 4.6 The design of your camera not only dictates how comfortable the camera is, but what types of shots you'll be able to get. While a small hand-held camera (a) may be more portable, a larger camera (b) will facilitate more complex cinematography.

Similarly, if you're shooting a feature, a smaller camera makes it easier to shoot scenes without being seen (drawing a crowd with your production can often slow things down). If you're shooting without a city permit or permission, the "tourist" look of a smaller camera may be just what you need to keep from getting hassled.

Larger cameras usually sport three CCDs for better image quality while their heavier weight makes for easier shooting and smooth, steady camera moves. And, let's face it, they look cooler.

Don't ignore the camera's physical feel. To get the footage you need, you must be able to move the camera with great precision. If a camera is too heavy (or light) or too bulky for you to pan and tilt comfortably, you may not be able to get the shots you want. The camera's weight can also have budgetary consequences, as a heavier camera will require a more sturdy—and therefore more expensive—tripod.

Manual Override

The most important feature for the serious videographer is manual override. Controls for manually setting the camera's focus, aperture, shutter speed, audio levels, and white balance are essential for flexible shooting.

The problem with automatic mechanisms is that they're not too smart and they have no artistic flair. Rather, they are designed to produce a good picture under common, ideal shooting situations.

Focus

With manual focus controls, you can choose what to focus on, and compose your shots the way you choose. Similarly, manual aperture controls (sometimes referred to as *iris* or *exposure*) let you compensate for difficult lighting situations such as harsh backlighting (Figure 4.7).

FIGURE 4.7   Manual controls give you more freedom for composition. In this example, we used manual focus and aperture controls to go from an image with a sharp, focused background to one with a soft, blurry background.

Lower-end cameras typically provide electronic manual focus controls that are accessed through a menu system or from buttons on the camera's control panel. Higher-end cameras will have lens-mounted rings just like the rings on a 35mm still camera.

Lower-end cameras usually don't have values marked on their focus or aperture controls; instead, they display simple slider graphics in the camera's viewfinder. While this is effective, the lack of quantifiable settings can make it difficult to get the same settings from shot to shot. Such electronic controls are not necessarily suited to changing aperture or focus on the fly, making it difficult to do *rack focus* or *pull focus* shots (see Chapter 7, "The Camera," for more on these types of camera moves).

 ### *Manual What?*

We'll discuss the theory and use of manual iris and shutter speed in Chapter 7.

Shutter Speed

Most cameras automatically select a shutter speed based on the aperture setting, a process called *shutter priority*. Many cameras also provide manual shutter speed control, which gives you an extra degree of creative control. By switching to a higher shutter speed—1/200th to 1/4000th—you can stop fast-moving action such as sporting events. A faster shutter is great for picking out fine detail, but faster speeds eliminate most motion blur, which can result in an image with very strobic, stuttery motion (Figure 4.8).

Unfortunately, digital video camera manufacturers frequently provide fast shutter speeds but they often skimp on slow ones. If you are ultimately planning to transfer your finished video to film, it's a good idea to look for a camera that can shoot at 1/60th of a second. At this speed, you'll tend to get a better film transfer.

Frame Rate

As explained in Chapter 3, "Video Technology Basics" frame rates for video can vary a lot these days, depending on where you live and whether or not you're shooting HD. Earlier, we said that film has a frame rate of 24 fps. Actually, 24 fps is just the frame rate at which film is usually shot and projected. In fact, most film cameras offer variable frame rates. Sometimes, if a project is shot on film and destined for video, film is actually shot at 29.97 fps, to match the frame rate of analog NTSC video.

It used to be that video cameras only had one frame rate available—29.97 fps if you live in North America or Japan and 25 fps if you live in the rest of the world. Now, inexpensive video cameras are available that can switch from 29.97 fps to 25 fps (described as "NTSC/PAL switchable") and HD cameras can sometimes also record at film frame rates (24 fps/ 23.976 fps) in addition to the NTSC and PAL frame rates. (See Chapter 3 for the lowdown on all the possible frame rates of HD.)

A

B

FIGURE 4.8   (a) At a somewhat "normal" shutter speed of 1/60th of a second, the moving car has a pronounced motion blur. (b) At 1/4000th of a second, moving objects in each individual frame are frozen. When played back, the video can have a somewhat "stroboscopic" look.

The ability to choose between frame rates can save a lot of time and trouble later on. If you know you will have your video blown up to 35mm film, shooting at a frame rate that is the same as that of film will result in a better video-to-film transfer. (See Chapter 19, " Rotoscoping and More Compositing," for more details on 35mm blow-up.) Some people argue that shooting at 24 fps results in more of a "film look" even if

Progressive Scan

you are not going to transfer the video to film. But beware that you'll eventually have to transfer the 24 fps video to either 29.97 fps (NTSC) or 25 fps (PAL), depending on where you plan to distribute it.

In Chapter 3, you saw how current video standards such as PAL and NTSC are interlaced; that is, each frame of video consists of two sets of scan-lines, or *fields*, which are separately painted onto the screen every 60th of a second.

Some cameras can shoot in a non-interlaced, progressive scan mode. Progressive scanning—painting the scan lines on, in order, from top to bottom—is what your computer monitor does, and it typically produces a clearer image with a more film-like sense of motion. (Some companies refer to this as "Movie mode.") However, on some lower-end cameras the clarity of the frames also means that fast-moving images sometimes have a strange, stroboscopic quality to their motion. On these cameras, progressive-scan mode is really intended for still photo use.

On higher-end cameras (like that shown in Figure 4.9), progressive-scanned video usually looks much more "film-like" than interlaced video. The reason for this is not grain or texture, but, rather, the lower frame rate itself. Since progressive scanned video is running at 29.97 whole frames per second, it's closer to film's 24 fps than interlaced video's 60 half-frames per second.

FIGURE 4.9   Higher-end cameras like the JVC GY-DV500 provide a full set of manual controls, pro-level audio inputs, high-quality progressive scan modes, and more.

Some film transfer houses claim that progressive scan yields a better film transfer, and many transfer houses recommend shooting this way. Others are more comfortable with interlaced, because that's what they're used to transferring. Similarly, some "film look" software packages prefer one form of video over another.

Be sure to do many test shoots before you commit to shooting in progressive scan mode.

Faux Progressive Scan

On some cameras, the progressive scan mode doesn't shoot a true 30 full frames per second. Instead, they shoot a single field, and duplicate it to create a full frame. Very often, they do this at a much slower frame rate of 15 frames per second. Though this can look a lot like a regular progressive scan, you're only getting half the vertical resolution. Stay away from these faux progressive modes.

Aspect Ratio

Many cameras include a "widescreen" mode that lets you shoot in a 16:9 aspect ratio à la HDTV or widescreen film. These features work by cropping the top and bottom of the frame to letterbox the image down to 16:9.

The downside to this "hacked" 16:9 effect is that you lose a lot of vertical resolution. If your CCD only has 360,000 pixels and you're using a third of them for black areas above and below your image, you're effectively shooting with much lower resolution than your camera is capable of (Figure 4.10).

FIGURE 4.10 The "widescreen" feature on many cameras simply masks the top and bottom of your image, effectively wasting a third of your vertical resolution!

Some formats can shoot a true 16:9 aspect ratio because they use rectangular CCDs that actually have a full 16:9 ratio's worth of pixels. DV and other formats that don't provide a "true" 16:9 mode, can usually output a widescreen, non-letterboxed image to a widescreen TV, but this is only useful if you know that your project will be delivered and viewed on a widescreen device.

Another route to shooting wide screen is to leave your camera in its normal shooting mode, and do what film users do: get a special lens.

An *anamorphic* lens optically squeezes the image horizontally to fit a wider image onto the CCD. If you look at an individual frame of film shot with an anamorphic lens, you'll see a squished image that's greatly distorted. But project that image back through a projector that's been fitted with an equivalent anamorphic lens, and you'll get an undistorted, really wide picture. Similarly, you can use your editing software to unsqueeze your anamorphic footage to create a true widescreen image (Figure 4.11).

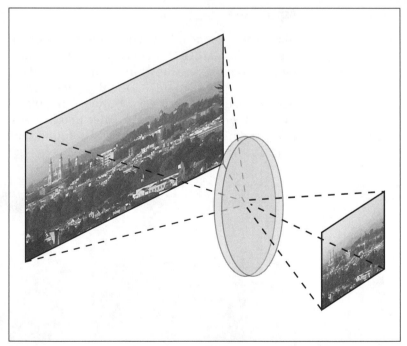

FIGURE 4.11   An anamorphic lens optically squeezes a wide image down to the aspect ratio of your CCD. To look right when viewed, it must be correspondingly de-squeezed.

Several manufacturers make anamorphic attachments for camcorders. If you're determined to use one of these, however, you'll need to make sure it works with your camera. Check with your vendor for compatibility. Also, if you're planning on transferring to film, check with your service bureau or film lab to make certain that they can handle anamorphic footage.

Audio

It's pretty safe to say that the microphones included on almost all camcorders are lousy. Low-quality to begin with, their usefulness is further degraded by the fact that they often pick up camera motor noise, as well as the sound of your hands on the camera itself. Consequently, an external microphone jack and a headphone jack are essential for quality audio recording. In addition to replacing the lousy onboard mic on your camera, an external mic jack lets you mix audio from a number of mics, and feed the result into your camera. We'll discuss audio hardware more in Chapter 9, "Production Sound." Ideally, you want a camera that has XLR mic connectors that can be switched between mic and line level inputs. Make sure the connectors are positioned so that mic cables and connectors won't get in the way of moving the camera and shooting (Figure 4.12).

FIGURE 4.12   Be sure to determine what jacks your camera provides. This Canon GL-1 provides a headphone jack (bottom) on its rear panel, and a mini mic jack on a side panel (not shown).

A headphone jack is a must-have to ensure that you're actually recording audio (you'll be surprised at how easy it is to forget to turn on a microphone).

Manual audio gain controls let you adjust or *attenuate* the audio signal coming into the camera, making it easy to boost quiet voices, or lower the level on a roaring car engine. At the lower end, very few cameras have audio meters and manual adjustments. This isn't a deal-breaker, but they're nice to have if you can get them.

Many cameras have an *auto gain control* or *auto limiter,* which will automatically try to limit loud noises. Unfortunately, like many automatic features, since you have no control of an auto gain feature, you can't always be sure that it's not limiting your sound more than you'd like. Again, these features aren't deal breakers, but if your camera is outfitted with such an limiter, you'll need to experiment with it to learn how sensitive it is.

Viewfinder

Most video cameras have two viewfinders, an eyepiece viewfinder and a flip-out LCD viewfinder. Because you can tilt an LCD into different viewing angles, flip-out LCDs afford you a wider range of shooting options. However, because an LCD drains your battery quickly and can be difficult to see in bright light, you might not be able to use it all the time. Yes, you want a high-quality LCD, but don't let LCD quality weigh too heavily when choosing a camera.

Some higher-end cameras include a feature called Zebra that displays diagonal black and white lines in areas of your image that are overexposed. These lines are not recorded to tape; they only appear in the viewfinder. If you're manually setting your shutter and iris, Zebra is a must-have for situations when you don't have an external monitor to look at (Figure 4.13). Top-of-the-line cameras let you set the brightness level at which the Zebra stripes appear. This is useful if you are trying to shoot with a low-contrast ratio, as is sometimes recommended for video-to-film transfers.

Most professional video cameras and film cameras do not have LCD displays, but in some cases there are special separate LCD viewfinders that can be added onto the camera. Often, a field monitor is used to see what the camera is shooting on a larger display. If you are shooting HD, this field monitor needs to be HD as well or else you won't really be seeing the image that is actually being recorded. Having an on-set HD monitor is another costly element of high-end HD productions.

FIGURE 4.13   The diagonal lines in this viewfinder are the "Zebra" marks that indicate overexposure.

Image Stabilization

Because it's difficult to hold a one- or two-pound camcorder steady, most cameras now provide some sort of image stabilization feature to smooth out bumpy, jittery camera movement. Image stabilization technology—though no substitute for a tripod—is very effective and (usually) has no ill side effects.

There are two kinds of image stabilization: electronic and optical. Electronic image stabilization (EIS, sometimes called *digital image stabilization*) requires a CCD with a larger imaging size than the actual image size that is displayed. EIS works by detecting camera motion, analyzing it to see if it's intentional or not, and then digitally moving the image to compensate for unwanted motion. Because the camera is overscanning the actual field of view, there are enough extra pixels around the edges to allow for this kind of movement (Figure 4.14).

Since the camera is constantly moving the image about the screen to compensate for shake, electronic stabilization can often result in softer, slightly blurred images. We've also seen some cameras show a slight color shift when using EIS. However, most EIS functions in use today do an excellent job of stabilizing the image without noticeably degrading the quality.

Optical image stabilization (OIS) doesn't alter your image, but instead, changes the internal optics of the camera to compensate for motion. Rather than solid prisms, cameras with optical stabilization use prisms composed of a transparent, refractive fluid sandwiched between two flat pieces of glass. Motors around this prism sandwich can move the glass panels to reshape the prism. Light passing through this mechanism

FIGURE 4.14   In electronic image stabilization, the camera scans an oversized area and then pans about that area to compensate for shake.

can be redirected onto the correct part of the CCD to compensate for camera shake (Figure 4.15).

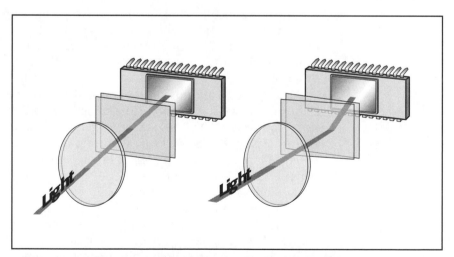

FIGURE 4.15   Optical image stabilization works by reshaping one of the lens elements on the fly to correct for camera movement.

Since OIS doesn't ever touch your image data, there's no chance that it will corrupt your image. On the downside, because it's more complicated, optical stabilization costs more than electronic stabilizing. Also, because the stabilization is tailored to a particular lens, if you add wide-angle or other attachments that change the focal length of your lens, OIS will stop working.

When evaluating a camera, try some motion tests—both slow and smooth, and fast and jittery—to see how each camera's stabilization feature affects overall image quality.

Direct-to-Disc Recording

As shooting on film gives way to recording onto videotape (for many applications), recording to videotape is slowly giving way to recording directly to a hard drive, or optical disk. Hard-drive recording has many advantages to tape recording, especially for post-production. If your footage has been captured directly to a disk, then you don't need to spend time capturing or digitizing—just move the files from the disk to your computer and start editing. Also, you can record over the footage stored on your hard drive with no quality concerns for the new footage, something that can't be said about recording over used videotape.

Direct-to-disc recording also has many on-set advantages. Speedy review of what you've just shot; quick non-linear access to other scenes you've shot without having to fast-forward and rewind; easy generationless backup and duping.

On the downside, direct-to-disc recording is still expensive, requires extra gear and power, and if you run out of disk space, you might have to switch back to tape anyway, possibly creating problems for shot logging and organization later on.

At the high-end, you can buy direct-to-disc cameras that can output uncompressed HD video directly to a hard drive, but these systems are incredibly expensive, and probably not within the budget of the users of this book.

At the low-end, you can buy cameras that record directly to DVDs. Unfortunately, these cameras don't simply store normal DV video files on their DVD disks, instead they produce DVD-video disks, which are compressed using MPEG-2 compression. In other words, they don't save simple, discreet files that you can move into an editing program in a non-linear manner. Instead, you'll have to capture the MPEG-2 footage in real time, just like you do with videotape.

So, for the types of production you're probably doing, the best direct-to-disk options are outboard DV recording decks—special units that include a hard drive and a FireWire port (Figure 4.16). To use them, you plug your FireWire camera into the device's hard drive, and then use it just as you would a tape deck: hit record to start recording, and then start up your camera. Your video and sound will be stored on the deck as standard DV files. Later, you can connect the device to your computer to transfer the files for editing.

Panasonic's P2 format is specifically designed as a direct-to-disk format. You can read more about it in Chapter 3.

These devices usually include a small LCD status screen and special controls that you let you sort through the media you've shot, delete unwanted files, and play video to an external monitor connected to your camera (or, sometimes, to the device itself).

FIGURE 4.16   The Firestore is a FireWire hard drive with a built-in controller and simple OS that lets you record from any camera directly to disk.

Priced anywhere from $600 and up, these devices give you all the advantages of direct-to-disk recording, but work with your existing camera. For documentary work, or any shoot that's on a tight deadline, hard-disk shooting can be an incredible timesaver and workflow simplifier.

When choosing a disk recorder, consider the following:

• How noisy is it? Some larger devices include built-in cooling fans that can make a fairly loud whirring sound. Though not a problem for shooting outdoors, for intimate interior work, they might be too loud.
• What kind of files does it output? Some devices export raw DV files, which should work with any DV editing system. For the ultimate in workflow ease, though, you might want to consider a device that is capable of writing your files in the native format of your editing software.
• Does it require recapturing? Some early direct-to-disk recorders were unable to transfer finished files directly to a computer. Instead, you had to capture from the device into your computer, just as you would

with a regular video deck or camera. Though these devices still provide benefits—quick field review, easy back up of your media—the ability to transfer without recapturing is a feature to hold out for.

For a list of specific hard disk recorders, check out *www.dvhandbook. com/directtodisk*.

Special Effects

Most video cameras, especially lower-cost cameras, include a number of special effects ranging from sepia tinting to "arty" posterizing looks. We don't recommend using any of these features. It's better to shoot unprocessed video so as to have the greatest flexibility during post-production.

Similarly, many cameras also provide a number of wipes and dissolves. If you plan on editing your entire project in the camera, or without using a computer (by hooking two cameras together), then these wipes and dissolves might be useful. But, as with effects, better to shoot clean footage and add the transitions later in post-production.

Batteries

Having a battery die during a shoot is more than just an inconvenience, it's a waste of time and money. Unfortunately, most cameras ship with batteries that won't last over a long shoot. When purchasing, find out what other batteries are available, and how long they will last.

Ideally, you'll want enough battery life for several hours of shooting. Battery cost should be factored into your assessment of final camera cost. Note that using an LCD viewfinder will consume your batteries faster. If you know you'll be using the LCD a lot, you'll need more batteries.

Third-Party Batteries

For extra-long life, consider a battery belt such as those made by NRG Research. With enough juice to power a camera and light for several hours, a battery belt is a great—though bulky and costly—solution to short battery life.

Use Your Director of Photography

If you have already chosen a director of photography (DP), talk to him or her about your camera needs. Your DP may have ideas about how to shoot your project that will not only make for better-looking video, but help enhance the emotional impact of your scenes. Depending on what sort of effects you want to achieve, some cameras might be better than others. If you'll be shooting your feature yourself, then consider the same questions you would ask a DP:

- Is there a particular "look" that you are striving for? Grungy old film? Super saturated and glossy? Muted and subtle?
- Are you planning on certain camera movements? If you know that you will be shooting from a Steadicam or other specific camera mount, you'll need to consider the size and weight of your camera.
- Do you have special post-production needs? If you know, for example, that you will be shooting blue-screen footage, then you'll want the best image quality you can afford.
- Does your shoot require more than one camera? If so, you may need to consider going with cheaper cameras.
- Are you going to rent a high-end, professional camera? If so, you may need to hire a professional operator. Consider this in your budget.

ACCESSORIZING

As with any piece of gear, there are loads of accessories available for your camera. And, while many are fun frivolities, others are necessary for a serious production. Pick out your camera before you start shopping for any of the following items, though. Different cameras have different needs, and you don't want to buy an expensive accessory only to find it has the wrong type of connector, or is the wrong shape for your camera.

Tripods, Steadicams, and Dollies

There is absolutely *no* substitute for a good tripod. A tripod is also essential for some complex camera motions such as smooth pans with simultaneous zooms. Camera movement is part of your visual vocabulary, and most camera movements require a tripod. Shooting without one limits your vocabulary.

The ideal tripod has a fluid head for smooth movement, and easy-to-find handles for locking and unlocking each axis of the tripod's motion (pan, tilt, and pedestal). Check for stability and sturdiness and make sure the tripod can support the weight of your camera, along with anything else you may need to have onboard (audio mixer, microphones, small lights, etc.).

Steadicams/Glidecams

Normally, when you want to move the camera through a scene—rather than having it pan and tilt from a fixed location—you must lay tracks along which your crew will slowly push a camera dolly. In addition to the hassle of laying tracks and smoothly moving the camera, you have to be sure you don't capture the tracks in your shot.

Nowadays you can—if you have enough money—perform many of these shots with a Steadicam. A clever arrangement of gimbals and counterweights, Steadicams, Glidecams, and other similar stabilizers work by mounting the camera on an apparatus that has a lot of rotational inertia, but little reason to rotate. Though the physics are complicated, the result is simple: a camera that mostly floats in place, but that can be adjusted and moved in simple, tiny movements.

Both Steadicam and Glidecam produce a number of different types of units for cameras of different weights. These devices are not cheap, and if you really need one, you'll probably do better to rent. Note that if you have a very large camera that requires a large Steadicam, you'll also need to spring for a trained Steadicam operator.

Dollies

Dollies are special camera-holding carts that travel along special tracks, and are used for creating tracking shots. Dollies and tracks require some extra effort to set up and use, but they're often the only way to achieve certain shots. Most good production houses rent dolly gear at very reasonable rates.

Microphones

All video cameras—even at the higher end—have marginal microphones, so you'll need to replace these with professional units designed for the type of shooting you'll be doing. We'll discuss mics in Chapter 9, "Production Sound."

Filters

You can use filters to change the color or optical properties of the light in your scene. Most filters screw directly onto the threads on the end of your lens, though some have special mounting brackets.

We'll discuss filters more in Chapter 7, "The Camera."

All That Other Stuff

There are any number of other cool and useful accessories ranging from bags and trunks for protecting and transporting your camera, to housings for shooting underwater. Depending on the nature of your shoot, you might very well need to budget for extra pieces of gear.

What You Should Choose

When it comes down to it, most digital features are shot on one of a few different higher-end cameras. The Canon XL-2 and the Sony VX 2000 have been the workhorse cameras of the DV "revolution" because they offer professional features, very good image quality, and a reasonable price. Both cameras are affordable and readily available for rent. Recently, many independent films are opting to shoot on HD because of the high image quality and success in video-to-film transfers.

Down from these are several 3-chip cameras and both offer small packages and low prices while maintaining a pro-quality level. If you want full-featured, professional controls, though, you'll want to stick with a higher-end camera.

All of these cameras are DV cameras, and so are well-suited to feature or documentary productions that will be delivered on video or transferred to film. Quality-wise, though, they're not your best choice.

Summary

If you can afford it, you should consider shooting on a higher-quality format such as DVCPro or DVCam. These cameras offer improved image quality and professional features, but you may want to plan on transferring your footage to a format such as DV for editing because of the ease of using FireWire-based technology.

5

PLANNING YOUR SHOOT

In This Chapter

- Storyboarding
- Location Scouting
- Production Design
- Effects Planning
- Exercises
- Summary

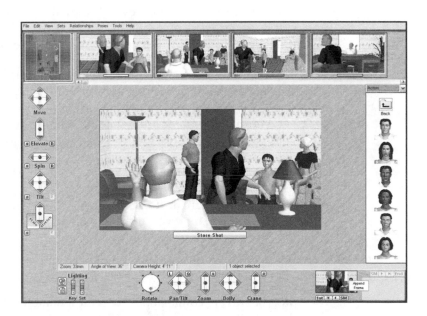

It's been said that making a movie is a lot like going to war, and while you most likely won't be risking life and limb during your production, as a producer or director you will be managing a large group of people, all with diverse talents and goals. In addition, you'll be trying to balance these talents and goals against budgetary constraints, scheduling problems, inclement weather, temperamental actors, and any number of impossible-to-predict problems. Each one of these problems and issues will end up slowing down your shoot and that will translate directly into a financial impact. The best way to steel yourself against these problems is with meticulous, thoughtful planning.

There's no correct way to plan, and different types of shoots require different degrees of planning. In Alfred Hitchcock's *Vertigo*, there is a scene in which Jimmy Stewart spies on Kim Novak as she shops in a San Francisco flower store. Observers of the shoot reported seeing Hitchcock meticulously plan and arrange all of the cars that were passing by the window in the background of the shot. Color, shape, speed, order—he planned and calculated it all. Hitchcock was also an avid storyboarder, utilizing his accomplished draftsman skills to create detailed illustrations of exactly what shots he would get.

At the other end of the extreme are directors like Woody Allen, who don't storyboard at all, but choose to plan and block their shots on-set, with the actors. However, even if they don't storyboard, these directors still do meticulous planning by working with their camera and production crews to prepare sets and costumes, determine a "look" for their work, and much more.

As a director, you're responsible for everything the viewer sees on-screen, whether it's good or bad. With a little preparation, you can improve your odds that the viewer is seeing something good.

Your main tool for preparing for your shoot is the *storyboard*. Because storyboarding requires you to perform the first serious visualization of your project, the storyboarding process forces you to answer some questions that you might not have dealt with during the writing of your script. From choosing locations, to the look of your production, to how your project will be edited, storyboarding is where you'll make many practical decisions about how you'll shoot your script.

STORYBOARDING

Storyboards are comic-book-like representations of the images in your production (Figure 5.1). How well they're drawn and what they look like

FIGURE 5.1   A picture can be worth a thousand words when drawn by a professional storyboard artist.

doesn't matter, just as long as they convey to you and your crew a reasonable approximation of how the composition, framings, and cuts in your production will play out. The amount of detail in your storyboards will depend on the type of scene you are creating. For a scene of three people talking around a dinner table, your storyboards will probably be less detailed, and will serve more to help you plan framing and cutting. For a special effects-heavy shot of a spaceship flying into a spaceport on an alien planet, your storyboards will include more detail to help your art department and visual effects crews plan and prepare for their work, and to help you make sure that what you shoot on location can be accurately merged with effects that will be created months later after your sets may already be gone.

It doesn't necessarily matter if you shoot exactly what you planned in your storyboards. More important is the information that you will learn while storyboarding. Until you meticulously start to plan things on paper, you might not know how much *coverage* you will need for a particular scene, or that you're going to need a particular set piece or prop.

Whether or not you choose to draw storyboards, you still need to go through a "storyboarding" process. That is, you need to methodically plan the visual images and details that you will use to create your final product. This planning ranges from deciding how to frame and shoot a scene, to choosing a location, cast, set, and props for your shoot.

You don't have to storyboard, and many great directors don't. However, if you decide not to storyboard, you should at least create a list of shots for each scene. The last thing you want to do when you get to a location is to keep your cast and crew waiting because you haven't spent any time thinking about how to shoot.

You'll often start storyboarding before you've chosen any locations or built any sets. Obviously, if you already know the location of a scene—the Golden Gate Bridge, for example—then you can storyboard somewhat accurately. Generally, though, you'll first create somewhat abstract, non-location specific storyboards. Later, if the shot calls for it, you can go back and refine your storyboards after you've chosen locations, built sets, created props, and so on.

In addition to visualizing the movement of your camera, you'll also use storyboards to explore the motion of elements within your scene. For complicated effects or action shots, your storyboards will be your first opportunity to choreograph your scenes.

Shots and Coverage

Once you start shooting, your main concern will be to get all of the *coverage* that you will need when you're in the editing room. The term *coverage* refers to the number and types of shots you need to shoot to "cover" a particular scene. How much coverage is necessary? That all depends on your tastes, the needs of your script, and how much shooting you can reasonably manage to do.

It's important to realize that, although you might have written a very "visual" script, you probably didn't write out specific shots (in fact, you shouldn't have written out specific shots; it makes your script much less readable).

How Many Shots Does It Take to Make a Scene?

When a scene is well shot and expertly edited, you won't even be aware of one shot turning into the next. In fact, unless you actually choose to look at the number of shots, you might not ever have any idea of just how many shots it takes to create a scene.

Let's take a look at a real-world example. Perhaps you've seen the James Bond movie *Tomorrow Never Dies*. Like all James Bond movies, this one begins with an action sequence that takes place before the main credits. One could describe this sequence as follows:

> On top of a snow-covered mountain, a group of terrorists have met to sell weapons. Having snuck in to the location, James Bond has set up a small video camera, which is relaying images back to headquarters where M and a number of generals are watching. After a lot of fighting and a daring air battle, Bond manages to escape with a nuke-laden airplane before a missile launched by the generals strikes the mountain.

As you can see, it's your basic "excuse me, I have to save the world" type of James Bond scene and the entire thing lasts about nine minutes. However, take a look at this list of the first 19 shots in the scene:

1. Wide-shot—Terrorist arms bazaar. Pan down to reveal a video camera.
2. Reverse-angle of the video camera.
3. Shot of what the camera sees (called a "point-of-view" or POV shot).
4. Shot of the camera lens zooming.
5. Another POV shot. We zoom in to a group of terrorists.
6. Another shot of the video camera panning and zooming.
7. Another POV shot. This time, we see a fat, bearded man.
8. Another shot of the video camera.
9. Another POV shot. This time, some trucks.
10. Yet another shot of the video camera.
11. And yet another POV shot. Two terrorists making a deal.
12. Again, a shot of the video camera.
13. A POV shot of some guns.
14. Now, we see three big-screen monitors showing the videos we've just seen. The camera pans down to reveal a man speaking.
15. Medium shot of two men in military uniforms. They watch the screens.
16. The speaking man again.
17. Reverse shot showing the whole room including the men, and the big screens.
18. Close-up of a woman.
19. 2-shot of the woman and the speaking man.

There you have it, 19 shots, each completely different, and almost every one of them requiring a different camera setup—that is, the camera had to be moved and rearranged for *each* of these 19 shots. What's really amazing, though, is that these 19 shots account for only *one minute* of screen time! And this is a two-hour movie!

If we imagine what the terrorist arms bazaar set looked like, we can get a good idea of all of the different locations where they would have to put the camera to get the first 13 of those shots (Figure 5.2).

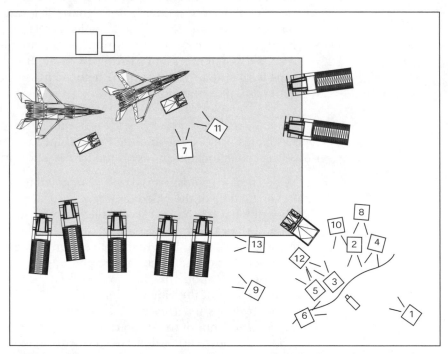

FIGURE 5.2 This map shows a rough approximation of the set for the first scene of the James Bond movie *Tomorrow Never Dies*, including camera positions and orientations for the first 13 shots. Note that these 13 shots take up only 40 seconds in the final scene! That's a lot of work for 40 seconds of finished film.

Two things are interesting about this scene: first, you can see that it can take a *lot* of different angles and setups to get the coverage you need to make the scene you want. Second, when you watch this scene, you don't ever think "man, there sure are a lot of different camera angles here." In other words, if you shoot and edit well, your audience won't necessarily even realize how many different shots they're seeing.

CAMERA ANGLES

Here's a list of the types of shots or camera angles you can use to compose a scene. Figure 5.3 shows samples of each type of shot and how you might represent such shots, framings, and cuts within your storyboards.

FIGURE 5.3   Camera angles.

Master shot: A master shot is usually a wide, static shot that covers all the action in a scene. Often it is used more as a "safety" shot or a backup in case the planned coverage doesn't work. Master shots "establish" the scene—its location, participants, and tone. They are what gives the viewers their first, big hit of information in a scene.

2-shot: A shot used to cover a dialog scene between two actors. Both actors are visible, usually from mid-torso up.

Over-the-shoulder (OS): Also used to cover dialog scenes between two actors. The shot focuses on one actor, but contains the silhouette or partial view of the second actor in the foreground.

Reverse: A view 180 degrees from the previous shot. Usually used in combination with a POV shot or an OS shot.

Point of view (POV): A shot where the camera shows the point of view of one of the characters. Often a dolly move.

Extreme close-up (ECU): A very tight close-up, such as a shot of someone's eyes or a bug on his or her nose.

Close-up (CU): A tight shot where the subject fills the entire frame. If the subject is a person, a shot of his or her head.

Medium close-up (MCU): A slightly wider shot than a close-up. Usually like a sculptured "bust"—head, neck, shoulder, upper torso.

Medium shot (MS): On a person, usually a from-the-waist-up view.

Wide shot (WS): A shot that shows a whole area, usually full-figure in the case of people.

Tracking (or dolly): A moving shot that uses a camera dolly (a wheeled cart that travels along special tracks) to push the camera through the scene. Often an opening shot or a POV. Depending on how they're designed, dolly shots can travel from side to side or forward and back.

Crane: A moving shot that uses a camera crane to move the camera through the air, allowing movement on an X-Y-Z axis.

Pan: A side-to-side movement of the camera, where the camera rotates around its base. The resulting motion is what you would see if you stood in one place and turned your head from side to side. Often used to follow a figure across frame.

Tilt: Similar to a pan, but the camera tilts up and down. Analogous to tilting your head up or down. Usually used to reveal something, like a character who just ripped his pants.

Pedestal: Raising or lowering the camera, usually by adjusting the tripod on which the camera is mounted. Creates a "rising periscope" point of view. Very rarely used in features.

Zoom: A lens movement from a tight to a wide shot (zoom out), or a wide to a tight shot (zoom in).

Dolly counter zoom: A shot where a dolly and a zoom are performed at the same time. In the resulting shot, the framing of the image stays the same, but the depth of field changes dramatically. Objects in the background foreshorten and appear to float backward. The most famous example is in *Jaws*, when Roy Scheider sees the shark in the water on the crowded beach. His POV of the shark is a dramatic dolly counter zoom.

Slow reveal: Usually a pan, tilt, or dolly that reveals something that at first wasn't apparent. A woman laughs at a table, pan over to reveal that her husband just spilled his wine.

COMPUTER-GENERATED STORYBOARDS

There are a good number of computer-based storyboarding tools that can make your storyboarding chores much easier. Ideal for people with limited drawing skills, these programs let you create professional-quality storyboards with detailed sets, characters, and symbols. Even if you're an experienced illustrator, the convenience and speed of CG storyboards can be a real time and money saver. Many storyboarding apps include the ability to automatically import your script from a screenwriting program, sophisticated web-based storyboard sharing, and more. These are some of the top apps that are currently available.

PowerProduction Software's Storyboard Quick: Available for Mac or Windows, Storyboard Quick has been around longer than any other dedicated storyboarding app. Providing a simple interface, the program lets you drag and drop characters, props, and locations to create nice-looking colored line-drawings. Offering robust import of screenplay formats and export of finished boards to print or the Web, Storyboard Quick is an excellent solution to your storyboarding needs.

PowerProduction Software's Storyboard Artist: Offering sophisticated 3D storyboard generation, Storyboard Artist allows you to create more complex storyboards than what you can build with Storyboard Quick. In addition, the program lets you create *animatics* complete with multi-track audio. An excellent tool for any type of pre-visualization, Storyboard Artist is especially good for complex action and special effects scenes.

FrameForge 3D Studio: Also a 3D storyboard app, FrameForge (shown in Figure 5.4) provides easy tools for building 3D sets, and plenty of characters and props for populating your virtual venues. Offering excellent controls for specifying lens focal length, FrameForge also boasts easy-to-position characters that automatically know how to sit on objects, hold other objects, and perform other automatic actions.

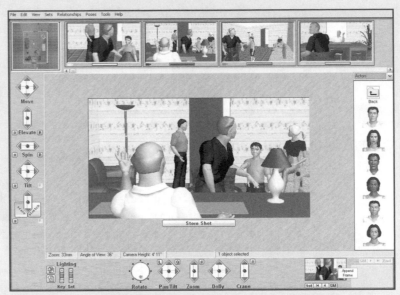

FIGURE 5.4 FrameForge 3D provides a true 3D environment for quickly building sets, blocking positions, and adding storyboarding symbols.

SketchUp Film & Stage: SketchUp is an excellent 3D modeling program that was originally designed to provide a way for architects and designers to quickly create 3D visualizations of their designs. The new Film & Stage plug-in (shown in Figure 5.5) provides a few extra features that add additional storyboard and pre-visualization functionality. In addition to its simple interface, SketchUp scores over the other products mentioned here for its beautiful "sketchy" rendering quality, which yields storyboards that look much more like real hand-drawn images.

FIGURE 5.5   The Film & Stage option for SketchUp 3D combines a simple-to-use architectural CAD program with pre-built objects that are ideally suited to shot planning and storyboarding.

Less Is More

Remember, storyboards are a visualization tool, not an end product. If you show crew members detailed, photorealistic storyboards, they'll be inclined to think that those images are what your final scene will look like. Better to give designers, costumers, set builders, and actors rough, sketchy storyboards. Let them use their expertise to design and create the details for which they're responsible.

Storyboarding is only one of your previsualization tasks, and you'll probably refine and change your storyboards throughout your pre-production and production phases.

Camera Diagrams and Shot Lists

For scenes that have a lot of complicated action like the James Bond scene mentioned earlier, you might find it useful to create a camera diagram. This is a simple visual reference that will help you understand what camera setups you need once you're on-set. In addition to helping you plan your shoot, camera diagrams can help ensure that you get all of the coverage that you need. Camera diagrams can also include information about light placement, to help your lighting crew stay organized.

Take a look at the scene in the sidebar below.

INT. THE UPTOWN BAR - DAY

A woman, DEBRA, sits drinking alone at the bar. She doesn't look up as JOE, a greasy-looking character in his mid-thirties, enters.

MAX, the bartender, comes out from behind the bar.

Joe stops dead in his tracks.

JOE

I thought you quit. Left town. Something about cleaning up your act.

Debra looks uneasily from Joe to Max.

MAX

Doesn't look that way, does it?

JOE

She's with me. Arent' you, Deb?

Debra nods nervously.

MAX

I don't think so.

Max pulls out a gun and, without waiting for Joe's reaction, shoots. Joe falls to the floor, dead.

According to the corresponding storyboards in Figure 5.6, this scene needs a master shot, three close-ups, and a two-shot.

FIGURE 5.6   A storyboard of the scene scripted in the sidebar on page 110.

These storyboards are based on *master shot* style coverage. Shot 1 is a master shot that covers the entire scene and serves as the foundation onto which you will add the close-ups (shots 2, 3, and 5) and other shots in the editing room (Figure 5.7).

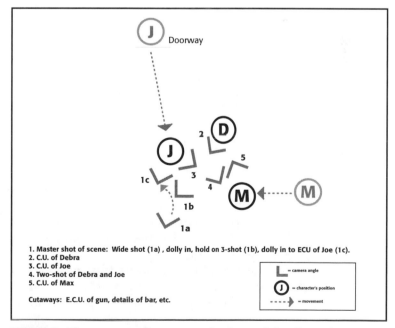

FIGURE 5.7   The corresponding camera diagram and shot list to the storyboard in Figure 5.6.

Camera diagrams can also include information about light placement and other crucial objects. Figure 5.2 is an example of a much more complicated camera diagram.

LOCATION SCOUTING

The locations and sets on which you choose to shoot will convey some of the most vital visual information in your story. Sometimes, set and location will convey even more than your script or your actors.

There's no real rule for finding a location; you simply have to get out of the house and start looking around. There are, however, some things to remember and some questions to ask when looking for and selecting a location. Moreover, depending on the type of equipment you will be using, your location needs might vary. Consider the following when scouting locations:

- **Will the owners of the property let you shoot there?** You should, of course, always ask permission before shooting on private property. Though many people will let you shoot for free simply because they'll be excited by the idea of a movie shoot, in other situations you might have to work a deal—either for cash or donations of improvements to the property. If you are planning to sell your finished project to a distributor, you'll need to get a *location release* from the owners of the property.
- **Do you need a permit to shoot?** For shooting on civic or government-owned property, you'll often need to get special permits from your local city hall or municipal government. Most larger cities have film commissions whose primary purpose is to help film production crews get permits. Permits do cost money, though, so you'll need to add this into the cost of shooting at a particular location. You can often get away with shooting clandestinely, without a permit, but there can be risks to this. Here in San Francisco, we've heard stories of permit-less production crews having all of their equipment confiscated by the local cops.
- **Do you need both the inside and outside?** You may not necessarily need access to both the inside and outside of a location. After all, you can always shoot your interiors on a set, or in a building to which you have better, less expensive access. Storyboard carefully for these situations.
- **Can you find the same type of location in a cheaper town?** The inside of an office is the inside of an office. See if you can find office space nearby, but in a cheaper location.

- **Is the location a reasonable distance from the rest of your shoot?** Lugging equipment, cast, and crew to faraway locations can quickly become prohibitively expensive, particularly on a union shoot.
- **Does the location require redressing or modification?** Removal of signs, addition of new signs, changing the look or "period" of the environs. This can be done through practical set dressings or through digital "dressing" and post-processing, but it will add expense to that particular location.

FILM CREW IN THE 'HOOD

For his movie *Do the Right Thing*, Spike Lee made major modifications to an entire city block in Brooklyn. With a clear idea of the storefronts he needed for his set—as well as their proximity to one another—his set designers proceeded to modify existing buildings to fit his needs. Because he had the use of an entire city block, he got all of the "in-between" locations (sidewalks, street corners, etc.), in addition to getting the individual storefronts he needed, and all within walking distance of each other. In the process of preparing the set, his location security guards cleared out and renovated a crack house, a set change that, obviously, made a lasting improvement in the neighborhood.

- **Does the location afford the coverage you need?** If the shots you plan require many different angles, you'll need to consider your location carefully. For example, although your location might look great, be sure you can shoot it from multiple angles and reverse angles without getting unwanted scenery (Figure 5.8).

A   B   C

FIGURE 5.8   (a) This Spanish-style mission might be just the location for some exteriors in your turn-of-the-century drama. (b) Unfortunately, it sits on a very busy, four-lane thoroughfare, which will make shooting clean audio very difficult. (c) Also, across the street from the mission are very modern buildings and parking lots, which will make reverse angles difficult. (On the other hand, this location—San Francisco's Mission Dolores—was good enough for Hitchcock! He featured it prominently in *Vertigo*. Of course, it wasn't a period piece, and there was much less traffic in 1958.

- **Does your location have the physical space required for the size of your shoot?** In addition to your equipment, don't forget the support needs of your crew (power generators, trucks, dressing rooms, catering, porta-toilets, etc.) (Figure 5.9).

FIGURE 5.9 These cozy little houses could make a great location; however, the narrow street could make things difficult if you're expecting to use a large crew. In addition, clearing the street of cars could require expensive city permits, making what seemed like a cheap location into a big expense.

- **Does the location have access to sufficient practical resources such as power?** Remote locations pose other logistical problems, such as access to restrooms and refrigeration.
- **Is the location too noisy?** Refrigerators, outside traffic, and air-conditioning are just a few things that will add a hum to your sound recordings. Overhead airplanes and other intermittent noises will require constant halting of your production while you wait for the noise to pass.
- **What are the location requirements of your equipment?** If you are shooting at night, you might be able to get away with more or less lighting depending on the type of camera you are using. In addition, video cameras can have difficulty dealing with certain repeating patterns and textures. Closely spaced horizontal or vertical lines can create annoying interference patterns on your screen. Does your location contain such textures? If so, can you shoot around them?

LEARN FROM OTHER PEOPLE'S HIDEOUS NIGHTMARES

You can learn a lot from making mistakes. Unfortunately, the mistake-making process can be really uncomfortable and expensive. However, there are lots of other people out there also making mistakes, so there's no reason you can't exploit their misfortune for your own edification. Terry Gilliam, director of *Brazil*, *The Fisher King*, and *Time Bandits*, made a whole sling of mistakes while trying to make a movie version of Don Quixote. From choosing locations on an Air Force training ground to having his equipment wash away during a flash flood (in an area of Spain known for freak storms), his decisions on this film make fine examples of how *not* to make a movie. Fortunately, the movie *Lost in La Mancha* does an excellent job of documenting the entire debacle, giving you a chance to vicariously experience movie making gone awry. Other good "don't do this" examples can be found in the documentaries *Hearts of Darkness*, about the making of Francis Ford Copolla's *Apocalypse Now*, and *Burden of Dreams*, about the making of Werner Herzog's *Fitzcarraldo*.

- **What about light and sound?** Can you adequately light and mic your location for the needs of your particular equipment? Different cameras and formats have different needs in regard to light and sound. Plan for these accordingly.
- **Can you improve the authenticity of your set with sound effects?** Adding some simple ambient sounds to a shot—adding the cries of a circus barker to a shot of a tent, for example—can improve the authenticity of your set.
- **Can you fake it?** Cutting from a good, convincing establishing shot of a sun-dappled vineyard with appropriate ambient sound effects to an interior set that's been properly decorated might be all you need to make your audience believe that you paid for a long shoot in the hills of Tuscany (Figure 5.10).

Talk to your principal crew members when scouting locations. Does the production designer agree with your assessment of the feel of the set? Can he or she dress it accordingly? Does the cinematographer feel that he or she can shoot it in the way that you want? And can it be done affordably? Does your gaffer think the set can be outfitted? Careful storyboarding will help you explore these issues and formulate questions to present to your crew.

FIGURE 5.10 (a–c) A few well-planned establishing shots combined with the right audio can quickly establish a Mid-Eastern location. (d) When, in fact, you've only gone as far as a busy American street corner.

PRODUCTION DESIGN

An important part of pre-production is the chance to work with your crew to create the "look" of your movie—from the elements on the set, to the way the movie will be shot and cut—a process also known as *production design*.

Whether you do it yourself or attach a professional production designer or art director to your project, defining the look is more than just creating a style; it's a chance to explore how all of the elements at your disposal can be used to strengthen your visual image and, consequently, your story.

The goal of production design is to enhance the story by adding to the available visual palette. For example, in *Trainspotting*, every wall is painted a striking color often covered in a thick layer of grime: turquoise, red, green, mustard yellow. This dark, rich palette conveys an atmosphere of opiate sensuality appropriate to the film. In the film *Red,* the color palette is biased toward occasional touches of bright reds against a background of charcoal grays and rich dark browns. In *American Beauty*, the sets are dressed in typical suburban furniture just verging on "kitsch." The comfortable excess of the main family's house lies in sharp contrast to the austere, traditional Americana furniture in the house of the family next door. In *Do the Right Thing*, bright reds in the sets and clothing are used to increase both the feeling of hot summer and the emotional intensity of the drama.

Just as the director of photography is head of the camera department, the production designer is head of the art department. The production designer usually starts working early in the process, helping to generate storyboards and an overall "look" for the project. The title of this position might vary—you might use an art director or a set designer instead of a production designer, but their duties will be relatively the same. On a big movie, the production designer is responsible for the overall vision, while the art director implements that vision and manages the art department crew, which includes set designers, set dressers, prop masters, modelers, scenic painters, set construction workers, and production assistants.

Art Directing Basics

Good art direction is a combination of the symbolic and the practical. If your story is about a young girl growing up in Kansas in 1850, you'll be limited to certain types of buildings, furniture, and clothes. However, you still have the choice of giving her a sunlit, whitewashed bedroom with furnishings upholstered in bright calico fabrics, or an age-darkened room with no direct sunlight and dull, dark fabrics. These simple details tell two very different stories.

One of the easiest ways to add visual symbolism to a scene is via lighting. Colors also have strong connotations for people. Black often connotes death, while red conjures feelings of blood and violence, but also love and passion; blue is peaceful and calming, but can also create a feeling of sadness, and so on. Similarly, styles of furniture and clothing can say a lot about a character. An elderly woman living alone in a house decorated in sparse Eames furniture from the 1960s might indicate someone who won't let go of the past. Change the character to a young man, and the same furniture indicates a trendy sense of style. Clutter can be comfortable or claustrophobic; sparseness can be clean or indicative of emotional emptiness. In addition to externalizing the themes of the story, production design should also aid in focusing the viewer's eye, a challenge that goes hand in hand with lighting and framing the shot.

Building a Set

If your location needs are very specific, it might be easier to build a set than to find the right location. Whether you build your set on a stage or at a location, you'll need to spend some extra effort to make it look real. Sets are usually built out of *flats,* large, hollow wooden walls that are held up from the rear with supports. If you rent a soundstage, you might find that several flats come with the stage rental. You can paint them the color of your choice.

Typically, a room built on a stage will have three solid walls and a fourth wall on wheels for use when needed. Many flats have doors or windows built into them. When shopping for a soundstage, look for one that has the type of flats you need. If your needs are very specialized, you may have to built your own flats, and color or texture them appropriately. For example, you can easily create a stucco or adobe look by gluing foamcore to a flat and then spray painting it (spray paint dissolves foamcore). Hiring a set carpenter can save lots of time and trouble.

Retail Therapy

Good set dressers and wardrobe people spend a lot of time browsing in the shops in their city. A thorough knowledge of where to buy odds and ends is one of the secrets of their profession.

Set Dressing and Props

Whether you have a found location or a built set, the next step is to dress it. Because they're completely empty, dressing a built set takes more work than handling a found location. On the other hand, your options might be limited when dressing a found location because you'll want to avoid disturbing the occupants or ruining their property. Either way, a good prop (short for *property*) can really sell a weak location. A giant gilded Victorian mirror, a barber's chair, a mirrored disco ball—the mere presence of these objects tells you where you are and makes the location believable. Props can be very expensive to rent, but if you can find that one key piece, it might be worth the money. In addition to prop rental houses, you can sometimes rent props from retailers. Usually, this will involve a hefty deposit and the requirement that it be returned in perfect condition.

If your film involves weapons and fight scenes, you'll need special props such as breakaway furniture and glass, fake knife sets, and realistic-looking guns. Fake knife sets usually include a real version of the knife, a rubber version, a collapsible version, and a broken-off version. Renting a realistic-looking gun usually involves some extra paperwork, and you are required to keep it concealed at all times. If you have a really specialized object that you need—like the *Get Smart* shoe-phone—you'll probably need to have a fabricator or modeler make it for you.

ART DIRECTING EQUIPMENT CHECKLIST

- Staple gun
- Hammer, screwdriver, and other tools
- Nails, tacks, and push-pins
- Various types of glue
- House paint and spray paint, various colors including black
- Paint brushes and rollers
- Bucket
- Dark brown and amber water-based stains, Streaks and Tips, etc.
- Dulling spray (to take the shine off reflective objects)
- Contact paper
- Window cleaner (with ammonia)
- Cleaning products
- Rags, towels, cheese cloth
- Dust mask

PRODUCTION DESIGN EXAMPLES

Your local video rental store is a great source of production design examples. Here's a list of rentals that are worth watching in their own right, but that we've included here as examples of particularly good production design.

Matewan. John Sayles's 1987 tale of union troubles among West Virginia coal miners is an all-around example of excellent filmmaking. For the independent producer, it's especially informative as it shows that a convincing period piece (a type of movie that can be very expensive) can be produced with an indie budget. You can read more about the production design of this movie in John Sayles's excellent book *Thinking in Pictures: The Making of the Movie Matewan.*

Narc. This gritty tale of undercover narcotics agents is set in modern-day Detroit, but the lack of modern props and recognizable establishing shots give it a timeless, placeless feeling: this is a story that could happen anywhere in America.

Eyes Wide Shut. In his last film, Stanley Kubrick used the religious images and iconography of middle ages, particularly the works of Hieronymous Bosch, and their famous depictions of hell to create a frightening but fascinating secret world.

The Incredible Adventures of Wallace and Gromit. Animated works offer the most extreme production design examples, because *everything* that you see on-screen had to be designed. Even if you've already seen these excellent animated shorts, take a look at them again with an eye toward the production design. From the custom-designed wallpaper themes to the characteristic "industrial era" look of Wallace's inventions, these works are masterpieces of production design.

EFFECTS PLANNING

If your shoot requires any special effects, then you have a whole extra planning job ahead of you. Special effects must be carefully planned out for all the reasons that any shot needs to be planned (to save time on the set and to make sure you get the footage you need), but effects planning is also the time when you have to figure out how you're going to create the effect you want.

Your first question when creating a special effect shot should always be, "Do I really need it?" Effects are time-consuming, complicated, and expensive. You should never include anything in a story if it doesn't really belong there, but you *definitely* shouldn't include something as complex as a special effects shot if it doesn't really belong there.

If you decide that you do need the effect, your next question is to determine if the effect is going to be created digitally (in the computer), or practically (using "real" props and sets, and clever camera work), or some combination of both. As amazing as digital effects can be, it's often easier and faster to create an effect using special props and backdrops on the set.

Obviously, to determine the best way to create an effect, you need to know something about creating effects, both digital and practical. We talk much more about effects creation in Chapters 17, "Titling and Simple Compositing," and 18, "Rotoscoping and More Compositing." Hopefully, if you're not comfortable with effects work, you can find someone who is and get him or her to help you with your effects planning.

Once you've determined how to create the effect you need, you might want to shoot some simple test shots and see if the effect really works. Alternatively, maybe you'll want to create *animatics*, animated shots (usually 3D) that serve as a "moving storyboard." Animatics can provide good visual references for everyone, from designers to effects crews to actors. For example, you can use a 3D program to create animatics that can be shown to actors and crew and that can even be used as placeholder video while you're editing.

Perhaps the best way to understand the importance of effects planning is with an example. The shot in Figure 5.11 is from a short film about a guy with a remote control. In one scene, the script calls for a painting of the Mona Lisa to appear on the wall behind the man, and for the wall to change color.

When shooting, we first thought about compositing the Mona Lisa in digitally, but then realized it would be easier to simply create a Mona Lisa prop (which we did by printing a digital file of the Mona Lisa on a large-format printer, and then mounting it inside a rented frame).

The change in wall color, though, was achieved through a digital effect called *rotoscoping*. Simply put, we simply re-painted the wall color in post-production. Unfortunately, the first time we shot, we didn't realize that the actor's head needed to remain in front of the painting at all times, to ease the rotoscoping process.

FIGURE 5.11   Due to bad effects planning, this shot was unusable. Since the actor's head did not remain in front of the Mona Lisa at all times, repainting the wall became prohibitively difficult.

With better planning and some good tests, we could have avoided this. As it was, we had to reshoot, or face an incredibly difficult rotoscoping job.

Creating Rough Effects Shots

If your feature requires complex effects shots—battling spaceships, giant flying insects, waving computer-generated cornfields—you'll want to start preparing such shots early in production. There's no reason you can't have your effects department quickly rough-out low-res, low-detail animations that can serve as animated storyboards. With these rough animations, you can more easily plan and direct shots. Having low-res proxy footage also means that you can go ahead and start editing before your final effects are rendered.

EXERCISES

ON THE DVD

1. **Storyboarding:** In Chapter 2, "Writing and Scheduling," you were introduced to a scene from Shakespeare's *Richard III*. If you performed the script breakdown exercise at the end of that chapter, then you've already acquainted yourself with that scene. The script is located in the Chapter 2 folder on the companion DVD. Though it's a simple dialog scene between two characters, there's a lot of dramatic tension and rhythmic interplay. Finding a way to shoot this scene to showcase the actors, enhance the drama, and reveal the tension is an excellent exercise. (After all, this is one of the rare instances as a director where you know you can trust your material.) Create a set of storyboards for this scene. In addition to planning your shots, go ahead and give some thoughts to how and where you might like to stage it. Do you want to shoot it in a traditional period British setting? Or re-stage it for a different location. Because it's primarily talking heads, you don't need any exceptional rendering skill, even stick figures will do.

2. **Shot Lists:** Now that you've created a set of storyboards for the *Richard III* scene, create the associated camera diagrams and shot lists. In addition to helping you understand where you're going to want your camera, this process will also give you an idea of how many times you might have to run the scene to get the shots you want, and when you might need to shoot some things out of sequence. Remember, to get all the angles that you need, your actors will have to be prepared to perform many takes.

3. **Production Design:** Don't worry, we're not going to send you shopping or set-building. Rather, we're simply going to ask you to write up a narrative description of how you might design the *Richard III* scene. You should have already chosen a setting during the storyboarding exercise. (If you really want to exercise your skills, go ahead and scout

around for some locations, take some pictures of them, determine if you think you could shoot your storyboarded scene there.)

Now you can start thinking about how you might want to dress your location, what kind of wardrobe you might want the actors to wear, what sorts of props you'll want to use. In addition, give some thought to overall color palette and tone of the scene. The obvious palette and tone choice is dark and muted, but perhaps there are other options—not so obvious—that are equally as powerful.

4. **Budget:** You've now done the bulk of the planning that you need to actually pull off a shoot of this scene. Now, with your breakdown sheets, production design, and shot lists in hand, give some thought to how much it would cost to shoot it. Write up a budget to generate a cost estimate to cover the shoot. Obviously, you'll need a camera, and possibly lights, as well as two actors and a crew of at least one person and a camera operator. In addition, you might need to rent props or costumes, or pay for access to your location. If you're really going gung-ho on this, then you might even need to budget for set dressing or construction. (Bear in mind that it's also possible to do this scene for free with a skeleton crew. That's one reason we picked it. One great thing about Shakespeare, everything you need is in the text, so you can pull off this scene with minimal production. Nevertheless, it's fun to imagine a lavish production as well.)

SUMMARY

Filmmakers have always had to engage in meticulous planning before rolling their cameras. As a digital filmmaker, you have a decided advantage. With digital tools for storyboarding, you can more easily try out different visualizations. Moreover, with digital editing, your storyboards, animatics, and early work files can actually be repurposed to save time in post-production.

6

LIGHTING

In This Chapter

- Lighting Basics
- Film-style Lighting
- The art of Lighting
- Types of Light
- Lighting Your Actors
- Tutorial: Three-point Lighting
- Interior Lighting
- Exterior Lighting
- Video Lighting
- Special Lighting Situations
- Exercises
- Summary

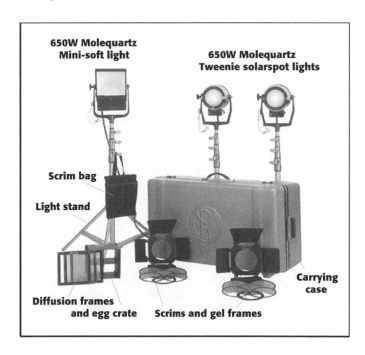

650W Molequartz
Mini-soft light

650W Molequartz
Tweenie solarspot lights

Scrim bag

Light stand

Carrying
case

Diffusion frames
and egg crate

Scrims and gel frames

LIGHTING BASICS

Camera choice, of course, has a huge impact on the quality and look of your final project. But picking the right gear is only half the shooting battle. It doesn't matter how good your camera is, if you do a lousy lighting job, you'll get a lousy final product. A well-lit scene shot with an inferior camera can look much better than a poorly lit scene shot with a great camera. Fortunately, of all of the things that can affect the look of your production, lighting is something that you can actually control.

Lighting is not just a way of making your video look better. Lighting is an essential element in your visual vocabulary. Lighting conveys mood and atmosphere, and is the key to a successful video-to-film transfer. In this chapter, we will discuss tips for film-style lighting (whether you're shooting video or film), basic lighting setups, lighting for different exterior and interior situations, the unique challenges of lighting for video, and lighting for special situations, such as video-to-film transfers and blue-screen photography.

FILM-STYLE LIGHTING

If you've done any research on using video to shoot feature-length projects, you've probably encountered this piece of advice: "If you want your video to look like film, you need to light it like film." What's the difference between lighting for film and lighting for video? (If you're just starting out and don't know anything about "lighting for video" then you're in great shape, because you have nothing to unlearn, and no preconceived notions to jettison.)

Shooting on film is technically more challenging than shooting on video, because film stocks are much less forgiving of bad exposure, and proper film exposure requires lots of light. But film lighting specialists, known as *cinematographers* or *directors of photography* (DPs), do more than just pile lots of lights onto the set, they use special equipment to control the path of the light, the quality of the lights, the brightness of the lights, and the color of the lights. The amount of light coming from every light source is meticulously measured with a *light meter* in order to achieve the desired *contrast ratio* between the highlights and shadows. By controlling these elements, the cinematographer is able to direct the viewer's eye within the frame.

Lighting, along with focus and framing, which we cover in Chapters 7, "The Camera," and 8, "Shooting Digital Video," all add to the visual vocabulary used in filmic storytelling. Film-style lighting is not so much a distinct visual style as an artistic choice that helps tell the story and it is useful for traditional film cinematographers and videographers alike.

Video Lighting

In the past, it has been generally accepted that video looks lousy when compared to film. There's good reason for this prejudice. Just turn on the TV and take a look at any talk show, news show, reality TV show, and even most sitcoms, and you'll see footage shot with garish lighting—or no lighting at all. Rarely will you see the type of moody, subtle, expressive lighting that you'll see in a movie. These examples, though, don't mean that video *has* to look garish, harsh, and ugly.

First, a film look is not appropriate for all projects. News footage and other documentary-style productions that use run-and-gun, shot-on-the-fly footage are designed simply to convey some specific factual (hopefully) content. Style is not a concern. Similarly, producers love reality shows because they're cheap, and the reason they're cheap is that they have such low production costs thanks to their simple shooting needs. Similarly, your production may not need a traditional film look either because the material doesn't need such a look, or simply because you can't afford the time and expense of shooting with complex lighting setups. These are decisions you'll need to make early in your pre-production process.

However, no matter what type of lighting you ultimately decide to use—even if it's none at all—a knowledge of film-style lighting can be very important. Though you may not be setting actual lights, you can still make decisions about where to position your camera, or choose to use some simple lighting implements such as reflectors, that can make a substantial difference in your image quality.

Finally, shooting video that is destined to get transferred to film for theatrical projection offers yet another set of special circumstances and technical considerations. Throughout this chapter we'll cover both film-style lighting and also the special needs that arise when lighting for video, especially when circumstances do not allow for traditional film-style lighting. But first, the basics . . .

Test Your Lighting

When dealing with unfamiliar territory, professional directors of photography don't just light a scene and hope for the best. Instead, they do a test shoot and check the results at the film lab or video-to-film transfer facility. Although shooting tests requires an investment of time and money, you'll save a lot of both in the long run, by ensuring you're getting footage that will make for a good film transfer.

THE ART OF LIGHTING

Lighting is one of the most powerful yet subtle filmmaking tools available. *Film noir* classics, such as *The Maltese Falcon,* are known for their creative use of light and shadow, while modern comedies often feature a bright, simple lighting style that is similar to television. No matter what your film is about, creative lighting can enhance the mood and emotion of your story.

Three-Point Lighting

Three-point lighting is the basic, jumping-off point for more complicated lighting setups. Three lights are used to light a single subject—usually an actor—from three directions (or points). The primary light source, called the *key light,* is used to illuminate the subject and is usually positioned at an angle (Figure 6.1). The key light is a strong, dominant light source and is often designed to replicate a light source in the scene such as the sun or a lamp (Figure 6.2a).

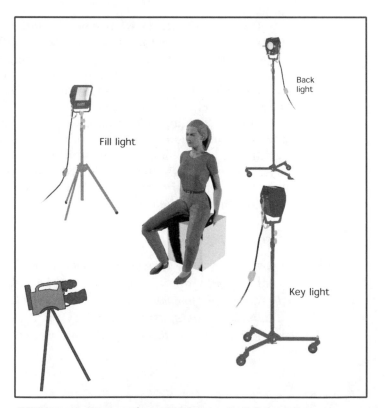

FIGURE 6.1 A diagram of a typical three-point lighting setup, including camera placement and subject.

The second light, called the *back light* or sometimes the *kicker*, is positioned behind the subject and is used to separate the subject from the background (Figure 6.2b). This separation lends a sense of depth to the image and helps make your subject "stand out" better. You can see the effect of the back light in just about any type of video production, even the evening news. Note that well-lit newscasters usually have a ring of light

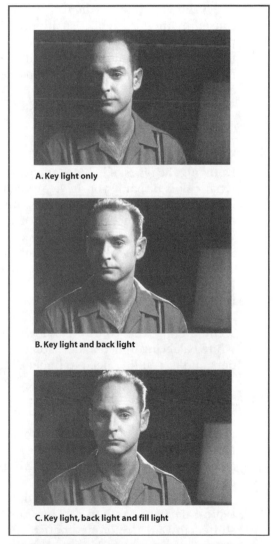

A. Key light only

B. Key light and back light

C. Key light, back light and fill light

FIGURE 6.2   In this example of three-point lighting, the actor is first lit with a diffuse key light (a), then a hard back light is added (b), and a soft, subtle fill light brings out the left side of his face without losing the high-contrast look (c).

around the top of their heads, or at least a good strong highlight on the top of their head. This rim lighting is created by the back light, and serves to give their head a more discernible shape. Sometimes the back light is a different color—bluish or orange. Making choices about the relationship between the key, fill, and back lights is part of the art of cinematography. After we present a few more key lighting concepts, you'll be ready to try your hand at the three-point lighting tutorial later in the chapter.

A third light, called the *fill light*, is used to "fill in" the strong shadows caused by the key light. Usually the fill light is quite a bit dimmer and more diffuse than the key light (Figure 6.2c). The idea is not necessarily to get rid of the shadows, but to achieve a pleasing contrast ratio between the lights and shadows on the subject, so that neither bright lights nor dark shadows are dominant.

TYPES OF LIGHT

Knowing the types of lights that are available for shooting is like knowing what colors of paint you have available to paint a portrait. Professional lights fall into two basic categories: tungsten balanced (or indoor lights) and daylight balanced (or sunlight). These two categories represent two very different areas of the color spectrum. The light from a conventional indoor light bulb tends to look orange or yellow, whereas the light outside at midday tends to appear more white or blue. Your camera probably has a setting that lets you choose a light bulb icon (for tungsten) or a sun icon (for daylight). By informing your camera whether you are in daylight or tungsten light, you are letting it know the overall color-cast of the scene. Setting this control is known as *white balancing*. We will discuss white balancing in detail in Chapter 7, "The Camera," but in order to understand it, you first need to understand how light and color are related.

Color Temperature

First, a quick science lesson: Light is measured in terms of *color temperature*, which is calculated in *degrees Kelvin* (K). Indoor tungsten lights have a color temperature of 3200° K, whereas daylight has an approximate color temperature of 5500° K.

Color Plate 1 shows the color difference between tungsten light and typical daylight. As you can see, tungsten light at 3200° K is heavily shifted toward the orange part of the spectrum, which results in the warm, golden cast of household lights. On the other hand, daylight at 5500° K is heavily biased toward the blue part of the spectrum, which results in more of a bluish-white light. Be aware that as the sun rises and sets, its color temperature changes and it decreases into the orange part of the spectrum.

While you might not be able to discern that household light looks orange and sunlight looks blue, the main thing to realize is that daylight is much stronger. (Think of the hotter, blue flames in a burning fire.) Daylight-balanced lights are over 2000° K stronger than tungsten lights, and if you try to mix them together, the daylight will certainly overpower the tungsten light. If you can't avoid mixing tungsten and daylight—for example, if you're shooting a day interior scene that absolutely requires that a real window be in the shot—you need to account for the color temperature differences by *balancing* your light sources. Balancing your light sources means that you'll use special lighting gels to change the color temperature of some of the lights (or windows) so that they are all either tungsten-balanced or all daylight-balanced. We'll talk more about lighting gels and mixing daylight and interior light later in this chapter.

Other Types of Lights

Tungsten lights and daylight-balanced lights aren't the only types of lights. *Fluorescent* lights have a color temperature that ranges from 2700° to 6500° K, and *sodium vapor* lights, with a color temperature of about 2100° K, are yellow-orange. *Neon* lights vary wildly in temperature. All of these lights introduce special challenges.

Fluorescents are notorious for flicker and for having a greenish tint, which can be exacerbated on film or video. You can buy or rent special *Kino-Flo* tubes that fit into normal fluorescent fixtures, and get rid of the flicker and the green color. Yellowish-orange sodium lights use a very limited section of the visible color spectrum. The result is an almost monochrome image. If you try to color correct later, you'll have very little color information with which to work. Neon lights can easily exceed the range colors that your camera can capture, (these lights produce colors that are outside of the NTSC color gamut) especially red and magenta neon. Even though they tend to be quite dim in terms of lux or foot-candles, neon lights appear bright and overexposed due to their extremely saturated colors. (See Color Plate 10 and Figure 13.14).

Wattage

Lights are also measured in terms of the amount of electric power they require, or *wattage*. The higher the wattage, the brighter the light. Typical film lights range from 250 watts to 10 K (10,000 watts). The powerful HMI lights used to mimic the sun and to light night exteriors require as much as 20,000 watts, whereas a typical household light needs a mere 60 watts. The professional lights best-suited for use with video are those with a wattage of 2 K or less. Figure 6.3 shows a typical video light kit.

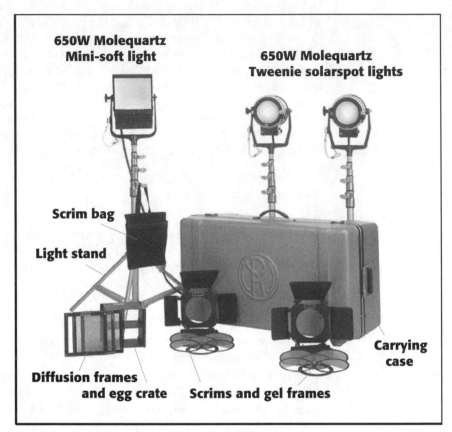

FIGURE 6.3   This Teenie-weenie/Softlite combo kit from Mole-Richardson is a good example of a typical video lighting kit.

Camera Mount Lights

Camera mount lights, also called sun guns, are a great quick fix for run-and-gun photography. However, if a film look is your goal, save the camera mount light for your next documentary-style project. If you do need to use them, try adding some diffusion fabric to reduce the "hot spot." Shining a light directly into someone's face is just about the least-flattering light that you can contrive, so it's best to use these types of light sparingly.

THE BASIC LIGHT KIT FOR VIDEO

A basic light kit for video provides the minimum lighting equipment necessary for three-point lighting. The typical cinematographer won't be happy with it, but it's a considerable step above single source lighting. A basic video kit costs around $40 a day to rent and includes something like the following:

- Two 650-watt lights (with fresnel lenses)
- Two single scrims
- Two single half-scrims
- Two double scrims
- Two double half-scrims
- Two sets of barndoors
- One 1 K or 650 W softlight
- One egg crate (used to make the softlight more directional)
- Three gel frames
- Three light stands

MEASURING LIGHT

The intensity of a light stays the same no matter how far the subject is from the light; what changes is the amount of illumination given off by the light. Illumination is measured in either footcandles (based on the English measurement system) or lux (based on the metric system) as expressed in these formulas:

$$\text{Illumination in lux} = \text{Intensity (in candelas)}/D2$$

where D is the distance in meters between the light source and the subject.

$$\text{Illuminaton in footcandles} = \text{Intensity (in candelas)}/D2$$

where D is the distance in feet between the light source and the subject.

Light meters are devices that measure light in footcandles and/or lux, and translate the measurements into f-stops.

If you've ever used a still camera that provides manual controls, you're probably familiar with f-stops. F-stops are defined as the ratio of the focal length of the lens to the aperture of the lens. The aperture is one of the controls that governs how much light passes through the lens and onto the imaging surface, or focal plane. When you adjust the f-stop control on a camera, you are opening or closing the aperture of the lens. Many professional video cameras also have f-stop marks on their lenses, or in their viewfinder displays. Because of how they relate to exposure in film, f-stops are often used in video to describe increments of light.

There are two types of light meters: *Reflective light meters* measure the light that is bouncing off the subject and *incident light meters* measure the light that is falling on the subject. Many handheld light meters offer both modes of light metering. Digital video cameras do not have built-in light meters but they do have features such as *zebra stripes* that let you know that part of the image is going to be overexposed. However, it is best to rely on a field monitor rather than your camera's viewfinder to check the lighting on your set.

Controlling the Quality of Light

In addition to having different color temperatures, lights have different *qualities*. They can be direct or *hard*, they can be soft or *diffuse*, or they can be *focused*, like a spot light. Figure 6.4 shows the same subject lit with a diffuse key light (a) and a hard key light (b).

There are all types of lighting accessories that can be used to control the quality of professional lights. A special *fresnel* lens attachment lets you adjust the angle of the light beam from flood to spot light. *Barn doors* attach to the light itself to help you control where the light falls. Round *scrims* fit into a slot between the light and the barndoors and allow you to decrease the strength of a light without changing the quality. Single scrims (with a green edge) take the brightness down by one-half f-stop, and double scrims (with a red edge) take it down a whole f-stop. (See the sidebar "Measuring Light" for more about f-stops.)

Lighting gels are translucent sheets of colored plastic that are placed in front of the light not only to alter the color of the light, but to decrease the brightness (Color Plate 2). The most common use of lighting gels involves converting tungsten to daylight, or vice versa. *Diffusion* gels are usually frosty white plastic sheets that make the light source appear softer. *Gel frames* allow you to place lighting gels behind the barn doors, but it's usually easier to use clothespins to attach gels directly to the barn doors.

Bounce cards (often just pieces of white foamcore) are also used to create soft, indirect lighting, while *reflectors* (shiny boards) are used to redirect lighting from a bright light source, such as the sun.

C-stands (short for *Century stands*) hold *flags, nets,* and other objects in front of the lights to manipulate and shape the light that falls on the subject (Figure 6.5). We'll talk more about how to use these items as we cover traditional interior and exterior lighting.

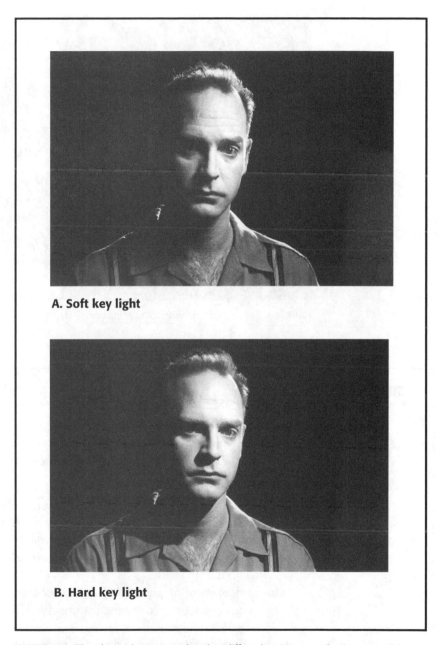

A. Soft key light

B. Hard key light

FIGURE 6.4 The choice between a hard or diffuse key is an aesthetic one—this actor is lit with a diffuse key (a) and a hard key (b).

FIGURE 6.5   A soundstage with lots of flags on C-stands to control the light.

LIGHTING GELS

Gels are an indispensable tool if you're serious about lighting. Rosco and Lee make swatch books like the one in Color Plate 2 that contain samples of the different gels they produce. Gel swatch books are usually available at any professional camera store.

Colored gels can be used to add just about any color in the rainbow to your light sources. It's a good idea to have a choice of colors on hand. Remember that the brighter the light shining through the gel, the less intense the color will be. Adding colored gels will always decrease the brightness of the light.

Color temperature orange (CTO) and **color temperature blue** (CTB) gels can change the color temperature of a daylight-balanced light to tungsten, or tungsten to daylight.

Neutral density gels cut down the intensity of light without changing the color temperature. These gels are extremely useful when shooting video, where too much light is often a problem. They are especially handy when it's necessary to shoot in front of windows.

LIGHTING YOUR ACTORS

Lighting a person is always a bit more challenging than lighting an object—the human face has many angles, and it's easy for bright lights to cast strange and unflattering shadows. In addition, bright lights can magnify every little flaw on a person's face, while the wrong color lighting can result in an unnatural-looking skin tone. Whether your goal is to make your actors look beautiful or ugly, the right lighting will enhance your characters and story. The following three-point lighting tutorial provides a tried-and-true method for lighting an actor.

TUTORIAL	THREE-POINT LIGHTING

This tutorial assumes you have access to a typical video light kit (like the one described in the sidebar "The Basic Light Kit for Video"), a selection of gels (see the sidebar "Lighting Gels"), and a suitable subject to light, preferably a person. If possible, you should also have your camera set up on a tripod in order to see how the different lighting possibilities look through the lens. If you have a field monitor, you should use that too. If you don't have a field monitor, consider recording a videotape as you experiment with your lighting, so that you can later view the results on a full-size monitor. You'll also need a pair of work gloves for handling hot lights. Finally, you should start with a large, dark room. A sound stage is ideal, but any dark room will work. If you're doing this tutorial at home, see the following tip on how to avoid blowing a bulb.

Step 1

To begin, set up your key light. Take one of the 650-watt lights from your kit and set it up on one of the stands. Attach the barn doors to the light itself—they usually just slide into place. Direct the light toward your subject and turn it on. Don't worry about the background yet; we'll deal with that later. For now, focus on lighting your subject as best you can.

Now that you have light on your subject, find a pleasing angle at which to place the light. The human eye is used to seeing light that comes from a high angle, usually from over our shoulder, so low-placed, low-angle lights often yield results that look a little strange. Extend the stand to its full height and then aim the light down at your actor. Experiment with different heights to see what works best. Try placing the light at different distances from your subject. Does it look better close or farther away? You can set up the lights any way that looks good to your eye. Just make sure that the light is not so bright that it overexposes in your viewfinder. (If your viewfinder provides a Zebra display, turn it on to help identify hot spots.)

Because of the shadows cast by a person's nose, the key light is usually placed about 30 to 45 degrees off-center from the person's face. This position gives definition to the features of the face and allows the shadow from the nose to fall to the side without becoming huge or distorted. (Consult the diagram back in Figure 6.1 to re-visit a typical three-point lighting setup.) Once you're happy with the angle, play with the focus knob on the fresnel lens. Does it look better tightly focused or flooded? (Figure 6.4 shows the difference between a hard key and a soft key.) Try adding some diffusion. Play around until you find a look you like, and then move on to the next step.

Don't Waste Expensive Light Bulbs

Avoid touching high-wattage light bulbs, (or globes, as they are professionally known). The oil from your fingers can overheat and cause them to explode (the globes, not your fingers).

Step 2

Now it's time to add the back light. As with the key light, set it up on a stand and play around with different positions. Back lights are usually quite bright and often filtered with lightly colored gels. Usually, the best position for a back light is either high overhead pointing down at the back of the subject's head, or way down near the ground pointing up at the back of the subject's head. The reason for this is that you need to avoid having the light itself visible in the shot as well as avoid having it pointed directly at the camera (which will cause a lens flare). Figure 6.6 shows the actor illuminated with the back light only, and Figure 6.2b shows that actor illuminated with the back light and key light.

Fire Hazards

Avoid putting diffusion gels, lighting gels, and any flammable materials too close to professional light globes—you might end up with a stinky, smoldering mess stuck to your light, or worse, you might start a fire!

In addition, use your gaffer's tape to tape down your light's power cords. It can be easy to trip over cords and pull over your lights as you work around them. Finally, use sandbags to weigh down light stands so that they aren't easily knocked over.

FIGURE 6.6   The actor lit with a back light only.

Step 3

Now you are ready to set up the fill light. Take the 1 K soft light from the kit and set it up on the stand. Your goal with the fill light is to make the shadows cast by the key light less severe. Usually, this means placing the light on the opposite side of the subject from the key light, typically at a 30- to 45-degree angle directed at the unlit side of the actor's face (see the diagram in Figure 6.1).

The brightness of the fill light is very important, since this is how you control the contrast ratio of your scene. Remember that video doesn't handle high-contrast lighting as well as film does. Try placing the light at different distances from the subject to see how the contrast ratio changes. It's often nice to have a fill light that's a different color than the key light. Experiment with different colored gels until you're satisfied with the fill light. Figure 6.7 shows the actor illuminated with a soft 1 K fill light only, and Figure 6.2c shows a subject lit with key, back, and fill lights.

Step 4

Now that you have your three lights set up, it's time to look at the overall scene. Are colored areas washing out to white? Are there hot spots, bright reflections from cheekbones or foreheads? In other words, is it overlit? Try adding single or double scrims to the lights that seem too bright.

FIGURE 6.7   The same actor lit with a fill light only.

How does the background look? It's pretty hard to light the subject and the background with only three lights, but see if you can move the fill light so that it fills in the background as well as the shadows on the subject. Is there too much light falling on the background? Try using the barn doors on the key light to direct the light onto the subject only. If you have barn doors for the fill and back lights, adjust them as well. Remember to wear gloves when you're adjusting lights that have been on for awhile—they get very hot. If your lights are still too bright, try moving them further from the subject, or add more scrims or diffusion to your setup.

Lighting for Darker Skin Tones

When an actor has darker-toned skin, it can be difficult to get enough light on their face without overlighting the background, because darker complexions simply require more light. If you can, keep the actor farther away from the background so that the light falls on the actor but not the background.

INTERIOR LIGHTING

Lighting an interior scene can present all sorts of challenges, not the least of which is choosing a location that can facilitate your lights. Ideally, you would use a soundstage with an overhead lighting grid, lots of available power, and plenty of space for setting up lights as far from your subject as needed. Shooting in a normal house or office building will save you the trouble of having to build a realistic set, but you'll be hampered by less space, a limited power supply, and less control over how much exterior light enters the set.

Power Supply

If you're using professional lights at a location, you'll have to be careful not to overload the electrical circuits. A little pre-shoot prep work can save lots of headaches later. First, you need to map out the electrical circuits at the location. Arm yourself with some masking tape and a socket tester or an easily moveable household lamp. Plug the lamp into the first outlet and turn it on. Go to the breaker box and turn the circuits on and off until you find the one that controls the lamp. If the circuits aren't labeled, use the masking tape to label each with a number. Then, use the masking tape to label the outlet to correspond with the circuit number. Work your way around until you find and label several outlets on different circuit breakers. To be safe when lighting, use one light for each 10-amp circuit. Most household circuits range from 10 to 40 amps, and the amperage of each circuit should be clearly engraved on the switches in the breaker box.

Mixing Daylight and Interior Light

Because of the different color temperatures of daylight and interior light, mixing them together can present a challenge. The simplest solution is to choose which light source you wish to have dominant, and balance the other light sources to match the color temperature of that source.

For example, if the dominant light source in your scene is the light streaming through a window, you should balance your light sources for daylight by using daylight balanced lights. You can also use Color Temperature Blue (CTB) lighting gels on tungsten lights, but remember that CTB gels decrease the intensity of the lights and might render them useless. If your dominant light source is a 650 W tungsten light, you should balance your light sources for tungsten light using Color Temperature Orange (CTO) lighting gels on daylight balanced lights and windows with daylight streaming through. You might also need to add neutral density (ND) gels to control the brightness of the daylight coming through the window. In general, shooting a daytime interior against a bright window is best avoided.

Using Household Lights

Because video requires less light than film does, you can often get away with using normal household lights. Generally, household lamps are less than 3200° K and lean more toward the orange side of the spectrum.

Unfortunately, ordinary household lights are not directional, which makes it harder to control where the light falls in your scene. There are a couple of ways to make household lights directional. You can buy directional or "spot" light bulbs, or you can surround the bulb with tin foil or some other light-proof material. Filter manufacturers such as Rosco and Lee sell *black wrap*, a heavy-duty tin foil with a black matte coating that can be used to create makeshift barn doors.

Even if you're not concerned with the light being directional, replacing low-wattage light bulbs with brighter bulbs is a good way to create "practical" lights. "Practical" lights are those that are actually visible in the scene, such as a household lamp that the actor turns on. You can hide diffusion materials or gels in the lamp shade for more lighting control. By using a low-wattage bulb and keeping it several feet away from the actor, the household lamp in the background of Figure 6.2 does not cast any light on the subject.

Clamp Lights

Cheap clamp lights available at any hardware store can be a good way to get some extra, low-budget illumination. Replace the bulbs with high-wattage directional bulbs, and use black wrap to make them even more directional.

EXTERIOR LIGHTING

The concept of exterior lighting might sound silly—who needs lights outside when you have the sun? However, if you're bent on a film-style look for your project, you'll need to do more than just point and shoot. Daylight, defined as a combination of skylight and sunlight, is an intense source of light—often too intense for video, especially if you're going for a video-to-film transfer. Think of the sky as a big giant bounce card reflecting the sun. It's a powerful light source in its own right, comparable to a 30,000 watt fixture on the ground and more than 50 times the illumination of a 650 W tungsten light. Your light kit will be useless on an exterior shoot unless it includes a 2 K light at the very least. The art of exterior "lighting" has to do with blocking, diffusing, filtering, reflecting, and controlling the light of the sun and sky.

LIGHTING EQUIPMENT CHECKLIST

You should have the following items on-hand and easily accessible during your shoot:

- 2 cloth tape—to tape down cables so that people won't trip over them.
- Power cables and heavy-duty extension cords (25¢, 50¢, 100¢).
- Three-prong to two-prong adapters for older locations.
- Clothespins—used to attach lighting gels or diffusion to barndoors, and so forth.
- Heavy work gloves—for handling light globes and hot equipment.
- Lighting gels.
- Diffusion materials.
- Reflectors.
- Bounce cards—often nothing more than a big piece of white foamcore, bounce cards can help you get more mileage out of your lights.
- Duvetine, black felt, or black garbage bags for blocking windows.
- Kino-Flo bulbs—these color temperature-corrected, flicker-free light bulbs are used to replace standard fluorescent light tubes in location fixtures.
- Clamps with rubber handles—similar in function to clothespins, but with more grip.
- Extra light globes—650 W and 1 K bulbs to go with your light kit, household bulbs in high wattages, and so forth. You should have at least one extra globe for every light in your kit.
- C-stands.
- Flags and nets.

Enhancing Existing Daylight

If you're shooting outside on a sunny day at noon, you'll get a brightly lit image with very harsh shadows. If you're armed with the items listed in the "Lighting Equipment Checklist" sidebar, you will be able to exert some control over the harsh conditions of bright daylight. Here are a few tips for brightening up those dark shadows:

- Try positioning a piece of foamcore below your subject and off to one side, so that the light of the sun bounces off the white foamcore and up into the shadows on your subject's face. This is a variation of three-point lighting—think of the sun as your key light, and the bounced light as your fill. Use a C-stand to secure the foamcore.
- Use flags, black screens, and diffusion to cut down the intensity of the sun on the subject.
- Use a reflector or a bounce card to create a back light.
- If the contrast ratio is still too high, you need a stronger fill light. Try placing the sun behind your subject, and use the bounce card as a soft key light from the front.
- Change locations. If you can't get the look you want in direct sunlight, try moving to a shadier location and using a bounce card to add highlights or positioning a large silk over your subject.

Golden Hour

The hour or so before sunset, also known as "golden hour," is one of the best times of day to shoot exteriors. The warm cast of the light is very flattering to human skin tones, and the chance of your scene being overlit is reduced. In addition, the low angle of the sun creates sharp, dark shadows, throwing everything in your scene into sharp relief. Unfortunately, you'll have to work fast to take advantage of this quality of light, as it does not last long.

VIDEO LIGHTING

Today's digital video cameras have an impressive ability to shoot in low-light situations. As a result, one of the challenges of shooting video is that there is often *too much* light. In Chapter 7, "The Camera," we discuss *neutral density filters* and other ways to control the amount of light that your video camera records but it's also good to know some of the ways to limit the light on your set. Whether you're shooting a daytime or a nighttime interior scene, it can be hard to avoid overlighting the set, especially if you're in a small room. "Flat" lighting means there is not enough contrast between your key and fill lights, which will result in a lack of sculpting. Here are some ways to deal with an overlit scene:

Block out sunlight. Because sunlight is so powerful, it might be the cause of your overlighting. *Duvetine* is a black light-blocking fabric that can be used to cover windows. A cheaper alternative is to cover them with black plastic garbage bags. If windows are in the shot, you can use ND gels (see the sidebar "Lighting Gels" earlier in the chapter) to tone down the light coming through the windows.

Turn off lights, especially overhead fixtures. If your set is small, you simply might not be able to use all the lights you want without overlighting the scene.

Move lights away from the subject. If space allows, move your lights back. The farther they are from your subject, the less illumination they'll cast on your subject.

Black nets and black flags. Black nets and black flags attach to C-stands and are versatile tools for controlling and blocking light.

Studio wallpaper. Shooting in a room with white walls is like having four giant bounce cards surrounding your scene. You can buy different colors of studio wallpaper to tone down the walls or to create blue/green backdrops for compositing. If you're shooting a night scene, use black studio wallpaper to make a room look bigger than it is—but be careful not to allow any light or hot spots to fall on the black paper.

Scrims. If one or more of your lights are too bright, add scrims to take them down. Most lights will take at least two scrims at once.

Barn doors. Narrow the opening between the barn doors to make a light more directional.

Video and Low-Light Situations

Modern digital video cameras can do a good job of producing an image when there's very little light. Unfortunately, they accomplish this by electronically boosting the gain of the camera, which adds noise. If you turn off the gain boost, you'll have noise-free video, but probably little or no image. The only solution in this case is to use lights. You'll have to weigh the benefit of noise-free video against the difficulty of lighting. If your eventual goal is a video-to-film transfer, noise should be avoided at all costs. (More on gain in Chapter 8, "Shooting Digital Video.")

Battery-Operated Lights and Generators

Renting a generator might be out of your league, but for those situations where electrical power is unavailable, try using battery-operated lights.

SPECIAL LIGHTING SITUATIONS

Lighting does more than illuminate actors and locations. It also plays a key role in creating a believable setting, pulling off some types of special effects, and producing successful blue- or green-screen photography.

Using Lights to Create a Scene

With a little imagination, lights can be used to suggest a location. Here are a few typical ways to create a scene with lights:

Car interiors: A nighttime driving scene can be shot on a soundstage using a few focused lights placed outside a car, along with a fill light. The focused lights should be gelled to match the lights of passing cars, street lights, and brake lights. Each light (except the fill) needs to be manned by a grip who will move the light past the car at irregular intervals to replicate passing lights.

Day-for-Night: Use slightly blue-colored gels to create light that looks like nighttime, and ND filters on your camera to make the image darker. Later, use digital compositing tools to matte out the sky and tweak the contrast ratio. There are several vendors that make day-for-night software plug-ins that can be used to treat your daylight footage so that it will look like it was shot at night. Check out *www.dvhandbook.com/dayfornight* for more info.

Firelight: Dark orange gels can make your light source the same color as firelight. Wave flags in front of the light source to create a fire-like flicker. A fan with paper streamers in front of the light can add hands-free flicker.

Other illusional spaces: Carefully flagged lights in the background can create the illusion of space, such as a doorway.

 Smoke and Diffusion

Fog machines and diffusion spray are used to create an atmospheric haze in a scene, which can be very heavy or very subtle.

Lighting for Video-to-Film Transfers

Lighting for video-to-film transfers can be a little tricky if you've never done it before. This is because the way your lit set looks to the naked eye will bear very little resemblance to how it will look after it's been transferred to film. There are many theories on how to achieve the best results, but here are a few guidelines to help make your shoot a success:

Avoid high-contrast lighting: Transferring your video footage to film will increase the contrast ratio between light and dark areas so it's important to avoid too much contrast in the original video footage. Low-contrast lighting won't look very "film-like" when you view your original video footage but it will acquire a higher-contrast, film-like look after you transfer it to film.

Make sure your images are sharp: Sharpness, or focus, is related to your camera and the lens, but it's also dependent on good lighting. Any softness in your video image will be exacerbated once it's transferred to film and projected on a big screen. Often, you won't be able to see that your image is out of focus until it's blown up and projected onto a big screen.

Light to avoid video noise: Low-light situations require that you boost the gain on your video camera, which in turn increases video artifacts or "noise." Noise is similar to *film grain* but larger and more distracting, especially when transferred to film and projected so be sure to make sure that your on-set lighting is sufficient enough to avoid video noise.

LATITUDE AND VIDEO-TO-FILM TRANSFERS

Latitude refers to how many gradations of gray there are between the darkest black and the brightest white. When you stand in an unlit room in the day and look out the window, you can probably see details in the room, as well as in the bright sunlit areas outside and the outside shadows. In other words, your eye sees all the shades of gray from black to white. Because the latitude of film and video is too narrow to handle both bright areas and the dark areas, you'll have to choose to expose one range: either the sunlit areas or the shadows. Film has more latitude than video, but neither comes anywhere near what your eye is capable of seeing. The challenge for cinematographers is to shoot so that the resulting image looks more like what the human eye would actually see.

If you're planning on eventually transferring your video to film, latitude will be an important consideration. Because the latitude of video is smaller than that of film, any overexposed whites or underexposed blacks might look clipped. In other words, they will appear as a solid area of black or white, without any depth or detail. DV format cameras are exceptionally good at recording in low light situations. As a result, the black areas tend to have plenty of information, and look fine when transferred to film. However, bright whites and hot spots look terrible. (If you know how to read a waveform image, see Color Plate 7 and Figure 13.12 for an example of clipped white levels.) The effect of clipped whites or blacks is especially distracting when a filmed image is projected.

Shooting Video for Film

If you are going to finish your video project by transferring it to 35mm film, you should research and find a film recordist now. Each film recording company uses a different process, and they'll have specific tips for how to light and shoot in order to achieve the best look for your project. (More on transferring video to film in Chapter 19, "Output.")

Lighting for Blue and Green Screen

If you will be shooting blue- or green-screen shots for later compositing with other elements, it's critical that you light your screen smoothly and evenly. For best results, consider the following:

Choose your compositing software before you shoot. Different apps have different needs. Becoming familiar with your compositing software and its specific needs will save you time and headaches later. See Chapters 17, "Titling and Simple Compositings," and 18, "Rotoscoping and More Compositing," for more on compositing apps.

Place your subject as far from the blue/green background as possible. If your subject is too close to the background, you'll end up with blue spill (or green spill)—reflections of blue light that bounce off the blue screen and onto the back of your actor, resulting in a bluish backlight. This can make it extremely difficult to pull a clean matte later. If you can't avoid blue spill, try to make up for it by adding a hotter orange back light to cancel it out.

Light your subject and the background separately. This also helps avoid blue spill and makes it easier to create the matte. The set in Color Plate 3 shows how much trouble a professional crew has to go to in order to light the set and the green screen separately.

Light to minimize video noise. Video noise can make pulling a matte difficult. Be sure the scene is well lit so that there's no need for gain-boosting on your camera. If you can, disable the automatic gain boost feature.

Try to make sure the blue/green screen is evenly lit. Because you want an even shade of blue across your entire blue-screen background, having consistent lighting across the surface of your screen is essential. A spot meter reads reflective light instead of incident or direct light, and can be a real asset when trying to even out the light levels on your blue screen. Most camera shops rent them on a daily or weekly basis.

Art direct to avoid blue or green in your subject/foreground.
This might seem obvious, but blue can be a hard color to avoid,
which is why the option of green screen exists, and vice versa. In
Color Plate 4, the warm oranges and browns of the set lay in
sharp contrast to the green screen in the background.

Dress the floor. If you're going to see the actor's feet in the shot, it
will be much easier to dress the floor with something that
matches your final composite shot—carpeting, wood, stones,
etc.—rather than attempting to composite it later.

Screen correction shots. Several compositing applications can use
a screen correction shot to make creating a matte easier. Either
before or after every take, get a few seconds of footage of the
empty blue/green screen with the same framing as the action.
Refer to your compositing software documentation for other specific tips regarding screen correction shots.

Have a visual effects supervisor on set. They might see problems
you won't notice.

Pay attention to shadows. Shadows can tend toward blue, which
can make creating a matte difficult.

Light to match your CGI material. If you're going to be compositing live action and CGI environments, be sure the live-action
lighting matches the CGI environment lighting. If your digital
background has an orange hue, it will look strange if your subject
is lit with a blue backlight. The green screen set in Color Plate 4 is
lit to match a CGI background.

EXERCISES

1. **Make a lighting plot.** Obviously, lighting is a very hands-on stage
   of production. However, there's still plenty of planning that you can
   do to make sure you have the gear you need and to make the best
   use of your time on-set. Once you've chosen your locations, meet
   with your lighting crew or director of photography and try to plan
   exactly what type of lights you'll want where. Try to rough out some
   floorplan sketches and determine where you'll need each piece of
   equipment. This is also a good time to assess how much power you'll
   need, and whether you'll need extra power generators. If your shoot
   involves any special effects, you'll want to take extra care in planning
   the lighting for those shots.

2. **Use a 3D program to practice lighting.** Believe it or not, 3D applications like Maya and Studio Max are great tools for mapping out
   lighting, because their lights do a great job of simulating real-world

lights. You can use pre-programmed figure models in the place of your actors and try out different kinds of lighting on them. You can even use a 3D application to do the three-point lighting tutorial earlier in this chapter. You can download an evaluation copy of Maya from *www.alias.com*. These types of 3D packages are complex, but learning enough to perform simple lighting studies is fairly simple, and worth the investment in time.

3. **Do a test shoot.** Big budget features test everything before they shoot—they even use "screen tests" to determine if the actors are photogenic, and whether they have "screen chemistry" with each other. Spending a weekend testing your lighting and other tricky elements of your production can be invaluable. For blue/green screen shoots, start out by familiarizing yourself with the blue (or green) screen compositing software that you'll be using. Follow any recommendations in the software manual, such as shooting a reference image. Use miniatures or stand-ins against a blue or green background and try different lighting set-ups. Be sure to follow the tips listed earlier in this chapter but play around with some of the variables to see what works best.

4. **Do the three-point lighting tutorial.** If you don't have access to a simple light kit at school or through a friend, you can rent one at most professional still photography suppliers as long as you can provide a credit card for a deposit. They generally cost about $40 for a weekend. Be sure to avoid light kits with high-wattage lights if you're shooting video—it's likely they'll overpower your set.

SUMMARY

Lighting provides the backdrop in which your story will take place. Once you've tackled it, you're ready to move over to the other side of the set—the camera.

7

THE CAMERA

In This Chapter

- Using the Camera
- The Lens
- White Balance
- Lens Filters
- Other Camera Features
- Technical Tips
- Exercise
- Summary

The sweeping panoramas of *Lawrence of Arabia*, the evocative shadows and compositions of *The Third Man*, the famous dolly/crane shot that opens *A Touch of Evil*—when we remember great films, striking images usually come to mind. Digital technology has made visual effects and other post-production tasks a hot topic, but shooting your film is still the single most important step in a live-action production. Shooting good video requires more than just recording pretty images. As a director, the ability to unite the actors' performances with the compositions of the cinematographer, while managing all of the other minutia that one must deal with on a set, will be key to the success of your project. Central to all of the above is the ability to use the camera.

USING THE CAMERA

The camera is the primary piece of equipment in any type of production, so in this chapter, you're going to get familiar with your camera. Professional cinematographers know their cameras inside and out. Many of them will only work with certain types of cameras, and some will only work with equipment from specific rental houses. The advantage of most digital video cameras is that you can point and shoot and still get a good image. However, if you want to get the most from your camera, you should follow the example of the pros and take the time to learn the details of your gear.

FIGURE 7.1   In addition to excellent image quality, the Canon XL-2 provides a full complement of manual controls and overrides.

Shooting good footage involves much more than simply knowing what button to push and when. There are many creative decisions involved in setting up your shots, and in this chapter, we're going to cover all of the controls at your disposal, and learn how they affect your final image.

We're biased toward cameras that offer manual override of all key camera functions: zooming, focus, white balancing, f-stop/iris control, variable shutter speeds, and gain controls (Figure 7.1). As you'll see, each of these features plays an important role in successful shooting. Even if your camera only offers automatic controls, you need to know how each of these parameters affects your final image to better understand the choices the camera is making.

CAMERA EQUIPMENT CHECKLIST

You should keep these items in your camera bag for easy access at all times:

- Your camera's original owner's manual
- Lens tissue
- Lens cleaning fluid
- Blower brush
- Measuring tape
- Rain cover, umbrella, or plastic garbage bags
- Sun shade
- Head cleaning cartridge
- Extra lenses (if applicable)
- Lens filters
- Extra batteries (charged)
- A/C adapter
- Flashlight
- Standard tool kit
- Slate (see Chapter 8, "Shooting Digital Video")
- White pencil (for temporarily marking settings on the lens)
- Colored tape (for marking blocking, camera, and light placement)
- Gaffer's tape (for who-knows-what, but when you need it, you need it)
- Small bungee cords
- Small alligator clamps
- Large black cloth (to hide camera from reflective surfaces)

The Lens

Camera lenses fall into two categories: *prime* lenses and *zoom* lenses. Prime lenses have a fixed focal length, measured in millimeters, that determines their angle of view. Prime lenses are known for producing a sharper image than zoom lenses do, and DPs who work in feature films are used to having a selection of high-quality prime lenses for their 35mm film cameras. However, most video cameras are equipped with zoom lenses (Figure 7.2) that offer a range of focal lengths from telephoto (or close-up) to wide angles, and are more suitable to documentary-style photography.

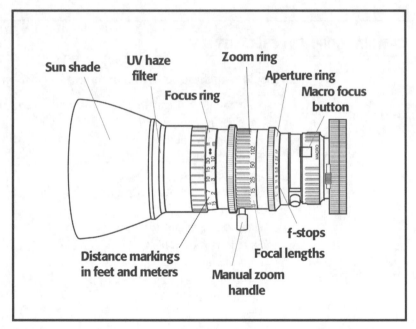

FIGURE 7.2 A professional zoom lens will be equipped something like this.

Focal Length Equivalency

There is about a 7:1 ratio when figuring what a DV lens correlates to in terms of focal lengths on a 35mm film camera—the focal lengths that most of us are used to. The 5.5–88mm zoom lens that comes with the Canon XL-2 is the equivalent of an approx. 39–600mm lens on a 35mm still camera.

Focal Length and Camera Position

The great thing about a zoom lens is that it provides great flexibility when you frame a shot. Without changing your position, you can quickly zoom in to a subject to get a tighter view and a different framing. However, it's essential that you pay attention to the elements of your image that change when you zoom in and out.

It's easy to think of your zoom lens as a big magnifying glass and, to a degree, that is what it is. As you zoom in, your subject appears larger. This is why digital video camera manufacturers label their lenses with a magnification factor—2x, 3x, and so forth. However, a few other things happen to your image when you zoom.

Focal Length Defined

Focal length is the distance from the lens to the camera's CCD, usually measured in millimeters.

As you go to a longer focal length (zoom in), your field of view gets narrower. The human eye has a field of view of about 50 to 55°. This is considered a "normal" field of view (Figure 7.3).

More important, though, is to pay attention to the way that a lens magnifies different parts of your image, and how it compresses depth overall as you zoom in and out.

At wider focal lengths (that is, when you are zoomed out), objects that are closer to the lens get magnified *more* than objects that are farther away. *Telephoto* lenses, on the other hand, magnify all objects in a scene equally, no matter how far away they are.

An example: At some time, you've probably looked at a photograph or video of yourself and thought "that doesn't really look like me." One reason for the poor result might be that the photographer was using a wide-angle lens. Shooting a portrait with a wide-angle lens is problematic because some parts of your subject's face are closer to the lens than others are. Consequently, those parts, particularly the nose, will be magnified more than the parts that are farther away.

Check out the pictures in Figure 7.4. The image on the left was shot with a slightly telephoto lens and really does look like the actual person. The image on the right is not a very good likeness (though it might be truer to this person's character). The nose is too big and the ears have been rendered too small. In addition, the distance between the nose and ears—the depth of the picture—is too long. In other words, the sense of depth in the second image has been expanded, and the results look a bit weird.

22mm

50mm

480mm

FIGURE 7.3 The middle, 50mm image displays roughly the same field-of-view as the naked eye. As the focal length shortens to 22mm, the field of view gets very wide. Conversely, as the focal length extends to 480mm, the field of view gets very narrow.

FIGURE 7.4   These two pictures show what a difference focal length can make. The image on the left was shot with a slightly telephoto focal length, while the image on the right was shot with a very wide-angle focal length. The camera's position was adjusted accordingly.

Now consider the images in Figure 7.5. For these images, we zoomed the lens in, *but we also changed the camera's position to keep the framing the same*. In other words, we adjusted the camera's position (by moving it farther away) to maintain the same field of view as we zoomed the camera in. Therefore, the man appears to be the same size in each image, but notice what happens to the tree. It gets bigger! This is because, as we zoom in, we're compressing the sense of depth in the image, just as we compressed the face of the man in Figure 7.4.

The lesson here is that there's a price to pay for being lazy. Many people think "great, I can stand here, zoom in and get the shot I need, rather than having to take my camera all the way over there." However, as you can see, the camera's position and distance from the subject has a huge effect on the final image. A tight shot created by a zoom can feel voyeuristic, while a tight shot created by moving the camera up close can feel more intimate. In other words, your choice of camera position and corresponding focal length can greatly change the sense of space and atmosphere in your scene.

Next time you watch a comedy, pay attention to the focal length of most shots. If it's a particularly wacky comedy, you'll probably notice that most close-ups and many scenes are shot with a really wide-angle lens.

A. Very wide angle   **C. Normal angle**

B. Wide angle   **D. Telephoto**

FIGURE 7.5 These four images were shot using four different focal length lenses: (a) very wide, (b) wide, (c) normal, and (d) telephoto. Notice what happens to the tree in the background.

The fact is: wide-angle lenses make people funny-looking. You'll be able to spot a wide-angle shot because actor's faces will appear distorted as they are in Figures 7.5a and 7.5b. You'll also probably notice that objects behind the actors appear very far away, and of course, you'll have an extremely wide angle of view that encompasses a lot of the set or location.

To sum up: As focal length increases, the sense of depth in the image decreases, so it's very important to carefully choose your focal length and camera position.

You'll learn more about the importance of focal length when we discuss composition and framing later in this chapter.

Care of the Lens

Always keep your lens cap on when your camera is not in use. Keep a UV haze filter on your lens as a protective layer. Avoid touching the lens with your bare hands, since the oil from your fingers can etch a permanent mark on the glass. Never clean a lens with dry fabric or tissue. Instead, use a lens tissue dampened with lens cleaning fluid to wipe it off.

Zoom Control

In addition to letting you choose an appropriate focal length when you frame a shot, zoom lenses allow you to change focal length *during* a shot, using either a mechanical control button or by manually turning the zoom ring on the lens itself. Unless you're trying for that "caught on tape" look, a good zoom needs to start out slowly, ramp up to the desired speed, and then gradually slow to a halt. You can also conceal a zoom by combining it with a pan or tilt.

The mechanical zooms found on most high-end consumer DV cameras can be difficult to control—they tend to start awkwardly, go too fast, and respond jerkily to any fluctuations in pressure on the button. And unfortunately, many DV cameras have lenses that do not have a manual zoom ring. In either case, practice makes perfect—give your camera operator (or yourself!) time with the camera before the shoot to get a feel for how the camera's zoom works. A word to the wise—if your camera doesn't let you to make a smooth zoom, then zoom as quickly as possible. A *snap zoom* has two advantages: it hides shakiness and it takes up a minimal amount of time, making it easier to cut around later when editing.

Most DV cameras also have digital zooms, which are accessed through a menu display. Digital zooms are best avoided, since they work by blowing up the image rather than moving the optics of the lens, resulting in a low-resolution, *pixelated* image.

Aperture

Aperture refers to the opening at the rear of the lens. The camera's lens focuses light through the aperture and onto the image sensor mounted on the *focal plane*. The size of the aperture is controlled by the *iris,* a series of interlocking metal leaves that can expand and contract like the iris in your eye. The size of the opening of a camera's iris is measured in *f-stops.* Higher-numbered f-stop values stop more light. That is, a higher-numbered value represents a *smaller* aperture, which provides *more* light stoppage, resulting in less light passing through the lens (Figure 7.6).

Most high-end video cameras show f-stop markings on their lenses, which make it easy to set a particular aperture. Mid-range cameras do not have f-stop markings on their lenses, but provide control of the lens aperture with special dials, and with f-stop settings that appear in the digital menu display. Lower-end cameras do not display f-stops, but allow for manual iris adjustment and iris locking. Bottom-line cameras do not allow for any manual control of the lens aperture, and rely solely on automated iris settings.

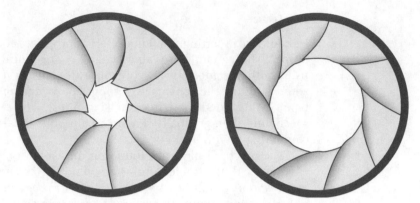

FIGURE 7.6   The iris on the left is stopping more light than the iris on the right is. Therefore, it has a higher f-stop value, and makes a smaller aperture.

All video cameras include an auto-iris function, which constantly adjusts the size of the camera's iris according to the current lighting conditions. While the auto iris function might work fine in "normal" lighting situations, it's usually the wrong choice in more complicated scenes. For example, if you have a subject who is in the shade, but a background that is sunny, the auto iris will probably expose for the bright background, since it fills the majority of the frame (Figure 7.7a). Because the camera is exposing for the bright part of the image, the shadowy person in the foreground ends up underexposed and difficult to see. In order to expose for the darkened foreground figure (Figure 7.7b), you'll need to use the manual iris control to overexpose. This will blow out the background, while keeping the subject exposed correctly.

As your camera moves, or the subjects in your scene move, your camera might re-evaluate what it thinks is a proper exposure. For example, as people walk in front of light sources in your scene, the iris will fluctuate causing your scene to get lighter and darker. Though what the camera is doing is technically "correct," it will look awful. If your camera allows it, you should usually work with the auto iris function turned off, and control the iris manually while shooting.

Having control of the iris also gives you the freedom to control the *depth of field* in the image, which allows you to separate the subject from the background. Depth of field refers to how "deep" the range of focus is in an image. In Figure 7.8a, the depth of field is shallow and only the subject is in focus. It is easy to focus your attention on the actor because he is completely separated from the background. In Figure 7.8b, the depth of field is longer, and more detail shows in the background.

A

B

FIGURE 7.7   In the upper image (a), the camera's automatic exposure exposed for the sunlit background, leaving our subject in shadow. In the lower image (b), we used the manual exposure control to expose for our subject. Although the background is blown out, at least now we can see our subject's face.

Both of these images were shot under the same lighting conditions with the same lens. In Figure 7.8a, the depth of field is shallow because the lens aperture is wide open. In Figure 7.8b, the lens aperture is closed down all the way, resulting in a less shallow depth of field. Moreover, depth of field is shallower at longer focal lengths. Therefore, if you want a really shallow depth of field, you need to position your camera farther from your subject, zoom in, and open the iris as far as possible.

A. Shallow depth of field

B. Less shallow depth of field

FIGURE 7.8 By controlling the depth of field in your image, you can selectively blur out parts of your image.

However, as you open your aperture, you'll be letting in more light, which means you'll need to go to a faster *shutter* speed. A faster shutter speed might result in more stuttery motion, so you'll need to carefully balance your depth-of-field and shutter-speed concerns. As you'll see later, you can also use special neutral density filters to reduce the amount of light entering the camera, allowing you more shutter speed flexibility.

It's difficult to judge focus, exposure, and depth of field on a very small monitor, like your camera's viewfinder or LCD screen. Instead, you should use a larger *field monitor*.

A SHUTTER BY ANY OTHER NAME

Most digital video cameras don't have a mechanical shutter that opens and closes. Instead, they use an "electronic" shutter; that is, the image sensor inside the camera simply turns itself on and off for the appropriate duration.

Focus

Before you can focus your camera, you need to make sure the viewfinder is adjusted to match your vision. Most cameras, like the ones in Figure 7.1 and 7.9, have an adjustment ring, or *diopter*, on the viewfinder. (Refer to your camera documentation for specifics.) Set the camera lens out of

FIGURE 7.9   The JVC GY-DV500 DV camera has manual override for everything and many high-end features.

focus, then look through the viewfinder and move the viewfinder focus adjustment until you can see the grains of glass or the display information in the viewfinder itself.

If your camera allows, you might want to turn off the autofocus mechanism. Autofocus will always focus on the middle of the frame. Since you might want to be more creative than this, stick with manual focus.

To focus a zoom lens manually, zoom all the way in to your subject, and focus the image. Now you can zoom back to compose the shot at the focal length you desire. As long as your subject doesn't move forward or backward, your image will be in focus at any focal length available.

You can also focus by composing your shot first and then adjusting the focus ring on the lens, the same way you would with a prime lens. The only problem with this method is that the wider your shot, the harder it will be to tell if your subject is truly in focus.

Measuring Focus

If your camera lens has a focus ring with distance measurements marked on it, like the lens in Figure 7.2, you can measure the distance between your subject and the lens to ensure perfect focus. (Note that you can't be sure of the focus markings on your lens unless you've tested them and found the marks to be accurate.)

If you plan to eventually transfer your video image to film, proper focus is critical. When the image is projected and blown up to 25+ times its normal size, what looked in focus on a small video monitor might appear out of focus. Luckily, most images have a *depth of field* that exceeds the depth of focus. In Figure 7.10, the depth of focus is eight feet from the camera, but the depth of field—the part of the image that *appears* in focus—starts a couple of feet in front of the subject and extends to infinity. Anything behind the subject will appear in focus, even though they're not on the plane of focus.

If you're having trouble focusing, use your manual iris control to iris down (go to a higher f-stop number). This will increase your depth of field and improve your chances of shooting focused. Under most normal, bright lighting conditions, especially daylight, the field of focus will extend from your subject (i.e., the plane of focus) to infinity (Figure 7.10).

Generally, focus won't present much of a problem. In fact, one of the biggest complaints about the look of digital video is that the focus is too sharp throughout the image. Film typically has a much more shallow depth of field than video, so often only the subject is in focus (Figure 7.8). One way to get more of a filmlike image is to control the lighting and exposure so that the depth of field is shallow. With a video camera, this is very difficult to do under bright, uncontrolled lighting conditions such as daylight.

FIGURE 7.10   In this illustration, the plane of focus is eight feet from the lens, but the depth of field is much bigger. Everything behind the plane of focus appears in focus as well.

The only time you're likely to encounter a focus problem is when you're shooting in low light conditions. When there isn't a lot of light, the field of focus becomes very small, and it's hard to judge focus in the viewfinder or LCD display when there isn't much light on the subject.

If you're planning on a video-to-film transfer, maintaining perfect focus is crucial. Things that look focused on a small TV monitor might in fact be slightly out of focus. When these images are blown up to the big screen, the focus problems will become visible.

Cinematographers shooting on film often make certain that the subject is in focus by calculating the field of focus mathematically using *depth of field charts*. Unfortunately, depth of field calculations for consumer video cameras are complicated by the lack of f-stop or distance markings on their lenses, and by the fact that their focal lengths don't yield the same field of view as lenses used for a 35mm film camera. As such, standard depth of field charts, such as those found in the *American Cinematographer's Manual*, do not apply to the typical video camera. To check for good focus after the shoot, use a video projector to view your video footage on a bigger screen.

Use a Field Monitor

Feature film directors connect "video assist" monitors to their 35mm film cameras so that they can see what the camera operator sees through the viewfinder. A field monitor lets you do the same thing with a video camera. Even if you'll be operating the camera yourself, a field monitor can be an asset, making it much easier to focus and frame your shots, and, of course, it lets others see what the camera operator is seeing.

Pulling Focus

Film camera operators compensate for shallow depth of field by having a camera assistant *pull focus*. As the camera moves on a dolly, for example, the camera assistant manually moves the focus using the focus ring on the lens. To make pulling focus easier, some lenses have a place to attach a knob, but either way, it requires a steady hand. You need to be able to pull focus in order to do a *rack focus* shot. Unless you have a camera with high-end features like the one in Figure 7.9, pulling focus is almost impossible.

Faking Focus Pulls

Red Giant Software's Image Lounge includes a rack focus filter that you can use to fake some rack focus shots in post-production. Obviously, you'll need to do some experimentation and planning before you rely on such post-production effects.

White Balance

As you saw in Chapter 6, "Lighting," different types of lights shine at different temperatures, or colors. One of the amazing characteristics of your eyeballs is that they can adjust automatically to all of these different temperatures, and can even understand mixed lighting temperatures—sunlight shining through a window into a fluorescent-lit room, for example.

Film and video cameras are not as sophisticated. Film has to be specially formulated for different types of light to accurately represent color. This is why there is film for daylight and film for tungsten light.

Digital image sensors have the same trouble. Fortunately, though, a digital camera's understanding of color is entirely dependent on how the data coming off the sensor is processed by the camera's internal computer. Therefore, by telling the camera what kind of light you're shooting in, you can make sure that the camera interprets color data correctly.

White balancing is the process of getting a camera to accurately represent white. Because white light contains all other colors, if a camera can accurately reproduce white, then it can accurately render every other color. Color Plate 12 shows an example of an image that was incorrectly white balanced.

Your camera probably has an automatic white-balance setting that tries to white balance correctly on the fly. Automatic white-balance mechanisms can work very well, but for best results, you should take control of the white-balance process yourself.

Pay Attention to Auto White Balance

Be aware that because the auto white-balance mechanism is constantly white balancing, a sudden change in the luminance or color content of your scene can cause the camera to re-white balance, resulting in a weird color shift. For example, a giant pink elephant entering the frame might be enough to throw off the white balance for the entire scene. If you think your scene might be susceptible to such problems—or if you notice them when shooting—then you'll want to use a manual white balance as described next.

Most cameras offer white-balance presets for different types of light. Therefore, you'll have an option to select preset white-balance settings for daylight, or tungsten, or fluorescent lights. These can often prove better than auto white-balance settings, especially if you're shooting in a mixed light situation (Figure 7.11).

White Balance in °K		
3000°K	—	**White Tungsten**
3700°K	—	**Yellow Tungsten**
4000°K	—	**Flourescent**
4500°K	—	**Flourescent**
5500°K	—	**Sunlight**
6500°K	—	**Cloudy**
7500°K	—	**Shade**

FIGURE 7.11 On some cameras, you set white balance by specifying the temperature of your current lights in degrees Kelvin.

For the absolute best results, though, you should use your camera's manual white-balance control. Getting yourself in the habit of always manually white balancing will help you shoot better footage, and is essential for mixed-light situations.

To manually white balance, first set your lights. Then, place something white in-frame, like a piece of foamcore, or the back of a white script page. Make sure the white object is illuminated by the dominant light source(s) in your scene. Frame the camera so that only white shows in the viewfinder, and activate the camera's manual white-balance control.

Remember that you'll need to re-white balance every time you significantly change the lighting, especially if you switch from daylight to tungsten light, or vice versa. Also, note that some cameras lose their manual white-balance reading if they are switched off, or even placed in standby mode. If your camera functions like this, then you must remember to manually white balance when you restart the camera.

Alternative White Balancing

You can use the white-balancing feature on your camera to achieve different color effects. White balancing against a bluish surface will result in a warmer-looking image, while balancing against an orange-ish surface results in a cool-looking image. Since white balancing affects the scene's overall color temperature, it is sometimes easier to adjust the white balance than it is to place colored lighting gels on all your light sources. However, you'll be hard-pressed to get your footage back to a normal color if you decide later that that's what you need. As such, it's almost always better to shoot good, normal-looking footage and then add any color effects later, in post-production.

Lens Filters

If your camera has threads on the end of its lens (Figure 7.2), you can attach special *filters* that will help you better control color and composition, as well as create special effects. Filters are simply specially prepared pieces of glass housed in a screw-on attachment. Most filters are threaded so that you can screw filters onto other filters to stack up effects. Filters come in different sizes, so the selection of filters available for your lens size might vary. Many filters come in different "strengths" whose values are usually measured with a simple number scheme—the higher the number, the stronger the effect you'll get from the filter.

UV Filters

As mentioned earlier, you should get at least one UV filter to protect your lens. In addition, UV filters will stop ultraviolet light from coming into the lens, and will help reduce haze. There are a number of variations of UV filters, including stronger haze filters and warm UV filters, which will add warmth to your image.

Polarizing Filters

Polarizers are used to deepen saturation and improve contrast. Shooting with a polarizer will greatly improve images of cloudy skies, and are valuable for all landscape shooting.

Polarizers can also be used to eliminate reflections when shooting through glass or windows (Figure 7.12) and to eliminate hot spots on a reflective surface created by a light source.

FIGURE 7.12   The window reflections in the first image can be easily eliminated with a polarizing filter.

Neutral Density Filters

Neutral density (ND) filters reduce the amount of light entering the lens in single f-stop increments, without changing the quality or color of the light. Therefore, if you're shooting in bright sunlight (which normally requires a small aperture), but you want to shoot with a very shallow depth of field (which requires a large aperture), you can use ND filters to cut out enough light to facilitate a smaller f-stop value. ND filters can also be used to slow shutter speeds from fast, stuttery speeds to something a little more natural looking.

Your camera might have a built-in electronic ND filter. Check your manual to see how many f-stops this feature provides.

Contrast Adjustment

High-contrast filters can be used to improve the contrast ratio (and therefore, apparent sharpness) in an image, while filters such as Tiffen's ProMist and Black ProMist can be used to reduce contrast to achieve more of a film look (Figure 7.13).

In addition to filters, a *sun shade* attached to the end of your lens will prevent the sun from shining directly on the lens and creating lens flares.

Sharpening

In Figure 4.5 you saw how an image can have annoying jagged edges that jitter and move. This is almost always the result of the camera applying too much sharpening. In addition to creating jagged lines, over-sharpened images gain a lot of contrast, which can be a problem if you're going for a film look.

Most lower-end cameras lack a manual sharpening control. Hopefully, you were able to afford a model that does have such a feature. Because your camera's built-in LCD is a poor gauge of sharpness, you'll need to connect your camera to a monitor and experiment with the setting to find an acceptable level of sharpening. While testing, point the camera at high-contrast areas (power lines against a bright sky are always a good test) and slowly move the camera. Jagged edges should be readily apparent if your camera is over-sharpening. You can then dial the sharpening down to find an acceptable level.

Film-Look Filtering

There are many ways to achieve a "film look" from your video, including post-processing filters or actual transfer to film. There are also some things you can do while shooting to make your video look a little more

FIGURE 7.13   Tiffen's ProMist and Black ProMist can be used to reduce the contrast in an image, and make light flares bloom, creating a more film-like image.

like film. In addition to shooting in your camera's progressive scan "movie mode" (if it has one) you can use diffusion techniques, which will reduce the harsh sharpness that video often yields.

One of the challenges of a successful video-to-film transfer is delivering an image that looks sharp on film, but using lots of filters or diffusion might result in an image that isn't sharp. If you're committed to transferring your video to film, it's a good idea to consult with your film transfer house before you shoot. Ask them if they think it's okay to use lots of filtration or diffusion. In addition, we recommend that you avoid using diffusion materials, such as softening effects filters or stockings and other fabrics over or behind the lens itself. Use diffusion spray, fog machines, and diffusion on the lights to soften the image, but avoid overusing these items as well.

We'll discuss film look more in Chapter 19, "Output."

Other Camera Features

If your camera allows it, you should opt for a slow *shutter speed* when shooting for a film look. Usually, the slowest speed available on a DV camera is 1/60th of a second, which corresponds with the fastest shutter speed available on most film cameras. In Figures 4.8a and b, you can see the difference between a fast shutter speed and a slower shutter speed. The resulting motion blur of the slow shutter speed will help make your video look more like film. (Refer to your camera manual for instructions on manually adjusting the shutter speed.)

Many DV cameras will allow you to choose between *progressive* and *interlaced* scanning. (See Chapter 3, "Video Technology Basics," for an explanation of progressive and interlaced scanning.) Progressive scanning— sometimes called "movie mode"—will also make your video look more film-like, since, as discussed in Chapter 3, it's effectively a lower frame rate than interlaced video. Progressive scanning often produces a stuttering look when used for shooting fast action or with quick camera moves. Some people switch freely between interlaced for fast action, and progressive for shots that are more static. Some high-end HD cameras can shoot 60 progressively scanned frames per second, ideal for sports and other fast-moving subjects.

When shooting regular DV formats, you can freely mix and match interlaced and progressive footage on the same tape. Your editing software won't know any difference and your post-production workflow will proceed normally. If you're shooting on HD formats you should be more careful. HD formats include a number of different combinations of resolution and progressive/interlaced shooting, but switching freely among these on the same tape can make for troubles in the editing room. Resolution and scanning changes can often make breaks in your timecode, which will make capturing into your computer much more complicated. If you want to shoot both interlaced and progressive HD footage, shoot each type on a separate tape.

See the Difference

To see the difference in progressive versus interlaced scanning, check out the ProgScan movie located in the Chapter 7 folder of the companion DVD.

All newer video cameras come with a *gain boost* feature for low light situations. Gain boost makes everything in your image brighter, including the black areas of your image. A good video image should aim for dark, solid blacks, and bright, clear whites. If the gain is boosted, the blacks tend toward gray. With many digital video cameras, the color cast of the image tends to go red when you shoot with the gain boosted. In addition, video *noise* is introduced. Noise is the video equivalent of film grain, except it is much more noticeable and distracting. If you are planning to go to film later, you should avoid any gain boosting. Instead, use proper lighting to get a good exposure on your videotape, and turn off the gain boost feature (Figure 7.14).

FIGURE 7.14   Thanks to a little gain boost, it was possible to shoot usable footage in this completely dark theater. However, gain boost is no substitute for good lighting. Dark is dark, and boosting the gain can only recover so much image. In addition, as can be seen here, boosting the gain dramatically increases the amount of noise in your image.

Aspect Ratios

Choosing an aspect ratio is an artistic choice. Needless to say, composing a shot for 1.33 video (4:3) is very different from projected film at 1.85 or High-Definition television at 1.77 (16:9). (See the aspect ratio table in Chapter 3 as well as Figure 3.4.) Be sure to keep this in mind when you shoot. The DV format's 1.33 aspect ratio is perfectly suited to the current broadcast standard, although the number of TV productions shot in the HD 1.77 format continues to grow. If you're planning to transfer to film, 16mm film shares the same 1.33 aspect ratio as DV, but to get the 1.85 aspect ratio of North American theatrical release format for 35mm film, the top and bottom of the 1.33 image will be cropped out.

If you want to take advantage of the 35mm film format, you'll need to shoot in the 1.77 widescreen aspect ratio. An aspect ratio of 1.77 is still slightly smaller than projected film, but the difference is negligible. Most 35mm film cameras have lenses that can be fit with removable ground glass attachments for viewing crop marks that indicate various aspect ratios through the viewfinder. This helps camera operators compose the shot for the aspect ratio desired (even if it doesn't match the native aspect ratio of the format with which they're shooting). Unfortunately, the concept of removable ground glass attachments hasn't quite trickled down to the video camera world yet.

Buyer Beware

Just because a camera can switch between 16:9 and 4:3 doesn't mean that the camera records a true native 16:9 image. The change in aspect ratio might simply mean that the image is being reshaped to fit that ratio (Figure 4.10). If your camera doesn't shoot native 16:9, you can add an anamorphic lens attachment to it that will squeeze the image (Figure 4.11).

TV Title Safe and Action Safe

The portion of the video image that is visible varies from one TV set to another. To ensure that all viewers can see the action and read the titles, there are standard guidelines for the *action-safe* and *title-safe* areas of the image. If any elements of your image fall outside of these lines, there's no guarantee that they'll be visible on all TV sets.

Professional lenses have visual guides visible in the viewfinder that show where the title-safe and action-safe boundaries lie, much like the guides shown in Figure 17.1. Unfortunately, not all DV camera manufacturers have included these guides in their viewfinders. When shooting, it's imperative to remember that your LCD viewfinder is showing the *entire* image, much of which will not be visible on many TVs. If your viewfinder doesn't have action-safe and title-safe guides, you'll simply have to try to approximate where the safe areas are and remember to try to keep important action within them. Also, remember to frame your subject appropriately if you think you might need to put any text over the image.

Action and title safe concerns are just another reason why it's best to use a field monitor when shooting, to see an accurate view of what you're actually recording.

Know Thy Camera

By now, you should be comfortable with the idea of experimenting to discover what your camera is capable of, and how it reacts in different lighting situations such as low light, night exteriors, and backlight situations. Try to learn where the camera's controls are by feel. While shooting, you might want to switch a feature on or off without taking your eye from the viewfinder. It's better to learn about your camera during test shoots, rather than during your production.

TECHNICAL TIPS

Planning a Test Shoot

If you're really worried about how your footage is going to turn out, you should plan on a simple test shoot prior to going into production. This will give you a chance to look at the quality of your footage and determine if you need to make any changes in your shooting plan. If you're transferring to film, you might also want a film recordist to do a film print of your test shoot. Obviously, to be a useful test, your test shoot should replicate the lighting and shooting conditions of your real shoot.

Preparing Your Equipment

Video equipment is relatively easy to use compared to film equipment. Nonetheless, you'll need to do a little equipment preparation before your shoot.

Preparing the Tape

Before you shoot or edit onto a new videotape, you should fast-forward it to the end and then rewind it back to the beginning. This ensures that the tape has been stretched as much as it will stretch under normal use, and that it is tightly and evenly spooled. Stretching and winding the tape will reduce the risk of drop-outs, tape jams, and even tape breakage.

Bars and Tone

You should use your camera or computer to record at least a minute of bars and tone onto the head of the tape before you shoot (note that not all cameras can generate bars and tone). Bars and tone are important references for use in post-production. They are explained more thoroughly in Chapter 13, "Preparing to Edit," and Color Plate 5 shows a picture of standard NTSC color bars. Refer to your camera user's manual for instructions. In addition to providing a reference for editors and sound editors, there's another reason to record bars and tone: you should *always* avoid recording anything important on the first minute or two of your tape—this is the part of the tape that is most prone to damage. If your camera doesn't generate bars and tone, then record one to two minutes of tape with the lens cap on, to get past the first part of the tape.

Environmentally Incorrect

Even though you can re-use videotape stock, you should avoid doing so. Videotape gets physically worn the more you use it, becoming more susceptible to drop-outs and degradation. If you must recycle tapes, be sure to "degauss," or magnetically erase, your tapes. In addition, avoid using the end of a tape from a previous shoot. This reduces the risk of accidentally recording over your previously shot footage. It sounds silly, but it happens all the time. Tape stock is relatively cheap—budget some extra money and avoid the potential pitfalls of used tape.

Timecode

Timecode is an important part of editing and is discussed more thoroughly in Chapter 13. Most DV formats automatically record *DV timecode* on the tape, although higher-end formats, such as DVCAM offer more options as to how the timecode is recorded on the tape.

For example, your camera might allow you to set the hour at which the timecode starts. If so, it might be useful in post-production to have your timecode start at different hours on different tapes. You might have tape 4 start at hour 4 which will help you and your editor stay organized later on.

When shooting, every time you turn the camera on and off there will be a break in the timecode. These *timecode breaks* can make capturing footage difficult later when you are preparing to edit. Pausing the camera or leaving it in standby mode will not result in a timecode break unless you are *using time of day timecode* (see below), in which case timecode breaks are unavoidable.

Most DV cameras include special controls (usually in the form of buttons on the camera) that will search forward or backward for the last piece of stable timecode. The camera will then cue the tape to the last frame of stable timecode and begin recording from there. If your camera doesn't have such a feature, you can protect your tape from timecode breaks by always letting the tape run for a few seconds after the end of your shot. Then, before you begin taping again, back the tape up so that recording begins on top of your extra footage. *Note that if you have to switch your camera into VCR mode to do this, you might lose your manual white-balance setting! Be sure to set it back when you switch back to record mode.*

Some cameras automatically use *time-of-day timecode*. The camera uses its internal clock to record timecode that corresponds to the actual time of day. A shot that has a starting timecode of 11:07:40:15 was shot at about seven minutes after 11 A.M. This can be useful information for time-sensitive material, such as news footage and certain types of documentaries, but it can make editing difficult later if the camera is paused frequently between shots. Unless having a timestamp on your tape is crucial, time-of-day timecode is best avoided.

Heads and Tails

Many editing functions will be easier if, when you're shooting, you allow a few seconds to roll before the action starts and a few seconds to roll after the director calls "cut."

EXERCISES

Do a camera test: depth of field, focal length, lens filters, white balance, and camera movement are all cinematic tools that you have at your disposal when composing a shot. Good composition involves balancing these choices along with the placement of your subject and background within your scene.

Here, then, is a simple checklist that you should get in the habit of following when setting up your shots:

1. **Consider depth of field.** Think about how deep or shallow you want the depth of field in your image. If you want a very shallow depth of field, then you're probably going to need to use a longer focal length, so you might need to move your camera away from your subject to get the framing you established in step 1. Remember also to manually control your camera's aperture, as described earlier.

2. **Pay attention to the affect of your focal length.** Whether or not you're trying to control the depth of field in your scene, you should take a minute to consider how your choice of focal length is affecting the sense of depth in your image. Are you trying to create a large sense of space? If you are, then you probably want a shorter focal length to reduce depth compression. However, if you go too short,

you might distort your actor's faces. There's no right or wrong to focal length choice, but it is important to pay attention to how focal length is affecting your image.

3. **Double-check exposure and shutter speed.** Most of the time, your camera will be calculating at least one of these parameters, often both. If you're manually adjusting aperture to control depth of field, then make sure the camera hasn't switched to a shutter speed that's too high. Or, perhaps you want to make your images darker, or to expose them in a particular way. Or, perhaps you're worried about your actor's movements interfering with your camera's automatic exposure mechanism. If so, you'll want to manually pick an exposure that works well for the scene and set the camera to that aperture.

4. **White balance.** Assuming your set is already lit—and assuming you've decided to shoot using manual white balance—it's now time to white balance. Have someone hold something white in an appropriate spot, and take your white balance. You might not have to do this every time, but remember that if your camera has shut off or been placed in stand-by mode, or if your lighting setup has changed, you need to take a new white balance.

If you follow the preceding steps when setting up your camera, you'll stand a better chance of using all of the creative tools at your disposal.

Summary

Like any other tool, when you're very familiar with how to use your camera, your hands will simply do what they need to do without you having to think about it. With all of the other things you'll have to think about when on-set, worrying about a particular camera setting is a luxury you won't be able to afford. As such, a thorough working knowledge of your camera is essential.

SHOOTING DIGITAL VIDEO

In This Chapter

- Preparing to Shoot
- Managing the Set
- Shooting
- Keeping On-Set Records
- Exercises
- In the Can

Preparing to Shoot

This is it. You have a script, treatment, or outline. You've determined a production schedule based on your budget. You've selected a film or video format, aspect ratio, and chosen a camera to purchase or rent. You've planned the shoot, using storyboards, shot lists and camera diagrams. You've secured a location or created a set. You've researched and tested tricky lighting set-ups and any special effects shots that you might need. You've learned how to use the camera and carefully selected the audio equipment necessary for your production. You may have even devoted a day or two to a test shoot.

Now, all the hard work you've done is about to pay off. You're ready to start using your camera to shoot some footage. In many ways, shooting is the best part of the entire movie-making process. You get to go out to fun locations, you get to boss people around, and you get to use cool gear. It's also the first time that you can start to see the ideas in your head turn into something real.

Unfortunately, shooting can also be really difficult. Many things can go wrong, there's lots to keep track of, and you're usually working against the clock. During the shoot, you're going to have to muster all of your artistic, logistical, and managerial sensibilities to create each shot.

In this section, we'll cover how to deal with all of those concerns, as well as learn how to get the best-looking footage for your project. Not everything included in this chapter is necessary for every type of project, but we've offered options for any type of shoot, from feature-length scripted projects to on-the-fly, handheld documentaries to carefully planned industrial videos.

Up to this point, everything in the book has been about preparing to shoot, and there still are some things to do in the week, days, or even hours before the shoot begins. Arriving on-set fully prepared will save you time and money, and you won't have to worry about appeasing a bored, frustrated cast and crew.

Table Reading

The reading of a script from start to end using either actors or non-actors. Called a "table reading" because usually the group reads seated at a table rather than standing or going through the motions of acting.

Rehearsals

Film and video productions are notorious for scheduling little or no rehearsal times for the actors. However, rehearsals can be a valuable experience for both actors and directors.

Most big budget Hollywood movies set aside two weeks to rehearse an entire feature film. Other directors, like John Cassavetes, are famous for rehearsing for months. How you decide to work with actors is up to you, but at the very least, plan on spending some time choreographing the movement of the actors—also known as *blocking*—for the camera. The more action you have in your scene, the more time you should spend blocking. Blocking a fight scene in a way that looks realistic but also fits with the visual style of your film can be a big challenge. If your film has an important fight scene, consider using a *fight choreographer*. If you have time, consider shooting the rehearsals to get a feel for the flow of the scene, and for planning a shot list. If you can, avoid waiting until the day of the shoot to start blocking. Working out the blocking of a scene can reveal many unforeseen problems in advance of the shoot itself.

Sometimes, actors aren't the only ones who need to rehearse. If you have complicated lighting effects or camera movements or challenging special effects scenes, schedule some time with the camera, lighting and special effects crewmembers for a *tech rehearsal*.

Rehearsals aren't necessary for documentary-style productions. However, commentators, on-camera hosts, and voice-over talent can benefit from a quick warm-up or read-through of the material. Seasoned producers often take a few minutes to speak with interview subjects before they shoot to break the ice and make sure everyone is on the same page before the interview begins.

The Shooting Script

By now, it's been a while since the final draft of your script was completed. You've probably gotten comments on the script from higher-ups: producers, your boss, your professor, etc. The script has been read by the cast and crew and you've heard their opinions as well. Now is the time to decide if you want to incorporate or ignore their ideas and suggestions. It's also the time to a take a good look at the dialog in your script and revise it if needed. Perhaps the age of a character has changed due to a casting choice. Or you have to shoot a love scene in an apartment instead of a castle because of budgetary constraints. By this point you should have staged a table reading and read-through a rehearsal of (at the very least) the key elements of your script. If you noticed actors tripping over too many words, awkward phrasing, and unnecessary repetition, now is the time to fix it. Finally, you may need to resolve technical issues, logistical problems, or reorganize the order of the scenes.

Once you've made these types of content changes it's time to "number" the script (if it's a feature). Each scene gets a number. (In case you're confused, if it has a slugline, it's traditionally considered a separate scene.) Later on, if you decide to omit a scene, you can cross it out on the script and write "Omit" on the scene, but you do not have to renumber the script.

When you are done, clearly date the draft and label it the "shooting script." Distribute copies of this revised script to anyone who needs it: actors, producers, the director of photography, and other crewmembers. Everyone on the set should have read this version of the script by the time you are ready to roll.

Putting Plans into Action

In Chapter 5, "Planning Your Shoot," we discussed storyboards, camera diagrams, and shot lists. Now they'll come in handy. It's possible that weeks or months have gone by since you first planned your shoot, so it's likely that you'll need to revise them so that they match the shooting script. If any changes are made to the script, traditionally the shooting script is updated with new pages in a different color for each set of revisions.

Whatever the nature of your project, you should always arrive on set with a shot list. Documentary filmmakers will find it useful to second guess what will happen during the shoot and plan their coverage in advance. Is a close-up of a sign or other object needed? An establishing shot? A shot list serves as a simple checklist detailing the day's plan and it can go a long way toward helping you achieve your goals and communicating your vision to the crew so that you get the coverage you need for each scene.

Get Releases on the Set

For documentary producers and anyone else shooting in a "real" location, it is important that you get releases from anyone in the shot and from the owner of the location. It is much easier to obtain releases as you shoot than it is to go back later and track people down. If you succeed in selling your project to a TV network or other distributor, their legal department will require these releases. For locations filled with lots of people, it is standard to post a sign at the entrance of the location informing those who enter that they will be taped. For legal purposes have your cameraperson get a quick shot of this sign.

MANAGING THE SET

There are many things to keep track of during a shoot, no matter how big or small your production. If you're directing a small crew, you might find yourself performing many of the tasks that would be delegated to others on a bigger crew. If you have a large crew, then you'll have crewmembers who can take care of some of your management concerns but you may feel like you're losing control of your own project. Whatever the size of the crew, good on-set management skills are always an asset. Part of good management includes setting a tone for the day—is it going to be casual and relaxed or tightly scheduled and serious? It's worth considering the tone of the material you are shooting on that day, and take cues from there to establish an appropriate mood for the actors. As the director or producer, the cast and crew will look at your attitude and act accordingly. If you spend twenty minutes chatting socially with a friend who's helping out on the set, you'll give the impression that there's plenty of time to get what you need, whether or not this is actually true.

When you first get to your set or location, you (or the person with the appropriate job—usually a producer or production manager) need to ensure that all crew and cast members have arrived with their gear. In addition, you need to check that you have all power, cables, lights, and other necessary pieces of hardware. Make certain that nothing unexpected has developed at your location—bad weather, noisy construction workers, and so forth. Finally, talk to the actors and key crewmembers to find out if they have any questions about what they'll be doing in the scenes that you'll be shooting.

CAMERA CREW WHO'S WHO

Lighting and shooting a feature film is a big job that requires many people. Here's a list of the camera and lighting crewmembers you'll find on a typical big-budget film set:

Director of photography (D.P.), a.k.a. cinematographer: This is the person in charge of all camera operations and lighting. With a skeleton crew, the D.P. might operate the camera. With a bigger crew the D.P. will hire a camera operator.

Camera operator: This is the person behind the camera, who works in tandem with the D.P.

First assistant camera (A.C.): The first A.C. is responsible for loading the camera, setting up the lenses and filters for each shot, and making sure the shot is in focus.

Second A.C.: The second assistant camera (A.C.). is responsible for keeping camera reports, slating each shot, and sometimes loading film or videotape into the camera.

Gaffer: The gaffer is the head electrician on the set and is responsible for directing the setup of the lights and other electrical equipment.

Best boy and electricians: The best boy is the first assistant under the gaffer and is responsible for managing the other set electricians in the setting of lights and other electrical work.

Key grip: The key grip assists the gaffer with lighting, and is responsible for coordinating the placement of grip equipment (flags, nets, etc.), special riggings, and the hardware used to move the camera.

Dolly grip: Big movies have special grips who are employed to operate cranes, dollies, and other heavy equipment.

Camera department production assistant (P.A.): The camera department often needs a production assistant (or two) to run errands to the equipment rental house, purchase film stock or videotape, and so on.

The Protocol of Shooting

Because a movie shoot requires the coordination of many people, each with unique job concerns, it's important to stay organized and follow a regular procedure on your set.

Believe it or not, there is a very specific protocol to follow when calling "Action" on a traditional film shoot. Shooting a shot begins when the assistant director yells, "Roll sound." The sound recordist starts the sound recorder and replies "Speed" when his equipment is ready. Next, the assistant director calls "Roll camera" and the camera person answers "Speed" once the camera is ready. The assistant director calls "Marker" and the slap is clapped for synchronization. Finally, the director calls "Action!" Even if you're not using a sound recordist, assistant director, or a camera operator, it's still good practice to warn everyone on the set vocally that you're about to start shooting, and give your camera and audio equipment a few seconds to get going before you call "Action." Additionally, actors and crewmembers are expected to keep going until the director calls "Cut." If the tape or film stock runs out in the middle of a take, the camera or sound operator calls "Roll out" to end the take.

Respect for Acting

In the sea of technical details, you might forget the most important thing on your set: the cast. Here are a few quick tips on how to help them give a great performance:

- Try to maintain some type of story continuity as you shoot. It's often necessary to shoot out of sequence, but at least try to stay continuous within each scene.

- Have a closed set if you're doing a scene that involves highly emotional performances or nudity. In addition, try to keep your crew as small as possible for these shots.
- Respect actors' opinions about the characters they're playing. Even if you wrote the script yourself, you might find that they have new ideas that make your script even better. Remember, they've probably spent the last week or two thinking a lot about that character, and they might have come to a deeper understanding than you have.
- Try to remain sensitive to the mood and material of the scene. If the actor must play a sad scene when everyone is joking around on the set, the actor might have a hard time concentrating or getting in the right mood.

SHOOTING

However complicated your set may be, there's one thing on it that's more important than everything else: the camera. If you don't shoot it, it won't exist later on—it's that simple. If you walk away from your shoot with video or film footage and no sound, the project might still be salvageable. But without picture, your project is over.

In Chapter 4, "Choosing a Camera," we explained how digital video cameras work, in Chapter 5, "Planning Your Shoot," we discussed different types of shots, and in Chapter 7, "The Camera," we showed you how to use the various features of a typical film or video camera. In this section, we'll discuss how to put it all together using strong compositions, camera movement, and exposure to tell your story.

Composition

Composition is simply the way that elements on-screen are arranged. Composition determines which visual elements are included in the image and how they're arranged. While shooting, you'll *frame* each shot using your camera's viewfinder to create compositions. Composition is essential to creating moving images that are attractive, and that serve to tell the story.

Good composition skills let you do far more than simply create pretty images. By carefully crafting each shot, you can convey important information to your audience. For example, look at the images in Figure 8.1.

In the upper image, the man looks confident and powerful, while in the lower image, the same man looks lonely and possibly afraid. In both of these images, the man is striking a similar pose and a somewhat neutral expression. Your sense of how powerful or weak he is comes mostly from the composition and framing of the shot.

FIGURE 8.1 The different compositions of these two shots present two very different impressions of this man.

In the upper image, he has been shot from below and framed so that he fills the frame. In this image, he is a very strong-looking, imposing figure. By contrast, the lower image shows a man who seems small. He is literally lower than we are, and therefore appears to be overwhelmed and weak. When used well, compositional differences can add a lot of depth to your story.

Mastering composition requires not only study, but also practice. Great camera operators are able to compose beautiful shots on the fly, a skill that's crucial for documentary-style shooting. Nevertheless, there are some basic compositional rules that you can learn quickly:

Headroom. One of the most common mistakes that beginning photographers and cinematographers make is that they don't pay attention. Your brain has an incredible ability to focus your attention on something. If you pay attention to what your brain is "seeing" instead of what your eyes are seeing, you might end up with a shot like the one shown in Figure 8.2a.

A

B

FIGURE 8.2   (a) Framing with too much headroom is one of the most common compositional mistakes of beginning cinematographers. (b) Less headroom brings more focus to your subject.

If you were intending to show a wide shot of the entire scene, then this shot might be okay—boring, but okay. If you were intending to show the person in the scene, though, you'd be better off with something like the image shown in Figure 8.2b.

When composing a shot, it's very important to get in the habit of looking *at* the image in the viewfinder, rather than looking *through* the viewfinder at your scene.

Figure 8.2a has too much extra space around it—its subject is not clearly presented and framed. If you get in the habit of checking the edges of your frame when you're composing, then you'll force yourself to notice any extraneous space that needs to be cropped out.

Framing Interviews for Television

If you are shooting a documentary that is destined for television broadcast, be sure to frame your interviews with enough room for "lower thirds." Lower thirds (also called Chyrons) are titles in the bottom third of the frame that state the person's name and job title (Figure 8.3).

John Smith
Director of Public Relations

FIGURE 8.3 A "lower third" is a title that identifies an interview subject used in television shows and documentaries. Remember the text must fall within the "title safe" guidelines. The figure on the left looks fine but when a lower third is added it becomes apparent that the subject is framed too tightly.

Lead your subject. Composition and framing can also be used to help your audience understand the physical relationships of the people and objects in your scene—to help them better understand the space in which your scene takes place. When you have a single shot of someone speaking, you should usually "lead" them by putting some empty screen space in front of them.

For example, Figure 8.4 shows a person talking to another person who is off-frame. If we put the blank space in front of them, we get a much more comfortable sense than if we put the space behind them.

FIGURE 8.4   By "leading" your subject with empty space, you give your audience a better understanding of the physical relationships of the actors in your scene.

Following versus anticipating. Both documentary and scripted projects will include very mundane events and actions that present a challenge for the camera operator: sitting down, standing up, opening a door, following a subject as they walk. Often these sorts of movements happen spontaneously and unpredictably. In general, the rule is that the camera should slightly *follow* any action of the subject. If your actor decides to stand suddenly in a scene that you blocked as seated, it will look okay if the camera is a little behind the movement of the actor, *following* their movement. But if the camera operator senses that the actor is about to stand and tilts up before the actor actually stands, then camera will be perceived as *anticipating* the actor's movement, which will result in footage that looks awkward and sloppy. If you do accidentally anticipate a movement, resist the urge to correct the movement by moving back to your original position unless you are fairly certain the movement you anticipated isn't going to happen in the next few moments.

Don't be afraid to get too close. Although it's important to have the proper headroom and leading in a shot, there are times when a shot calls for something more dramatic. Don't be afraid to get in close to the actors and to crop their heads and bodies out of the frame, as shown in Figure 8.5.

FIGURE 8.5   You can increase the drama and suspense of a scene by getting in really close to your subject. Although this "tight" framing cuts off some of our actor's head, it's still a well-composed, effective image.

This is a very "dramatic" type of framing. In Figure 8.5, tight framing is used to heighten suspense. In a more dramatic moment, it could be used to give the audience the perspective to see an actor's mood change or develop.

Listen. It might sound funny, but listening is one of the most important skills of any camera operator. Whether you're shooting a documentary or a scripted drama, listening and paying attention to what is going on *beyond* the visual elements of the scene is often the key to achieving the most brilliantly captured moments or performances. Many camera operators think that anything that isn't visual is not of their concern. This is a big mistake and the result is that the camera operator fails to capture the moments of the high drama, emotion, or spontaneity.

Eyelines. If you're shooting a conversation between two or more actors, you need to make sure the eyelines in each close-up match, so that when the shots are edited together, the performers appear to be looking at each other (Figure 8.6). It's also a good idea to shoot separate close-ups within a dialog scene using the same focal length and from the same distance, so that the shots match in terms of scale, composition, and lens distortions as well.

FIGURE 8.6   The upper images have eyelines that don't match, while the lower images have eyelines that match.

Clearing frame. When framing a static shot that might be used to start or end a scene, have the actors enter the frame from off-screen, perform, and then exit the frame entirely. You might not need to show them both entering and exiting frame in the final edited project, but you'll at least have the option.

Beware of the stage line. Crossing the 180° axis, also known as the *stage line, or axis of action*, is jarring. If you think of your set as a theatrical stage, the 180° axis falls along the proscenium (the front of the stage). Once you've set up your camera on one side of the axis, avoid moving it to the other side or you might end up with camera angles that don't cut together (Figure 8.7), as well as mismatched eyelines. Be aware that this primarily concerns action and dialog shots. Cutaways and establishing shots can often get away with crossing the stage line, as can handheld moving shots in documentaries.

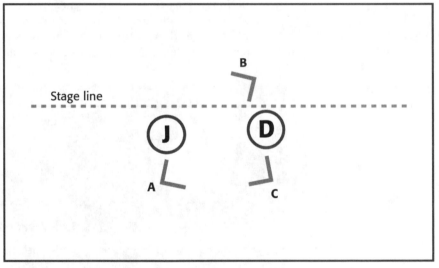

FIGURE 8.7 This camera diagram corresponds to the images in Figure 8.6. Camera angle B is on the wrong side of the stage line, which results in the mismatched eyelines in Figure 8.6.

Breaking the rules. In Western culture, our ideas about good framing are heavily dependent on the tradition of fine art painting. The shape of the film and video frame is similar to that of a traditional landscape painting, and the concept of how a medium close-up should be framed is similar to a traditional portrait. Breaking from these traditions can be interesting and exciting when it looks intentional, but beware: it can be disastrous when it looks like you didn't know any better.

Shooting for the Web

It used to be that shooting video for the Web required a lot of care to avoid compression artifacts. Today, thanks to high-quality CODECs such as MP4, H.264, and Sorenson, that's no longer the case. If you've ever watched a movie trailer on the Internet, you know how good video on the Web can look. If small file size is an absolute must, though, try to limit the amount of motion in your image (both subject and camera motion), and stay away from sets and locations with lots of different colors and lots of fine detail. These will all contribute to the size of your final file.

Camera Movement

As if composition wasn't complex enough, we're now going to complicate things and consider camera movement. Pans, tilts, zooms, dollies, and other types of camera movement are important parts of the language of film. (See Chapter 5, "Planning Your Shoot," for definitions of these types of shots.) As with composition and editing, good camera movement is something that you don't always notice when you're watching a movie. When planning your shots, your goal is simply to create movements that will allow you to cover the action in your scene in an elegant, attractive manner.

Panning and Tilting

Pans and tilts are movements around the camera's axes. When you swivel the camera from side to side around its center, you are panning the camera. When you swivel it up and down around its center, you are tilting the camera. These are the most common camera movements you'll make, especially if your camera is locked down on a tripod. Like most camera moves, good pans and tilts are smooth and slow, never jarring or sudden. They always start with a static image and eventually come to rest on a static image, even if these static parts of the shot are edited out later on.

Zooms and Dolly Shots

These types of shots use movement that goes forward and backward along the Z-axis. We've already discussed zooms and techniques for zooming in Chapter 7, "The Camera." It's important to know that, aesthetically, zooms are considered the low-rent cousin of *dolly shots*. *Dollying* the camera means to move it closer or farther from the subject. The feeling is similar to walking through space, rather than simply magnifying it. As we saw in Chapter 7, when you zoom the camera, you change the sense of depth in your scene, which results in the objects in your scene appearing to have a different spatial relationship to one another. Consequently, dolly shots usually appear more natural. Dolly shots require a camera dolly or some type of wheeled conveyance. Therefore, if you really need to pull off a good dolly shot, you'll want to rent some extra gear.

Tracking Shots

Tracking shots are akin to dolly shots, in that you physically move the camera, but tracking shots are used to follow action, or to create a camera movement parallel to the action within the scene, such as following a car by shooting from another car. As with dolly shots, you'll need some type of wheeled camera dolly to create a tracking shot.

Handholding

Traditionally, handheld shots were used in documentaries because it's easier to capture unscripted events when the camera person isn't bogged down by a tripod. In features, this *verité* style of shooting is often used intentionally to give a raw, documentary feeling that implies that the camera operator was involved in the scene—think of dramatic footage you've seen on the news where the cameraperson starts running without turning off the camera, in an obvious attempt to escape personal danger. Even big budget movies occasionally have their camera operators handhold shots to capture moments of extreme action or violence. In the hands of a skilled operator, a handheld shot can be indistinguishable from a shot on a tripod, but a wobbly handheld camera draws attention to itself and makes the audience question whether the event was real or fictional (think *Blair Witch Project*). Nowadays, handheld cameras have additional meaning within the lexicon of visual literacy. Thanks to "reality" TV shows, home-video TV shows, and amateur news footage, we've learned to see handheld shots as amateur, caught-on-tape *verité* footage. As more and more people shoot more and more video, the lines between real and fictional, professional and amateur continue to blur.

Handheld shots often imply a point-of-view change. If you use a tripod to shoot a scene of a scared person walking fearfully through a dark, deserted house, the audience will feel like they're simply watching that action. If you shoot the same scene handheld, though, the audience will feel like they're watching the action from the point of view of someone else—probably someone rather unsavory. This can greatly heighten the tension in your scene. Switching from locked down to handheld is often a way of switching the viewer's perspective from outside the action to inside, from objective to subjective.

Handholding a lightweight video camera can be a challenge. Some prefer to hold the camera at waist level, balanced against their torso; others prefer at eye level. You can also use the shoulder strap to try to steady the camera, while standing with your legs shoulder-width apart to help steady your stance. As with most camera-operating skills, practice makes perfect. Handholding a medium-sized 16mm film camera or a professional video camera is actually a little easier because the weight of the camera helps the operator hold it steady. Many gear-laden 35mm and HD cameras are not designed for handholding at all, and projects that use these cameras often use a secondary camera for any handheld shots.

In many ways, the camera operator who handholds is free from the restrictions that others face when using tripods, dollies, jibs, and steadicams. But there are many challenges as well. Perhaps one of the most difficult things to shoot handheld is a subject who "walks and talks." Generally, the camera operator must get in front of the subject and walk backward, shooting the subject as they walk toward them. Believe it or not, skilled handheld operators can shoot footage in this manner that looks fluid and smooth. One trick of the trade is for the camera operator to match his stride to that of the subject. Not only does this ensure that the camera operator walks at the same pace but it also ensures that the bobbing motion of a camera matches the bobbing motions of the subject. The result is that the subject's head stays in approximately the same place within the frame, which makes the footage appear "smoother" and less jarring than it would if the camera were moving up and down out of sync with the subject.

Deciding When to Move

Choosing when to use a camera movement can be tricky. Not only do moving shots require special gear (dollies, cranes, jibs, steadicams, etc.), and a skilled cameraman, they can also be challenging to work with in the editing room. Editing moving shots into static shots, or moving shots that travel in different directions or at different speeds can be difficult and may result in scenes that lack the emotional tone you were looking for.

A camera movement is usually used for two reasons:

1. **It's the only way to get the shot.** Sometimes, the decision to use a moving shot is obvious, as it's the only way to cover the action in your scene. If you're having trouble blocking your scene because you can't keep it all framed from one camera position, then try some very simple camera movements. Sometimes, even a short tracking movement is all you need to get the camera into a new position that frames the rest of your action.

2. **A moving camera changes the level of tension in a scene.** Think of the extremely tense moments in a soap opera. A character has just learned some horrible news and we're getting ready to break for a commercial. The music builds, the actor looks traumatized, and what happens? The camera slowly zooms into their face. (Never *ever*

zoom for this type of effect. Dolly the camera in instead.) Camera movements are not just used to create tension, they can also be used to *release* tension. A swirling camera movement that circles two excited lovers as they finally embrace and kiss on a crowded street corner at rush hour, can be a tremendous release of tension (since they were probably on the outs just a few scenes earlier).

It *is* possible to move the camera too much. A scene of an intimate private discussion between two people may not be served by lots of camera movements. In fact, the moving camera may simply distract the audience and upstage the action happening on-screen.

A well-conceived camera movement will be invisible to the viewer, which makes it hard to learn from skilled directors, because you simply won't notice their best work. Nevertheless, studying and practicing camera movements are the best ways to learn how to use them.

Corporate and industrial works usually benefit tremendously from moving cameras. Because these types of productions often include lots of footage of mundane actions, spicing up your shots with some nice camera work not only allows you to show the same mundane actions in different ways, it can also inject a lot of visual energy into what might be dry material. Next time you have to shoot an office worker talking on the phone or filing, consider renting a small jib or dolly, and try shooting them a little more dynamically.

Exposure

Both film and video need to be properly exposed to produce a good image. Video is much more sensitive to light than is film, and video has less *latitude*, so it's easier to over- and underexpose. However, unlike film, with video you can use a field monitor to immediately see if the image is properly exposed. We recommend *always* using a field monitor when shooting video—think of it as your first and only line of defense against poor image quality.

With a field monitor, you can make an immediate decision as to whether or not an overexposed image is acceptable for your project. You might decide, for example, to purposely overexpose the sky, in favor of keeping a good exposure on an actor's face. Be aware that the auto-exposure mechanism in your camera will make exactly the opposite decision, and will properly expose the sky, causing the actor's face to fall into shadow.

Underexposure usually results in a dark or muddy-looking image, whereas overexposure causes bright areas to turn white, or get "blown out." Properly exposed film or video footage usually contains some areas of overexposure—usually reflective highlights and bright whites. With film, overexposed images are easier to fix than underexposed images because the brightness can be pulled down in the film lab. If your video project is destined for videotape delivery, a little overexposure or under-exposure can usually be corrected in post-production. However, for video-to-film transfers, overexposed video can cause many problems because blown-out white areas contain no visual information. Once transferred to film, they will look like glaringly white "hot-spots." In that case, under-exposure is preferable to overexposure. Of course, proper exposure is always best of all.

Recognizing Proper Exposure

If your video camera has a Zebra feature, overexposure will be particularly easy to spot. Underexposure, though, can be hard to see, especially in a tiny viewfinder or LCD screen. Ideally, every image will contain a range from very dark areas to very light areas, even if you're shooting at night. If your entire image looks dark in your viewfinder, chances are it's underexposed.

Auto-Exposure Troubles

As with automatic white balance, auto-exposure features can be affected by a change in the content of your scene. If an actor walks into a frame and blocks some light, for example, you might see your camera iris up, resulting in a disturbing, overall contrast change. For this reason alone, you're usually better off controlling exposure manually.

Double-Check Your Camera Settings

Right before you shoot, go over all of the controls and settings on your camera to make sure they are all set appropriately. Be certain that any features you don't want (16:9 shooting, progressive scan, etc.) are turned off. Ensure that your sharpening and white-balance settings are config-ured appropriately. Bear in mind that some settings might change back to their defaults when you power down the camera, or even put it in standby mode. So you'll need to double-check your settings any time you change tape, or do anything else that takes the camera out of recording mode.

If you are shooting from a tripod or some other image-stabilizing de-vice, turn off any electronic or optical image-stabilization features on your camera. Electronic image-stabilization algorithms typically shoot at higher shutter speeds. In addition to producing a harsher image, you'll see a reduction in gain. Some EIS mechanisms will also soften your image, even when the camera is sitting still.

Optical image-stabilization mechanisms won't change your image quality, but they will drain your battery life. Since you won't need stabilization if you're using a tripod, turn off optical stabilization when your camera is tripod-mounted.

And don't forget to make sure your audio equipment is working properly as well.

SHOOTING BLUE-SCREEN EFFECTS

If you have a special effect that is dependent on blue-screen shooting, then there are a few things to remember when shooting. Most of the work of getting a good blue-screen plate comes in the lighting (as explained in Chapter 6). However, there are still some things to remember when shooting blue-screen shots:

- Use a field monitor and pay close attention to the quality of the blue screen in your shot. Are the actors casting shadows? Is the blue screen reflecting on their clothing?
- If you have access to a laptop computer, consider taking it to the set with you. There, you can shoot some quick test footage and do a simple composite on your computer. This is the best way to determine if your blue-screen effect is working.
- Finally, be very careful of your camera's built-in sharpening mechanism. One of the byproducts of sharpening is that high-contrast areas—like the border between an actor and a blue screen—can develop "halos" of color. These halos can interfere with your post-production compositing process.

As an example, consider Figure 8.8. This shot shows a custom-made prop—a "universal remote control" that was painted blue to facilitate compositing of a computer-generated control panel. Check the edge of the blue area, though. Because the camera over-sharpened, there's a discernable halo that is visible even after compositing.

By simply dialing down the camera's sharpening feature, you can usually eliminate these artifacts.

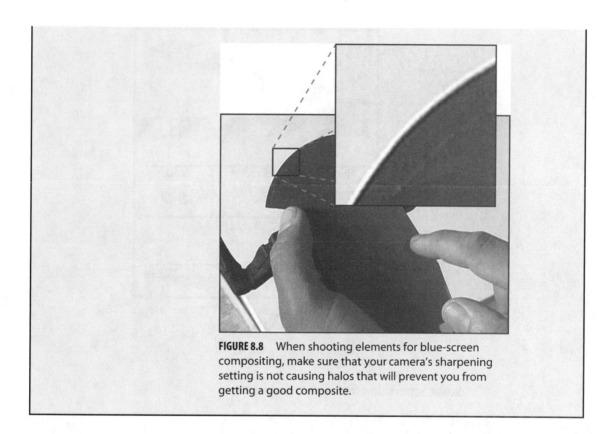

FIGURE 8.8 When shooting elements for blue-screen compositing, make sure that your camera's sharpening setting is not causing halos that will prevent you from getting a good composite.

KEEPING ON-SET RECORDS

All productions benefit from having someone keep a record of what happens on the set. The traditional Hollywood method uses a *script supervisor* to record all the shots as they occur, along with important details. Using a script supervisor is not necessary for non-scripted projects such as documentaries and corporate videos. Instead a *field producer* keeps careful notes about the shoot. Either way, on-set records are used later during post-production to help the editor and others who were not present on the set understand what was shot, how it was shot, and why it was shot. When problems occur during the shoot the script supervisor's or field producer's notes offer an explanation and often point to a solution.

FIGURE 8.9   A typical camera slate marked with the scene number and take number.

Script Supervising for Scripted Projects

The script supervisor's job is to keep track of the number of pages that are shot each day and to make sure that the camera angles and eyelines are framed correctly to cut together later on, that continuity is maintained, and that the camera slates are marked with the correct take numbers and other information (Figure 8.9). As if this weren't enough to keep track of, they are also responsible for creating a *lined script* during the shoot (Figure 8.10).

Continuity

During a shoot, the process of keeping track of dialog changes, matching camera angles, actor's positions, wardrobe and props so that the footage from shot to shot, and day to day, will cut together.

When a script is prepared for production, each scene is given a scene number. In turn, each shot in that scene is given its own shot number. Generally the master shot is named according to the scene number, for example scene 23, and each take is numbered consecutively: 23-1, 23-2, 23-3, etc. The next shot in the scene, say a close-up of the lead actor, would be called 23a, and so on. This information is recorded on the slate (Figure 8.9) and also on the notes kept on the shooting script by the script supervisor (Figure 8.10), usually handwritten on the facing page of the

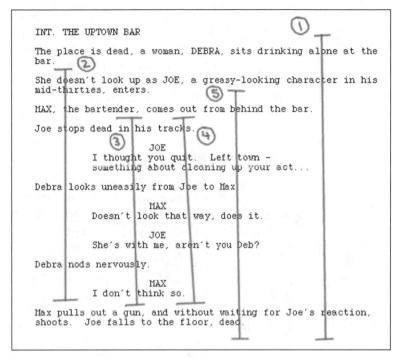

FIGURE 8.10   A lined script and script supervisor's marks.

shooting script itself. Usually, the best takes are marked with a circle around the shot number. These *circled takes* are the shots that the director thought were the best takes during the shoot.

For complicated scenes, a script supervisor's notes might include diagrams of the set, still images for continuity, and more. In addition, the script supervisor lines the script, drawing lines with arrows to show the portion of the script that each shot covers (Figure 8.10). Be aware that these lines indicate the dialog that was *actually* covered during the shot, as opposed to the director's idea of what should be covered.

Clearly, script supervising isn't necessary for every shoot, but the longer your project and more complicated the shoot, the more valuable this information can be later on.

Documentary Field Notes

For documentaries, there is no such thing as a script supervisor, however there is usually someone on the set to take *field notes*. Field notes are not as formalized as script supervisor notes but they contain the same sorts of information: content, technical notes, etc. If the shoot involves multiple takes—such as the taping of an on-camera host—the takes are numbered and the director selects circled takes, just as they do on a scripted project. With documentaries, separate "takes" don't always exist—rather the camera operator(s) simply cover the scene as best they can without stopping the camera unnecessarily. The field notes serve to describe what happened, and to give the timecodes of key moments so that later on, people working in post-production can quickly find important material.

Camera and Sound Logs

Have someone on the camera crew keep logs: a list of shots, lens focal lengths, and technical notes with timecode references. Similarly, have the production sound mixer keep track of the sound takes and any technical problems. For example, the camera logs might explain that the tape rolled out during a shot and that another take was shot on the next film reel or videotape. Moreover, a sound log might report a microphone problem. If you have trouble later, these logs can help you decipher the problem (and hopefully find the solution).

Roll Out

Don't forget to label your tapes as you use them, and depress the record inhibit tabs—you don't want to accidentally record over an already-used tape because it looked like new stock! Also, beware rewinding to look at the footage you just shot in the viewfinder—you might end up accidentally recording over it!

EXERCISES

1. **Stage a table reading.** Before you shoot your project, gather a group of actors or friends to do a *table reading* of your script. Try to avoid having anyone play more than one character in the same scene, and cast a separate person as the narrator who will read the stage directions in the script—often the majority of the reading. Invite friends and colleagues and either hand out a questionnaire or initiate an informal discussion of the project afterwards. Use this information to revise the shooting script.

2. **Make a shot list.** Take your shooting script or outline and use it to make a shot list. Think about how you want the final edited project to look and make sure the shots you've listed will get the results you desire. Take into account the assets and limitations of the crew, locations, cast, and other key elements. Take the most complicated scene in your script and make a camera and lighting diagram as well. If you

already have storyboards, shot lists, and camera diagrams, go over them and make sure they are appropriate for the actual conditions of your pending shoot.

3. **Think about framing.** Begin your shot setup by roughly positioning your camera. This is your first stab at getting the composition you want. Make sure you can frame and position all of the elements the way you want them. Is the subject and action best shown in a static shot or in a moving shot? Make a choice and take a rough camera stance. You might need to reposition the actors and props to get the framing you want. What's more, you might need to reposition them in a way that is completely unrealistic; that is, in positions that wouldn't occur in real life.

4. **Practice handholding.** Video cameras are pretty easy to come by these days—if you don't own one yourself, you can probably borrow one from a friend or your school or your office. Start out by learning how to hold the camera steady by picking a static object and shooting it. The longer the shot, the harder it is to hold the camera without shaking. Next, try panning, zooming, and following moving objects—cars, your cat, birds, or airplanes in the sky. Try to make each pan part of a composed shot that starts and ends. Remember to keep the center of gravity in your body low even if your arms are holding a camera pointed up overhead. Sometimes slightly bending your knees helps. If your camera has electronic image stabilization, try shooting both with and without it.

5. **Study camera movements.** Watching camera movements in movies can be a great way to understand how they can be used, how they edit together, and what emotional impact they can have on a scene. As we mentioned earlier, a well-orchestrated camera movement won't necessarily be visible, so you may have to pay close attention to notice them. This means focusing less on the story, which is often easier with a movie with which you're very familiar. Being a little less compelled by the story will make it easier to concentrate on technical specifics. For complex movements, you'll probably need to watch a scene repeatedly. For an interesting comparison, rent *Dr. Strangelove* and *The Shining*, both of which were directed by Stanley Kubrick. In *Strangelove* pay particular attention to the scenes between Mandrake (Peter Sellers) and Ripper (Sterling Hayden). Note Kubrick's use of extremely wide-angle shots that contain no movement at all. Also, note how he's willing to only show Hayden's back. Now consider *The Shining*, a movie that is stunning for its dynamic camera movements, and that is well known for being the first prominent use of a steadicam. Two very different approaches to camera movement, from the same director.

6. **Practice camera movements.** Even if your script isn't ready, you can still practice the use of a moving camera. Choose some mundane actions—a person opens a letter and reacts to the contents while sitting down in a chair—and practice shooting with different types of camera movements. Try some versions of this shot with multiple angles, and then try editing them together so that you can get a feel for how moving shots can be pieced together.

IN THE CAN

Once your project is shot and you've got it "in the can," it's time to move on to post-production. The rest of this book covers building a workstation for post-production, editing picture and sound, color correction, titling, rotoscoping for special effects, and outputting your final project.

PRODUCTION SOUND

In This Chapter

- What You Want to Record
- Microphones
- Setting Up
- Recording Your Sound
- A Good Approach
- Exercise: Gear Checklist
- Summary

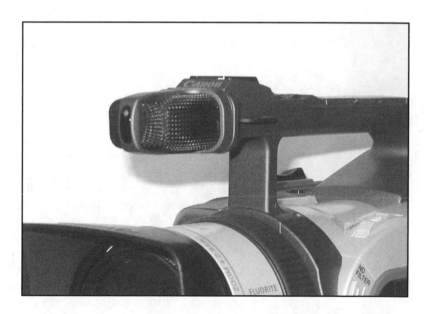

With all this talk about storyboarding, cameras, and image quality, it's pretty easy to become something of a "visual chauvinist" and end up scrimping on your project's sound. Therefore, at this point, it's important to be reminded that *sound is one of the most powerful tools in your creative palette*. With the right music and sound effects, you can do everything from evoking locations to defining moods and building tension. In fact, in many ways, good sound is *more* important than good video.

As an example, there are plenty of movies that adopt a grungy, low-quality image as a stylistic choice. The makers of *Three Kings and I* went to great lengths to create a very rough-looking, grainy, noisy image style. However, did they choose an equivalent low-fidelity for their audio? No way! (You'll regularly see similar visual styles in music videos—grungy, beat up video with high-fidelity sound.) Audiences are very forgiving of low-quality video—they even find it visually appealing—but if they can't understand the audio, especially the dialog, they won't be engaged in the story.

Editing, mixing, adding music, and creating sound effects are each a crucial part of your post-production process, but to be successful in those tasks, you have to have clean, high-quality audio recordings. In this chapter, we'll cover the basics of good production sound recording, including how to choose and use microphones, as well as what the best recording options are for different types of projects. Finally, at the end of this chapter we'll detail simple recording setups for common shooting situations.

What You Want to Record

Most of your audio recording tasks will involve dialog. (Obviously, if you're shooting a nature documentary or action sequence, dialog is probably not as prevalent.) Therefore, your entire strategy when planning your audio recording will be built around the specific problems of recording dialog.

Although it is possible to edit the quality of your audio in post-production, don't expect to be able to make the type of content changes that you can make when editing video or still images. If you have extra sound, such as background noise, or low recording levels, correcting your audio will be extremely difficult. Your goal when recording audio is to get high-quality recordings of just the sounds you want. Although dialog will make up the bulk of your audio recording, there are times when you'll want to record other things, such as actions that are critical to your story; for example, a hand turning the clicking dial of a safe, or the philandering husband trying, unsuccessfully, to quietly creep into his house late at night.

It's difficult or impossible to correct a sound, or remove an unwanted sound from a recording, but it's easy to mix sounds *in*. Therefore, if you've recorded high-quality sound of your primary *foreground* elements, you can always add *background* sound later.

For example, say you're recording two people talking in a crowded restaurant. You can spend a long time shooting multiple takes, trying to get a version where you can hear every word over the din of other diners. Alternatively, you can ask everyone else in the restaurant to be silent—but continue to pantomime talking—while you record your actors. Afterward, let your restaurant patrons go back to speaking, and record a few minutes of their sound (in the business, crowd noise is referred to as *walla*). In post-production, you can mix together the sounds of your characters with your separately recorded background walla, and have full control over the loudness of the background, letting you mix the background to more easily hear your foreground characters.

Similarly, any other sounds—doorknobs, car doors opening, windows breaking—can be added later, during a process called *foley* (named for Jack Foley, the man who pioneered the technique). Foley is simply the process of recording all of the other incidental sounds that your scene needs, and mixing them in during your final sound mix.

Recording good audio requires a lot of preparation, and begins with selecting the right microphone.

MICROPHONES

Although your video camera has a built-in microphone, you shouldn't use it for most feature and documentary work. On-camera mics are typically low quality, and produce tinny sound recorded from all directions. In addition, because of their location on the camera, they frequently pick up camera noise such as motors and hand movements (Figures 9.1 and 9.2). Consequently, to record good audio, you'll want to buy or rent one or more high-quality microphones, which you will connect to your camera or to a separate audio recorder such as a DAT or MiniDisc recorder.

Different types of microphones are designed for different recording situations, so your choice of microphone will be based on matching microphone characteristics to your shooting needs.

What a Mic Hears

Just as different lenses have different angles of view—some wider, some narrower—that define what they will see, microphones have different "directional" characteristics that define what they will hear. The directional "coverage" of the mic that you choose will have a lot to do with both the content and quality of your recorded sound.

FIGURE 9.1 On-camera mics are frequently housed inside the camera's body, where they are susceptible to picking up camera noise.

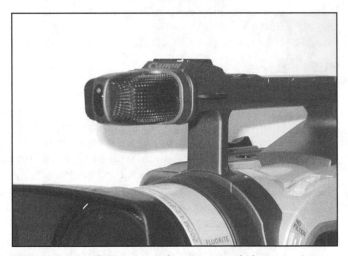

FIGURE 9.2 Even if your camera has an external, shotgun mic, you'll still want to get a higher-quality, better-sounding mic for your shoot.

Omnidirectional Mics

As their name implies, omnidirectional mics pick up sounds from all directions. While this might seem like a good idea for recording the sound of an entire room, omnidirectional mics are often not practical. With their wide coverage, omni mics can pick up far more sound than you might want, including camera noise (and camera operator noise!), as well as ambient sounds such as passing cars or people. Because they listen in all directions, omni mics tend to record echoes within the room, which makes for a much more "boomy" sound.

Omnidirectional mics work well if they are held close to the subject of the sound—within 12 inches or so—because the subject tends to over-power any background sound. However, keeping a mic in this position can be very difficult, particularly if you want it hidden, and especially if your subject is moving.

On the positive side, omnidirectional mics have a low sensitivity to wind and breath sounds, and many provide a "shaped" response that boosts higher-frequency sounds while dampening lower, rumbling sounds. Shaped-response mics are good for preserving the sound of a voice that is being recorded against loud sounds such as traffic or construction.

Unidirectional Mics

Unidirectional (or just "directional") mics, as you might expect, pick up sound from one direction. Because you can point a unidirectional mic at a particular subject, they are well suited to feature and documentary production, as they allow you to selectively record a particular person or event. Moreover, because a directional mic can be farther from the recording subject than an omnidirectional mic can, they are better suited to some feature production sets, where keeping a mic close to the subject is difficult. Some directional mics are more directional than others, and which type to choose depends on your shooting task.

Most directional mics are sensitive to sound in a *cardioid* pattern (so named because it looks vaguely heart shaped—see Figure 9.3). A cardioid microphone is more sensitive to sound coming from the front of the mic, and typically *attenuates*, or drops off, sounds around the sides of the mic. Typically, a cardioid pattern is wide enough that a cardioid mic placed more then seven or eight feet from its subject will pick up unwanted sounds.

A *supercardioid* mic has a tighter pickup pattern than a cardioid and is similar to the pickup pattern of the human ear. Supercardioid mics pro-vide good results when used at a distance of 6 to 15 feet from the subject.

Finally, *hypercardioid* mics have an even narrower pickup pattern that rejects most sounds that are "off-axis" from the direction the mic is pointed. Hypercardioids are, in fact, so directional that they can be some-what difficult to use. If they stray even a little from their subject, they will not pick up the desired sound. You'll need a diligent mic operator to use a hypercardioid mic.

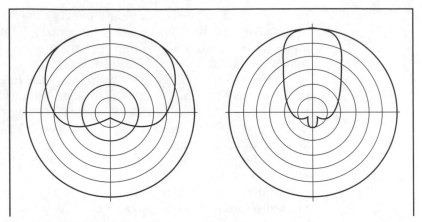

FIGURE 9.3   The cardioid patterns for an omnidirectional and a supercardioid mic.

Contrary to common sense, it's the holes on a microphone that make it more or less directional. Take a look at a typical handheld or clip-on omnidirectional mic. You'll see that most of the holes in the microphone's case are in the very top of the mic, with just a few holes around the sides. Now look at a typical hypercardioid mic and you'll see a very long tube riddled with holes along its entire length. What's the deal?

The holes in a directional mic cause the sounds coming in from the sides of the mic to cancel each other out, leaving only the sounds from the front (and sometimes, back). In fact, you can turn a hypercardioid mic into an omnidirectional mic simply by covering up the holes along the sides (Figure 9.4),

FIGURE 9.4   Extremely directional mics such as this Sennheiser ME66 are ideal for mounting on a boom or fishpole or, in a pinch, mounting on the top of your camera. It is the holes in the side of the mic that give its directional qualities.

If you can't afford multiple mics or arrange for a *boom operator* on your shoot (more on this later) and you need to shoot dialog scenes, then an omnidirectional mic will be the best choice. Ideally, though, you'll want a mic with a supercardioid pattern, and the personnel and equipment to use it right. Later in this chapter, we'll discuss how to mic your scene.

Most microphones come with a coverage chart that indicates the directional pattern of the microphone, and how different parts of the field of coverage respond to different frequencies (Figure 9.5). Although interesting, don't lose any sleep over trying to understand these charts. Most mics are clearly rated as cardioid, supercardioid, or hypercardioid.

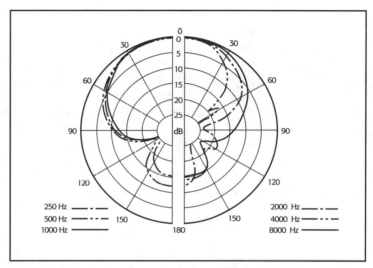

FIGURE 9.5   Most microphones include a polar chart that diagrams their directionality and sensitivity. The polar chart shows a cross-section of the mic's pickup-pattern, with the mic laying in the middle of the chart, pointed toward the top. This chart diagrams a supercardioid mic.

Hands Off That Mic!

Because a mic's directional characteristics can be affected by the way you handle the mic, be very careful when attaching a mic to a stand or pole with a clamp or tape (or when holding a mic in your hand). Be certain you don't cover up any of the holes in the mic's case. Similarly, don't think that you can make a mic more directional by cupping your hands around the front of the mic.

Finally, *parabolic* mics are extremely directional mics that use a large parabolic dish to gather and focus sound onto the head of a unidirectional microphone. Parabolic mics are sensitive to sounds over 200 feet away and are not practical for most feature shoots. However, for difficult shooting situations where a subject is extremely far away (climbing the side of a mountain, for example), a parabolic mic might be the most reasonable way to record sound.

How a Mic Hears

All microphones work by converting sound waves into electrical impulses. There are different mechanisms for performing this conversion, and each has its own advantages and limitations. Typically, different mechanisms are used for different types of microphones.

A *dynamic* microphone is the most basic mechanism, consisting of a simple diaphragm attached to a coil of wire that is surrounded by a magnet (it is, literally, the exact opposite of a speaker). When the pressure of a sound wave hits the diaphragm, it moves the coil of wire within the magnetic field of the magnet. This generates a small electrical current that is fed out of the microphone.

Because of their simple design, dynamic microphones are incredibly rugged and require no external power or batteries. The dynamic mechanism has a very short range, and so is typically only used in handheld mics. Their short range makes dynamic mics well suited to narration and voice-over recording (they tend to pick up only the voice of the speaker), but frequently impractical for on-set recording.

In a *condensor* mic, a metal plate and a metal diaphragm are separated by a thin gap of air. Both plates are electrically polarized by an external power supply. Because of a property called "capacitance," an electric charge is created between the plates. As incoming sound waves move the metal diaphragm, the amount of charge between the plates changes. The electrical charges produced by this mechanism are tiny and must be amplified using power from either a battery or a *phantom power supply* housed externally. Because the diaphragm in a condensor mic is so small, it requires very little acoustic pressure to make it move. Consequently, condensor mics are much more sensitive than dynamic mics.

An *electret condensor* is a somewhat cheaper, lower-quality version of the condensor mechanism. Electret condensor mics use a small battery to create a polarizing voltage, and so don't require an external power supply.

Because their pickup mechanisms are so tiny, condensor mics can be made very small—most clip-on mics use electret condenser mechanisms. Most condensor mics also include a small *pre-amplifier*, either built into the mic itself, or located outboard in a small box.

Ideally, you'll want to choose a condenser mic simply because they deliver the best quality. However, for recording voice-overs or narration, or for doing interviews in more harsh conditions (bad weather, extreme humidity, etc.), a handheld, dynamic mic might be a better choice.

Types of Mics

No matter what type of pickup element is used, mics typically fall into three categories: handheld, lavalier (clip-on), and shotgun. Which to choose depends on your set, and you might find yourself using multiple mics of different types. Obviously, for a dramatic production, keeping the mic hidden is your primary concern (after getting good audio!). However, even documentary producers might want unobtrusive mics, both for aesthetics and to record their subjects more clandestinely. (Note that we're not advocating illegal wiretapping! Rather, we're simply trying to remind you that a microphone can be a very intimidating object to someone who hasn't spent a lot of time "on-camera." To keep an interview or documentary subject calm and more spontaneous, a less-intrusive type of mic might be preferable.)

We've all seen the handheld mics used by talk show hosts, rock stars, and karaoke singers. Usually omnidirectional dynamic mics, these are the least useful mics for on-set use. Because they typically operate at short range, they have to be held close to the speaker's mouth, making it nearly impossible to keep them hidden (Figure 9.6).

FIGURE 9.6   A handheld mic on a microphone stand.

Lavaliers

Lavalier, or clip-on mics, are the small condenser mics that you see clipped to the front of newscasters. Lavaliers are usually omnidirectional mics, but because they are kept so close to the speaker's mouth, they rarely pick up extraneous sound, making them well suited to recording individual performers. Moreover, because of their small size, they can easily be hidden under clothing (Figure 9.7).

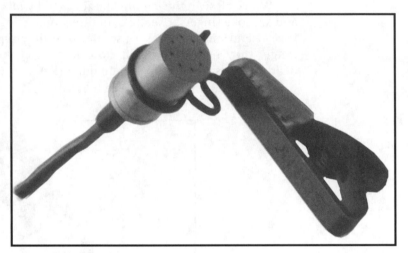

FIGURE 9.7   A clip-on, or lavalier, mic.

Although laveliers are omnidirectional, they might still have some directional characteristics. A somewhat directional lavalier will produce a very clear recording, but might lack some ambient sound that makes for a full, realistic sound (these lavs are typically used for newscasting where the sound of an authoritarian voice is all you're interested in recording). A more omnidirectional lav can record a more natural sound, but you'll have to worry about controlling extra ambient noises on your set.

For scenes involving many actors, you'll probably need a separate lav for each performer, which means that you'll have to deal with the requisite logistical troubles such as wiring multiple performers, and managing lots of mic cables. (You'll also need a *mixer*, which we'll discuss later in this chapter.) Because keeping cables hidden (and keeping actors from tripping over them) can be a problem, *wireless lavaliers* are a good solution for complex shoots involving lots of mics. A wireless lav system consists of a normal lav microphone attached to a small transmitter worn by the actor. A receiver picks up the audio and routes it on to your recording device.

Although a great solution to the "obtrusive cable" problem, wireless lavaliers have complications of their own. First, you'll want to be sure you get a system that uses an FM transmitter, for higher quality. In addition, you'll have to worry about radio interference from other devices, cell phones, overhead power lines, and so on. These problems can be easy to solve, but they can take time.

Shotgun Mics

Those long, skinny microphones that you often see sticking off video cameras are referred to as *shotgun* mics. Although varied in pickup mechanism and directional characteristics, shotgun mics provide the greatest flexibility for miking. Most shotgun mics record stereo audio, usually by having two pickups inside, one each for left and right channels (Figure 9.8).

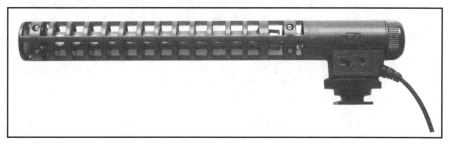

FIGURE 9.8   A typical shotgun mic.

If your camera already has a shotgun mic attached, odds are it's not very high quality. Whatever its quality, the front of your camera is not the best location for a mic. Ideally, you'll want a supercardioid or hypercardioid shotgun mic attached to a *boom pole*. We'll discuss using a boom later in this chapter.

A Little of Each

The ideal audio setup involves several microphones, frequently of different types. If you can only afford one mic, then you'll want to get a directional shotgun mic and attach it to a boom. However, for better sound and greater post-production audio editing flexibility, fitting actors with lavaliers while simultaneously miking them with a boom mic provides your sound editor with more options for mixing and correcting difficult-to-understand audio.

No matter what types of mics you choose, you'll ideally want to listen to them before you buy. Just like loudspeakers, different mics provide different sounds. Some will boost low frequencies to help create authoritative, booming voices. Others will have more of a "flat," realistic response. Although you can look at frequency response charts for a mic, such stats don't reveal everything about how a mic will sound. Your ear is the best judge of whether or not a mic is right for you.

Mixing

As you might have noticed, most cameras and tape decks only have one place to plug in a microphone. Therefore, if you're using multiple microphones, you'll have to plug them into a *mixer* to mix their signals down to a pair of signals that can be plugged in to the stereo input on your camera or deck.

When choosing a mixer, you'll need to pick a unit with enough inputs (four is usually plenty) for the number of mics you'll be using. You might also want to select a unit that has a built-in *graphic equalizer*. As we'll discuss later, an equalizer will let you slightly modify the sound coming through a mic to add more bass or treble. Equalizers are a great way of improving the sound of a weak voice, or removing certain problems such as "shushing" S sounds or hisses.

Headphones

Headphones are the audio equivalent of a field monitor—you need them to hear (or "monitor") the audio as it's being recorded. Headphones serve a dual purpose: they block out ambient noise from the set and allow the sound recordist to monitor the audio directly. Because the sound recordist is listening to what is being recorded, as opposed to what the human ear would hear on the set, he will often notice extra noises such as crackling mics and distracting background sounds. Even though you can use small "walkman" type headphones, it's best to use big, professional padded ones that block out as much ambient noise as possible.

Connecting It All Up

Unfortunately, connecting your mics to your camera, mixer, or deck involves a little more than just matching connectors. Although you might have the right-shaped plug on your microphone, it might not be wired properly for the jack on your deck or mixer.

There are two different types of inputs on a recording device: *line-level* inputs and *mic-level* inputs. Mic-level inputs are designed to receive weak, quieter audio signals. A *pre-amplifier* inside the mic input boosts the incoming signal to increase its level. Line-level inputs are designed for more powerful signals. Most video cameras provide a mic-level input, while most mixers or tape decks provide both mic and line. Note that you can't tell the level of an input by its connector—RCA, Mini, or 1/4" phono connectors can all be either mic or line level. However, most jacks are clearly labeled *mic* or *line*, and some can be changed from one to the other by flipping a switch, usually located near the jack. If your recording device has only line-level inputs, then you'll need to buy a microphone pre-amp to boost the signal from your mic up to line level. The pre-amp will sit between your microphone and your recorder.

There are two types of microphone connectors: *balanced* and *unbalanced*. You can generally tell whether a mic is balanced by looking at the type of plug it uses. RCA, 1/4" phono, and mini plugs are all unbalanced connectors, while three-prong XLR plugs are usually balanced. One is not better than the other as far as audio quality goes, but if you want to use cables longer than about 25 feet, you'll need balanced connectors (Figure 9.9).

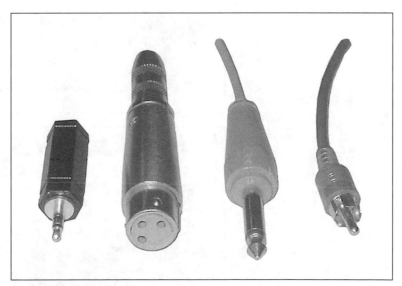

FIGURE 9.9   Mini, XLR, 1/4" phono, and RCA plugs.

Most likely, your camcorder has an unbalanced connector, usually a mini jack. If you're using a mic with a balanced connector (usually a mic with an XLR plug), then you'll need to get a special adapter that not only provides an XLR jack, but also alters the mic's signal. Studio 1 Productions' XLR adapters provide balanced XLR and mini jacks that are switchable between mic and line levels. The XLR-Pro also provides separate level controls for each input. With its small size, the XLR-Pro can easily be attached to the tripod mount on the underside of your camera, or sit between your camera and your tripod.

With a product such as the XLR-Pro, you're free to use higher-end, professional quality mics with a lower-end camera—at any cable length—with no concern for distortion or incompatible connectors (Figures 9.10 and 9.11).

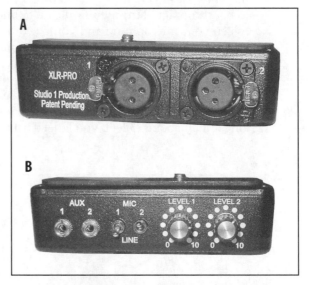

FIGURE 9.10   (a) The Studio 1 Productions' XLR-Pro adapter provides a simple mic mixer on the front, and XLR jacks on the back. (b) A single mini-jack attaches the device to your camera's external mic jack. (c) The XLR-Pro can be easily mounted between your camera and tripod.

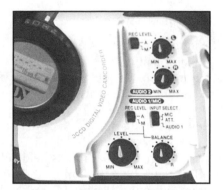

FIGURE 9.11   Higher-end cameras provide manual mic level adjustments. However, they might still need an XLR adapter to connect balanced, professional mics.

Double-System Recording

Although your DV camera can do a great job of recording audio, there will be times when you'll want to record audio onto a separate recording device. On some occasions, it's simply a hassle—or outright impossible—to have a microphone plugged into your camera. For these instances, recording your audio on a separate audio recording device, such as a hard disk recorder, MiniDisc, or DAT recorder, is the only way to go.

When You Should Use Double-System Recording

Recording audio separately from your video makes your shoot more involved and your post-production more complicated. Double-system recording requires extra gear and crewmembers, and editing nonsynchronized audio requires extra steps to synchronize your audio and video. As such, we only recommend this technique for times when it's necessary. Some examples:

- If you have a very small video camera and are planning on doing a lot of handheld camera movements, it might not be practical to have an external microphone or mixer plugged into the camera.
- Any scene in which actors are inside a car having a conversation, but you're shooting the exterior of the car from a chase vehicle. In this case, you'll need to have an audio recorder inside the car with the actors.
- Any scene in which the logistics of your set or camera movements make it impractical to keep your camera cabled to your microphones.
- Any scene in which the action is a long way from the camera—action scenes, wide landscape shots, or any time when you want to shoot something from far away.
- Multi-camera shoots—of a concert or play, for example.

Shooting Double-System Sound

Shooting double-system sound is, obviously, more involved than shooting automatically synched audio, and requires the careful cooperation of a number of people. First, you'll want to have an operator for your audio recording device. This person, the *production recording mixer*, will monitor the recording levels and take care of starting and stopping the recording device. You'll also want a camera assistant to handle the *slate*.

We've all seen the classic shot of the black-and-white chalkboard with the clapper bar that is held before a camera. "Scene 1, take 1" says a voice, and then the top of the board is clapped down to make a loud cracking sound. *Slating* is used both to label the shot and to provide an audio/visual cue that can be used to synchronize the video and audio. Once in the editing room, the editor looks for the frame where the clapper bar is down, and lines this up with the sharp crack of the audio. If all has gone well, the rest of the scene will be in sync. You can use this same method when shooting DV.

Today, most productions that shoot with double-system sound use a timecode slate. These are electronic devices that, in addition to displaying scene, shot, and take numbers, also display an electronic timecode readout. The electronic slate is connected to a timecode-capable audio deck through a special cable. When editing, rather than having to look sync your audio manually, by looking at the clap of the slate, you can simply read the timecode display on the slate to see how much of an offset you need between your audio and video.

Timecode audio recorders are expensive to buy or rent, and a timecode slate adds even more money. It's easy enough to sync audio the old-fashioned way, but many indie producers opt for spending the extra money on timecode audio equipment because of the time it saves later on when editing.

If you're not going to invest in timecoded audio recording, buy or build yourself a clapping slate board, and be sure to enlist a responsible person to handle the job of filling out and clapping the slate. When slating, make sure the slate fills the frame clearly so that you can read what it says, and make sure the clap is quick and loud, so that it will appear as a sharp spike in your audio track. In addition, don't forget that if you missed slating the head of the shot, you can always *tail slate* at the end of the shot, as long as camera and sound are still rolling.

Finally, be sure that you've chosen the right audio sampling rate (usually 44.1 kHz or 48 kHz) and that the frame rate on your audio recording device matches the frame rate on your video or film camera.

The Sound of Two Hands Clapping

As long as you can see it clearly through your viewfinder and hear it from your recording device, clapping your hands together can be a sufficient slate for synchronizing video and audio later on. While not ideal, it's better than nothing.

Setting Up

Getting good sound requires much more than just clipping a mic on an actor and pressing the Record button. Good sound recording also involves choosing appropriate mic setups for the type of image you're shooting, and careful management of your set or location.

Placing Your Mics

As we've seen, different types of mics have very different characteristics, both in terms of sound quality and in what they can "hear." To get the most from your mic, you need to place it correctly.

Handheld Mics

Because they're usually omnidirectional, handheld mics need to be placed close to your subject to ensure that they record more of your subject than anything else. Handheld mics can be placed on a microphone stand, either a tall, floor-standing device or a small desktop stand. Your talent should not speak directly into the top of the mic; rather, tilt the mic at about a 30° angle.

Windscreens

No matter what type of mic you're using, you might need a windscreen—a foam covering that slips over your mic—to cut out the sound of wind, or particularly breathy voices. Some camcorders include an electronic windscreen which automatically cuts out certain frequencies to reduce wind sounds. Although these features can work well, they can also cut out more frequencies than you might want. You'll need to test in your particular situation to ensure that it's not degrading the quality of your audio.

Lavalier Mics

For feature film production, you'll usually do more than simply clip a lavalier onto someone's collar or tie. To keep the microphone invisible, you'll most likely want to hide it under the talent's clothing, or somewhere on-set—in a plant, on the dashboard of a car, on a prop. In these cases, try to choose a location that's roughly at mouth level to the actor, and in the direction in which the actor will be speaking. For close-ups, the easiest way to hide a mic is simply to place it out-of-frame. Wherever you attach a lavalier, consider the following:

- Try to position the mic so that it sits about 8 to 12 inches from the performer's mouth.

- As the speaker turns her head back and forth, she might tend to speak more or less into the microphone, making her voice get louder or softer. When attaching her mic, try to predict which direction she will favor, and place the mic on that side. For example, if the actor will be "cheating out" a bit to stay open to the camera when talking to someone on her right, then her head will probably be turned a little to the right side. Place the mic more to that side of her body. The clip on most lavaliers is reversible, making it easier to clip the mic in one direction or another.

- If you're trying to hide the mic inside of clothing, you'll need to make sure that it doesn't rub against skin or clothing when the actors move, as this will create extremely loud noise. With some cleverly placed gaffer's tape, you can usually secure the mic and any surrounding clothing. If the talent is moving a lot, or wearing tight clothes, a lav mic might not be the best choice.

- After clipping the mic to a shirt, arrange the cable as shown in Figure 9.12 (obviously, we're not concerned about hiding the mic in this shot, but you'll want the same cable arrangement, even if it's inside someone's shirt). With the cable looped as shown in the figure, the sound of cable bumps or movements will not be conducted up the cable to the microphone.

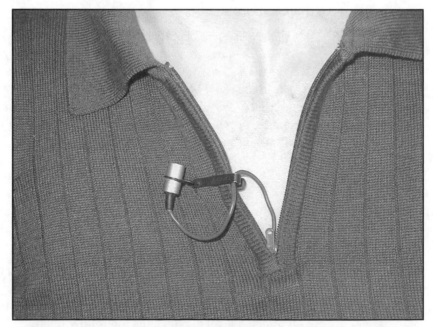

FIGURE 9.12 When placing a lavalier mic, make sure the mic cable is secured to prevent cable noise and bumps.

- Run the rest of the cable down the inside front of the talent's shirt, and around the waist to the back.
- For most work, you'll need to attach the connection end of the mic cable to a cable extension. These couplers are usually large, and just a little bit heavy. Place the connector in the subject's back pocket or attach it to his waistband using gaffer's tape, clothespins, or binder clips. If clipping the cable, be careful that the clip is not so strong that it damages the cable.
- Once you've wired the talent, let them move around to test their freedom of movement. Make certain that your rigging holds. When you test the level of the mic (more on this later), make sure that you've positioned the mic well to get the best recording of their voices. You might need to move it.
- If you're using a wireless lavalier, then you'll need to test the reception of your system. Make sure you're getting a clean signal on your receiver. Noise or other interference might be caused by cell phones, other pieces of equipment, or any large transmitters that might be in the area. In addition to the difficulty in keeping the transmitter hidden, wireless lavs are also prone to picking up static when the actor's clothes move across the antenna.

Wireless lavaliers can also be confused by transmitter reflections, wherein the transmitter's signal, and reflections of that signal, are both picked up by the receiver. Moving the receiver can often alleviate these troubles.

Shotgun Mics

Because they're usually very directional, it's crucial that you pay attention to what a shotgun mic is pointed at. This means taking note of not just your foreground elements, but your background as well.

For example, if there is a shotgun mic attached to your camera, it will be pointed at your subject when you've framed him or her with the camera. Unfortunately, it will also be pointed at everything *behind* your subject. Whether it's other sounds, or an echo-producing wall, there will be little differentiation between the sounds of your foreground and the sounds of your background. Because you can always add background sound in post-production, your primary concern when recording is to get good audio from your foreground elements. Consequently, a shotgun mic mounted on your camera is not the ideal shotgun setup. Although fine for stand-up interviews where the subject is directly in front of your camera, a camera-mounted shotgun is a bad choice for recording dialog.

A better choice is to mic your scene from above with the microphone pointed down toward the ground. The easiest way to do this is to attach the mic to a *fishpole* or *boom* and have it held in position by a *boom operator*. A fishpole is a long, telescoping pole with a super- or hypercardioid mic attached to one end. The boom operator holds the mic above the performer, and tries to keep the mic as close to the performers as possible, without letting it dip into the shot. Because the mic is above the performers and pointed down toward the ground, there is little or no background noise for it to pick up. Consequently, you'll get a very clean recording of just your actors. In addition, this type of miking affords your cast much more freedom to move around without worrying about hitting a microphone or tripping over a cable. Because it's overhead, the mic will also pick up a good mix of footsteps, prop sounds, and other environmental noises that will make for a richer soundtrack. For almost all situations, a fishpole or boom mic will be the best miking option.

(Although people will use the terms *boom* and *fishpole* interchangeably, technically a *boom* is a beefed-up version of a fishpole and is usually only used in a studio situation. Booms are typically much larger than a fishpole, with a capacity to extend a mic over 100 feet. Frequently hydraulically controlled, they're not the sort of apparatus the independent filmmaker will take on location.)

Operating a mic fishpole can be difficult work. In addition to the physical strain of holding a long pole overhead for hours at a time, the boom operator must be very focused and diligent to ensure that the best sound is recorded. Remember, because the microphone that is used is typically very directional, even a little mic movement can change the quality of the sound. Moreover, if your subjects are moving, boom operation gets even more difficult.

 The boom operator must wear a set of headphones to monitor the audio that is being recorded!

In addition, consider the following:

Properly rig the pole. Although you can try to get away with a makeshift pole, a commercial boom has a number of advantages. First, a shock-resistant mount attaches the mic to the pole and reduces noise from the boom itself. In addition, in a professional boom pole, the inside of the pole will often be insulated to reduce sound conduction along the length of the pole. To keep the cable from slapping against the pole, you'll want to hold it taut against the pole when in use, and you'll need to secure any cable slack at the end of the pole to ensure that the cable doesn't slide or move. Professional boom poles come with clips to hold the mic cable against the pole.

Mounting the mic. Although the mic will be pointed at the actors, don't forget that directional mics pick up sounds from the side and back as well as the front. Therefore, be aware of where other parts of the microphone are pointing. In some situations, you might need to angle the mic to ensure that it's not picking up sounds from other directions.

Directional mics are more susceptible to wind noise than other types of mics are. You might need a special "blimp" or "zeppelin" style windscreen (Figure 9.13).

FIGURE 9.13   A supercardioid mic and windscreen.

Choose the right amount of extension for the shot. How long your pole will need to be depends on how wide the shot will be. For most feature work, a pole between 8 and 15 feet will be adequate. Experiment with the mic and pole before shooting to learn where its center of gravity is, and what is most comfortable. To be able to grip the pole more toward its center, you might want to extend the pole farther than you actually need for the shot. This will provide a more balanced grip. Many poles have locking mechanisms at each extension. Extending to a point just short of these locks will usually make for a stronger pole.

Choose your position. Make sure you choose a position that affords you access to the entire shot, allows you to get the mic as close to the subject as possible, and isn't so uncomfortable that you'll be unable to do your job.

Watch your grip. Remember, noise from your hands—scraping, drumming, and so forth—can be transmitted up the pole to the mic, so you want to get a good grip on the mic before you start shooting, and then hold it for the duration of the shot. Gloves are often a good idea in extreme temperatures, both for comfort and to eliminate the sound of your skin sticking to the metal pole.

Holding the pole. The pole should be held parallel to the ground with your arms straight up, close to your head, and your elbows locked. Microphone poles aren't too heavy, and you should be able to hold this position for a while. Your lead arm will act as a fulcrum for the mic, while your trailing arm can be used to steer. From this position, you can quickly get the mic into the right position. In addition to tilting the pole around, you might need to spin the pole to point the microphone in the right direction. Make sure your grip and stance allow for all the motions you'll need.

Positioning the mic. Remember: if you're a boom operator, your job is to get the best audio possible, and this means getting the microphone *close to your subject!* Don't be shy, get the mic in as low and close as you can. Depending on the framing of the shot, your mic can be a few inches to a few feet above the talent's head. Although you might screw up some takes by dipping the mic into the shot, this is better than discovering later that the audio is lousy because the mic was too far away. To make the mic easier to see in the frame, use a brightly colored windscreen or place a bright-colored label on the front of the windscreen.

Booms don't have to be held above your subject. Remember that you can also hold your mic boom below your subject and point it upwards. This is often easier on your boom operator, and sometimes less intimidating to your talent (particularly in a documentary shoot). However, if you're outdoors or in a high-ceilinged room, overhead positioning will probably sound a little better. Have your sound person do some tests before committing to a particular boom positioning.

Adjusting for echo. If the surface that you're standing on is hard tile or stone, there is a chance that it will reflect sound back up toward the microphone. In your mic tests, if your sound is a little too echoey, consider putting cardboard, carpet, or some other sound-absorbing surface on the floor, below the frame.

Talk to your director and cinematographer! You'll need to maintain good communication with both of these people to ensure that you're not letting the mic enter the frame, and to remind them that you're only trying to get the best audio you can. With all the troubles present on a shoot, it's easy for nerves to get a little frayed. Stay in communication with the rest of your crew to ensure that everyone stays calm.

Hanging Mics

Mics can be hung to record large groups of people, or presentations. Typically, an omnidirectional or cardioid mic is best, and you might need more than one if you're covering a large area. You usually need a lot of cable when hanging a mic, so you'll need balanced mics and connectors. Alternatively, a high-quality, omnidirectional wireless lavalier can be used—obviating the need for lots of cable—if you're not miking an area that's too large.

Multiple Mics

If your subjects are too far apart to reach with one boom, consider using multiple mics. Some sound people like to use multiple mics as backups. For example, you can feed a lavalier mic into the left channel, and a boom mic covering the same actor into the right channel. When mixing and editing, you can select between channels to get the best sound.

Think Batteries

Accept it right now: at some point in your moviemaking career, a mic battery will die in the middle of the best take you've ever shot. Your sound will be useless. Although frustrating, the situation will be more frustrating if you don't have any extra batteries! Always pack several extra batteries for each type of mic you plan on using, and be sure to test your mics throughout the day to make sure their batteries haven't died. For shots where you only get one take—pyrotechnic or other special effects shots—consider using more than one mic so that if a battery dies in one mic, you'll still get sound from the other.

Using Your Mixer

If you're feeding multiple mics through a mixer, then you might want to consider "arranging" the different mics onto the separate left and right channels that you're feeding to your camera. This will allow you to keep different actors (or groups of actors) on separate channels. If there are two people who have a lot of overlapping dialog, then consider using your mixer's *pan* control to place one person at the extreme left and the other person at the extreme right. This will help you maintain separation during overlapping dialog, which will ease your audio editing chores.

Getting the Right Sound for the Picture

No matter which type of microphone you use, it's important to consider what the audio "feel" of the shot should be. An extreme wide shot, for example, should sound far away, while a close-up should have a more intimate sound. Consider this when selecting the type of mic to use for a shot.

When using an overhead mic, you'll tend to automatically compensate for these types of shot changes. Since the mic will have to be farther away from its subject during wider shots, but can afford to be brought in closer during close-ups, your audio recording will have a natural shift of audio "space."

The bass response of any microphone drops off over distance. Consequently, handheld mics and lavalier mics often have a richer, bassier tone—sometimes too rich and bassy—than an overhead mic. This difference in bass tone is called the *proximity effect*, and some microphones have special filters to reduce the amount of bass response in the mic. It's important to be aware of the proximity effect while miking so that you don't create mixing hassles in post-production. If a bass-heavy lavalier is used in a close-up, but a less-bassy overhead mic is used in a cutaway, the actor's voice will sound distractingly different from shot to shot. A good pair of headphones and careful attention to EQ while shooting will help you prevent such problems.

Testing Sound

After connecting your mics, you'll want to do a *mic check* to ensure that the microphones are working and that their *input levels* are set properly. Your camera might not have manual control of input levels, in which case, there's little you can do in the way of testing and preparing to record. Simply connect the mic to your camera, attach headphones to your camera, ask the subject to speak, and make sure you can hear her in your headphones. If her voice is too quiet, consider moving the microphone closer to her mouth, and then test again.

Hopefully, you're running your audio through a mixer. A mixer will not only allow you to use multiple microphones, but will also provide you with level controls—for adjusting the volume of each microphone. Level adjustment is crucial to getting good audio. If the record levels for a mic are too low, then the resulting sound will be too quiet. If they're too high, however, then distortion and noise can be introduced, and the resulting sound will be ugly and unintelligible.

Sound is measured in decibels, although there are two types of decibel scales. *dBSPL* (or *decibel sound pressure loudness*) is a measure of the actual acoustic power of a sound. This is the sound that we hear with our ears. A faint whisper from a few feet away might register at about 30 decibels, while a jackhammer usually meters at about 85 decibels. 135 dB is considered painful, and is the point at which permanent hearing damage can occur.

dBm (or *decibel milliwatt*) measures sound as units of electrical power and is measured using a VU meter that is displayed on your camera, record deck, or mixer. Through careful use of a meter, you can ensure that your audio level is set properly (Figure 9.14).

FIGURE 9.14 A digital VU meter.

Analog audio meters—the type you'll usually find on a video camera or deck—can seem a little strange at first, because they place "0" in the middle of the scale. The zero point does not mean *no sound*, but rather, *ideal sound*. Your goal when setting a level is to keep the VU meter readout as close to the ideal as possible. Using your mixer controls, you'll set the level when you test the mic, and then *ride the level* during your production (but not too much!), adjusting the level control to compensate for changes in the loudness of your subject.

With digital audio, the ideal level is somewhere between –12 and –20 dBm. This is the point where you'll want your audio level to *peak* on your VU meter. Try to set the level so that any spikes in the audio level don't go beyond this point. When digital audio peaks, the parts of the signal that go *into the red* are clipped out of the signal altogether. (If you're recording on an analog recording device such as an analog video camera or tape deck, then you'll want the audio to peak a bit higher, at 0 dBm.)

It is during the mic test that you'll also perform any *sweetening* of the subject using a graphic equalizer (if your mixer has one). We'll discuss this type of EQ in detail in Chapter 15, "Sound Editing."

Reference Tone

Not all pieces of hardware and software use the exact same scales and meters for measuring the loudness of audio. Consequently, "ideal" sound on your camera might be too quiet on your editing system. Fortunately, there's a simple way to work around this. Just as you record color bars on your videotape to help calibrate color when editing, you should record some 60 Hz *audio reference tone* on your videotape before you start shooting. You can then use this tone in post-production to set your audio levels (more on this in Chapter 13, "Preparing to Edit").

Any camera that can generate color bars should be able to generate reference tone as well. If you're shooting double-system sound, you'll also need to record tone with your DAT or miniDisc recorder. If your camera can't generate bars and tone, then you can use your editing software to pre-record the tapes with bars and tone before you shoot.

Managing Your Set

Although it is possible to edit your sound in post-production, you simply can't do many things. For example, you're not going to be able to remove the sound of a passing semi truck, or of that obnoxious couple that was having an argument across the street from your shoot. Consequently, you're going to have to pay close attention to what your set sounds like.

This involves more than just yelling "Quiet on the set!" and then waiting for everyone to stop talking. Your ears have an incredible ability to adjust to—and eventually tune out—sounds that might ruin an otherwise good shoot. You'll need to stop and listen to—as well as look at—the set to pick out any potential audio troubles. Once you start paying attention, you might be surprised at all the "white noise" you didn't hear before: air conditioners, refrigerators, fans from computers and equipment. Any one of these things can render a soundtrack muddy and useless.

Selecting an Audio Mode on Your Camera

Different tape formats have different options for audio recording. While most formats are capable of recording stereo sound, DV provides a couple of other options.

With DV cameras, you can choose to record two channels of 16-bit audio, or four channels of 12-bit audio. Sixteen-bit audio sounds better than 12-bit audio, and you really only need four audio channels if you're planning on performing video or audio editing in your camera. Since you're going to be editing using your computer, set your camera to the higher-quality 16-bit setting.

Some analog formats let you activate Dolby noise reduction, or switch between stereo and mono recording. Consult your manual for details.

RECORDING YOUR SOUND

With all your preparations complete (not just of sound, but of lighting, blocking, camera movement, cast preparation, costuming, set dressing, and so on), you're finally ready to start shooting. First, you'll need to get everything quiet on your set or location. When recording, "quiet" doesn't mean "no sound," but rather means to reduce the sound of your set to the natural ambience that belongs there. For example, if you're on a busy street, quiet will mean the sounds of car and foot traffic.

If you are recording your dialog separate from the background—for example, a conversation being held in a crowded room full of people—the "quiet" might mean completely quiet. As explained earlier, after recording your dialog takes with the crowd pantomiming silent conversation, you'll do a final take to record the sound of the crowd talking. These two elements will be mixed together later.

Once you've achieved quiet, you're ready to begin:

- Tell your tape operator to start rolling. If you're recording sound onto your camera, then the camera is all that will roll, but if you're recording non-sync sound on a separate recording deck, then that deck will have to be started also. For non-sync sound, you'll next need to use a slate, as described earlier.
- Tell your performers and crew to get ready. At this point, if you have a boom person, he or she will need to position the mic and double-

check with the director of photography to ensure that the mic isn't in the frame.

- After the call to *action*, your boom operator will begin following the sound, while your sound person will monitor your audio levels (if you have such hardware) and adjust them to ensure proper recording.
- Finally, with your take completed, *all* your decks will need to be stopped. Next, you do it all again, and again, and again.

If there is a pause between takes, your sound person should take the opportunity to ensure that sound was properly recorded. He or she should rewind the tape and play back a little bit of both the beginning and end, and listen to the sound on headphones. This will help to ensure that good sound was recorded throughout the take. If sound was not recorded, it's the sound person's job to fix the problem and break the bad news that another take will be required.

Documentary filmmakers frequently don't have the downtime between multiple takes that narrative filmmakers have. Consequently, whenever he can get a break, the sound engineer should listen to ensure that the recorded audio sounds good. If there's no break during the day, then he should double-check different sections of the entire tape to make sure it's all usable. If not, then another day at the location might be required.

Room Tone

At some point during your shoot, your sound recordist will need to record 30 seconds to a minute of *room tone*. Room tone is nothing more than the sound of the room when no one is talking or making sound. This "empty" sound will be used by the sound editor to patch gaps in the soundtrack and to cover rough sound edits.

Because you are trying to record the natural ambient sound of your location, be sure to record your room tone after your set has been fully dressed. Recording it before might produce a different quality tone, as there will be fewer sound-absorbing set pieces and props. The end of your shooting day is usually the best time to record room tone. Simply ask everyone on the set to be quiet, and start your recorder.

Run-and-Gun Audio

If you're shooting corporate videos, documentaries, "reality" productions, or any type of project where you need to shoot quickly, on-the-fly, then you won't have the time or opportunity for complex audio setups. At best, you might be able to get people outfitted with wireless lavs, or be able to give them a handheld microphone. Ideally, you'll want to have a boom mic and operator, but if you're a single-person crew, or don't have the budget for a boom, then you should at least invest in a quality, very directional shotgun mic, and mount it on your camera.

As we said earlier, one problem with shotgun mics is that they can also pick up sounds coming from behind your subject. A directional mic will minimize these problems, and you can further improve your chances of getting good audio by moving in close to your subject. (Obviously, you don't want to get so close that you must use a wide-angle focal length that will make their face look weird.)

A CREW OF ONE

If you're really working on a shoestring you might not have a crew of any kind, leaving yourself in the position of having to do *everything* while shooting. If you're shooting a scene with actors, you can often get your performers to assume some of your crew duties, but if you're shooting a low-budget documentary on your own, you'll usually have access to only your own two hands. Unfortunately, lack of personnel doesn't mean you can scrimp on the issues and details presented here. However, you might want to adjust your gear if you're shooting on your own.

Obviously, managing multiple recording devices is going to be more complicated than recording audio to your camera so, unless there's some special reason for outboard audio recording, stick to recording directly into your camera.

Since you don't have a boom operator, you'll be forced to rely on lavaliers or a high-quality on-camera shotgun mic. Lavaliers are the best option in this instance because they can deliver excellent quality with little work on your part. (Wireless lavs are even better for single-person shoots, as they save you the trouble of managing cables.) If you must use an on-camera mic, opt for a very directional microphone, so as to minimize the recording of extra background sounds, echoes, and room noises.

(Because audio is so critical, when budgeting your project, you should prioritize the purchase or rental of a good mic and boom over just about anything else. Finally: hire, beg, cajole, bribe, blackmail—use whatever techniques you have to get someone to operate your boom for you so that you don't have to face a single-person shoot.

As with any kind of audio recording, your most important task will be to monitor the audio recording through headphones while shooting. Because this can make things more difficult if you're conducting an interview, you might opt to only periodically monitor your audio, but you should check in on it fairly regularly. Dead batteries, the unnoticed activation of an air conditioner, power problems—all of these things can cause your audio to turn bad. Monitoring is the only way to ensure you're recording the sounds you need.

EXERCISE: GEAR CHECKLIST

Your audio equipment usually requires a big assortment of little items. Cables, adapters, batteries, stands, the microphones themselves—if you forget any of these things, you'll be severely audio challenged when you get to your set. Before you walk out the door, set up all of your audio equipment and make sure it works. Then, make a list of every item—even the smallest adapters and cables. If you want to be extra secure, get some tape and mark each item with a number, and code each item appropriately on your list. Then, when you're in a hurry, you can simply make sure you have the right number of items. If a number is missing, a quick glance at your list should tell you what you need to find.

SUMMARY

We recommend taking the same approach to audio that you should take to video: record the cleanest, least-modified sound you can. Then, in post-production, add whatever modifications, effects, grunge, and extra sound you want. In addition to more flexibility (if you decide you don't want a particular sound, you'll be able to move it), this approach will probably yield higher-quality results. We'll cover sound editing in Chapter 15.

10 BUILDING A WORKSTATION

In This Chapter

- First Things First
- Choosing a Platform
- Choosing a Video Interface
- Choosing a Computer
- Exercise: Know What You Need
- Summary

First Things First

Digital video cameras deliver better quality for less money than any other video or film technology. But that's just part of the reason that DV productions are so much less expensive than productions based on other technologies. While film producers have had to face the tremendous costs associated with film processing and duplication, and video editors have had to face the costs of expensive deck and editing console rentals, DV producers have access to inexpensive editing software that delivers capabilities that used to require hundreds of thousands of dollars worth of dedicated gear. In addition, computer-generated effects and compositing tools allow you to create images that would have been extremely expensive or even impossible with traditional film and video technologies.

Obviously, to make use of all of these advantages, you've got to have the right computer hardware. Once you've selected a tape format, you're ready to start thinking about your computer workstation. Odds are you already have a computer of some kind. However, your current system might need some upgrades and add-ons to get it up to digital video snuff. If you are starting from scratch, or buying a completely new system, you might have an easier time than the user who is trying to upgrade an existing system, since you can buy a package of components that are guaranteed to be compatible. Depending on which tape format you're using, you might need some extra hardware for capturing and outputting your video. In this chapter, we'll cover all the questions you need to answer to build the right digital video workstation for your needs.

Choosing a Platform

Your first hardware decision is one you have probably already made: What operating system (OS) do you want to use? Because you probably already have an OS of choice, we're not going to spend a lot of time on this question. However, if you are starting from scratch, or if you are wondering what might be in store for you, we'll quickly go over the pros and cons of each OS.

Macintosh OS

As with desktop publishing, video and film production is still somewhat Mac-heavy in its OS preference. Consequently, Mac users will have an easier time finding post-production houses that support (or possibly, *demand*) Macintosh compatibility. In general, setting up and configuring a Macintosh to recognize and use various cameras, capture interfaces, and storage options will be much easier than configuring any other platform. FireWire DV support is built into all new Macs, and the current OS/Quick-

Time combination provides thorough, robust support for FireWire-based DV I/O and device control. What's more, every Mac comes bundled with iMovie and iDVD, excellent applications for video editing and DVD authoring, as well as GarageBand for soundtrack creation. If you're using an older machine, you can buy Apple's iLife package which includes iDVD and GarageBand, for under $100. Apple's pro-level video editing and special effects software—from Final Cut Pro for editing, to Motion and Shake for compositing and effects—have become industry standards, used for major feature film work. Apple's commitment to this industry means that you'll have access to market leading hardware and software.

On the negative side, if you need to use a particular application for your project—such as special Webcasting software, or particular 3D animation or effects packages—then you'll need to make sure the Mac platform supports those packages.

Windows

There's a lot of good editing software for Windows and, because the platform is ubiquitous, you should be able to easily find tech support. In addition, because there are a number of different software and hardware options in a variety of price ranges, it's simple to fill every niche in your production process. What's more, many high-end 3D and effects packages are only available for Windows.

Newer versions of Windows (Windows 2000, XP, and XP Professional) provide built-in support for FireWire-based DV capturing, but older versions of Windows do not, which means you might have trouble combining different pieces of digital video hardware and software. As with any potential editing system, you'll want to pay close attention to the hardware requirements of your editing software and your video capture hardware.

Windows machines are much more difficult to set up and maintain, although they've gained a toehold in professional post-production houses thanks to Avid Technology's development of Windows-based products. Nevertheless, if you are planning on moving your data to a post-production facility for additional editing or film transfer, be sure that they can support your hardware and file formats. If you want to attach multiple monitors, you'll need to go with at least Windows 98.

If you're a stickler for very high image quality, then you might want to choose the Windows platform simply because of the availability of less-expensive uncompressed video capture boards. Though the cost of equivalent hardware for the Mac is coming down, working with uncompressed video is still cheaper for Windows, at the time of this writing. (Working uncompressed is still an expensive proposition for both platforms because of the video hardware and storage requirements, and is not a necessity for most productions.)

You might be more concerned about using a particular piece of software than a particular platform. For example, if you already know Adobe Premiere and want to do your editing there, then you can choose either Mac or Windows. Which platform to choose will depend on your OS preference, budget, and hardware/software requirements. Or, perhaps you already know Apple Final Cut Pro, in which case you will need a Mac, or Sony Vegas, which requires Windows. In either case, the software you are comfortable with—editing, painting, compositing, special effects, custom compressors, and so forth—should be the driving force behind your OS choice.

CHOOSING A VIDEO INTERFACE

Your biggest concern when building a workstation for editing is ensuring that you have the right video interface. The video interface determines the way that video is moved in and out of your computer and it is defined by the combination of cable, connectors, digitizers, and compressors that link your camera, video deck, or monitor to your computer. There are two video interface categories: analog and digital. Analog video interfaces *digitize* the video signal and save it on a hard drive, whereas digital video interfaces simply transfer the digital media your camera has captured directly to a hard drive. The type of video interface you choose will inform all of your other buying decisions, from processor speed to type of disk storage and should be based primarily on the video format you have decided to work with.

Digital Video Interfaces

One of the great advantages of any digital video format is that it is already digital; the camera digitizes the video before it ever writes it to tape. Therefore, to edit, all you have to do is move that digital file into your computer. This process is typically done through either a FireWire interface or *Serial Digital Interface*, also known as *SDI*. There are two variations of SDI: Standard Definition SDI (SDI) and High Definition SDI (HD-SDI). Lower-end DV, DVCAM, DVCPro and HDV equipment use FireWire interfaces, while higher-end DV, DVCAM, DVCPro, Digital-S, Digital Betacam, and D1 use SDI and HD format cameras and decks use HD-SDI.

FireWire (a.k.a. i.Link or IEEE1394)

FireWire was developed by Apple in 1986 as a replacement for several older interfaces: serial, parallel, SCSI, and, to a lesser degree, Ethernet. Nowadays, many computers only have two interfaces for connecting peripherals: USB for slow devices such as keyboards, mice, and printers, and FireWire for high-speed connectivity to mass storage, cameras, scanners, and even networks. (USB-2 offers close-to-FireWire speed, but has not been adopted by video camera makers.)

FireWire allows you to daisy-chain up to 64 devices, with none of the settings or ID concerns that you have with SCSI devices. In addition, FireWire devices are true *peers;* that is, they don't need a computer to know how to talk to each other. Therefore, you can easily connect two cameras together via FireWire to create digital dubs, or even to edit!

If you're going to use FireWire to capture your video, check to see if your computer has FireWire ports on its motherboard. If not, you'll need to get a FireWire interface for your computer. There are two types of FireWire connectors: 6-pin and 4-pin (Figure 10.1). The larger, 6-pin connectors can carry power as well as data, making it possible to have a single cord that provides everything a device needs. Most video cameras have 4-pin connectors, which take up considerably less space than a 6-pin connector does. Your computer probably has a 6-pin port, in which case you'll need to get a 6-pin to 4-pin cable.

These days, the FireWire ports on most computers transfer data at up to 400 Mbps. These ports are backward-compatible with the 100 Mbps ports that are typically used on cameras. FireWire 800 ports offer double the speed and use the special connector shown in Figure 10.2. DV cameras don't support (or need) these faster connections, they are used purely for connecting speedy hard drives. More and more high-end formats, such as Panasonic's DVCPro HD, are adding FireWire I/O to their decks and cameras.

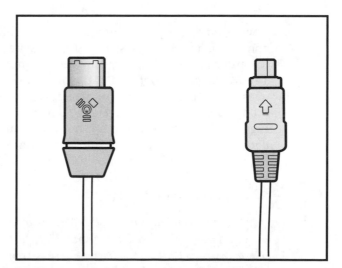

FIGURE 10.1   FireWire connectors come in either 6- or 4-pin versions. Six-pin versions carry power as well as data, which makes it possible to connect some devices—such as 2.5" hard drives—without having to use an additional, external power.

FIGURE 10.2   On the left, a regular 6-pin FireWire port—the type that you connect to a video camera. On the right is a FireWire 800 port, which provides access to high-speed FireWire hard drives.

SDI and HD-SDI

Developed by Sony as an interface between high-end digital video formats and non-linear editing systems, SDI (for Serial Digital Interface) is designed to handle uncompressed digital video and provides a data rate ranging from 140 Mbps to 570 Mbps. SDI supports much longer cables than FireWire does which is useful for post-production facilities that keep their equipment in a special climate-controlled machine room and need to send high-quality video signals to other rooms in the building. HD-SDI has a data rate of 1.485 Gbps (Gigabits per second) which is necessary for moving uncompressed HD data.

Serial Device Control

If you are using anything besides FireWire to capture your video (and audio), chances are you'll also need a serial device control interface for your computer, in the form of a serial port or a USB port with a serial-to-USB converter. The device control cable allows for remote control of a video deck from your computer. (For formats that use a FireWire connection, device control is managed through the FireWire cable.) More about video decks and device control in Chapter 12, "Editing Hardware."

Analog Video Interfaces

Analog cameras (such as those that record onto Hi8, Betacam SP, or VHS) do not digitize their video before storing it on tape; they simply store analog signals. This means that you'll need special hardware in your computer to digitize the analog signal produced by these decks and cameras. For these formats, you'll need to add an analog video capture card to your system to get video into and out of your computer (Figure 10.3).

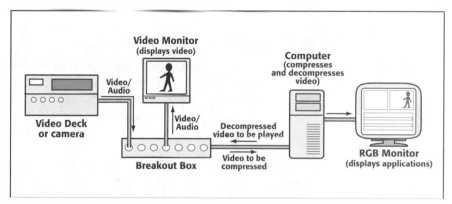

FIGURE 10.3   In an analog digitizing system, special hardware installed in your computer takes care of compressing and decompressing video in real-time.

Analog cable connections—such as composite RCA, S-video, or BNC connectors for video and audio—are usually provided through a special "break-out box" that attaches to the video card itself. Many analog video cards also offer FireWire I/O, but be aware that these systems will re-digitize the DV video signal that is coming through the FireWire cable using a CODEC other than the DV CODEC—usually MJPEG—resulting in a *recompression* of the video (remember, it was compressed once by the camera). Recompression can often degrade image quality.

You'll also use analog video and audio connections when connecting your deck or camera to a monitor, and sometimes when dubbing, if you're dubbing between formats that don't provide compatible digital connections.

Analog Composite Video

The simplest type of analog video interface is called *analog composite video*. Composite video connections pack the entire video signal—luminance and chrominance—into one cable that usually uses a standard RCA connector. Composite video offers the lowest quality of all of the analog video interfaces.

Analog S-Video

S-video cables carry your video's luminance and chrominance information separately, allowing for slightly higher quality than a composite connection. S-video uses a special, proprietary connector. (See Figure 12.10.)

Analog Component Video

Component video connectors use a separate cable for each color channel (red, green, and blue). Component video offers the highest quality of any analog video interface, and usually uses three BNC connectors.

Audio Interfaces

Remember, the cables and connections listed in the preceding section are for carrying digital and analog video. Audio usually requires a separate connection although the compressed, digital stream that is sent over a FireWire connection carries both video and audio.

Most interface cards and monitors use RCA connectors for audio input and output. Some higher-end decks and cameras, though, use BNC or XLR connectors. If you find yourself trying to connect an RCA-equipped device into something that only has BNC or XLR connectors, then you'll need to get appropriate adapters.

If you're capturing audio from a DAT or MiniDisc, your player might have a digital interface such as SP/DIF or AES/EBU, in addition to an RCA or XLR interface. SP/DIF and AES/EBU are digital interfaces, so if your capture card supports them, they are a better choice for audio capture. (Note that some SP/DIF or AES/EBU connections use the same cables—RCA, BNC, or XLR—to carry a digital audio signal.)

If you need to take audio from a mixer, or microphone, you'll probably need XLR connectors. As many lower-end capture cards do not provide XLR inputs, you'll probably need to adapt your mixer's XLR connectors to something else.

If you'll be capturing from your DV camera, then you'll probably need a special cable, usually provided with your camera. Most cameras typically provide a single mini jack that carries video and two channels of audio. Vendors typically include a special cable that has a mini jack at one end and three RCA plugs at the other (one for video, and one each for left and right audio channels).

FireWire Users, Take Notice!

Remember, even if you're using a FireWire-based system, you'll still need to use analog video cables to attach your DV camera or deck to an external video monitor. Therefore, you'll have FireWire carrying video and audio from your deck/camera to your computer, and an analog cable carrying video and audio from your deck/camera to your video monitor.

HOW A DV EDITING SYSTEM WORKS

When you press "play" on a DV deck (or camera), the compressed digital information is read from the DV tape. The deck does two things with this information. First, it decompresses the signal into analog video, which is sent through the unit's analog outputs—usually either S-video or composite. These outputs can feed a video monitor, an analog tape deck, or an analog digitizing system. Simultaneously, the camera or deck sends the raw, compressed digital stream out through its digital interface (FireWire or SDI). If you have a computer attached to the other end of that digital interface, you can capture that compressed stream (remember, it's *capturing*, not *digitizing*, because the video has already been digitized) and store it on a hard drive. Not all computers have the processing speed to completely decompress the incoming video stream for playback. As such, the image displayed on your computer screen by your editing program is usually a low-res proxy of your final video. The only way to see a full-resolution playback of your captured video is to attach a video monitor to the analog output of the video deck (Figure 10.4). Because the camera/deck is capable of fully decompressing the video, you'll get full quality on your analog monitor.

The video passing into and out of your computer is in a raw digital form, so it's possible to shoot, edit, and print back to tape with no loss of quality (unlike analog systems, which experience *generation loss* each time you make a new copy). Note that we said "it is *possible*." Depending on the type of effects and edits you are making, you might inadvertently recompress your video, resulting in loss of quality through recompression.

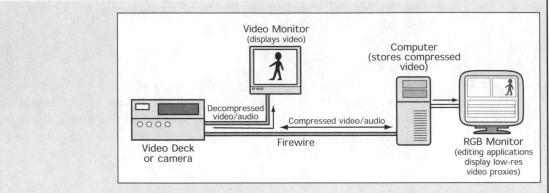

FIGURE 10.4 With digital video formats, the camera takes care of the digitizing and compressing. When you get ready to edit, you use a digital interface to capture the digitized, compressed video from your camera or deck into your camera.

Manufacturer's Recommendations

No matter what platform you're using, you'll need to be concerned about compatibility between your computer and video hardware. Fortunately, most vendors are diligent about publishing compatibility lists. Such lists include approved drives, interfaces, and CPUs. Before you make any purchases, you'll want to be sure to check out each vendor's compatibility claims. In addition, make sure that your dealer has a good return and exchange policy.

CHOOSING A COMPUTER

Once you know what type of video interface you'd like to use, you need to buy a computer. You have two options when selecting a workstation: piece together your own system, or buy a *turnkey system* from a vendor that packages equipment.

If you build your own system, you'll be able to use any hardware you might already have, and you'll be able to create a system that is tailored to the exact needs of your project. However, depending on your experience and the complexity of your intended project, doing it yourself might take a lot of time and experimentation. If you're not comfortable with installing hardware and software in your computer, this is not the best choice.

With a turnkey system, you'll get a computer that will work properly right out of the box, with no compatibility questions or installation troubles (Figure 10.5). Avid and Media 100 offer several cross-platform turnkey systems. Promax Systems packages excellent Mac and Windows turnkey systems that have been pre-configured and pretested. If you have the money, buying a turnkey system might be the simplest solution to your hardware needs, although these systems might be overkill for your project, as they typically offer tremendous amounts of storage and special video cards.

FIGURE 10.5 Turnkey systems like this Velocity HD package are ideal for Windows users who want a powerful editing system, but don't want lots of setup hassles.

These days, the easiest solution might just be to buy a new computer. Any new Mac that you buy, be it a laptop or desktop machine, will come with built-in FireWire ports and a hard drive that's fast enough to handle any DV editing tasks. Similarly, just about any Windows machine that you buy that includes built-in FireWire ports will also include speedy disk storage that will be suitable for video editing. What's more, you can easily expand your storage options with external FireWire drives. As mentioned before, these machines will also have basic editing software like Apple iMovie or Windows Movie Maker preinstalled.

No matter which approach you decide to take, it's important for you to understand the issues discussed next. A firm grasp of these concerns will make your current purchase, as well as any future expansion, much easier.

Standalone Editors

There is a third choice when choosing an editing system: standalone-editing hardware. Systems such as the Casablanca line from DraCo provide full DV editing with storage, editing software, and digital I/O in a single, plug-and-play video appliance. Such systems are great for the user who absolutely does not want to hassle with a computer. These systems are also ideal for classrooms.

CPU

Working with video requires a lot of processing power. How much depends largely on the type of video interface you're using. If you use an analog digitizing card, you can often get away with a less powerful CPU than if you're using a digital video interface. Check the requirements of your video system for more details.

Don't forget that you'll be doing more than just editing video. Be sure to get enough computing muscle to run the various image editors, compositing, and special effects programs that you'll want to use.

In addition, consider the other hardware that you might want. If you plan to add accelerator cards, real-time video processors, or special audio cards, you'll need a system with a good number of expansion slots.

When we wrote the first edition of this book, it was still possible to buy a new computer that didn't have enough processing power to handle a DV stream. Nowadays, you'd have to look really hard to find a new machine that was similarly hobbled. For the most part, any CPU you buy today should be plenty speedy for video editing.

RAM

Fortunately, video editing is more disk intensive than RAM intensive, so you don't need a huge amount of memory for simple editing tasks. A safe bet is 256 to 512 MB of RAM for most editing applications.

However, if you're going beyond simple editing with basic dissolves and effects, you should spring for extra memory. To prepare titles and special effects, you might be depending on an image editor such as Photoshop. In addition, specialized applications that load video segments into RAM—After Effects and Commotion, for example—need *lots* of memory.

Therefore, shoot for 512 MB, but if you can swing it, go ahead and spring for a gigabyte or more. We guarantee that no one who edits video has ever said, "gosh, I wish I hadn't bought all that extra RAM."

Storage

Buying enough storage used to be the bane of digital video editing. However, with recent changes in technology and pricing, storage has become surprisingly affordable. How much storage you'll need depends largely on the nature of your project.

If you are shooting a feature that's two hours long, odds are your shooting ratio will be at least 3:1; that is, you'll shoot three times as much video as you'll use in your final product. Therefore, you'll need enough storage for at least six hours of footage. You'll also need storage for project files, graphics, special effects, and audio editing. Better to play it safe and increase your storage estimates to something like 8 to 10 hours worth of storage. Check your video interface manufacturer's specs for information on how much disk space is needed for storing an hour of video. Figure 10.6 gives a rough guide to various video formats and their storage requirements. Don't forget that you'll also need space for your OS and your applications. If you are shooting a documentary, keep in mind that your shooting ratios are probably much higher—10:1 or more—but effects and graphics needs might be lower.

Different video input systems have different storage requirements. If you are planning to use a FireWire interface to capture your video, you're in luck! Since FireWire has relatively low throughput requirements, you can get away with using slower, IDE drives. If you are using an analog digitizing system, odds are you'll need faster storage—usually some type of fast SCSI—configured into an array. For HD projects, you'll need a RAID—several SCSI or IDE drives configured together for optimal performance. Consult your system's documentation for details.

Format	Data Rate	1 Gigabyte holds...	1 hour of video requires...
DV	25 Mbps	5.5 minutes	11 gigabytes (Gb)
DVCPro/ DVCAM	50 Mbps	2.75 minutes	22 Gb
HDV (720p30)	19.2 Mbps	7.5 minutes	8 Gb
SD (480i60)	170/210* Mbps	48/39* seconds	75/92* Gb
HD (720p30)	440/550* Mbps	18/15* seconds	195/240* Gb
HD (1020i60)	990/1240* Mbps	8.5/6.5* seconds	435/545* Gb

* First number is for 8-bit video, second number is for 10-bit video.

FIGURE 10.6   Digital video formats and storage.

Estimating Storage

If you're capturing digital video through a FireWire port, you can count on needing 15 GB of disk space for every hour of footage. If you're using an analog digitizing system, consult your documentation to determine storage needs.

DRIVE DEFINITIONS

SCSI: The Small Computer Systems Interface has been around for a while, and now exists in many flavors such as SCSI-2, Fast and Wide SCSI, and UltraWide SCSI. Video users will need to consider purchasing multiple UltraWide SCSI drives with a spin rate of at least 7200 RPM. Whether you're using a Mac or Windows computer, you'll need to buy a special UltraWide SCSI interface card for your computer. Up to seven SCSI devices (including the computer) can be chained off one SCSI interface. Obviously, you'll need drives that are UltraWide SCSI compatible.

RAIDs and arrays: A Redundant Array of Independent Disks—usually referred to simply as an array—consists of two or more identical hard drives that have been logically striped with indexing information so that they can be treated as a single drive. For video, the advantage of an array is speed. Because the computer can interleave information between both drives, one drive can be reading or writing while the other drive is preparing to read or write. RAIDs are needed for high-bandwidth video such as uncompressed HD.

EIDE, UltraDMA, ATA, SATA, and UltraATA: All variations of the same spec, these drives are much cheaper than SCSI drives. Although not always as fast as a SCSI drive or array, they provide all the throughput you'll need for FireWire-based DV editing. You can chain two devices off one of these interfaces. Look for drives with a spin rate of at least 5400 RPM and as much capacity as you can afford.

FireWire: Hot-swappable, with up to 63 drives per FireWire chain, and no termination or ID issues, these drives are ideal for FireWire-based DV editing. Because many FireWire drives can take their power directly from the FireWire cable (meaning you don't need a separate power cable), they're ideal for portable editing.

Build Your Own

Frequently, the cheapest hard drive storage option is to build a drive yourself. Most good-size computer stores sell hard drive enclosures. These kits include a case, power supply, and either a USB or FireWire interface. Drop the appropriate type of drive into the enclosure and you have a stand-alone, external drive that can be attached to your computer. When shopping for enclosures, be sure you get one that has an internal interface that matches the type of drive you're buying (usually either IDE or ATA) as well as the appropriate external interface (in other words, don't buy a USB enclosure if you want to connect the drive to your computer's FireWire port). If you do some searching, you'll usually find that you can buy a drive and enclosure for slightly less money than a finished, packaged external drive. Assembling the drive is very simple and usually requires nothing more than a screwdriver.

Computer Monitors

Video applications tend to consume a lot of screen real estate. Consequently, you might want to opt for a video card and monitor that can work at a higher resolution. You may also want to add a second computer monitor, but be sure you can spare the slot required by a second video card. (External video monitors are discussed in Chapter 12, "Editing Hardware.")

2D or Not 2D

If your production will include a lot of 3D animation or fancy motion graphics, you'll want to consider a video card with 3D acceleration features and/or a lot of on-board video RAM. These cards can provide a mammoth increase in 3D rendering and motion graphics performance.

Accessorizing

The hardware we've discussed so far, combined with the right software, will provide you with a good, full-featured post-production workstation. However, depending on your editing application, it might be worth adding on some extra hardware.

You can install special co-processor cards in your computer to accelerate the rendering of complex effects filters, while other co-processors can be added that will provide real-time transitions and effects. Such co-processors can be expensive, so you'll want to take a close look at your workflow to decide if custom acceleration will save you any money.

For audio-intensive projects, or simply for more audio control, you might want to consider the addition of professional audio editing hardware. Systems such as ProTools from DigiDesign provide multichannel, high-quality digital recording with real-time effects and editing. We'll discuss these products more in Chapter 15, "Sound Editing."

Uncompressed

Nowadays, there's lots of fancy hardware on the market—accelerator cards, cards that offer dual stream processing, and cards that digitize uncompressed HD or D-1 quality video.

CAPTURE CARDS AND PERFORMANCE

If you're not using a FireWire-based editing system, then you need to buy a video digitizing card to get video into your computer. When shopping, consider these features:

Real-time playback and rendering: Some video cards require that you render before you can play back full-screen video in real time. Others support real-time cuts-only playback, and still others support real-time playback of two layers—usually a layer of video with transition effects like dissolves, a layer of video with a filter, such as color correction, or a layer of video with a superimposed effect, like titles. At the top of the line, you'll get real-time playback of video and several layers of effects, including 3D effects. No matter how good your card is, some rendering is inevitable if you have complicated effects, and the speed at which your computer renders is also dependent on your video card, the CODEC it uses, and the speed of your storage drives.

Audio I/O: Not all video cards come with audio I/O. Make sure your card offers audio I/O and if it doesn't, be aware that you might need to add an audio card to your computer as well.

Breakout box: Some video cards come with an external breakout box that has all the connections offered by the card itself. Breakout boxes allow for easier access to the inputs and outputs, so that you don't have to crawl behind your computer to change a cable.

NTSC and PAL switchability: If you want to be able to go from NTSC projects to PAL projects, make sure your video card supports both standards.

HD support: Editing in a native HD environment requires an HD card for video capture and playback.

Pixel shape: Your computer screen—as well as many video formats— uses square pixels. This means that a screen with a resolution of 640 x 480 pixels will have an aspect ratio of 4:3. DV, DVCAM, DVCPRO, D1 (sometimes incorrectly referred to as CCIR-601) all use rectangular pixels and require pixel dimensions of 720 x 486 pixels to achieve the same 4:3 aspect ratio. But wait, it gets worse. NTSC D1 formats use vertically oriented rectangular pixels, while PAL D1 formats use horizontally oriented rectangular pixels. Make sure your video card supports all the pixel shapes you'll be using.

Dual-stream processing: Some things, such as long edited sequences and many layers of effects, are very hard for most computers to handle—the current top-of-the-line solution is dual-stream processing. To get dual-stream processing, you must have two video cards—either a primary PCI video card with a daughter board piggy-backed onto it, like the Avid Meridien board set, or a pair of PCI cards that connect with a special bus, like the Velocity board set. By having two pieces of hardware dedicated to processing media, your computer can handle two video signal streams at a time. Usually, this means that you can play back more layers of video and effects at the same time, without rendering. However, be aware that you must also be using a software application that's optimized for dual-stream processing.

nVidia's SLI (Scalable Link Architecture) allows you get dramatically improved video performance by distributing your video tasks across multiple video cards on the same machine. With multiple graphics processing units (GPUs) to work with, your video crunching chores can go much faster. So far, this technology is only available for Windows and Linux users, and SLI cards may not work with your particular motherboard, so you'll want to do your research and check your specs very carefully. If you're not working with uncompressed video, or creating lots of computer-generated imagery, the extra expense and hassle is probably not worth it.

2D and 3D Graphics Cards

If you'll be doing a lot of graphics or special effects, your system might benefit from the addition of a 2D or 3D graphics accelerator card. Such cards offer additional real-time layers, faster rendering, and often include plug-in software that adds special effects to your editing application. Some graphics cards are designed to accompany a specific video capture card, while others stand alone. Be sure to refer to your software and video card manufacturers' recommendations before you buy.

Building a Macintosh System

If you want to build a Mac-based system from the ground up, your choices are simple. You'll need at least a 300 MHz G3 processor with a FireWire port and a fast hard drive. At the time of this writing, the slowest machine that Apple sells new is a 1.25 GHz G4 with 2 built-in FireWire ports and a fast hard drive, so you'll only need to worry about processor speed if you're buying or using a used computer. Any new Mac will be DV ready (Figure 10.7).

FIGURE 10.7 Apple's desktop Macs provide blazing fast processors and plenty of room for multiple drives, and their easy-opening case is ideal for configuring and reconfiguring a complex video editing workstation.

Your RAM needs will vary depending on your software, but we recommend a system with at least 512 MB of RAM. Although Apple's systems ship with good-size hard drives, you might still want to add some extra storage.

If you are using a Mac tower that provides internal drive bays then you can add more drives internally. For laptops, or Macs that don't include more internal space, you'll have to use external hard drives for additional storage.

If you need serial device control of a video deck, be aware that the Macs do not have serial ports, so you'll have to add a USB-to-serial-port adapter or a card with a serial port to allow for remote deck control of non-FireWire decks. Most HD decks require serial device control but more and more models are adding FireWire connections as well. (More about device control in Chapter 12.)

Co-processors, audio cards, or additional monitors can be added if you need them (and if you have a Mac that provides expansion slots—iMacs and laptops do not), but you won't need any of this gear for a DV-based editing system.

If you don't think you're going to need to add co-processors or huge amounts of storage, the iMac is a great editing solution. You won't be able to add any expansion cards or internal hard drives, but you can always add FireWire drives, or replace the system's internal hard drive with a larger capacity drive if you need more storage.

Building a Windows System

Assembling a Windows system yourself is more complicated than assembling a Mac system, largely because you have more options. If you've used Windows for very long, you've probably already discovered that in the Windows world there are a zillion manufacturers for every type of component and accessory. Getting all of these different components to work together can be difficult. If you're not comfortable with setting IRQs or moving jumpers and switches on peripheral cards, then you'll definitely want to consider buying a preconfigured, turnkey system.

Configuring a Windows machine for DV can be complicated. The trouble stems from the fact that your system has to be finely tuned to deal with the requisite throughput required by a video editing program. Because you don't want to drop one frame, you need to be sure that you have no bottlenecks in your hardware.

As with buying a Mac, these days, any Windows-compatible system you'll buy new will have more than enough horsepower to deal with DV workflow. If you've got older gear, or are going to buy something used, then you need to ensure that you're using at least a 350 MHz Pentium II. If you opt for a non-FireWire system, such as Adobe Premiere Pro configured for HD, you'll need to check the specifications of those products to determine your other hardware needs.

If you have an older Windows computer and you're going to go with a FireWire-based setup, your first choice will be to pick a FireWire card (if your computer does not already have one). Because support for the FireWire interface is not built into all versions of the Windows OS, FireWire cards for Windows typically come packaged with drivers and editing packages. Pinnacle Systems Studio packages, for example, provide a FireWire card bundled with all necessary drivers as well as an editing program.

Next, it's time to move on to storage. Your computer probably already has an IDE drive of some kind, so you might be able to slave additional IDE drives to your internal host drive. As with Macs, if performance is key, it's better to add a PCI card for a second IDE bus rather than slaving the extra drives off your hard drive. If you're working with uncompressed video, you'll need a SCSI accelerator card and an array of SCSI drives.

Of course, you'll need a good amount of RAM, as well as a sound card and any accelerators and co-processors that you might desire. Be sure to plan and manage your slot usage before you start buying equipment, and remember that DV requires fast throughput, meaning that you'll need to use PCI slots for expansion rather than slower ISA or EISA slots.

Once you've gathered all your equipment, it's time to start installing. Go slowly and install one piece of hardware at a time. Don't confuse the situation by throwing a bunch of cards into your PC and then seeing if they work. Debugging such a complex system can be time-consuming and perplexing.

If you are buying a completely new system, consider a pre-assembled turnkey system or a machine with built-in FireWire support. Sony's line of Intel-based systems provides hardware designed from the ground up for DV editing (Figure 10.8).

FIGURE 10.8 Sony's desktop, Intel-based workstations provide built-in FireWire and all the hardware and software you'll need to perform DV editing and output.

Portable Editing

In addition to allowing you to edit your feature at the beach or in the park, portable editing systems mean you can try rough edits of a scene while you're still on set! With this type of immediate post-production feedback, you can quickly and easily determine if you've gotten the coverage and performances you need.

Because they're based around laptop computers, assembling a portable system will be costlier than putting together a desktop system. Moreover, you might not be able to get all the storage and acceleration features you'd have on a desktop. Finally, you might wish to consider how portable the system really is—the laptop might be small, but will it still seem portable when you have an external video monitor, a deck, and a box of tapes to lug along with it?

Macintosh

Mac-based portable editing starts with a 300 MHz G3 (or better) laptop with FireWire ports. Any new iBook or PowerBook is well suited to DV editing, although you might need to add some extra storage if you want to edit a very large project. External FireWire drives are your best bet for storage expansion (Figure 10.9).

FIGURE 10.9   PowerBook with an external FireWire drive.

Windows

Several vendors make Windows-based laptop editing systems. Sony makes several VAIO systems that ship with fast processors, a good amount of storage, built-in FireWire (although Sony calls it i.Link), and a varying assortment of software.

Portable Turnkeys

Both Avid and Media 100 make portable versions of their professional, analog digitizing systems. Packed with the same features as their desktop cousins, these systems provide a true portable solution for the die-hard Avid or Media 100 editor. As you might expect, these systems are pricey and probably only for the big-budgeted user with special editing needs.

Edit Controllers and Custom Keyboards

Though you can drive an editing program with your mouse, keyboard control allows you to make edits without having to stop to move the mouse around. In addition to being much faster, driving your editor from the keyboard allows you to work more fluidly, and to develop a rhythm. Editing is a very tactile process, so good keyboard control is essential.

However, complex editing programs can have dozens of keyboard commands and shortcuts. Though a good program will have keyboard controls that are logically arranged, learning these layouts can take some time. A custom keyboard like the one shown in Figure 10.10 can make learning your system much easier. These keyboards feature color-coded keys with custom icons that allow you to easily see exactly what each key does.

FIGURE 10.10   A keyboard with custom-colored keycaps designed for your editing program of choice can make learning a new editing app much easier. Even experienced users might be surprised to be reminded of key commands they didn't know about. Shown here is a Bella Corporation DV Keyboard.

When editing, you'll spend more time searching and scrubbing through your video files than doing anything else. If you come from a linear editing background, where you use a special edit controller to control tape decks, then you're probably accustomed to jog and shuttle wheels which can be used to move forward or backward through a tape at variable speeds. Custom input devices such as the Contour Designs Shuttle Pro shown in Figure 10.11 provide shuttle wheels and programmable buttons that allow you to easily replicate the feel of a linear edit controller.

FIGURE 10.11   Contour Designs Shuttle Pro.

Backing Up

Everyone who's used a computer for any amount of time knows the importance of backing up. And, though losing that critical word processing document can be a drag, losing hours and hours of video captures in addition to your editing project file and weeks worth of complex 3D renderings can completely destroy a project. As you might surmise, good backup is essential.

Unfortunately, backing up an in-progress video project is difficult simply because of the huge amounts of storage that a video production can consume. Consequently, you should consider your backup strategy when constructing your system.

The easiest backup system to implement and use is to simply buy additional external hard drives, and copy your files over at regular intervals. Using hard drives as backup is also the speediest backup strategy. Hard drives are also fairly cheap to buy these days, making them a cost-effective backup solution.

If you've got many projects to back up and archive, buying lots of hard drives will probably be prohibitively expensive. Tape backup drives are more expensive than hard drives, but have a cheaper cost/megabyte over the long haul.

Recordable DVDs are perfectly reasonable backup devices, but if you have any large files—over 4 gigabytes for standard DVDs and over 8.5 gigabytes for double-sided DVDs—you'll have to segment them using special software, which can make backing up a little more complicated. If you're like us, "more complicated" translates into "something you'll never end up doing," so this may not be the best backup strategy.

If you absolutely can't afford a large capacity backup system like external hard drives, or a tape drive, then you should at least back up your project files. Project files created by editing systems are usually very small and can easily be backed up to a USB key, floppy disk, external hard drive, or even uploaded to Web-based storage, or an email server. If you have carefully logged all of your files, then your project file contains a database that tells exactly where each clip is on your original tape. (Having timecode on your tapes and discrete tape names is crucial in this case!) If your system crashes, you can simply restore from your backed-up project file, and then tell your editing system to recapture all your footage. This will be time consuming, but you'll be able to rebuild your project.

Archiving

Though it might seem a long way away at this point, your project will eventually be completed. At that point, you'll probably want to archive it somewhere. Obviously, you'll be creating a finalized master output of some kind, so you'll be able to create dupes of your final work, but you might want to create an archive of your actual project, just in case you ever want to make changes—like maybe a special "director's cut." Having access to an archive is also handy for times when you want to recall how you created a particular effect.

Thanks to the low cost of FireWire drives, it is possible to archive your project on a dedicated hard drive. Many editing apps can "consolidate" your final cut, saving only the media that's in the cut for archive purposes. Most projects are two hours or less, this will require about 30

Gigabytes of storage. Tape backup is good for archiving, but tapes don't have a tremendous longevity, so you'll want to dupe them at least once a year, a process that will involve restoring them to your computer, then back up to new tapes.

Recordable DVDs are more durable than tapes, are inexpensive, and make for a very good archiving solution. However, as with backups, you might need to segment some of your larger pieces of media to get them to fit onto a DVD.

Finally, you can choose the low-budget archive, which is to simply save your project files and work files (and any computer-generated imagery you've created) and keep your original DV tapes as your original footage archive. If you ever need to re-create your project, you can use your editing system to recapture your original footage.

Network Systems

Now that you've hassled out the details of picking a single computer, you might consider picking up a few more of them. Large projects often require more than one editor, and having multiple editing systems on a network allows for instant access to shared resources and, consequently, less downtime while waiting for files to transfer. High-end turnkey systems, like Avid's Media Composer, offer special network solutions, like the Avid Unity system, which includes hardware and special software. But just because you're not using Avid Unity doesn't mean you need to stay out of the loop if networking will benefit your project.

Storage Area Networks (SANs)

Storage Area Networks (SANs) let you share drives (and media) between multiple workstations. As with local storage drives, the key to choosing the right system is bandwidth. You want to be sure that you can move media quickly enough through your pipeline to maintain real-time video and audio A low-bandwidth format, such as DV or HDV, will be transferable over many different networking options including Ethernet networks and FireWire connections, a high-bandwidth format, such as uncompressed HD will only work with Ethernet 100/baseT or Fibre channel. Creating your own SAN will require special software such as Apple XSAN, Charismac Fibre Share, or Studio Network Solutions SANmp to help manage your drives and your media across multiple workstations.

Render Farms

If you plan to do lots of effects work, or if speedy workflow is an absolute essential for your production needs, a "farm" of networked computers will let you distribute your rendering tasks across multiple machines. With this type of system, separate ranges of frames are distributed to each machine for rendering. As each computer finishes its batch, the rendered frames are returned to the host system, which assembles them into a completed piece.

Most 3D applications offer network rendering, as do most high-end compositing programs. At the time of this writing, there are few editing programs that are able to distribute their rendering tasks, but these rendering chores are not usually as time-consuming as 3D and compositing rendering, so distributed rendering is not as critical.

If you want to build a render farm, you'll need networking gear in addition to a bunch of computers. Because they are so computing-intensive, 3D programs see a bigger performance boost from distributed rendering than do compositing programs. Fortunately, because 3D project data is so small, you don't need an especially speedy network to create a rendering farm. In most cases, even a DSL line or cable modem is fast enough for good 3D distributed rendering. This means that you can use your friend's computers for your rendering tasks, even if they're across the country.

Using a render farm for compositing tasks usually requires the movement of a fair amount of data, which means you'll need to use computers on your local area network. These can be connected using a standard Ethernet network, or wireless network.

No matter what type of distributed rendering you want to do, you'll need to install special client software on all of the computers that you want to include in your render farm. Most programs that provide a distributed rendering option include a license for installing render clients on an additional number of machines, or *nodes*. How many nodes you can install varies from package to package; check your particular software for details. Purchasing additional rendering nodes is far less expensive than having to buy a full copy of the software.

EXERCISE: KNOW WHAT YOU NEED

Before you head to the computer store (or before you start surfing online for a good deal), there are a few technical specs that you need to be sure of.

- How fast a processor do you need?
- How much storage will you need for your intended project?
- What type of video interface do you need?
- How much RAM will your editing and effects packages require?
- Do you want a second computer monitor?
- Do you need an audio card?
- Do you need an HD card?

- What backup system will you use for backing up your in-progress projects?
- How will you archive your project when it's finally finished?
- Do you have multiple workstations that you want to share media over a SAN?
- Does your editing, compositing, or 3D software support network rendering? If so, do you want to build a render farm?

SUMMARY

There are many products and options out there for the digital video user. If you're a feature filmmaker, you don't need to worry about most of them because your needs are fairly simple, so don't go overboard in building your system. If you are working on a project with lots of graphics and effects, you'll need a more robust system with all the bells and whistles. Stick with what will work best for your production, and aim for a system that can support the software that you prefer to use.

11

NON-LINEAR EDITING SOFTWARE

In This Chapter

Now that you've assembled your computer, it's time to choose the editing software that you'll run on your new workstation.

In this chapter, we'll cover all of the issues, concepts, and terminology you'll need to understand when choosing a non-linear editing application. Your editing software will be the heart of your post-production system, so choose carefully.

EDITING SOFTWARE BASICS

A typical non-linear editing program is a very complicated piece of software. However, by identifying the features you need for your project, you can more easily zero in on the package that's right for you. The following are factors to consider when choosing an editing program.

The Interface

Most editing applications share a similar interface. A project window contains *bins* or folders, which hold video clips and other media. Double-clicking on a clip will open it in the *source monitor,* a window on the left side of the screen. The source monitor lets you view the shot and select the part of it that you want to use in your final edited *sequence.*

You assemble shots into a sequence using a *timeline* window that displays representations of your clips in their edited order. The timeline window is divided into tracks that contain video or audio. When editing, you can *target* particular tracks, letting you choose to add only the audio and video from a clip into your project, or just the audio *or* video. For example, by targeting the video track, you can perform a *cutaway* from one piece of video to another, without altering the underlying audio (Figure 11.1). There are two common types of timelines: A/B-style timelines and single-track timelines. A/B-style timelines have two video tracks with a transition track in between (Figure 11.2a), while single-track timelines combine video and transitions on one track (Figure 11.2b). Just because a system offers a single-track timeline doesn't mean you're limited to one track of video; in fact most editing applications that have single-track timelines can support unlimited tracks of video.

On the right side of the screen is the *record monitor,* a window that displays the video from the timeline—that is, your edited sequence (Figure 11.1). Figure 11.2a shows the editing interface in Adobe Premiere with both source and record monitors. Some simpler, editing programs such as Apple's iMovie use a less-complicated interface with only one monitor.

For maximum flexibility, look for a package with robust editing controls (many of which are described next). For faster learning, look for a

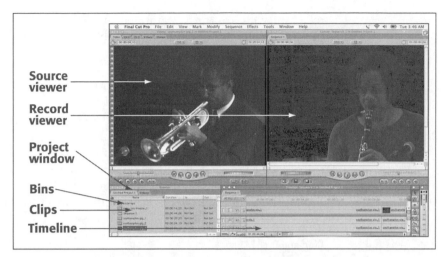

Source viewer
Record viewer
Project window
Bins
Clips
Timeline

FIGURE 11.1   Final Cut Pro 5 has all the standard interface elements: a project window, bins with clips, source and record monitors, and a timeline.

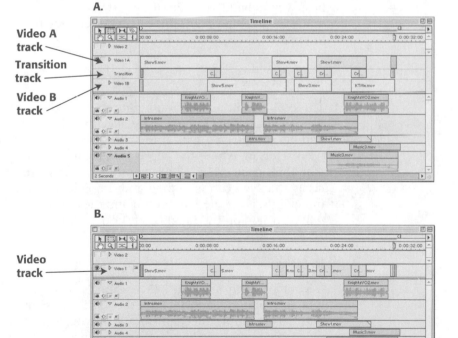

Video A track
Transition track
Video B track

Video track

FIGURE 11.2   The Adobe Premiere interface lets you choose between A/B-style timeline mode (a) and single-track timeline mode (b).

program with a more streamlined interface, but beware: with a simpler program, you might not get all the tools you need to produce high-quality audio and video.

Editing Features

One of the best things about a good non-linear editing package is that there are many different ways to make an edit. The following is a list of editing tools found in most editing applications. If you are new to editing, selecting a package with lots of these features will assure the most editing flexibility. If you have some experience editing, you'll want to be sure to find a package that provides the editing controls that you prefer.

Drag-and-Drop Editing

With drag-and-drop editing, you use the mouse to drag shots into the timeline window from a bin. Once there, you can rearrange shots by dragging them into the order you prefer. Drag-and-drop editing is often the best way to build your first rough string-up of a scene. You can arrange and select multiple shots in a bin and then drag them into the timeline all at once.

Three-Point Editing

Three-point editing lets you define the part of a source clip that will be used in your edited sequence, by selecting a beginning, or *in-point*, and an ending, or *out-point*, within the clip (these are the first two points), and then selecting where the clip will begin *or* end in your edited sequence (the third point). This allows you to build an edited sequence more precisely than you can with drag-and-drop editing. After setting the in- and out-points, press the Edit button and the selected part of your source clip will be placed on the timeline at the selected destination.

JKL Editing

If your program provides JKL editing controls, the J on your keyboard will play your video in reverse, the K will pause, and the L will play forward. This simple mechanism allows you to quickly shuttle around a video clip to find an in- or out-point. Since you can usually select an in-point with the I on your keyboard and an out-point with the O, JKL turns your standard keyboard into an efficient, one-handed edit controller (Figure 11.3).

FIGURE 11.3   Keyboard, or JKL, editing provides a simple, one-handed editing interface.

Insert and Overwrite Editing

Whether you're using drag-and-drop, three-point editing, or switching between the two, your editing package should provide for *insert* and *overwrite* editing modes. These two options allow you to choose *how* your footage is added into an already-cut sequence.

When inserting, all of the footage after the in-point is pushed down the timeline to accommodate the footage that is being added. In other words, the new footage—whether audio, video, or both—is *inserted* into the timeline.

Conversely, overwrite leaves all clips in place, but writes the new clip over any existing video or audio (depending on which tracks are targeted) (Figure 11.4).

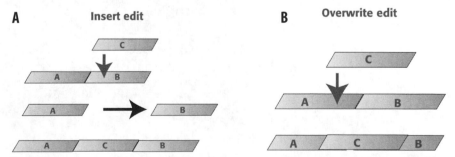

FIGURE 11.4   Insert edits allow you to add a shot between two existing shots (a), while overwrite edits allow you to easily add a cutaway (b).

Linear Editors Beware!

If you have experience editing on a linear editing system, be sure to note that insert editing on a non-linear system has no correlation to insert editing on a dedicated, linear edit controller (where insert means to overwrite a particular audio or video track).

Trimming

Once you have a decent rough cut of a scene, it's time to fine-tune it. For example, you might want to add beats of silence between certain lines of dialog to show a character's hesitation, or you might want to extend a shot of a character to show his reaction as another character speaks. One way to do this is by *trimming* the edit. A trimming interface has a familiar two-monitor window, but instead of source and record monitors, you see the last frame of the outgoing shot in the left monitor and the first frame of the incoming shot of the edit that you are going to trim in the right monitor (Figure 11.5). In trim mode, you can extend or shorten the end of the outgoing shot (the "A-side" of the edit), or you can extend or shorten the incoming shot (the "B-side" of the edit), or both.

FIGURE 11.5 The trimming interface in Avid Xpress DV.

Ripple and Roll, Slip and Slide

There are a number of different types of edits that you can make once you've built a sequence. The following are four advanced ways to fine-tune an edited sequence. Depending on your software, they can be executed in the timeline, in trim mode, or both (Figures 11.6 and 11.7).

- **Ripple and roll** are two ways to change an existing edit between two shots. *Ripple* allows you to extend or shorten either the outgoing shot (the A-side) or the incoming shot (the B-side). All of the shots in your sequence will move farther down in the timeline to accommodate these added frames. *Roll* lets you extend the outgoing shot and tighten the incoming shot simultaneously (or vice versa). The overall length of the sequence will remain unchanged, which makes rolling edits well suited to creating overlapping edits as in Figure 11.6.

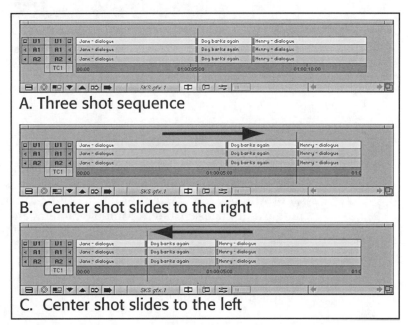

A. Three shot sequence

B. Center shot slides to the right

C. Center shot slides to the left

FIGURE 11.6   This dialog overlap was created using a rolling edit in trim mode, The edit in the video track rolls left as the A-side of the edit is extended and the B-side is simultaneously shortened.

- **Slip and slide** edits involve three shots, as in Figure 11.7a. If you use a *slide* edit to drag the middle shot forward in time, the first shot will automatically be extended to fill the gap, while the last shot will be automatically shortened to keep the overall length of the three shots the same (Figures 11.7b and 11.7c). *Slip* allows you to change the footage contained in the middle shot, starting it at a different place without affecting the shots surrounding it, or the duration of the sequence.

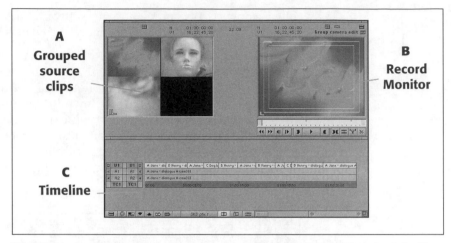

FIGURE 11.7 By using a slide edit, you can move the center shot in (A) to the right (B) or to the left (C) without changing the length of the overall sequence.

Multi-Camera Editing

If your software allows for multi-cam editing, you can *group* shots from different cameras together in your timeline and then select which video you want to see at any given time. Although most independent films are shot with one camera, multi-camera editing can be useful if you recorded audio and video separately. Multiple cameras are also sometimes used for concert footage, music videos, or effects shots involving pyrotechnics that can only be detonated once. You can group the audio and video for each shot using either matching timecode or a slate sync mark. Figure 11.8 shows multi-camera editing in Avid's Media Composer. For more on multi-cam editing, see Chapter 14, "Editing."

Other Features

In addition to their editing methods, there are a number of interface and utility features that you should look for when choosing an editing package.

Good keyboard controls are a must, as it's much easier to develop an editing rhythm by punching keys than by moving a mouse. Also look for multiple Undos (at least 15 levels) and automatic save and backup features, all of which will help you recover from mistakes.

Don't be taken in by packages that provide for dozens (or even a hundred) audio and video tracks. For most feature films, three or four

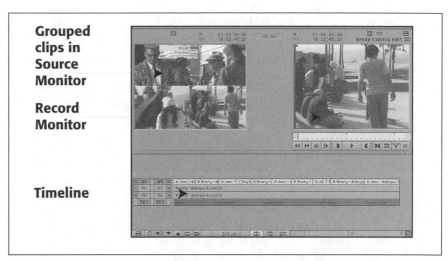

Grouped clips in Source Monitor

Record Monitor

Timeline

FIGURE 11.8   Multi-camera editing in Avid Media Composer.

video tracks and four to eight audio tracks are all you'll need. If you edit with more than 12 tracks total, you'll probably find you need a second monitor just for the timeline. Similarly, *nesting*, which allows you to place one edited sequence inside another, is not as useful as it sounds. If you're planning on exporting an EDL or passing on audio to a sound editor using OMFs, you'll have to un-nest your sequences first. (If you don't know what EDLs and OMFs are, don't worry—read on.)

In addition, look for the following features when assessing an NLE:

Matchframe: Instead of having to search through all your bins and shots to find a source file that you've already added to your timeline, if your editor provides a matchframe feature, you simply park your cursor on a frame in your timeline and then press the *matchframe* button. The source clip appears in your source monitor. Related to matchframe is the *find clip* or *find bin* command that opens the bin in which a shot is located.

Audio scrubbing: Most digital non-linear editing systems let you *scrub* through the audio, which means that as you slowly scroll through a clip, the audio plays back in slow motion along with the video. This is a must for finding a particular sound, such as a pause in a line of dialog or the beat in a piece of music.

Lockable tracks: Locking a track can prevent you from making accidental edits. If you follow the traditional motion picture workflow and *lock picture* before you begin fine-cutting your sound, then locking the picture track in your software will help ensure that the edited picture doesn't get changed.

Network editing: For projects that need multiple editors and workstations, software support for networked editing can save lots of headaches. The biggest danger with networked editing lies in accidentally writing over a project that someone else has worked on and losing all their work. Software support for networked editing helps prevent these sorts of mistakes.

Organizational Tools

A good non-linear editing system should provide you with tools that will help you keep track of all of the media in your project.

In applications with good organizational tools, bins will display columns showing information about each piece of media—start and end timecode, source tape number, frame rate, number and types of tracks, audio sampling rate, and more. For long projects, you'll want editing software that lets you customize and add columns for your own comments, keywords, and so on. You should be able to *sort* and *sift* bins according to your needs, and use *search* or *find* commands to locate clips (Figure 11.9).

FIGURE 11.9   Most editing applications let you add customized columns and headings when you view your clips in text view—shown here is Final Cut Pro.

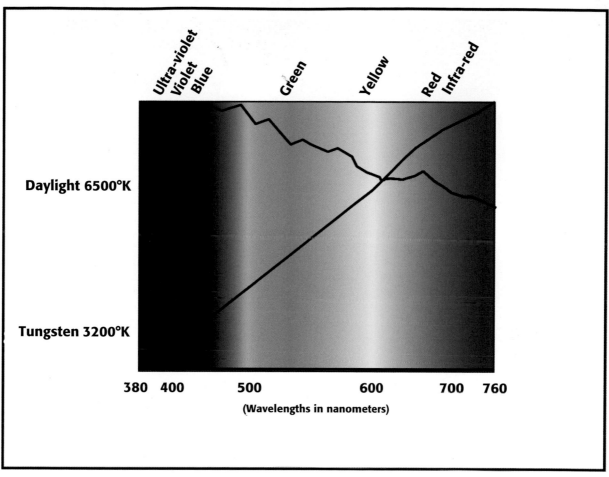

Ultra-violet
Violet
Blue
Green
Yellow
Red
Infra-red

Daylight 6500°K

Tungsten 3200°K

380 400   500   600   700   760

(Wavelengths in nanometers)

COLOR PLATE 1   Chart showing the visible color spectrum and the spectral energy distributions of sunlight and tungsten light. Both cover the entire range of color but sunlight has much more blue, whereas tungsten has more red.

COLOR PLATE 2   This swatch book from Lee Filters shows a selection of lighting gels and reflective materials.

COLOR PLATE 3 Lighting crews use a lot of equipment to light the green background on green screen sets.

COLOR PLATE 4 This greenscreen set was lit and art directed to match a CGI environment.

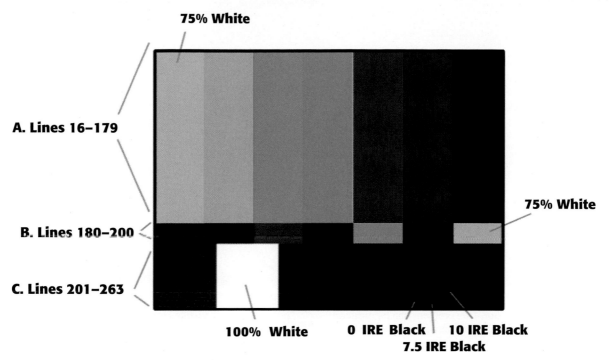

75% White

A. Lines 16–179

B. Lines 180–200

75% White

C. Lines 201–263

100% White   **0 IRE Black**   **10 IRE Black**
7.5 IRE Black

COLOR PLATE 5   Standard NTSC color bars contain three separate test patterns: A, B, and C in the image here.

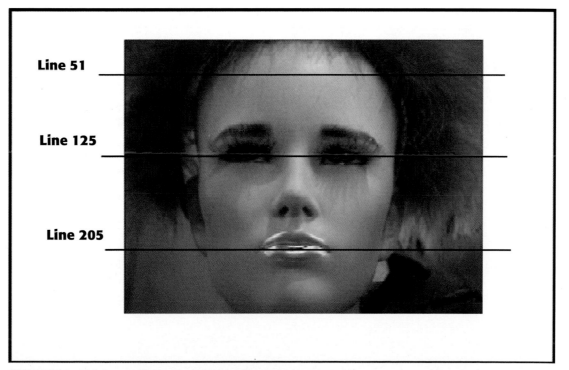

Line 51

Line 125

Line 205

COLOR PLATE 6   This image of a mannequin is well-exposed.

A. This image of a statue was over-exposed during the shoot. This problem can be reduced using the gain controls in your capture utility or hardware scopes.

B. The white levels are clipped in some areas, so "pulling down" the whites won't help much. But you can pull down the blacks, giving the image a better contrast ratio.

C. The vectorscope in Figure 13.12 shows that the image consists mainly of cyan. Increasing the red gain helps make the hue more balanced.

D. Finally, decreasing the blue gain helps bring out more of the warm tones of the statue that are lacking in the original image. Note that the greens in the plant look more natural now. The image is still overexposed but it looks much better.

COLOR PLATE 7 This image of a statue is over-exposed. We've taken some steps at correction.

A. This image of two teapots is dull and muddy.

B. Often the first reflex when trying to fix an image that seems too dark is to raise the black levels. But as this figure reveals, rasing the blacks only results in an even more washed-out image.

C. By raising the white levels, the brightness of the entire image is pulled up. This appears to be on the right track but if you pull the whites up this much, you'll most likely see artifacting in the image when it plays.

D. In this figure, the whites have been pulled up but not quite as high as in C. To compensate for this, the blacks have been pulled down, resulting in an image with better contrast. Now that the white and black levels are good, it's clear that the color balance doesn't need any adjusting.

COLOR PLATE 8   This image of two teapots is correctly exposed but under-lit.

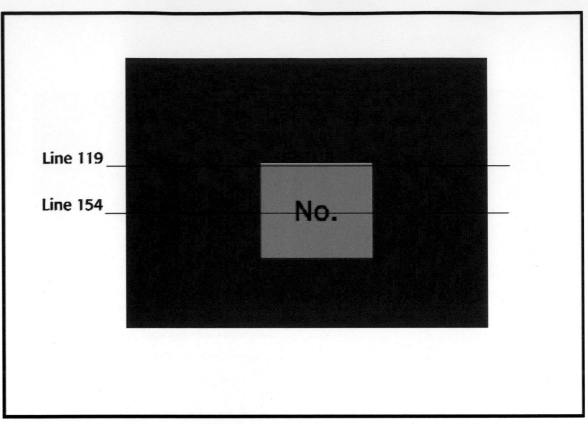

Line 119

Line 154

No.

COLOR PLATE 9 These colors exceed the NTSC color space and will bleed and smear when shown on an NTSC monitor. See Figure 16.4 for examples of how to spot these troubles on a waveform monitor and vectorscope.

COLOR PLATE 10 Neon lights tend to oversaturate even if they're exposed correctly.

COLOR PLATE 11 Recompressing your video with the DV compressor can result in severe quality loss. Our original image (A) was compressed 3 times (B) and then 6 times (C) to show the effects of overcompression.

COLOR PLATES 12 AND 13 Bad white balance (left) and corrected white balance (right).

COLOR PLATE 14   Bullet holes before and after. Here, we used color balance and blur filters to better integrate the bullet hole into the door.

COLOR PLATE 15   Backyard before and after. Through the use of a hand-cut matte, we can easily replace the sky in this video of a house.

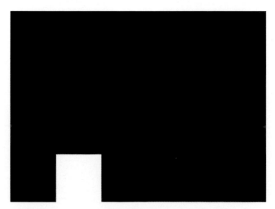

COLOR PLATE 16   If your monitor has a Blue Check control, you can use the blue bars for additional calibration.

EDITING HD AND HDV

Lately, every editing application seems to be adding the letters "HD" to their name—Avid Xpress Pro HD, Adobe Premiere Pro HD, Final Cut Pro HD—the list goes on. The reason for this is that most software-only applications are resolution independent. In other words, they simply add a CODEC (or several CODECs) and let the hardware in your system take care of the hardest part, i.e., providing the throughput and processing power needed to accommodate the high data rates of HD video and also the necessary video and audio interface. Dedicated turnkey systems or hardware/software combos like dpsVelocity and Media 100 HD provide the necessary video accelerator cards and video interfaces, usually in the form of a breakout box, to add the appropriate hardware support for HD to your computer.

HDV, on the other hand, has its own set of challenges and they are almost exactly the opposite of those of HD. HDV doesn't have the high processing needs that other HD formats have because it's highly-compressed, resulting in a low data rate. This means that media can be transferred via a FireWire interface without the need for special accelerator cards or breakout boxes. However, HDV uses a special type of compression called long GOP MPEG_2 that makes it difficult for editing software to incorporate native HDV editing. Long GOP MPEG_2 interpolates media in eight-frame sequences so that you can only make an edit on every eighth frame. (Figure 11.10). Editing applications that support native HDV editing use special algorithms to make this eight-frame limitation invisible to you, the editor. This tricky bit of computing is the reason that some editing apps have been slower than others to adopt native HDV editing and other require a special HDV plug-in. If you plan to edit HDV footage, make sure your software application supports it.

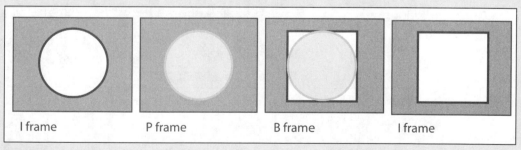

I frame   P frame   B frame   I frame

FIGURE 11.10   Illustration of HDV long GOP MPEG_2 media.

LOGGING, CAPTURING, AND IMPORTING

Most editing packages offer a capture utility to get video into your computer (Figure 11.11). The simplest packages will work like a tape recorder: tell them to start recording and they'll record any video that's fed into them. More sophisticated applications will let you specify which sections of a tape to capture, and can be configured for unattended capturing of whole batches of clips. (See Chapter 10, "Building a Workstation" and Chapter 12, "Editing Hardware" for more on video input hardware.)

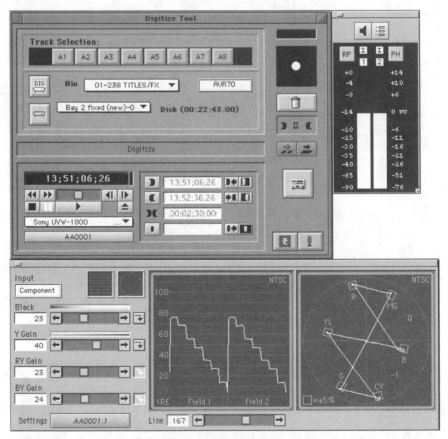

FIGURE 11.11 The capturing interface in Avid Media Composer.

Because your project might involve other types of media (audio, stills, animations), you'll want to be sure that your editor supports the file formats and specifications you need.

When looking at an editing package's capturing interface, consider the following:

Timecode support: If you plan to move from one system to another, reconstruct your project, or create an EDL, you need a package that supports timecode. If you plan to integrate with existing professional equipment, look for SMPTE timecode support. If you're going to stick with DV sources and equipment, make sure you have DV timecode support. (More on timecode in Chapter 13, "Preparing to Edit.")

HD and/or HDV support: If you're planning to work with HD or HDV video, you'll need software that supports those formats. HD requires extra hardware to handle the large files sizes, and HDV has special software needs due to the way it is compressed.

24 fps support: If your source media was shot at 24 frames per second and you plan to finish on 24 fps media, such as film or some types of HD video, you'll need software that either supports native 24 fps editing or uses a reverse telecine process to create 24 fps *cuts lists* or *EDLs* at the end of your editing session for use with a high-end 24 fps system to output a final master.

Audio level controls and meters: For maximum quality, you need to be able to see audio levels and adjust them while you capture. Look for meters with dB marks and sliding gain controls.

Waveform monitors and vectorscopes: A software waveform monitor and vectorscope are used to fine-tune your video signal to get the best quality possible (see Chapter 13, "Preparing to Edit," for more details).

Batch capturing: Batch capturing lets you log an entire tape and then capture all of your logged clips in one, unattended operation. This feature is also extremely useful if you plan to reconstruct your project on a different system or at a later date.

Importing files: Most editing systems can import and export a number of different graphics and sound formats. If you are dependent on a particular file type, be sure your app supports it.

Pixel aspect ratios: Depending on your video format, you need to make sure your editing app supports the right pixel aspect ratios. Chapter 3, "Video Technology Basics," covers the different formats and pixel aspect ratios in detail.

16:9 support: If you shot widescreen footage, be sure your package supports editing with 16:9 media—most newer products support this.

NTSC/PAL support: Most editing applications can switch easily between PAL and NTSC. Make sure the software you choose supports the video standards you need.

HD or SD?

If you are going to be editing an HD project using SD work tapes, you won't need special software and hardware to edit your project. Only later, when you are reconstructing your project in HD will you need the requisite HD equipment to finish your final master.

OTHER HELPFUL EDITING APPS

- Non-linear editing applications are designed to be all-in-one packages for capturing, organizing, editing, mixing audio, creating special effects, and outputting a final master. Sometimes, though, they can stand to have a little help from the outside:
- iView Pro (Figure 11.12)—For cataloging and organizing video, stills, and audio clips.
- Adobe Photoshop—For preparing still images (if you have any) and for certain types of graphics and titling operations.
- Special CODECS for HDV, HD, the Web, etc.
- SAN software—If you plan to work with a SAN.
- Backup software—Because you *don't* want to have a crash you can't recover from!

FIGURE 11.12 iView Media Pro cataloguing software is a great tool for cataloging and organizing all of the media that you'll use for a project, including video, stills, and audio.

EFFECTS AND TITLES

Most editing applications come packed with all types of fancy transitions and wipes. However, for a dramatic feature, you probably won't want to use anything more complex than a cross-dissolve. (Just think of those tacky wipes and iris transitions in *Star Wars* and you'll see what we mean.) However, if you're working on a project that's more stylized, or on a commercial or corporate presentation, fancy transitions might be necessary.

Because transitions are notorious for quickly falling in and out of fashion, don't let the presence of the "wipe du jour" play too much of a role in your purchase decision—it might look tired by the time you're up and running. Instead, look for software that has a good practical effects package—color correction, internal titling, motion effects, and compositing.

No matter what your taste in effects, look for software that supports effects plug-ins so that you can add effects as needed. And if you're really serious about special effects, look for software that easily integrates with dedicated effects applications such as Adobe After Effects.

The following are basic effects features to look for:

Plug-ins: Because there are plug-in effect filters that do everything from sophisticated compositing to special effects such as lightning and "film-look," plug-in support is essential. On the Mac and Windows platforms, most plug-ins conform to the Adobe After Effects or Premiere specifications. Some packages have their own proprietary plug-in specifications.

Keyframes: Keyframes allow you to change the parameters of an effect over time. For example, if you are adding a superimposed video image of a ghost to your shot, you can use keyframes to make the ghost fade up halfway, hold for a second, flicker a few times, move across the frame, and disappear. The screen position, movement, and transparency of your ghost image are all controlled by keyframes that allow you to choose exactly when and how you want the image to look at each point in time. Keyframes are essential for effects work beyond simple transitions.

Real-time versus rendered effects: Most non-linear editing programs require that you render each effect and transition before you can play them back in full-motion. Some applications can provide real-time playback of certain effects, while others require special video boards to render effects in real-time. (Video boards are discussed in Chapter 10.)

Types of Effects

Nowadays, even the cheapest editing package includes a mind-boggling number of effects. In fact, sometimes the cheaper the software, the more effects you get! Nevertheless, all effects fall into one of the categories discussed next.

Transitions

Transition effects create a bridge from one shot to another. The most often-used transition is the *cross-dissolve*. Others include various *wipes* and *pushes, page turns,* and *white flashes,* to name only a few. If you're planning on using lots of these, look for software with plug-in support and keyframing (Figure 11.13).

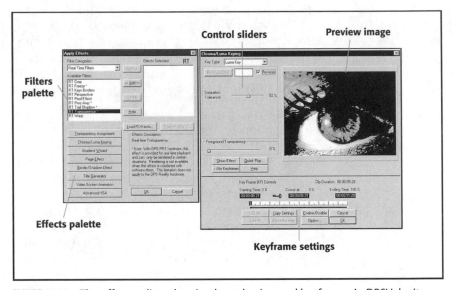

FIGURE 11.13   The effects editor showing luma keying and keyframes in DPSVelocity.

Image Enhancement Effects

There's a limit to how much you can improve poorly shot video, but your editing software should offer some control over the *brightness, contrast, saturation,* and *hue* of your footage (Figure 11.14). A lot of editing packages now offer elaborate color correction tools. These are especially useful if you are planning to finish your project using your non-linear editing system.

Motion Effects

One of the most basic video effects is the ability to freeze, slow down, or speed up a shot. If you're going to do lots of motion effects, look for soft-

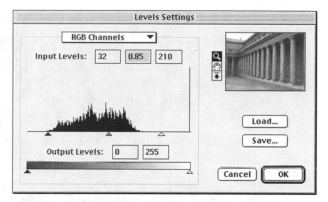

FIGURE 11.14   Color correction in Adobe Premiere. If you're used to Photoshop or After Effects, you'll recognize this standard Levels dialog for adjusting tone and color balance.

ware that lets you specify a variable frame rate from 0% (freeze frame) to 3000% (the maximum that most programs will allow).

Compositing

Compositing tools are used for everything from complex titling and video collage, to sophisticated special effects including virtual sets and locations. The compositing tools offered by most editing applications (*alpha channel compositing, luma keying, chroma keying, and matte keying*) are good enough for creating simple composites, but they lack the precision and control needed for serious special effects (Figure 11.15).

3D Effects

Another hot property these days is the ability to move a video layer in true 3D space. Used primarily for fancy transitions and simple effects, the feature filmmaker will find little use for these effects. If you want to create true 3D objects and environments, you'll have to use a 3D animation application such as Maya.

Titles

Most film projects need three types of titles: the opening title sequence, the credit roll at the end, and possibly subtitles. Most editing applications can create simple titles, subtitles, and credit rolls (Figure 11.16). An opening credit sequence is another story. Complicated title sequences

FIGURE 11.15 3D effects editing in Speed Razor.

such as the one in *The Matrix* or the famous title sequence of *7even* are really more like short animated films and will probably require using a dedicated 2D animation application such as Adobe After Effects.

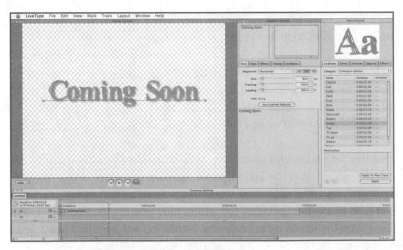

FIGURE 11.16 In addition to its built-in titling tool, Apple's Final Cut Pro ships with Live Type, an excellent stand-alone tool for building animated type effects.

AUDIO TOOLS

Audio editing can often make or break a film. Good audio can enhance atmosphere, create drama, and provide reason for what would otherwise seem like a bad edit. Editing software can tend to skimp on audio features, so if you're serious about sound editing, we recommend using a dedicated sound editing application, such as DigiDesign ProTools. We'll talk about sound editing applications in Chapter 15, "Sound Editing." That said, you'll still need some decent sound editing tools before the film is handed off to the sound editor.

The following are some things to look for that will help you create better sound tracks in your non-linear editing application.

Equalization

Good equalization features (or *EQ*) let you do everything from removing the hiss from a bad tape recording to adding presence to someone with a weak voice.

Audio Effects and Filters

Just like video effects, audio effects and filters let you change the nature of the sound in a clip. And, just like video effects, many programs support audio plug-ins for adding everything from echo, reverb, delay, and pitch-shifting, to specialized effects that make a voice sound like it's coming through a telephone. When selecting editing software, you should assess the audio filters that are included, and determine if the package supports audio plug-ins. See Chapter 15 for more on audio editing.

Audio Plug-In Formats

Although there are a number of audio plug-in formats, including TDM, SoundDesigner, AudioSuite, Apple's Audio Units, and Premiere, it's best to look for an editing package that is compatible with the plug-ins that you or your sound editor will use to edit the audio.

Mixing

No editing system is complete without the ability to set the audio levels on each individual piece of sound in your sequence, a process called *mixing*. Look for software that has a mixing interface with *gain sliders* and dB (decibel) markings. Some editing packages offer real-time mixing, which allows you to adjust audio levels while your sequence plays. This can be a time-saving way to get a rough mix that you can fine-tune later (Figure 11.17).

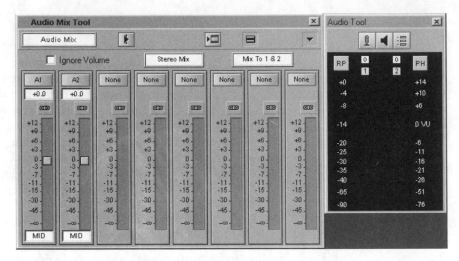

FIGURE 11.17 Audio EQ and mixing interface in Avid Xpress DV.

OMF Export

If you plan on using a dedicated sound editing application to complete the sound design of your film, software that can export *OMF files* will make your life a lot easier. OMF files contain the audio portion of your timeline and can be imported directly into an audio editing system such as Pro-Tools. OMF support saves lots of time if you need to reconstruct your audio in another application.

THE FINAL PRODUCT

Finally, the editing software you choose needs to be capable of creating an output of your final product. Outputting can be very complicated, and we've dedicated an entire chapter to it at the end of this book, but here are some guidelines for ensuring that an editing package meets your output needs.

Videotape Masters

Be aware that creating a videotape output involves both hardware and software—your editing software might claim that it can perform a certain type of output, but your hardware might not be up to the job. For example, some systems might have a hard time playing a 90-minute feature in its entirety, requiring you to break your project into smaller sections for output. If you think you might need to lay off your feature in segments (which is a good work-around if you don't have enough disk space to hold all your footage), then make certain your software is capable of frame accurate device control and editing to tape. Be aware that these capabilities are dependent on having the right type of video deck. (Video hardware is covered in Chapter 12, "Editing Hardware.")

Digital Video Files

If your video is destined for the Web, DVD, or CD-ROM, you'll need to export it in the right format for the final product—usually a QuickTime movie using a highly compressed CODEC for the Web and CD-ROMs or the MPEG-2 CODEC for DVDs. We'll discuss multimedia and Web output in more detail in Chapter 19, "Output."

EDLs

If you plan on finishing your project in a high-end online editing or color correction suite, you'll probably use an EDL (short for Edit Decision List) to facilitate the move from your system to the online system.

An EDL is a text file that contains a numbered list of all the shots in your final edited sequence, including the name of the shot, the name of the source tape, the source timecode, and the timecode where it's placed in the master sequence (Figure 11.18). The EDL can be used to reconstruct that sequence on many different types of editing systems. For example, if you export an EDL from Adobe Premiere, Apple's Final Cut Pro can use that EDL to automatically reconstruct the sequence. EDLs can be used to recreate sequences on high-end online editing systems, color correction systems, other non-linear editing systems, and sound editing systems.

There are several different EDL file formats, but the default is called CMX format. If you think you might need an EDL, be sure that your software at least supports CMX-3600. If you think you might need to move your final sequence from one editing system to another, be sure that the non-linear editing software you choose can export CMX-3600 EDLs. If you think you might want to recreate sequences from other systems, make sure that your editing software can import CMX-3600 EDLs and construct new sequences from them.

The process of exporting EDLs is discussed in detail in Chapter 19.

Film Cut Lists

A cut list is the film equivalent of an EDL. If your final goal is a film print for a theatrical project, you'll need software that can generate a film cut list using the keycode numbers on your camera-original negative. For more on cut lists, see Chapter 19.

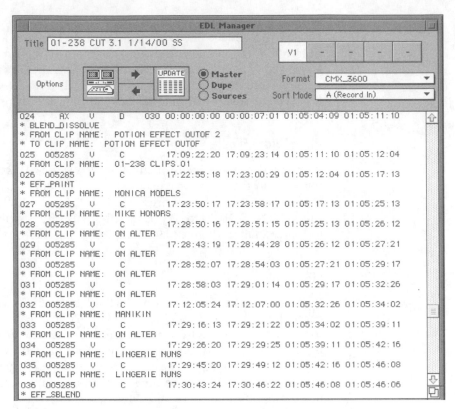

FIGURE 11.18 Avid Media Composer comes with the Avid EDL Manager utility for creating custom EDLs.

EDITING APPLICATIONS COMPARED

There are many editing applications on the market, so we decided to stick with some of the most popular, and, in our opinion, most successful products out there. All of these programs are capable of being the center-piece of a high-end, professional editing workstation. All of them share a similar, customizable interface with strong mouse support and lots of keyboard shortcuts. All of them offer drag-and-drop editing, three-point editing, and trimming. They have multiple levels of Undo, auto save and auto backup functions, as well as support for multiple video and audio tracks. They all offer decent audio editing tools and basic special effects capabilities, including title generators. Finally, they all support EDLs and the importing and exporting of QuickTime movies and are capable of high-quality videotape outputs. In short, any one of these applications is up to the task of editing a movie. If you're looking for a turnkey system, don't be put off by the apps that are software-only—most of these can be purchased as a turnkey package from a third party. Finally, be aware that this list is not comprehensive. We chose not to talk about the myriad low-end editing apps—from iMovie to Windows Movie Maker—simply because there are so many of them and they do not offer the advanced features necessary for longer format or more complex projects.

Adobe Premiere Pro (software-only or turnkey), the original QuickTime editing program, with its customizable interface and powerful editing tools, earns a place among the professional editing applications. Like many others, Premiere is weak when it comes to audio editing, but it offers impressive integration with Adobe's other products, Photoshop and After Effects. In addition, because Premiere has been around so long, there are many third-party add-on products. If you're interested in maximizing performance, you'll be glad to know that most of the real-time effects and HD boards on the market were designed with Premiere in mind. The current version of Premiere Pro is only available on the Windows platform and Adobe has partnered with hardware manufacturers like Dell, Intel, and HP to offer a line of turnkey Premiere Pro systems under the banner OpenHD that are specially designed for editing HDV or HD material.

Apple Final Cut Pro (software-only), Apple's entry in the professional editing world, is a complete, FireWire-based Mac platform-only editing system that has been steadily gaining popularity in the professional world which was, until recently, completely dominated by Avid's Media Composer. Packing a full collection of editing tools wrapped up in an interface with decent keyboard support, the latest version offers full HD and HDV support, multi-camera editing, real-time effects and transitions, improved multi-channel audio support, 24 fps support, and integration of Apple's CinemaTools for high-quality film output.

Avid Media Composer (turnkey) is a line of products that offer all of the features discussed in this chapter and then some. Designed for multiple users who need to manage large projects, Avid Media Composer sticks to the high-end market with optional support for HD-SDI I/O but no support for FireWire. Avid offers several variations of Media Composer for both Macintosh and Windows, and the professional price tag for this tool continues to drop. Avid Film Composer is the 24-fps cousin to Media Composer, which offers a native 24-fps editing environment for film editors.

Avid Xpress (software-only) is a family of products scaled-down from the high-end Avid Media Composer line available on both Windows and Macintosh platforms. Three applications—Xpress DV, Xpress Pro, and Xpress Pro HD—provide decent keyboard support, solid audio editing tools, and support for QuickTime importing and exporting, making these products a great solution for those who don't need the high-end features of the Media Composer line. Xpress DV offers native DV editing, Xpress Pro offers multiple resolution MJPEG CODECs and a choice of composite, component, or SDI video I/O. Xpress Pro HD (Windows-only) adds native HD editing and Avid promises HDV and Mac-platform support in the near future.

Canopus Edius HD (turnkey) is a high-end HD editing system that includes all the bells and whistles. This Windows-only system offers competition for similarly priced products like Avid Nitrus HD and dpsVelocity HD. Edius lacks customizable keyboard settings but can handle both SD and HD CODECS in the same timeline.

Velocity HD (turnkey/software-only) is a Windows-based editing system capable of capturing and outputting compressed and uncompressed, HD and D1 quality video, along with the full array of digital input and output formats including HD-SDI and HDV. Velocity offers real-time, dual-stream playback and effects in HD, with real-time eight-stream playback and effects in D1. The editing interface has everything you need to edit long-format, complex projects, but Velocity's true strength lies in its professional palette of real-time and rendered effects.

Media 100 (software-only, software/hardware combo) has always been ahead of the competition in terms of hardware/software integration as proven by their latest products, Media 100 844/X and Media 100 HD. Aimed at short-form, graphics-intensive editing, Media 100 is a high-end software app (Mac-only) with three PCI cards, known as the Genesis engine, which provides four streams of high-quality uncompressed video, each including an animated alpha channel, and at all a reasonable price.

Media 100 HD (Mac only) expands on 844/X by adding real-time uncompressed HD editing and an integrated offline SD to online HD workflow, including the capability of mixing SD and HD formats in the same timeline.

Pinnacle Liquid Edition Pro (software-only/software-hardware combo) offers native DV and HDV editing and allows you to mix SD formats (DV, etc.) with HD formats (HDV) in the same timeline. Liquid Edition Pro is a solid mid-range editing application (Windows-only) with an impressive array of 2D and 3D effects.

Sony Vegas (software-only/turnkey) is a mid-range Windows-only application with support for native HDV editing. Sony Vegas is limited in that it only allows one sequence per project; however this limitation is balanced by excellent audio editing tools.

EXERCISE: KNOW WHAT YOU NEED

By this point, you've thought long and hard about your project. Look at the following list of editing software features and decided which ones are important for your project.

- Do you need a customized keyboard for editing short cuts?
- Is trimming essential to your style of editing?
- Will your project require multi-camera editing? This is common for TV shows, especially talk shows, and concerts or other live performances.
- Will you need to network two or more editing workstations together?
- Do you want your software to be "scalable"? This means that you can start out small—DV with FireWire—and, by adding hardware, go big—uncompressed HD.
- Do you need native HDV editing?
- What kind of timecode will your media have and does the editing app support it?
- Do you need native 24 fps editing?
- Is color correction important for your project? If so, make sure your app provides a waveform monitor and a vectorscope in addition to strong color correction tools.
- Can the application import and export the file formats you need: Flash, Photoshop, etc.?
- Do you need support for both NTSC and PAL video?
- Do you need support for widescreen footage?
- If your project is HD, do you need both HD and SD outputs?
- What kind of special effects will your project require?
- Will you be doing your final mix in your NLE or in a dedicated audio editing app?
- Do you need to be able to export audio OMF files?
- Will you be finishing (or "onlining") your final masters out to videotape from your NLE?
- Will you need EDLs or film cut lists?
- Is easy output to DVD important for you?
- Do you want a turnkey system? (You'll still have to hook up the video hardware yourself—see Chapter 12 for more on that.)

Most software-only editing applications offer downloadable demo versions of their products, so try out the ones that sound promising. If you're thinking about buying a hardware/software combo or a turnkey system, the retailer probably offers demo models at their store. If you want to see a whole bunch of products at once, consider going to a trade show such as DVExpo.

SUMMARY

Your editing system is the hub of your production. Everything you record will go into it and come out of it in some way or another. However, don't expect your non-linear editing software to do everything—you'll need to add some external video and audio hardware before you can really call it an editing system.

12

EDITING HARDWARE

In This Chapter

- Hardware Peripherals
- Video Decks
- Audio Equipment
- Video Monitors
- Hardware Connectors
- Exercise: Hardware Checklist Before You Start
- Summary

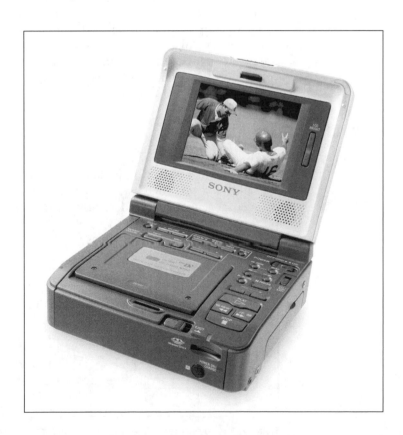

The cost of editing hardware can range from a few hundred dollars—your TV set, a pair of headphones and the cheapest DV camcorder you can find—to over a hundred thousand dollars for a high-end HD video deck and all the accessories that go with it, including expensive HD monitors. Most independent filmmakers fall into the lower end of this spectrum, while corporate media creators fall somewhere in the middle. But no matter what your budget is, every complete video editing system needs a video deck, speakers (or headphones), a video monitor, and possibly an audio deck. Even if you splurged for a turnkey system, you'll find that it only includes computer hardware and software.

Unfortunately, you can't just run out and buy any old piece of equipment. In addition to quality and performance differences, you'll also need to sort through some compatibility issues, because not every editing package is compatible with every video deck. By the time you're ready to purchase or rent video and audio equipment for your editing workstation, you should already have decided on a computer platform, video format(s) and editing software. At that point, you can make decisions about your editing hardware based on the needs of your editing software. Most software vendors publish a list of hardware that has been tested and approved to work with their software. If you already have some video hardware components, make sure that anything else you purchase is compatible with what you already own.

DON'T PANIC!

If you're building a FireWire-based DV or HDV editing system, you'll be able to get away with a simplified editing system (Figure 12.1). If you have specialized needs, such as the capability to edit HD or D1-quality footage or even analog BetaSP video, you'll need the components of the typical professional editing system (Figure 12.2). Producers on a tight budget can rent high-end video hardware as needed, such as when they're capturing and outputting their final master.

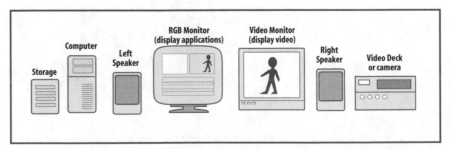

FIGURE 12.1   Components of a simple non-linear editing system, including peripheral audio and video hardware.

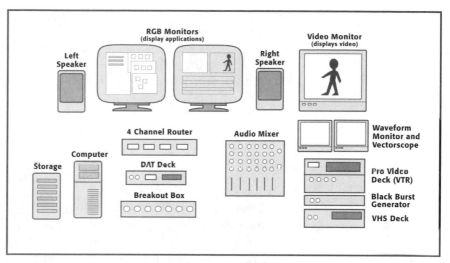

FIGURE 12.2   Components of a typical professional non-linear editing system, including peripheral audio and video hardware.

HARDWARE PERIPHERALS

In a perfectly budgeted world, your editing system would include a lot of specialized video hardware. However, as a low-budget producer, you may neither require nor care to spare the expense on most of the items shown in the following list. Don't worry! In many cases, you can rent these items, and most productions won't need all of them.

Whatever your needs, here is a list of the external hardware components that can make up an editing system:

Video decks (a.k.a. VTRs): Most editing systems have two video decks: a high-quality deck that can play original tapes from your camera, and a VHS deck to make viewing copies. Increasingly, as more and more people use DVDs for viewing copies, a VHS deck is less necessary.

Digital audio decks: DAT, Mini Disc, and so forth. Most likely, you'll be recording your audio on your camcorder, but if you record your audio separately, or add music or audio from other sources such as DAT, MiniDisc, or CD, then you'll need appropriate decks for playback.

Video monitor: An external video monitor is necessary for you to see what your final output will look like. This is the one component that you'll *have* to have throughout the post-production process.

Speakers: All editing systems need a pair of external speakers (or if you're really strapped for cash, headphones) so you can hear the sound in your project. If you use a mixer, you might also need a pre-amplifier.

Waveform monitor and vectorscope: Waveform monitors and vectorscopes are used to set proper video levels when capturing video. High-end systems use hardware waveform monitors and vectorscopes but low-budget productions can usually make do with the software "scopes" that come with most NLEs, especially when used with a FireWire-based editing system. In Chapter 13, "Preparing to Edit," we discuss how to maintain image quality when capturing.

Switcher, router, and/or patch bay: Most filmmakers will be using video from a single source: their camera. However, if you plan to use video from multiple sources—different formats and cameras, for example—then you might consider an inexpensive router, switcher, or patch bay. These make it easy to quickly switch from one format to another without having to re-wire your system.

Audio mixer: Mixing boards provide on-the-fly adjustment of equalization and gain to control the audio quality of your production and make it easy to manage multiple audio sources.

Transcoder: Transcoders change your video signal from one format into another. Any digital deck that has an analog video output performs some internal transcoding. External boards such as Blackmagic Design's Multibridge with PCI Express (Figure 12.3) converts video analog video to digital video such as HDV and HD. Transcoders are very useful if you frequently need to input and output several different types of video.

Black burst generator: High-end, professional video decks require a video black signal to use as a reference for setting the black level (more about black levels in Chapter 13), to keep sync, and to use for blacking tapes (see Chapter 19, "Output"). (Note: This sync is an electronic pulse that VTRs need in order to play properly, and is not related to synchronization of audio and video.) Low-end DV and DVCAM video decks do not use a black burst generator.

Battery backup: Many editing systems include a battery backup in case of a power failure. These batteries act as a central power switch for the system and, in the case of a power failure, keep the system running long enough for you to save your work and shut down properly.

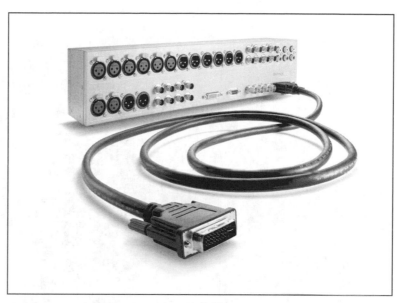

FIGURE 12.3   Transcoders like the Multibridge with PCI Express video converter by Blackmagic Design change video and audio signals from one format to another.

VIDEO DECKS

Probably the most important piece of hardware in a non-linear editing system is the video deck. Although you can use your DV camcorder as a deck for editing, camcorder tape mechanisms are not necessarily designed for the repeated searching and winding that editing requires. A relatively inexpensive video deck, such as the DV Walkman in Figure 12.4 will save a lot of wear and tear on your camera. Figure 12.5 shows the front of a high-end professional HD video deck.

The following sections list the features to consider when looking at decks.

Tape Format

This might seem like an obvious one. If you shot DV, for example, you should buy a DV deck. However, some decks are able to play a few different formats (Table 12.1).

FIGURE 12.4 A DV format video deck or camcorder, like this Sony GV-D1000 DV format Walkman, is essential to a FireWire-based editing system.

FIGURE 12.5 Front view of a professional HD format VTR, the Sony SRW-5500.

If you shot on DV, you can choose between DV, DVCAM, or DVCPro decks for editing and final mastering. A DV deck will be significantly cheaper (starting around $1,000) but will lack professional features and high-quality internal components that will save you time and trouble.

TABLE 12.1 VTR compatibility chart. Many digital video decks can play (but usually not record) multiple tape formats. Be sure to check each manufacturer's specifications if you need a VTR that plays back multiple formats.

TAPE FORMAT	CAN ALSO PLAY
Digital-8	Hi8
DV	DVCAM
DVCPro	DV* and DVCAM
DVCAM	DV*
Digital-S	S-VHS
MPEG-IMX	Digital Betacam and Betacam SP
Betacam SX	Betacam SP
DVCPro50	DV, DVCAM, and DVCPro
D5	D3
D9–HD	Digital-S
HDCAM	Digital Betacam

*DV tapes must be recorded in SP mode to play back on DVCAM and DVCPro equipment.

DVCAM and DVCPro decks will allow you to master to the larger and somewhat more stable DVCAM or DVCPro tapes, and might provide advanced features such as RS-422 device control and XLR audio I/O (more about device control and audio I/O later in this chapter).

SDI, FireWire, or Analog I/O

The deck you choose needs to have an interface that matches the one on your computer. For example, if your computer has a FireWire interface, you'll need a deck with a FireWire interface, and so on. See Chapter 3, "Video Technology Basics," and Chapter 10, "Building a Workstation" for more details on digital and analog video interfaces.

Not all companies are fully compliant in their implementation of the FireWire interface. If you're considering a FireWire-equipped deck, *don't* purchase it until you've checked with the makers of your editing software (and FireWire card, if applicable). They should be able to confirm whether a deck will be fully compatible with their software. Sometimes, one or two features of an editing package will not work with particular decks (or cameras). If you aren't dependent on these features, then go ahead and buy the deck.

Buyer Beware

Just because a deck uses a digital video format does not mean that it necessarily offers digital I/O. Some professional decks come with analog I/O only—you have to add an optional SDI board for digital I/O. This is also true of some FireWire-compatible decks.

Frame Accuracy

Frame accuracy means that when you tell your video deck to make an edit at 1:02:10:30, it will make the edit on that exact frame. If you plan to lay your final edited project off to tape in a single pass, then you don't need to worry about frame accuracy.

However, if you want to lay out your finished project in pieces—as you run out of disk space, for example—then you'll need a frame accurate deck; in other words, one with RS-422 device control and SMPTE timecode. Frame accuracy is also necessary for making *insert edits* onto tape. Most VTRs are rated by their manufacturers as to their projected frame accuracy, and many DV format VTRs are rated at +/–5 frames, meaning your edit could miss its mark by as many as five frames in either direction. If this isn't something you can live with, be sure to buy a VTR that is frame accurate, and uses RS-422 serial device control rather than FireWire-based device control.

Device Control

For more efficient logging and digitizing, your editing system needs to be able to remotely control your video deck to search through a tape, and to start and stop the playback and record processes. This is accomplished through a cable connecting your computer and your deck.

- **RS-422** is the professional industry standard and carries the SMPTE timecode signal, which, combined with the right VTR, is the only way, at present, to get true frame accuracy. RS-422 also allows the longest cable lengths—up to 1000 feet.
- **RS-232** and **LANC** (a.k.a. Control-L) are not capable of frame accuracy. You can, however, buy an external serial protocol converter to change your RS-232 or LANC into RS-422. However, if you already know you need frame accuracy, it's best to start with a VTR that offers RS-422.
- **FireWire-based deck control** is not capable of frame accuracy, but if you have a FireWire-based editing system, it's by far the easiest way to control the deck, since the deck control signal is contained—along with video and audio—in the single FireWire cable that goes from your deck to your computer.

If you have a FireWire-based editing system, then your software will most likely perform deck control through the FireWire cable. If you're using an analog or SDI interface, you'll need to string a serial cable between a serial port on your computer and a serial port on your deck. If your computer doesn't have a serial port, you can add a USB-to-serial converter to your system or you can install an internal PCI card with a serial port (or two) on it.

Audio Features

You might not have thought much about how a video deck handles audio, but as a rule, most of the audio you'll be working with when editing is production sound that comes, along with the video images, from your video deck. The higher the quality of your VTR, the more audio features it will come with. Audio level controls let you adjust the volume of sound as it comes into the VTR when recording. Audio level meters display the volume of the sound as the deck plays or records. This helps you identify whether the audio was recorded properly. Moreover, VTRs can differ in the types of audio I/O they offer. FireWire connectors include the digital audio signals, so FireWire decks have excellent quality audio I/O. Analog audio I/O can vary from very low-end composite connectors to high-quality XLR connectors. In addition, high-end decks offer AES/EBU or SP/DIF digital audio I/O.

VTR Checklist

Here are some questions to ask yourself before you start shopping for a video deck:

- **Will I be using this deck to create my final master?** If so, you'll want the best quality you can afford. If you shot DV, this means a DVCAM or DVCPro deck. These higher-end decks offer a very stable playback and recording architecture, which results in higher picture quality.
- **Will I be making lots of edits onto tape, or simply outputting my projects as one single edit?** If you chose the former, you'll need a deck that's *frame accurate*, a feature found only on higher-end VTRs.
- **What existing equipment do I need to be able to work with?** Do you need a deck with a FireWire connection, or do you need a deck with SDI connectors to interface with a high-end video capture board, or do you need analog component inputs and outputs? Does the audio I/O offered by the VTR match your needs?

- **Do I need an upgrade path to high-end equipment?** Some FireWire-equipped decks offer an upgrade path to SDI, others don't. If you think this is where your production is headed, don't lock yourself in to low-end equipment that you'll later have to replace. Similarly, don't waste money on high-end equipment that might be overkill for your project.

Whatever your answers to the preceding questions, the purchase of a video deck always involves weighing price versus performance.

Back to Front

The best way to see if a piece of equipment is right for your needs is to look at the rear panel. Usually, this is where all the hardware connectors reside. If the connector you need isn't there, the deck might not support it (see Figure 12.6).

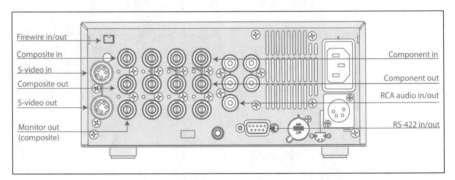

FIGURE 12.6 A diagram of the rear view of a typical professional VTR.

VTR CLEANING AND MAINTENANCE

Dust and other particles of debris inside your VTR can lead to drop-outs and glitches on your videotape. The smaller your tape format, the more destructive dust can be to the video signal. Most VTR manufacturers make head-cleaning products specifically designed for their VTRs. Cleaning the heads of your VTR should be done no more frequently than every 50 hours of use. A head-cleaning cassette works by running an abrasive material across the playback and record heads in your VTR. Overuse of head-cleaning cassettes can result in unnecessary wear and tear on the heads. After inserting the head-cleaning cassette, press Play or Record, depending on which head you want to clean. Be sure to stop the cleaning cassette after five seconds—the abrasiveness of the cleaning cassette generates heat and can actually damage the innards of your VTR. Never reuse the cleaning cassette once it reaches the end—it's the equivalent of washing with a dirty sponge. Always refer to your owner's manual for specific cleaning instructions before attempting to clean your VTR. In addition, remember that prevention is the best medicine, and keep your workspace free from smoke and dust.

Audio Equipment

As with video, using the analog audio inputs or outputs on any of your digital decks, cameras, or your computer will result in a digital to analog (D/A) conversion that might lower your audio quality. However, digital audio isn't an absolute necessity—good analog I/O using balanced XLR cables will prove satisfactory for most productions.

In general, the audio that you'll edit with will come from audio CD, DAT, or MiniDisc.

Audio CDs

An external audio CD deck is unnecessary these days because your computer most likely has a CD-ROM or DVD-ROM drive in it that you can use to import audio tracks from a CD. This is the best way to get audio from a CD into an editing system—if you lose your audio media you can easily reconstruct your tracks by re-importing the track from the CD and reconnecting the media in your editing application. If you digitize your audio CDs from a CD player, you won't be able to automatically reconstruct lost media, and you might be subjecting your audio to at least one unnecessary digital-to-analog conversion.

DAT and MiniDisc

You'll need a DAT or MiniDisc player if your production audio was recorded on either of those formats. As with VTRs, just because DAT and MiniDisc are digital formats does not mean that all DAT and MiniDisc decks have digital I/O—in fact, many of them don't. If they do have digital I/O, they probably use the SP/DIF or AES/EBU interface—formats that are unlikely to be supported by the video capture board in your editing system unless you have a high-end system with a hardware break-out box or break-out cable. If the only connector in your editing system is a

FireWire interface, you'll have to send the audio through a FireWire deck in order to capture it, or have the DAT or MiniDisc audio digitally dubbed to a DV format video cassette. You won't lose quality if you maintain the original sampling ratio.

Using Audio from MP3 Files

If you want to use audio from an MP3 player, be aware that not all players let you copy MP3 files to your computer. In theory, if you managed to get the MP3 file on there in the first place, you probably have a copy of it laying around somewhere. Most video editing programs don't accept MP3 files, so you'll need to convert your MP3 audio to AIFF. Technically, you'll take a quality hit here, though it may not be perceptible. If the MP3 in question was originally converted from a CD, it would be best to go back to the original CD and convert the track to AIFF from there.

Grounding Your Electronic Equipment

Heavy-duty electronic equipment, such as video editing system hardware, should always be grounded. This means using three-prong AC cables plugged into a grounded (three-prong) outlet. Some video decks also have an extra ground wiring input.

Audio Mixers

Audio mixers can save you the hassle of having to constantly recable your system every time you change audio sources. You probably have only one pair of speakers, but you might have a digital video deck, maybe an audio deck, a VHS deck, and the sound that comes out of your computer. By connecting all of these components to the mixer, and then connecting the mixer to the speakers, you can switch between one piece of hardware and another in an instant.

Mixers not only help you keep control of all of the sounds that go out to the speakers, they also give you control over the sounds that go into your computer or decks by offering *equalization*, *balance*, and *gain control*. In Chapter 13, "Preparing to Edit," we'll talk more about how EQ, balance, and gain control can be used to help improve problem audio while you capture.

As with the other hardware components, mixers can be digital, analog or both (Figure 12.7). You can now get mixers that connect to your computer via FireWire (Figure 15.2).

Speakers

Because the line-level audio that comes out of your computer or mixer isn't pre-amplified, it needs to be connected to either *self-powered speakers* that are capable of amplification, or standard speakers that are hooked up to an *amplifier*.

FIGURE 12.7   A typical analog eight-channel audio mixer, the Tascam M-08.

Self-powered speakers each have their own power supply. They fall into two categories: multimedia speakers that are sold for computer systems, and professional editing system speakers. If you want to use the type of speakers that come with a home stereo system, you can purchase an amplifier and hook the speakers up through it, or use your home stereo itself, by sending the audio from your computer or mixer through the Video/Auxiliary input. (Most newer home stereos will have this input.)

VIDEO MONITORS

A video monitor is a crucial component of every editing system. If you're using a FireWire-based DV editing system, you must have a video monitor to see full-motion, full-res video (don't rely on the LCD screen on your camera, it's simply not good enough). If you've ever looked at DV footage on a video monitor played directly off tape, you'll quickly see how different it looks from the version you see in your computer monitors or the playback in your camera's LCD monitor. Unfortunately, DV often looks better on your computer screen or camera LCD display—in order to know what kind of color correction and image enhancements your video needs, you need to see the real thing on a video monitor.

If you're using an analog digitizing system you'll need a video monitor to see a more accurate, interlaced output of your video. NTSC video is particularly notorious for its poor capability to handle saturated colors. Using bright colors that aren't *NTSC legal* is a common mistake—the saturated reds that look great on a computer screen will bleed, flicker, and generally look awful on an NTSC monitor. (PAL shares these problems, but to a lesser degree.) Having an NTSC/PAL playback monitor next to your computer monitor lets you keep track of how well your video is holding up, and is essential when adjusting color or creating graphics, special effects, or animations that will be output to tape.

Finally, if you are editing HD or HDV format video, you'll need an HD monitor to see the full-resolution, full-motion version of your footage. Filmmakers are often surprised—sometimes unpleasantly—at the level of detail visible in an uncompressed HD image. That electrical tape or microphone cable lying on the floor can become glaringly apparent. True HD monitors are one of the most expensive parts of the editing workstation equation. However, Blackmagic Design offers a product called HDlink that converts an Apple Cinema Display into a true HD monitor. Apple Cinema displays aren't exactly cheap either but they are cheaper than HD monitors and you save some money by having a single monitor.

Hot Air

The equipment described in this chapter, along with your computer processor and storage drives, can add up to a lot of hot air in the editing room. Invest in air-conditioning if you live in a warmer climate—your equipment will perform better, your computer will be less prone to crashing, and you'll be more comfortable.

Professional Video Monitor Features

Like all video equipment, professional video monitors offer extra controls and features that go beyond the typical consumer television monitor. Here's what you can get for the extra cash:

Better video quality: We're not just being snobs here, even a lower-end professional monitor will usually deliver much better quality than the average television can. Professional NTSC/PAL monitors have a horizontal line resolution ranging from 400 to 800 lines, which (simply put) means they are better than most consumer-grade monitors.

High-end I/O: Just like professional VTRs, pro monitors can have analog Y/C, analog component, and SDI I/O.

Switchable aspect ratios: Many pro monitors can switch between 4:3 and 16:9—a boon for projects shot with anamorphic lenses or on HD, although the image will be letterboxed (Figure 12.8). If you want a bigger image size, you'll have to spring for a true widescreen HD monitor like the one in Figure 12.9.

FIGURE 12.8   A typical professional NTSC/PAL monitor from JVC that supports both standard and widescreen footage.

FIGURE 12.9   A professional HD monitor from Sony designed specially for editing work.

NTSC/PAL compatibility: Many pro monitors can switch between NTSC and PAL. This is a great asset if you shoot your DV film in PAL but need to view NTSC video supporting materials such as trailers, press kits, and so forth.

Input switching: Most pro monitors allow for more than one input source, allowing you to switch from the "A" source, usually your NLE, to the "B" source, usually your primary VTR. This can be useful if you output your project to tape and want to compare what your computer is sending out to what your video deck is actually recording. *(Note: This doesn't work for DV-format editing systems, since all of your video will be coming through your VTR.)*

DV Decompression

A hardware transcoder, or "media converter" such as the Canopus ADVC-110, will let you capture analog formats through your FireWire port, and will also help you save wear and tear on your digital camera if you don't own a video deck. Because the transcoder can convert the digital information coming out of your computer into an analog signal for your video monitor, you won't have to use your camera or deck to preview your edits.

Underscan, horizontal delay, and vertical delay: These features let you troubleshoot any video signal problems you might be having.

Cheap Trick

If you can't afford to spend the money on a professional video monitor, you can settle for a cheap consumer television set. Just make sure it has the right inputs to work with your system. If you can afford it, at least spend the money for a TV with S-video input. The improvement in quality is worth the money.

HARDWARE CONNECTORS

The cables that connect the various parts of your editing system together serve to transport the video and/or audio signals from component to component, and are the key to maintaining signal integrity. Figure 12.10 shows the most common cables you'll encounter. Varying configurations of *BNC* cables are used to carry SDI and HD-SDI video, analog component video, analog composite video, AES/EBU digital audio, black burst, and VITC timecode signals. *RCA* cables are used to carry analog composite video, SP-DIF digital audio, analog audio signals, and LTC timecode signals. *XLR* cables are used to carry analog audio and AES/EBU digital audio signals. *Mini* cables carry mono or stereo consumer analog audio signals and the Sony LANC format device control signal. *1/4"* or *phono* cables are used to carry mono or stereo analog audio signals, particularly to and from headphones. *RS-422* (not shown) and *RS-232* (not shown) cables are used for serial device control. Proprietary *S-video* cables carry the Y/C video signal. Last but not least, 4- and 6-pin *FireWire* (a.k.a. IE1394) cables are used to carry DV video and audio, DV timecode, and DV device control signals.

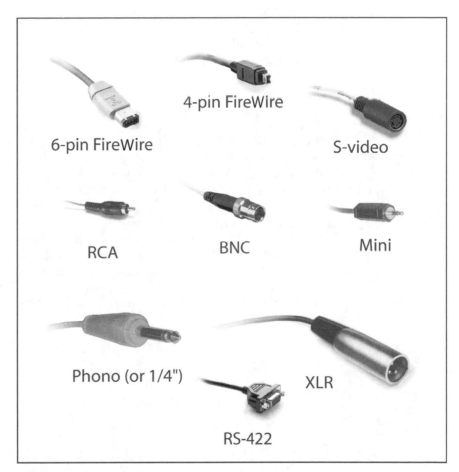

FIGURE 12.10   Standard video and audio cables.

Exercise: Hardware Checklist Before You Start

Before you begin your editing project, be sure to consult the following list to determine what components your particular project will require:

- Video decks (a.k.a. VTRs)
- Digital audio decks
- Video monitor

- Speakers
- Waveform monitor and vectorscope
- Switcher, router, and/or patch bay
- Audio mixer
- Transcoder
- Black burst generator
- Battery backup
- Cables and connectors

SUMMARY

If you've been shooting on DV and plan to edit on your computer using a FireWire interface, then your video hardware needs are fairly simple. At the very least, you'll need a good external video monitor, a set of speakers, preferably a deck for playback (rather than your camera), and all the right cables to connect it together. HDV is similar although a true HD video monitor can be a big expense.

If you want to go higher-end, you're going to have to spend a lot more money. Purchasing audio and video hardware is a lot like buying a car. You should research your options and the market thoroughly before you dive in. Consider rental equipment the equivalent of a test drive—you might save yourself the trauma of a dozen little nasty surprises later.

PREPARING TO EDIT

In This Chapter

G etting ready to edit is a three-part process: organizing your project, logging your tapes, and capturing media. It's also the part of
the process that is the most prone to problems, whether technical
or creative. Mistakes and judgment errors made at this stage of editing
might stick with you for the duration of your post-production phase, so
read this chapter carefully.

HOW TO ORGANIZE YOUR PROJECT

Because a typical editing project can contain hundreds of separate pieces
of media—video clips, audio clips, still images, and computer-generated
media—spread among dozens of tapes, disks, and hard drives, it's crucial
to have a cataloging system that lets you find any piece of media quickly
and easily.

Imagine this scenario: You've just finished whittling 30 hours of dailies
into a 90-minute feature film. You're about to output a master onto a rented
Digital Betacam deck (about $900/day) when your computer crashes. After
you restart, you realize that about thirty percent of your media is corrupted
or missing. What do you do?

If your project is well organized, you will probably be able to reconstruct your edited sequence in a few hours, possibly even using batch operations. If not, you'll have to reconstruct from memory. Depending on
the degree of disorganization, you might have to scroll through several
tapes to find the correct shots, recapture your footage, and so on. The resulting cleanup job could take days or even weeks.

The longer and more complex your project, the more likely it is that
you'll encounter problems such as corrupted or lost media, the need to
recapture or work on a different non-linear editing system, and the need
to conform your footage to multiple mastering formats such as broadcast
television, theatrical projection, or streaming Web media.

Even without these extreme troubles, staying organized will speed
your editing, and make later changes easier.

Create a Numbering System

As you capture video and audio into a project, your editing software will
prompt you to enter the name of the tape from which you are capturing.
If you ever need to recapture that media, the editing application will ask
for the specific tape by name. For that reason, it's crucial to give each
tape a unique name. The simplest way to do this is to number the tapes
consecutively.

When you import digital files, such as still images, audio from CD, or
effects shots that were created on a computer, the editing application will

use the existing filename and keep track of where it is on your drives. If you end up moving the file to another folder, the NLE will ask you where the file went. As a result, it's important to know the name of the file and also the location. Many applications will let you change the name of the file once you've imported it into a project, but the name of the original file on your drives will remain unchanged. This can lead to much confusion, so it's best to name your digital files intelligently from the beginning.

In addition, because there is always a chance that you might need to move your project to a high-end editing system for image enhancement before mastering, we recommend following the naming conventions used by many of those high-end systems: Use tape names or numbers of six characters or less and avoid spaces or other special characters. The reason for this is that there's a good chance that some piece of software down the line will cut off part of the name, or change the spaces into underscores.

Keep your names simple: AA0001 for your first tape, where AA is your code for the project. If you want to call your first tape "1," do yourself a favor and call it 000001. Write this number on the tape itself, not just the tape box. From that point on, label and number every piece of media that comes into your project—whether it's a DV tape, an audio CD, or a still photograph—*before* you start working with it.

Make Sure All Your Videotape Has Timecode

Every piece of video that goes into your editing system should have timecode. Without timecode, your computer will have no way of keeping track of where a particular clip is on a videotape. For the most part, only consumer videotape formats do not have timecode. It's generally worth the trouble to dub any non-timecoded media to a cheap timecoded format, like DV. What timecode is and how it works is explained in detail in the "Timecode" section later in this chapter.

Keep a Database of All Your Media

Your editing software will keep track of the tape name, timecode information, and comments for every clip in your project. At times, other people in your production might need access to this information—for example, your graphics person might need to know which take of a shot you're using. If so, you can usually print out a report from your editing software, called a *batch list.*

Before you start editing, you should also develop some keywords that will be assigned to clips. Keywords allow you to easily sift and filter your media bins to find categories of clips. Keywords can be an invaluable tool for organizing, logging, and finding shots later in the editing process.

Consider using the names of characters, topics in a documentary, the scene numbers or locations.

Storing Your Media

Remember, most digital media is magnetic, and as such, it should be treated with care. Keep it away from monitors, speakers, CPUs, carpeting, and video decks. Store your tapes in the plastic boxes they came in for extra safety.

Log Each Tape Thoroughly

By logging all of the shots, even the ones that you don't plan to capture, you'll have an accurate description of what's on each tape. This information can be a valuable resource later. For detailed instructions on how to log tapes using editing software, check out the "Logging and Basic Capturing" tutorial later in this chapter.

Use the Organizational Tools of Your Editing Software

It's a good idea to create a separate bin (or folder) for each source tape in your project. That way, if you want a reminder of what's on a particular tape, you can simply open that tape's source bin and see a list of all the shots on the tape. Figure 13.1 shows a Final Cut Pro bin that displays all of the information that was logged with each shot. As you can see, there's a lot of information there besides the tape name, timecode, and logger's comments—much of this information was added automatically by Final Cut Pro.

FIGURE 13.1 A Final Cut Pro bin in text view shows a complete tape log including clip name, tape name, start and end timecode, clip duration, the types of tracks contained in the clip and how the video was compressed.

Last but not least, sometimes it's important to keep your editing project from getting too big. If you have 50 tapes, and a bin for each tape in the project, plus some work bins and a bunch of edited sequences, your project file might grow to monstrous proportions. In this case, you should consider creating one project with all of your source tape logs and another with all of your rough cuts and work bins (or "selects" bins)—bins that contain copies of all the shots you're planning to use in a particular sequence, and so forth.

TIMECODE

One of the most common questions about video editing is, "why is timecode so important?"

If you've ever scrolled through a six-hour VHS tape looking for that TV show you missed a couple of weeks ago, you can appreciate the value of timecode. As you might have noticed, every time you remove the tape or turn the power off on your home VHS deck, the time counter resets itself to zero. As you scroll forward through a few hours worth of tape, the counter advances as expected. However, if you eject the tape and then put it back in, the counter will read zero, even though the tape was wound forward past the two-hour mark.

With timecode, if you're two hours into the tape when you insert it, the counter on the deck will read two hours. If you're 1 hour, 10 minutes, 3 seconds and 20 frames into the tape, the counter will read 01:10:03:20. Whenever the counter displays that number, you'll see the exact same frame on the tape. Not only does this make it easier for you and your editing system to find stuff on your tapes, it also makes it possible for the video deck to access any individual frame on the tape automatically, thanks to device control commands sent from your computer.

This fine level of control means that, with the right deck, you can accurately insert scenes or capture footage from any point on the tape. This allows you to reconstruct your edited sequence at any time. For moving a project from workstation to workstation, recreating a project after media has been lost or damaged, or recapturing media at a higher resolution, timecode is essential. (We'll talk more about low- and high-capture resolutions later in this chapter.)

Drop Frame and Non-Drop Frame Timecode

Because the frame rate of analog NTSC video is an odd 29.97 frames per second, *drop frame timecode* was developed to help round off the fractional frames to less awkward whole numbers. With drop frame timecode, the frame itself is not dropped, just that frame's number in the timecode counter. In other words, the frame rate is still 29.97 fps, but the counter is counting at 30 fps and making up for it by skipping a frame number every now and then.

Drop frame timecode is usually indicated with semicolons separating the hours, minutes, seconds, and frames—01;00;00;00. *Non-drop frame timecode* is indicated by colons—01:00:00:00. Unfortunately, this is not a standardized feature outside the realm of professional editing equipment, and not all VTRs display timecode in this manner.

Drop frame timecode is the standard for analog and digital 29.97 fps video for broadcast television in America, but if your project somehow ends up with non-drop frame timecode, don't panic—just make a note on the tape's label. Whether you choose to work in drop frame or non-drop frame doesn't matter, as long as others know which one you're using.

Timecode Standards

Just as there are different standards for video, there are several standards for timecode:

- **SMPTE timecode** is the professional industry standard in the United States, set up by the Society of Motion Picture and Television Engineers (SMPTE). All professional NTSC and HD equipment uses SMPTE timecode.
- **EBU timecode** is the European cousin of SMPTE timecode, used by all professional PAL equipment and set up by the European Broadcasters Union (EBU).
- **DV timecode (DVTC)** is the format developed by Sony for DV tapes, and only the DV format uses DVTC—not the DVCAM and DVCPro formats. If you plan to use only DV equipment, DVTC will be an acceptable alternative to SMPTE or EBU timecode. As the popularity of the DV format increases, DVTC is becoming more integrated into the realm of professional post-production.
- **RC timecode** is a format Sony developed for use with consumer Hi8 equipment. For all practical purposes, it is obsolete, but if you're planning to remain in an RCTC environment, it will do the job.

How Timecode Is Stored on Videotape

Timecode can be stored in a number of physical locations on the videotape:

- **Address track timecode (a.k.a. Vertical Integrated Timecode or VITC)** is encoded as a separate signal, in addition to the video and audio signals on a tape. It's the best of the three types of timecode listed here because it's invisible, accurate, doesn't interfere with the video image, and leaves all of the audio tracks available for audio.

- **Audio track timecode (a.k.a. Longitudinal Timecode or LTC)** is stored on one of the audio channels on a videotape. If you're working with a videotape format that doesn't support SMPTE or EBU timecode, such as VHS or DV, you can use one of the tape's audio channels to store SMPTE or EBU timecode. Of course, that means you can't store audio on that channel and you'll need an editing system that can understand audio track timecode.
- **Window burn timecode (a.k.a. Burn-in Timecode or BITC)** is usually reserved for work copies of master tapes because it's burned into the video image itself and isn't removable. Window burn timecode is commonly used for editing projects shot and finished on film or for low-res worktapes of HD footage.

Calibrating Timecode

If you're using a deck that uses serial device control (as opposed to FireWire), then some editing systems such as Apple's Final Cut Pro recommend that you "calibrate" the timecode before you start logging, and every time you change to a different video deck. Refer to your user manual for more information.

Keycode: Timecode for Film Sources

The film equivalent of timecode is called *keycode*. Each frame of film has a keycode number that is embedded on the film negative by the lab where the film stock originated (e.g., Kodak, Fuji, etc.). After the shoot, the negative is processed at a lab, and a film-to-video transfer is made, known as a *telecine transfer*. If you are planning to finish on film, the keycode numbers are very important—you'll need them in order to generate a *cut list* that will be used to by a negative cutter to edit the film negative prior to creating a final film print. The standard procedure is to add the keycode numbers to your videotapes in the form of window burn, along with window burn of the address track timecode that's been recorded on the telecine master (Figure 13.2). (It is standard to use non-drop frame timecode for film sources.) With both the keycode numbers and the source tape timecode numbers visible as window burn, it will be easier to check the accuracy of your cut list later on. Cut lists and film finishing are discussed in more detail in Chapter 19, "Output." Since the keycode is permanently superimposed over the video, this option is only viable if you are planning to eventually go back to film. If possible, you can have the window burned keycode and timecode placed outside of the image in the black letterboxed portion of the frame so that it doesn't overlap with the image. If you're not planning to go back to film, it isn't necessary to keep track of keycode numbers.

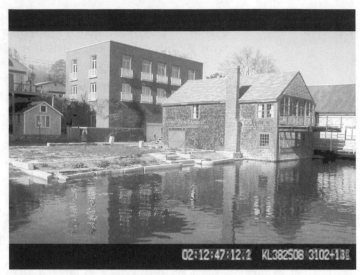

FIGURE 13.2 A typical frame of film transferred to video via telecine. Timecode and keycode numbers are "burned" into the image in the black letterboxed portion of the frame.

24 FPS EDITING AND 3:2 PULLDOWN

3:2 pull-down refers to the way in which 24 fps film or HD footage is transferred to 29.97 fps analog NTSC videotape. The first frame of film is "pulled down" to the first *two* fields of video, the second frame of film is pulled down to the next *three* fields of video, and so on (Figure 13.3). Unfortunately, in the resulting video a clean edit can only be made at every fifth video frame. Editing applications that support 24-fps editing use a *reverse telecine* process to provide an environment where edits can be made at each film frame.

Just to make things even more complicated, to achieve the 29.97 native frame rate of analog NTSC video, the film picture is slowed down .1% during the telecine process, to 23.976 fps. If you have synched audio transferred with your film to videotape, the audio will also be slowed down .1%, but if you have your film transferred to video without sound and capture the sound separately, you'll have to slow it down by .1% yourself in order for it to sync up with your telecined film.

If you're editing with PAL video, there usually is no pull-down process. The standard method is to transfer each frame of 24-fps film or HD video to one frame of 25-fps PAL video and accept the fact that it will play slightly faster at 25 fps during the editing process. Later, when you go back to film or 24-fps HD, the speed will return to normal. Many people consider the speed difference between 24 fps and 25 fps unnoticeable.

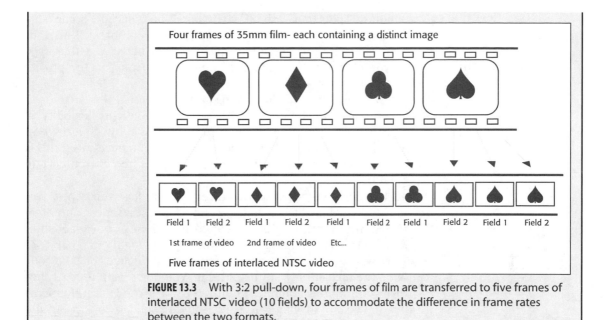

Four frames of 35mm film- each containing a distinct image

Field 1   Field 2   Field 1   Field 2   Field 1   Field 2   Field 1   Field 2   Field 1   Field 2

1st frame of video   2nd frame of video   Etc...

Five frames of interlaced NTSC video

FIGURE 13.3   With 3:2 pull-down, four frames of film are transferred to five frames of interlaced NTSC video (10 fields) to accommodate the difference in frame rates between the two formats.

LOGGING

Before you ever start editing your footage, you will have to *log* your tapes. Logging is the process of looking through each tape to determine which scenes, takes, and shots you will capture. Although much maligned as tedious and time-consuming, logging tapes is really the first step in the editing process. Whoever logs the camera-original tapes is, to some extent, deciding what will end up in the final project. The logger also, indirectly, decides which shots to leave out.

Following these technical tips can save time and frustration in the editing room, both now and later:

Log first, and then capture. Logging your tapes lets you skip unusable takes that would waste disk space if captured. Usually, it's best to log all the takes, whether good or bad, during a first pass. Then, you can capture only the good takes during a second pass. This way, you have a complete log of your tapes and can later easily grab additional takes.

Avoid logging across timecode breaks. The biggest troublemakers, when it comes to logging and capturing, are timecode breaks. Any section on the tape that displays no timecode in your deck's counter is a break. (We discuss how to avoid these in Chapter 8, "Shooting Digital Video.") Unfortunately, timecode breaks often go by so fast that you can't see them—some pro VTR models have "timecode indicator" lights that flash off when there's no timecode. Some editing applications cannot capture across timecode breaks; instead, they will stop capturing and display an error message. Other apps let you choose to "capture across timecode breaks" in the project capture settings.

Log with "handles." It's best to log each shot with a few seconds of padding at the head and tail. These *handles* give you flexibility to extend a shot or add dissolves. Some programs allow you to set up a predetermined handle length for your shots. In most cases, this is a bad idea unless you are positive your tape is free from timecode breaks.

Avoid logging extremely long takes. As you log your tapes, you might find yourself faced with a seemingly endless series of uninterrupted multiple takes. Rather than logging these as one giant shot, it's better to pick the best useable sections and log them separately. After you decide which take to use, you can delete, or take "offline," the media that you're not using. You don't want to log a shot that's ten minutes long if you only use five seconds of it. Remember, the goal of logging is to make some initial decisions about the content of your project. While it's nice to have lots of choices in the editing room, too many choices can bog down the editing process.

Log the blue-screen correction shot. If you're logging blue-screen footage, log the empty blue-screen shots that either proceed or follow each shot. These are important for compositing.

How to Log by Content

When logging, you should think about the footage that you'll need to properly edit each scene. If you're logging tapes that were shot film-style—in other words, with slates, scene numbers, and script supervisor notes—your job will be relatively simple: just look at each slate and name each shot accordingly. However, if you're logging something that couldn't be meticulously organized on the set, like a typical documentary shoot, you might benefit from the following tips:

Log the dialog first. Dialog is the framework of any scene, whether scripted or documentary. If the camera work is bad but the audio is good, it might be worth logging the shot as a backup.

Log cutaways that go with the dialog. These are usually reaction shots of the other characters in the scene. Sometimes, cutaways will be on the tape before or after the scene itself.

Log all the "action." Log all of the action necessary to complete a scene. For example, if a scene involves two people going out to dinner, make sure you get all of the "action" or movement in the scene (entering the restaurant, sitting, ordering, etc.). Make sure that you have all of the moments that set up the scene and that define how the characters are arranged physically.

If you're logging interviews, log each Q&A as a single clip. In other words, keep the question and the answer together, rather than only getting the answer, and don't include more than one question and one answer in a single clip.

Log the establishing and/or wide shots that set up the scene. Log all the "b-roll" or scenery shots of the location.

Log any particularly nice or interesting-looking shots. The camera operator might have shot something that's not in the script but that will prove useful later.

Log some "room tone." Room tone is the background sound at a location—whether it's party chatter or what sounds like "silence." You might need it for audio editing. Hopefully, the person who recorded the room tone voice-slated it so that you know what it is—room tone, naturally, often sounds like nothing.

TUTORIAL   **LOGGING AND BASIC CAPTURING**

Logging and capturing can be a simple process, once you've tried it a couple of times. Before you start this tutorial, check your editing software user manual to make sure you have all the correct settings for your particular system. This tutorial is designed to work with any standard non-linear editing application, such as those listed in Chapter 11, "Non-linear Editing Software."

Step 1: Open Your Capture Utility

Launch your editing software, open a new project, and navigate to the capture utility. Use the tape transport controls to find the first shot you want to log. The tape transport controls are a set of buttons that look just like those on a VCR: Play, Pause, Record, Fast Forward, and Rewind (Figure 13.4).

Step 2: Select a Clip

Find the *in-point* of your shot. The in-point is the first frame that you want to capture. Set the in-point using your software's controls. Most editing applications let you press "I" on your keyboard to set an in-point. You should see the timecode from your tape appear in the window next to the "In." Compare this timecode to the timecode reading on your deck or camera to ensure they match. Be sure to give a few seconds of *handles* if possible. You also need to be careful to leave enough *pre-roll* for your video deck. (See "Logging" earlier in this chapter if you don't know what

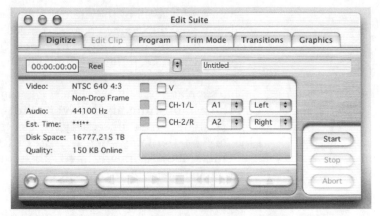

FIGURE 13.4 Most capture utilities let you adjust video and audio settings and provide tape transport controls similar to those on a VCR.

handles and pre-roll are.) Now, find the out-point and set it by typing "O" or clicking the "Out" button on your interface. Again, check your time-code. Don't forget to leave a couple of seconds of handles at the tail.

Step 3: Log the Clip

Now you need to enter a name for your shot. Most NLEs also allow you to add other information: the shot number, the take number, whether the take is good (g) or not good (ng), and comments. If you have keywords for your project, you can also add them here. Click on the button that says "log" to log the clip and add it to the bin. Note, however, that the clip has *not* been digitized. It is an *off-line* clip, but the computer knows exactly where it is located on the tape if it needs to be captured (Figure 13.5).

Step 4: Log the Rest of the Tape

Repeat this process until you've logged all of the desired shots on this tape. As you go through the tape, make a note of any quality changes or problems: drastic changes in lighting, changes in audio levels, and so forth. You might need to capture those shots separately so that you can adjust their audio and video levels independently.

Correcting Video and Audio Problems during Capture

If your non-linear editing software offers advanced controls during capture, you might want to check out the .pdf file called "Advanced Capturing" in the Chapter 13 folder on the companion DVD. You'll learn advanced techniques for setting video and audio levels and how to correct technical problems during capture.

ON THE DVD

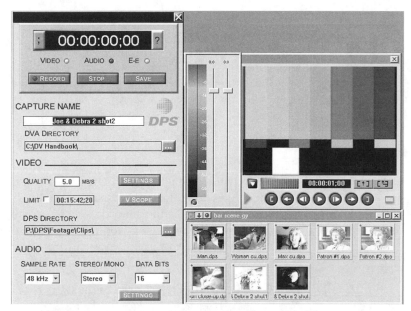

FIGURE 13.5   In addition to standard capture controls, high-end capture utilities display incoming video, audio levels and timecode and, they offer a digital waveform monitor and vectorscope to help you adjust luminance, hue, black levels, and gain on input.

Step 5: Select Capture Settings

Once you get to the end of the tape, tell the software to "batch capture." It will then work its way through the list of logged shots and capture each. Depending on your editing system, you might need to specify the resolution at which you want to capture. You also need to pick an audio sampling rate—48 kHz is the norm. Whatever you choose, make sure you stick with it throughout your project. Many editing applications let you save these preferences.

Calculate Available Disk Space before You Capture

There's nothing more frustrating than running out of room on your hard drive before you've captured all your material. Advance calculation of how much media will fit on your drives will save you from such hassles.

Step 6: Batch Capture

Before you press the Capture button, you should quit any background applications and turn off any networking functions that are not governed by your editing application. Once your system starts capturing, you can take a coffee break while the machines work. It's a good idea to not go too far away, however—editing systems tend to be fussy about capturing, and you might find an error message upon your return, instead of a bin full of media. If so, see the "Troubleshooting" section later in this chapter for tips on how to avoid logging/capturing errors. ✄

CAPTURING QUALITY

Of all the types of media you'll encounter in an editing room, the most complicated is videotape, because it's really three things bundled together: video, audio, and timecode. We've already talked about timecode in detail; now it's time to talk about video and audio and how to preserve their quality as you capture it into your non-linear editing system.

How Good Does Your Project Need to Look?

If you're editing a home video, the answer might be "Not very," but if you're editing a feature film shot on DV and you hope to transfer it to 35mm, the answer is "As good as possible." Always keep the end product in mind when you capture—you'll avoid worrying unnecessarily about image quality if it's not a big concern, and you'll also avoid having to re-capture everything if quality is crucial for you.

Digital Online and Offline

Although you might be used to the terms *online* and *offline* when talking about the Internet, those terms have a very different meaning to a video editor. Understanding the difference between online and offline editing is essential to understanding how to get the best possible quality when editing.

The concept of offline editing developed in the early days of television. Editing a rough cut with low-quality work tapes saved the camera-original masters from wear and tear due to heavy use and avoided *generation loss*. A typical project was shot on a high-quality tape format and then transferred with matching timecode to a lower-quality format for editing. Once the picture was locked, the project was then reconstructed using an expensive, high-quality editing system and the camera-original tapes.

Today, the offline/online workflow is primarily used for 35mm film projects and HD projects. With both formats, it is much easier and cheaper to edit with standard definition (SD) worktapes that have matching timecode and/or window burn (and in the case of film, keycode numbers). The cost of creating a set of worktapes can be expensive, but you'll save money by not having to edit on a native HD editing system that requires lots of computer processing power, high-speed disk storage, and expensive HD monitors. For film, the old-fashioned method of editing on film is so time consuming that it is almost never considered as a viable option anymore.

Offline Resolution

Another type of offline/online workflow involves the use of different capture resolutions. Offline-quality resolutions are the digital media equivalent of work tapes, but rather than preserving the quality of the camera-original tapes, they trade image quality for smaller file sizes, which in turn require less storage space. At the end of the editing process, the media is recaptured at the best possible online-quality resolution and then output to tape to create a final master (Figure 13.6).

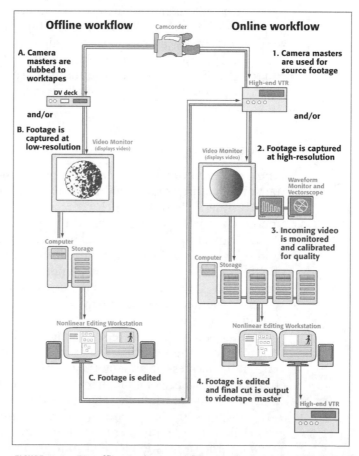

FIGURE 13.6 For offline/online workflows, camera original media is dubbed to worktapes and capture, possibly with a low-res CODEC. After editing, the footage is recaptured at high-res from the camera-original master tapes.

Sometimes, this recapturing process is done on the same system that was used to create the offline edit, and sometimes it's done on a much higher quality system. Because the media is only captured twice, the risk of wear and tear on the tapes is relatively small, so whether the camera-original tapes are analog or digital, there's rarely a need for a special set of work tapes. However tiny, miniDV tapes are quite fragile and if you can afford it, creating a set of *clones*—identical dupes of your masters is not a bad idea.

AUDIO QUALITY

When it comes to audio, the decision to capture your video footage at a high resolution or a low resolution is immaterial. That's because *nobody* recaptures their audio—at least not if they can avoid it.

Since audio files are much smaller, there's simply no good reason to capture low-quality audio. Even more importantly, by the time you get to the point of recapturing video at a high resolution, someone (probably you) has spent a lot of time editing the audio tracks, which includes setting the levels to get a rough sound mix. To recapture the audio might mean that you'd have to reset all the levels, a process that could be very time consuming.

Audio Levels

The perception of audio is very subjective, and what sounds loud to one person might not sound loud to another. The loudness of audio is measured in decibels (dB), which represent a subjective scale: an audible increase in loudness means that the volume of the audio has increased 1 dB. Software and hardware manufacturers put dB increments on the audio level meters that are a part of the equipment (Figure 13.7), but 1 dB on your video deck might sound louder than 1 dB in your editing application. Unfortunately, this is a good introduction to the ambiguities you'll encounter when working with audio. Despite attempts to define it, sound is very subjective.

Analog audio level meters, like the one in Figure 13.7a, place 0 dB in the middle of the scale. That's because 0 dB doesn't mean total silence; rather, it indicates the midpoint in the range of loudness and softness that this particular piece of equipment can handle. Digital audio meters place 0 dB at the top of the scale (Figure 13.7b), and the midpoint is placed at −12, −14, or −20 dB, depending on the manufacturer. Because it varies from one piece of equipment to another, this midpoint is also referred to as *unity*. The sounds louder and softer than unity might vary from one piece of equipment to another, but the sounds that fall exactly at unity should have the same volume on any piece of hardware or software.

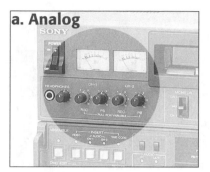 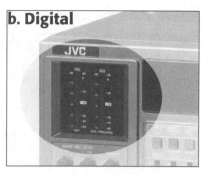

FIGURE 13.7   Hardware-based audio level meters can be analog (a) or digital (b).

You might be wondering how exactly that can work. It works because you, the editor, will use a 60 Hz audio reference tone to tell the equipment exactly how unity should sound. In Chapter 8 ("Shooting Digital Video") and Chapter 9 ("Production Sound"), you learned about the importance of recording bars and tone at the head of every tape. When you play a tape with tone at the head, the audio level meters on your video deck and in your software capture utility will indicate where on the dB scale that tone falls.

When capturing audio, you should adjust the level sliders in your capture utility until the tone rests at unity, and leave them there during capture until you change tapes. You'll have to reset the audio levels for each tape. If the audio was recorded properly, this process will ensure good audio levels for your captured media.

Clipping and Distortion

You might be wondering what that red area on the audio level meter is. To simplify, it shows sounds that are very loud. Digital and analog audio levels differ when it comes to this portion of the dynamic range. Basically, it's perfectly natural that very loud sounds—a door slamming, for example—go to the top of the scale, or *peak*.

With digital audio, the red area should be avoided at all costs, because digital audio that's too loud gets *clipped.* Instead of distorting, the loud parts of the audio signal will simply get cut off. If, for example, the sound of a man yelling peaks, the high frequencies will get clipped, but the lower frequencies that aren't as loud will remain. The result will be a very strange sounding yell (Figure 13.8a).

In analog audio, as long as only a few extremely loud noises go into the red, your audio will sound okay. If the sound goes beyond what your equipment or speakers can handle, you'll hear *distortion* (Figure 13.8b). If this is the case, you should adjust the levels appropriately.

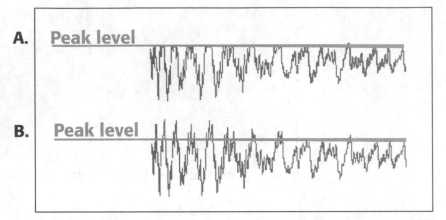

FIGURE 13.8 (a) Digital audio that goes above the peak level gets clipped. The part of the signal that is too loud simply doesn't play. (b) Analog audio that goes above the peak level gets distorted. The signal remains intact but it surpasses the capacity of the speakers.

Riding the Levels

Sometimes, the best solution to problems with audio levels is to adjust the levels on the fly as you capture, or ride the levels. If the levels are set perfectly except for one very loud sound five seconds into the clip, you can try to lower the levels for that sound and increase them again once it's over. The level sliders on an audio mixing board are designed to facilitate this process, but be aware that this process requires a gentle and conservative touch. If you ride the levels too aggressively, you'll hear it in your sound track, and correcting it in an editing application will be a nightmare.

So, what if you set the tone to unity and you still have sounds that go into the red and get clipped? That means that the audio wasn't recorded properly. Even though the sound recordist or camera operator added tone to the head of the tape, the audio itself was recorded with levels that were too high. You'll have to adjust the levels on your equipment accordingly.

Equalization

Adjusting the levels appropriately is the first crucial step in making sure that the audio you capture is of high quality. To improve your audio quality even further, you can apply *equalization*.

The sound of audio reference tone is a very simple sound—it only contains one 60 Hz frequency. However, most sounds in the natural world are complex and contain a range of frequencies. Think of them as a chord in music, rather than a single note. Equalizers let you control these different frequencies, boosting some and diminishing others (Figure 13.9).

FIGURE 13.9   On a hardware mixing board, EQ is adjusted with knobs that are easier and faster to work with than digital sliders. Each of the four knobs adjusts a different range of sounds.

When capturing audio, you shouldn't do much to the signal in terms of equalization; instead, you'll save the EQ for later, during the *mix*. For that reason, equalization is discussed in greater detail in Chapter 15, "Sound Editing." However, there are times when you will adjust the equalization as you capture: when you need to globally enhance a specific type of audio that you'll be using extensively in your project, and when you need to correct problem sound.

If you're capturing a type of sound that you'll be using throughout your project, like a voice-over recording, it might be beneficial to determine the type of equalization that sounds best, and adjust the EQ on input. It's much easier to make a global adjustment of the EQ settings when you capture than to go through your entire edited project later and adjust each piece individually. Moreover, if you have a mixing board, it's a lot easier to play with the EQ knobs on the board, rather than the controls in the average non-linear editing application. Your editing application might require that you render after adjusting the EQ, and it might only offer some standard EQ presets. The mixing board, on the other hand, will give a full range of possibilities in real time. If you're not comfortable making the type of delicate aesthetic judgments required for good equalization, save your EQ tasks for later, when you get ready to do your final mix. By then, you'll have spent some time working with the audio and you'll have a better idea of how it should sound.

Where's That Hum Coming From?

If you hear a hum when you play audio, it might have been recorded onto your original source tape, However, there's also a chance that it might be coming from your system itself. Faulty cables, loose connections, and power supply problems can all add a hum to your audio signal. Before you try to correct a hum with EQ, make sure your system isn't the culprit.

You can also use equalization to correct global audio problems such as hums and hisses. If the audio was recorded too low and you have to boost the levels to get a good signal, you'll probably hear *tape hiss*—the sound of the tape running across the play heads. Diminishing the high frequency can alleviate this. Similarly, if the audio was recorded in a room with a refrigerator or air-conditioner running, you might have a low hum in the background. A faulty audio cable can also result in a hum. You can try adjusting the low frequencies to minimize these hums.

There's one big caveat: *be very careful*. By diminishing a part of the audio signal, whether it's low or high, you might also diminish the good audio that you want to capture. Most of the audio that you'll be concerned with will involve the human voice, and you must be careful not to diminish the frequencies that contain voices. Human voice resides primarily in the middle frequencies, but can also dip into the low and high frequencies, meaning that you might not be able to get rid of the hum without damaging the voices. There's no magic fix when the problem part of the audio shares the same frequencies as the voices in the sound track.

VIDEO QUALITY

Many people think of *online editing* as an output process, but to get "online" quality, you have to be very diligent in how you capture your media. If you are eager to start editing, you can go ahead and batch capture according to the procedure described in the "Logging and Basic Capturing" tutorial earlier in the chapter, and start cutting. However, at some point before your final output, you'll want to go back and recapture your video at the highest quality. This means you'll probably need to forgo the convenience of batch capturing, and capture each scene or lighting change with custom settings. If you're using a system with multiple resolutions, you'll need to switch to a higher quality setting. Because you've already logged each scene, the computer knows where each clip is on each tape, so you'll simply need to adjust the settings and recapture.

Video Levels

Setting the video levels is more complicated than setting the audio levels, because a video signal is more complex than an audio signal. Luckily, there are several tools to help you set the video levels properly. *Waveform monitors* (Figure 13.11) display the brightness of the video signal.

By looking at the waveform display, you can see if the image is too bright (Figure 13.12) or too dark (Figure 13.13). In the tutorial later in this chapter, we'll show you how to set the white levels and black levels using SMPTE color bars (Figure 13.10). Generally, everything else will fall into place once you have these two key variables in place.

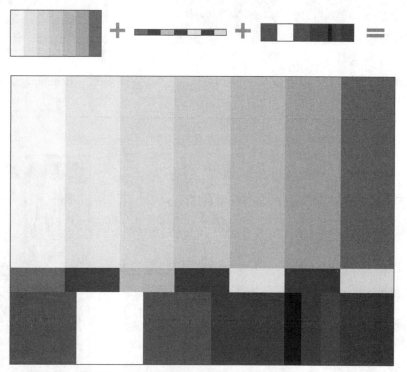

FIGURE 13.10   SMPTE color bars are a familiar sight although most people don't know what they are (see Color Plate 5). Each frame of color bars contains three different test patterns to help calibrate brightness and color in a video signal.

Vectorscopes (Figure 13.11b) display the color information, or hue, in the video signal. After setting the black and white levels with the waveform monitor, you can use the vectorscope to make sure the color information is set correctly (Figure 13.14). You can use either a hardware or software-based waveform monitor and vectorscope to check the video

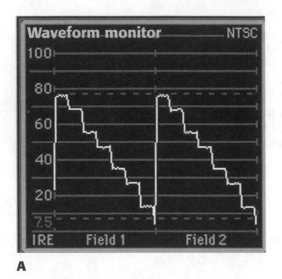

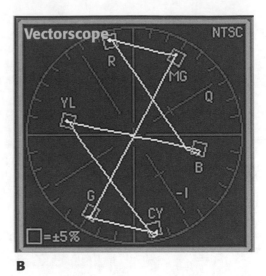

A

B

FIGURE 13.11 (a) The waveform monitor displays only the brightness, or luminance, of an image; (b) the vectorscope displays only the color, or hues, of an image.

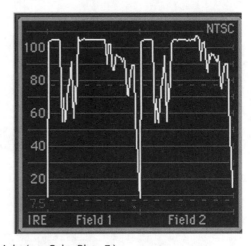

FIGURE 13.12 The waveform of this image shows that it's too bright (see Color Plate 7.)

levels. Be aware that waveform monitors and vectorscopes do not do anything to the video signal—they simply display it, just like regular video monitors. To adjust the video signal levels, you'll have to use controls on your VTR (if available) or controls in the capture window of your non-linear editing application (Figure 13.15).

 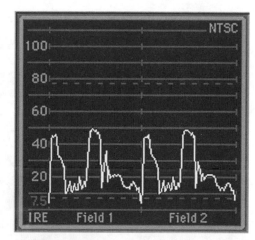

FIGURE 13.13   The waveform of this image shows that it's too dark (see Color Plate 8.)

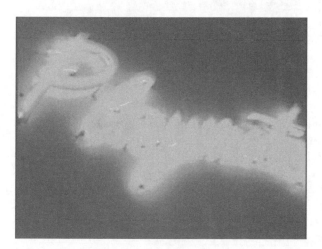 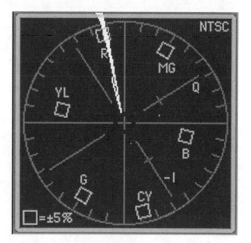

FIGURE 13.14   The vectorscope of this image shows that there is too much red (see Color Plate 10).

So, how do you know what these levels should be? The video equivalent of 60 Hz audio reference tone is the *SMPTE color bars* test pattern (Color Plate 5 and Figure 13.10). There are slightly different video test patterns for PAL and other video standards. The SMPTE color bars image actually contains three separate test patterns. This allows you to double-check the video level settings—a process covered in the tutorial later in this chapter and in the more complex tutorial called "Advanced Capturing" in the Chapter 13 folder on the companion DVD.

ON THE DVD

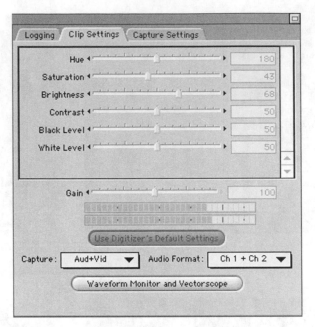

FIGURE 13.15   Video levels sliders in Apple Final Cut Pro.

As with audio reference tone, you'll need to check the color bars and adjust the input sliders every time you change tapes or input devices. Sometimes, you'll find that you've adjusted the bars perfectly, but the video still looks hot or underexposed. This means that the color bars weren't recorded properly. In order for color bars to be effective, they must be recorded by the same device that records the video image and with the same white and black balance settings. If a camera operator uses a tape that's been pre-striped on a VTR with timecode and color bars, these bars will not be relevant to what he records later on at the shoot. Rather, the bars must be generated by the camera itself and, naturally, only higher-end cameras are capable of generating their own color bars.

Capturing at "online" quality can be a lot of work. You'll need to closely watch your video as it goes into your computer to make sure there aren't any glitches, drop-outs, or other problems. If there are, you should try to recapture or make note of the problem so you can avoid using that footage later on. You'll also want to listen for glitches and distortion in your audio. It may be boring but your diligence will pay off in the quality of your final output.

TUTORIAL

SETTING YOUR VIDEO LEVELS

Before you begin digitizing and capturing, you need to adjust your NLE to correctly read the color from your videotape. To do this, you'll use your software's waveform monitor to help you adjust *white level* and *black level,* and the vectorscope to help adjust *hue.* You'll also need a videotape that has bars and tone on it. Some editing apps can send bars and tone out to tape (see your manual for instructions) or you can use the bars and tone located in the Chapter 13 folder of the DVD that accompanies this book. Import them into your NLE and edit them into a sequence. Making them at least ten minutes long will make the tutorial easier. Edit the sequence to tape and you're ready to go.

ON THE DVD

Bars and Tone

The companion DVD contains sample audio files of 60 Hz tone and still image files of different video test patterns in the Chapter 13 folder. You can import these files into your editing software and put them at the start of your sequence so that your final tape output can be calibrated when played on another editing system or VTR.

Step 1: Launch Your Capture Utility

Enter capture mode in your NLE and open your software waveform and vectorscope. Refer to your software documentation if you don't know how to do this.

Step 2: Put a Tape in Your VTR

Insert a tape with bars and tone at the beginning into your video deck. Your software should prompt you to enter the name of the tape. If you're not prompted, enter this information yourself.

Step 3: Play the Color Bars

Rewind to the head of the tape and play. When you get to the bars and tone on the tape, you're ready to start calibrating. First, take a look at your waveform monitor—if there's a box that indicates which horizontal line of video you are viewing, make sure the number in this box is set between 16 and 179 so that you are viewing data from the upper color bars test pattern (Figure 13.16a).

Step 4: Adjust the White Level

As the color bars play on your tape, watch the waveform monitor (it is very important that you do this while your deck is playing, not paused). Note that the waveform image in Figure 13.16b shows two identical stair-stepping patterns. Each stair-stepping pattern represents a separate field of video. Your waveform monitor might display either one field or two. The color bars in the upper test pattern start with white at the far left and progress to dark blue at the far right. Each bar of color is about 10% darker than the next, going from left to right, which is why the waveform looks like a set of stair steps going down. For now, though, we're only going to worry about the white bar.

Look at one of the fields (it doesn't matter which)—the highest stair step on the right corresponds to the white color bar on the left side of the upper test pattern. There are actually two variations of the upper test pattern—one with a bar that's 100% white and one with a bar that's only 75% white. They both appear white to the eye when playing on a video monitor but when you see them on a waveform display, you'll notice the difference right away. The bars we provided for you on the DVD and shown in the figures in this chapter are 75% bars, so you'll set the white level at 75%.

Now, look at the numbers along the side of the waveform display. These numbers are fixed and represent brightness in percentages. Use the luminance or white level slider in your NLE's capture utility to adjust the white bar in the waveform until it falls on the dotted line just below the 80% mark. The dotted line is there to help you set the white level at 75%.

Step 5: Adjust the Black Level

You might have noticed that there is no black bar in the upper test pattern. To set the black level, we'll use the middle test pattern instead (Figure 13.17).

Select a different horizontal line, between 180 and 200, and check your image against Figure 13.17a. This is the middle color bars test pattern and it consists of bars that alternate between different colors and black.

The black level for North American NTSC video is 7.5% (sometimes referred to as 7.5 IRE). Use the black level slider in your capture utility to adjust the black bars until they sit on the dotted line at 7.5%. If you are setting the black level for Japanese NTSC or for PAL, the black level should be set at 0 IRE. Your waveform image should look like the one in Figure 13.17b when you're done. You can also check that your white levels are still at 75% (Figure 13.17b).

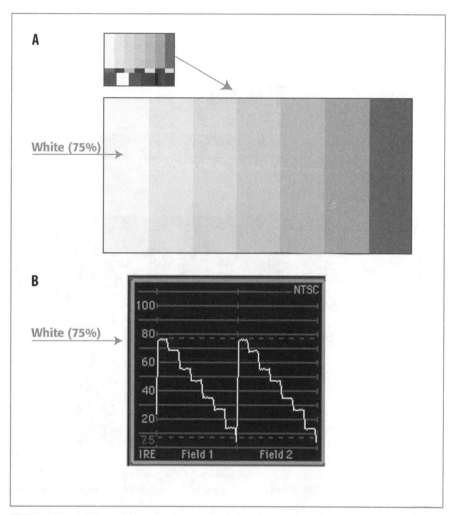

FIGURE 13.16   (a) The white color bar on the left in the upper color bars test pattern (b) matches the tallest bar to the left in the waveform display shown here. Adjust the brightness or luminance input level so that the top of this bar rests at the 75% mark.

Now, you can use the bottom test pattern to double check your black and white levels. Select a line between 201 and 263 and check your display against Figure 13.18a and 13.18b. The second bar from the left in the bottom test pattern displays 100% white and the second bar from the right actually contains three small bars that can be hard to see. They are there to allow for fine adjustment of black levels. In order from left to right, they are 3.5% black, 7.5% black, and 11.5% black and should match the three small notches in the waveform display.

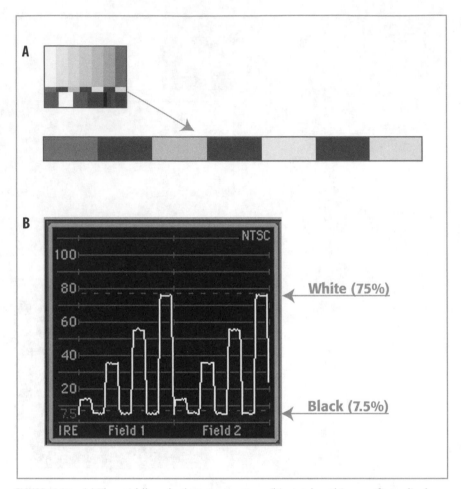

FIGURE 13.17 (a) The middle color bars test pattern (b) matches this waveform display.

Hardware Waveform Monitors and Vectorscopes

Hardware waveform monitors and vectorscopes are more accurate and easier to control. If you are serious about your video levels, and especially if your software "scopes" don't allow you to select different horizontal lines, you might want to rent hardware scopes on the days you want to capture high-quality material.

Step 6: Check the Color Levels

Now that you've defined black and white, the colors in between should fall correctly into place. To make sure, choose a horizontal line between

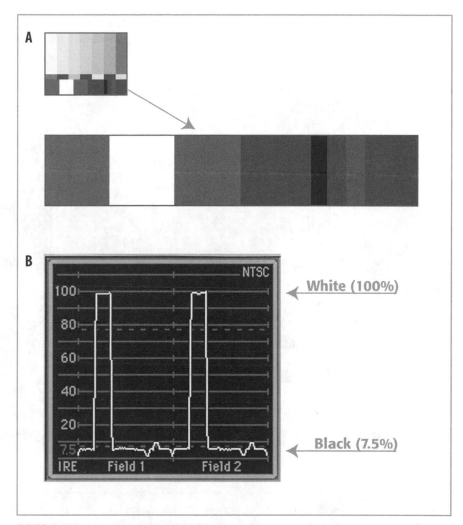

FIGURE 13.18   (a) The bottom color bars test pattern (b) matches this waveform display, which lets you adjust for 100% white and fine-tune black levels.

16 and 179 (the upper test pattern), then look at your vectorscope (Figure 13.19). The six little boxes each represent a different color, or hue: R for red, G for green, B for blue, M for magenta, Y for yellow, and C for cyan. Figure 13.19a shows the ideal pattern that color bars should show on your vectorscope for the upper color bars test pattern. Each point of color should fall in the appropriate box. Adjust the hue and saturation sliders on your capture utility to get as close to this pattern as possible.

Then, select a line between 180 and 200 and double-check your colors against the image in 13.19b, the middle color bars test pattern. The middle test pattern only shows three colors: blue, magenta and cyan. (The lower color bars test pattern contains no color information and is not shown.)

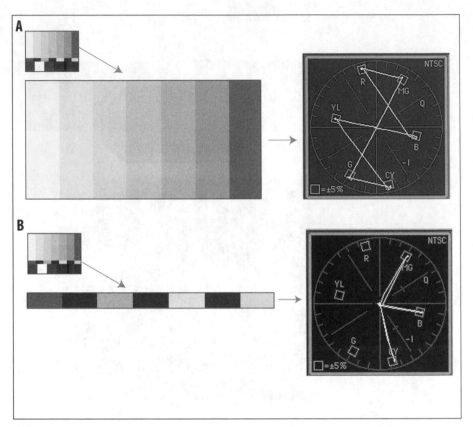

FIGURE 13.19   Shown here are the corresponding vectorscope images for the upper (a) and middle (b) color bars test patterns. The vectorscope displays only color, or hue, information.

Step 7: Save Your Settings

If your software allows you to save your video level settings, now is the time to do so. It's best to name these saved settings to correspond with the tape number. If your NLE does not allow you to save these settings, you might want to write them down for future reference.

Step 8: Set Your Audio Levels

Next, you need to set your audio levels using the 60 cycle (60 Hz) tone that accompanies the color bars. Open the audio level meters and move the sliders until the tone peaks at unity—refer to your software documentation for the correct dB setting (Figure 13.20). Now you're ready to start capturing from your tape.

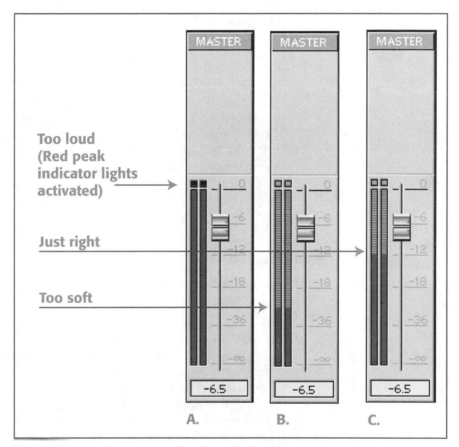

FIGURE 13.20   Use the sliders to adjust the audio levels.

Remember: You should perform these steps *any time you change tapes!* With practice, the process will only take seconds to complete.

TROUBLESHOOTING

Capturing audio and video is probably the most problem-fraught part of the non-linear post-production process. It's also the most difficult to troubleshoot because so many things can go wrong. Here's a checklist of what to look for when you're having problems:

Check your software settings. Be certain all preferences are set properly. Relaunch. Refer to your software documentation.

Check your computer. Do you have enough RAM for your editing software? Are other applications running? Are your drives full or fragmented? Mac OS 9 users should try rebuilding the desktop, zapping the PRAM, and restarting the computer. Remember, when you shut down your computer, count to 10 before restarting.

Check your cables. With your computer shut down, check all your cables, connections, and routers (if you have any), and make sure everything is secure. Check that cable lengths are within the approved limits. If you're using SCSI drives, check your SCSI IDs and termination.

Check your hardware. Check all the settings on your VTR and other peripheral hardware. Refer to your equipment documentation. If you're unable to record to tape, check for record inhibit tabs on your videotapes. Make certain all your components are receiving power.

Problems and Solutions

Most technical problems can be solved by thoroughly working your way through the preceding list, but that can take some time. Here's a list of common problems and probable solutions:

Dropped frames. Frame-dropping is often due to a hardware compatibility problem. Make sure all your hardware conforms to your software manufacturers' specs and recommendations. Dropped frames can also stem from performance bottlenecks: fragmented disk drives, an overtaxed processor, or lack of RAM. If your software manufacturer provides a hardware utility program, be certain that your system passes all of the tests. In addition, check for system conflicts, especially CODECs from different editing applications.

No video coming in. This is either a problem with your software settings or a problem with your cables. Check the software settings and preferences, especially video format and device control. Check the cable path from the VTR to your computer and make sure every connection is correct and secure. Finally, check the external video monitor to make sure video is playing from the VTR—it might be that you are looking at a black portion of the tape. Try another videotape that you know has an image on it to make sure the problem isn't the tape itself.

No audio coming in. Look at the audio level meters on your VTR, audio deck, and in your software to determine where the audio signal might be stopping. If there are no levels on your deck, make sure that you haven't accidentally muted the deck or changed other audio settings. Try another tape that you know has audio on it to ensure that the problem is not the tape itself. Check that your audio sampling rate in your software setting matches the audio sampling rate you recorded.

Audio is distorted. Compare the levels on your deck to the levels in your software—are they both overmodulating? If so, the problem is on the deck or the tape itself. If your deck has level controls, try to lower them so that they aren't peaking. Use a pair of headphones, or set your mixer to monitor the deck only. If the audio still sounds distorted, it was probably recorded that way, so there's little you can do. If the audio is fine on your deck but overmodulating in your software, check the level controls in your software—are they up too high? Does turning down the gain remove the distortion? If not, check the path your audio signal follows from the deck to the computer—is it getting amped more than once? Is there something wrong with the settings on your mixer? Are you using cables of the wrong impedance level?

Inaccurate timecode. If the timecode on your deck does not match the timecode in your software, you're going to have some serious problems. Some editing applications require that users calibrate timecode; see your user documentation for more on this. If the timecode in your software always starts at 00:00:00:00, your software is probably creating a default timecode for the media, also known as "bogus timecode," since it is effectively meaningless. This means that your editing software is not reading the timecode from your tape. Check the capture settings, device control settings, and device control cables. Make sure the timecode from the deck is compatible with your software. See your documentation for workarounds, or consider having your tapes "re-striped" with the correct form of timecode by a post-production facility.

Your software refuses to batch digitize a previously logged shot. This is almost always due to timecode breaks in the source footage. Set your software to "capture across timecode breaks" (if possible) or re-log the shot. See "Logging" earlier in this chapter.

Audio and video are out of sync. This is usually a playback problem. Some software apps are known to be unable to maintain sync in longer edits. Moreover, some low-resolution CODECs aren't capable of maintaining true sync. If none of those are the problem, it might be that the tracks in your timeline have accidentally gotten out of sync. Finally, listen to the audio directly from your VTR— perhaps the source tape is actually out of sync. If this is the case, you can adjust the sync in your NLE after you capture.

Audio plays too fast. Make sure the audio settings in your software match the audio settings at which you recorded your sound.

Video glitches and drop-outs. Check the camera-original tape—is the glitch on your tape as well? If the drop-out is only on your captured clip and not the tape itself, simply delete the damaged media and recapture the clip. If you've been using your VTR a lot it could need cleaning—refer to the section on VTR maintenance in Chapter 12, "Editing Hardware," and then recapture the clip. If the problem is on your tape and you're using a digital video format, there are a couple of ways to try to fix digital drop-outs. Try cloning the tape (see Chapter 19, "Output," for more about clones, dubs, and transfers). If this doesn't work, try dubbing the tape. If this doesn't work, try dubbing the tape while feeding the record deck an audio signal from another source—a CD player or other VCR. You can then record the audio separately and re-sync by hand in your NLE. All of these processes can help create a more stable video signal and possibly remove the drop-out. If it still won't go away, you're probably stuck with it. You'll have to try to fix it using your effects tools in your editing software— more about this in Chapter 16, "Color Correction."

Video looks bad on the computer screen. Remember, if you're capturing DV footage through a FireWire interface, your video *will* look lousy on your computer (see Chapter 10, "Building a Workstation," for details on why). Check your software settings and be sure that your editing system is echoing your video clips to the FireWire port. This will allow you to see full-quality video on an external video monitor attached to the deck. Footage captured with a low, offline resolution will also look bad until you up-res it at online quality.

IMPORTING DIGITAL FILES

Importing digital files is probably the easiest way to get media into your project. Compatibility issues aside, the main thing you want to avoid when importing digital media is accidentally lowering the image or audio quality.

QuickTime and AVI files: Make sure you have the right CODECs installed. For example, if you have QuickTime media that was created on a Media100 or Avid Media Composer, you'll need the Media100 Transcoder or the Avid CODEC, respectively, in order to play those QuickTime movies on a different system. Another thing to be very careful about is recompression. If you have a QuickTime or AVI movie, it has probably already been compressed. If you import it into editing software that uses a different CODEC, you'll compress it again. This could seriously degrade the image quality. To avoid this, compress all QuickTime and AVI movies with lossless CODECs, such as the QuickTime animation compressor.

WAV, AIFF, and other audio files: For optimal quality, the audio files you import into your editing system should have been saved with the same sampling rate as the rate you're editing with, usually 48 kHz.

MP3/4: Most editing applications cannot edit with audio that's saved in the MP3 or MP4 format. Others require that these files be rendered before you can play them back in real-time. In general, these files should be converted to WAV or AIFF files before you import them into your editing software. Be aware that audio saved in either format is highly compressed and might not yield the high quality some projects require. In addition, some MP4 music downloads are copy-protected if you bought them online, so you won't be able to edit them.

Keep a Database of Digital Files

If you're relying on lots of imported audio and graphics, you can easily lose track of those files. Use database software such as iView Media Pro or FileMaker Pro to keep track of your media.

Digital stills (TIFF, PICT, JPEG, PSD, BMP, etc.): Some editing applications will let you import images of any size, while others require that it fit the resolution and aspect ratio that you've set for the project. The standard resolution for video is 72 dpi, and the aspect ratio varies depending on what type of video you're working with. Always be certain that the pixel shape of the still image matches that of the video. Otherwise, the still image might get distorted on import. Some applications, like Adobe Premiere Pro import Photoshop files with the layers intact—they appear as elements on separate video tracks—others will flatten and convert them to a video clip on import.

Digital media (Flash, etc.) Many non-linear editing apps now allow you to import Flash and other animation files.

Moving Media from Mac to Windows

If you have to move media from one platform to another, be aware that different file naming conventions can cause your computer to rename your media files, which will in turn cause your NLE to lose track of your shots. This can cause big headaches so avoid switching platforms mid-project if you can and if not, take extra care to make sure your filenames are compatible with the naming conventions for both the Mac and Windows operating systems.

Getting Audio from a CD

Chances are that much of the audio you'll be using for your project will come from an audio CD. To import this audio directly into your non-linear editing system, you'll need some encoding software—that is, software that will take a track from a CD and encode it into the format that's compatible with your editing system. Apple's iTunes will do the job for those of you running Mac OS X or OS 9. Windows users will need Windows Media Player.

Whether you're using Mac or Windows, a favorite tool for this job is QuickTime Pro, the professional version of the Apple QuickTime utility (Figure 13.21). The QuickTime Player lets you open tracks from an audio CD and save them to your hard drive as QuickTime audio-only movies and export them into any format you wish (.WAV, .AIFF, etc.). Because the audio files are digital, you won't lose any sound quality when you do these conversions as long as you stick with the CD-quality, 44.1kHz sampling rate or greater.

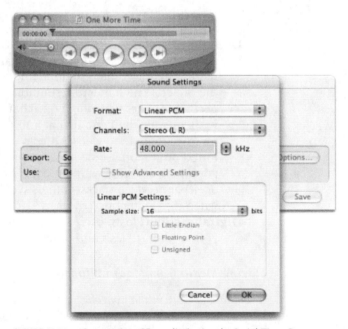

FIGURE 13.21 Converting CD audio in Apple QuickTime Pro.

Media Management

At the simplest level, an editing application acts as a link between you and the hard drive(s) where your media is stored. Exactly how does the computer handle the massive amount of data that is being processed when you edit?

Each project that you create is stored in a folder usually on the main hard drive. Some applications create a special folder for all the projects they create; others let you decide where to store the *project folder*. Inside the project folder are all the files that make up your project—some applications store a master *project file* that includes just about everything. Others, like Avid Media Composer, store a master project file, a file for each edited sequence, a file for each bin, and a settings file for each project and each user.

What you won't find in the project folder is the actual media for your project—the video and audio files that make up your source clips. How and where this data is stored differs from application to application. Refer to your software documentation.

EXERCISES

ON THE DVD

This chapter contains a few important tutorials, so be sure to work through each, and then try working with some of your own footage. There's also an additional tutorial called "Extra Tutorial.rft" on the DVD, in the Chapter 13 folder.

SUMMARY

Preparing to edit can be a huge undertaking, but if you start out with a well-organized project and log carefully, you'll have the building blocks for editing success. Capturing high-quality video and audio can be a difficult and highly technical process, but if you're concerned about quality, the pay-off is worth it.

Now that your project is logged and captured, it's time to move onto the next step: editing and locking picture.

14

EDITING

In This Chapter

THE INVISIBLE ART

By the time you get to this stage, you've probably been working on your project for a long time: writing, researching, planning, and shooting. Now it's time to play with it. The history of filmmaking is rife with examples of films that have been rebuilt, restructured, and sometimes resurrected in the editing room.

If the script is weak, it is the editor's job to try to find a way to make it work. If the director was tired one day and forgot to get the cutaways, it's the editor's job to cut the scene regardless. The notorious "cutting room floor" has saved many actors the embarrassment of a weak performance, and many cinematographers the embarrassment of poorly shot footage. There's a saying that editing is a no-win situation—if the editor saves the film, the director gets the credit, but if the editor fails to save the film, the editor takes the blame. While it's true that for many people, editing is an invisible art, it's also well appreciated by those who know better.

Editing Tutorials

In this chapter, we'll use a series of short tutorials to walk you through the basic concepts of editing. These tutorials use footage from a modern adaptation of Shakespeare's Richard III. *You can use any editing application, but we opted for Adobe Premiere which is provided on the DVD in the Apps folder. Basic editing functions are covered in Chapter 11, "Non-linear Editing Software," and also in the tutorials and manuals that come with most editing applications. If you haven't already, take the time to familiarize yourself with your editing application's interface before you continue.*

ON THE DVD

Building Blocks

Motion picture film was invented in the late nineteenth century, but editing as we know it today developed slowly over the next 40 years as new technologies were introduced, and more sophisticated ways to tell stories became the norm. The earliest films, like the Lumière brothers' *Workers Leaving the Lumière Factory* (1895), consisted of nothing more than *shots*, the most basic building blocks for an edited sequence. Turn-of-the-century French filmmaker Georges Meliès introduced the use of in-camera special effects such as *slow-motion*, *dissolves*, *fade-outs*, and *super-impositions*. These "magic tricks" developed into the rudiments of a filmic language: fade-ins to signify the beginning, dissolves to transition between one shot and another, and fade-outs to signify the ending.

Around the same time, Edwin S. Porter made *The Great Train Robbery* (1903), a film considered the beginning of modern editing. Porter developed the technique of jumping to different points of view and different locations, something we now take for granted. In the controversial *Birth of a Nation* (1915), D.W. Griffith took the concept of editing a step further, introducing the use of the *close-up*, the *long shot* (long as in length of time, not as in camera angle), and *panning* to develop story and intensify emotion. He also innovated the *intercutting* of scenes and parallel plot lines.

Russian filmmaker Sergei Eisenstein took Griffith's techniques even further and invented the concept of *montage*, as exemplified by the famous Odessa steps scene in *The Battleship Potemkin* (1925). In 1929 another Russian, Dziga Vertov, made the early cinema verité film, *Man with a Movie Camera*, documenting daily life in Russia with fast-cutting to create intensity and energy.

The invention of sync sound added an entirely new level of sophistication in filmmaking, and this turning point is exemplified by Orson Welles's *Citizen Kane* (1941), which used off-screen dialog, voice-over, overlapping dialog, and music to enhance the mood and power of the story. Editing styles and techniques have continued to grow and change since *Citizen Kane*, but the early history of film and editing is repeated on a small scale in every editing room as films are cut together using dissolves, close-ups, cutaways, intercutting, montage, and sound to build the final cut (Figure 14.1).

FIGURE 14.1   If we first show a clip of the *San Joaquin Valley Swiss Club* and then show a clip of our actor, he looks confused. However, if we show a clip of a knife-wielding maniac, and then show the exact same clip of our actor, the actor will appear terrified. The same images "edited" two different ways yield a very different emotional impact.

The Language of Film

Whether you prefer the quick-cutting MTV style, a more traditional film-cutting style, or something you come up with all by yourself, the goal of editing is to successfully tell a story. In this regard, editing can be considered a continuation of the writing process: now that the film has been shot, the editor needs to do a "rewrite" of the script using the footage that exists. Because the footage has already been shot, this rewrite, or *cut*, will be limited to what was recorded on film or tape. The editor might find that he can't always remain true to the original story—the dialog that looked great on paper seems long and tedious, the "montage scene" that was supposed to play for several minutes ended up consisting of a mere three shots, and so on. The editor's job is to use the screenplay as a blueprint for the final story that will emerge.

Applied 3-Act Structure

If you've studied screenwriting (or read Chapter 2, "Writing and Scheduling"), you've probably heard the phrase *3-act structure* tossed about. 3-act structure originated with the plays of ancient Greece and is the basis for most Western visual storytelling forms. 3-act structure, put simply, means that every story has a beginning, a middle, and an end. In a typical feature film, the first act, or beginning, ends about 30 minutes into the story; the second act, or middle, ends 45 to 60 minutes later; and the third act, or ending, comprises the last 30 minutes.

When editing, 3-act structure can be applied to each scene and each sequence of scenes, as well as the film as a whole. The beginning, middle, and end of a scene are referred to as *beats* rather than *acts*. Another way to think of these three beats is the *setup*, the *action*, and the *pay-off*. A typical chase sequence might start with a burglar breaking into a convenience store and setting off the alarm (the setup); he flees and is chased by the police (the action); but he escapes by gunning his car across a rising drawbridge (the payoff). Sometimes, there is an additional half beat at the end for comic effect—a shot of the frustrated cops sitting in their car on the wrong side of the bridge. If a scene is missing one of these elements it might seem odd, nonsensical, or boring. Keeping the idea of three story beats in mind can help if a scene or sequence you're cutting seems awkward or unwieldy.

TUTORIAL   **SETTING UP A PROJECT**

Step 1

Launch your editing application.

Step 2

Create a new project and call it "Richard ring". Set up the project according to the following specifications (Figure 14.2):

- NTSC video (Disclaimer for PAL editors—even though this footage is NTSC, you'll still be able to work with it in your non-linear editing application. However, you won't be able to view it on an external video monitor unless you have a professional PAL/NTSC switchable monitor.)
- 720 × 480 resolution
- 29.97 frames per second
- 48 kHz, 16-bit stereo audio
- Sorenson CODEC

You might need to refer to your software manual for instructions. If your software requires that you render the Sorenson compressed video before you can preview it, refer to the document called Compressed Media Tips in the Chapter 14 folder on the DVD for some work-arounds.

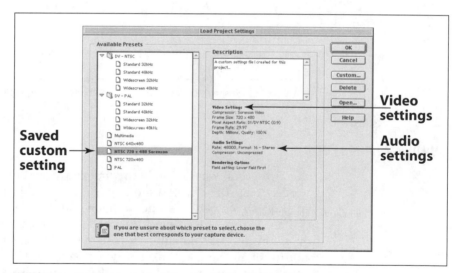

FIGURE 14.2   Custom project settings in Adobe Premiere.

Step 3

On the DVD, is a folder called Chapter 14 Tutorials—copy it onto your hard drive.

Step 4

From inside your editing application, import the media in the 04 Ring subfolder in the Chapter 14 Tutorials folder on your hard drive. Some editing applications will let you select an entire folder for importing, while others will require you to import each shot individually. If you're using Adobe Premiere, drag the 03 Ring folder into the "Bin" column in the project window and save the project.

Your project window should now look something like the one in Figure 14.3.

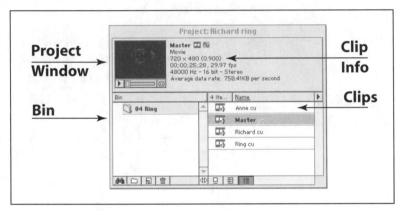

FIGURE 14.3   The window in Adobe Premiere containing the 04 Ring tutorial media.

BUILDING A ROUGH CUT

There are several ways to build the first cut of a scene using a non-linear editing system. The simplest method is known as *drag-and-drop editing*. If your shots are named by scene number, shot number, and take number, sort them in that order. Select the good takes of each shot, and drag and drop them into the timeline in your NLE. The result will be a rough string-up of all the good takes of your scene in the order you selected them. If your software allows, switch to a thumbnail view in your bin and visually arrange the shots in an order that you think will work, and then select and drag and drop them into the timeline. If your scene is a complicated montage or action sequence, you might want to use *three-point editing* to create a more refined first cut of your scene.

Radio Cuts

If the scene you're cutting is based on dialog, a good way to build the first cut is to create a *radio cut*. The idea of a radio cut is to create an edit that sounds good first, without worrying about how it looks. This method works equally well for scripted and unscripted projects. Using three-point editing, you can watch your footage, select the in- and out-points for each line of dialog, and then press the Edit button to add each line, in order, to your sequence in the timeline. Once you've created a rough string-up of all the dialog, go through the scene and make sure all the dialog edits sound good and that you're happy with the overall flow of the dialog. Now is the time to trim out extra lines, or add a pause where you think the content of the scene calls for it—such as after a particularly emotional, funny, or shocking line. If you find working with the choppy picture too distracting, you can turn off the video track monitor in your timeline.

TUTORIAL

ON THE DVD

CREATING A SIMPLE ROUGH CUT

Step 1

Open the Richard ring project you created in the last tutorial and drag the shot called *Master* into the source monitor (Figure 14.4). Press Play (space bar or L) and watch the shot.

Step 2

Set an in-point by pressing the "I" key right before the first line of dialog, about two seconds into the shot. Set an out-point ("O") after the line "Wear both of them, for both of them are thine," about 21 seconds into the shot.

Step 3

Make sure the Video 1 and Audio 1 tracks are targeted in the timeline, and that the cursor is at the beginning of the timeline. The cursor position indicates the in-point in the timeline. Complete the three-point edit by pressing the Overwrite button. Your timeline should now look like Figure 14.4. Save the project.

Auto Save and Auto Backup

Remember to save many copies of your sequences as you work. Use auto save and auto backup features if your NLE offers them.

FIGURE 14.4 Load the Master shot into the source monitor, set an in-point and an out-point, position the cursor in the timeline, and press the Overwrite button.

Master Shot–Style Coverage

If your scene was shot master shot-style (that is, a wide establishing shot and series of cutaways), you'll want to set up a series of multiple tracks. Start by editing the entire master shot into your sequence as a guide track. Your scene probably has a selection of camera angles that can then be worked into your master shot. By adding extra video and audio tracks, you can edit other shots into the sequence by laying them in higher tracks, rather than by cutting up the master shot. The next tutorial, "Editing with Master Shot–Style Coverage," shows you how to build a scene using master shot-style coverage.

After you build the rough cut of your scene, you're ready to take another pass: refining cuts, extending shots, adding reactions and cutaways, and making sure the whole scene plays smoothly.

Don't Be Afraid to Try Different Versions

Non-linear editing is nondestructive. As long as you save copies of your sequences, you can always go back to an older version if you don't like the changes you made.

| **TUTORIAL** | **EDITING WITH MASTER SHOT–STYLE COVERAGE** |

Step 1

Open your project from the previous tutorial, Richard ring. This part of the scene was covered in master shot–style. In the last tutorial, you edited the master shot into a sequence. In this tutorial, you'll add the coverage—close-ups of the two actors.

Step 2

Drag the shot called Anne cu.mov found in the 04 Ring folder into the Source monitor. She only has one line in this scene, which starts about FOUR seconds into the shot. Set in- and out-points around this line, "To take is not to give."

Step 3

Target the Video 2 and Audio 2 tracks. By targeting these tracks, you'll avoid overwriting the footage from the master shot on Video 1 and Audio 1. In the timeline, find the place where Anne's line starts and set an in-point, or place the cursor there. Perform an overwrite edit.

Step 4

Repeat the preceding steps with Richard's lines in the shot called Richard cu. Edit these lines onto Video track 3 and Audio track 3. You might have to add tracks to your sequence. In Premiere, select Add Video Track from the Timeline menu. When you're done with this step, your timeline should look like the one in Figure 14.5a.

Step 5

Now its time to choose between the shots—do you want to start the scene with the master or with the close-up of Richard? By turning the different video tracks on and off you can get an idea of how the different shots play. Work through each shot and remove the parts you don't need (Figure 14.5b) using the Razor tool. You can then drag and drop *within* the timeline to adjust the timing of each shot. Remember that your NLE will play your sequence from the top down, so the shot on Video track 3 will cover up any video on the tracks below it, and so on. Once you're happy with the layout and sequence of shots, you can collapse them into a single track of video (Figure 14.5c).

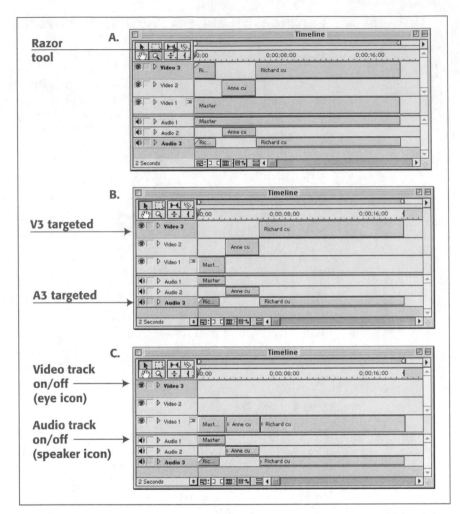

FIGURE 14.5 If your scene has a master shot and coverage, you can use multiple tracks in the timeline to help you build a rough cut (a). Once you've whittled down the shots (b), you can drag them down to V1 to create a single track edit (c).

REFINING YOUR ROUGH CUT

There's a saying that if you notice the editing, the film was poorly edited. Traditional Hollywood feature film editors strive for *seamless* edits—edits that don't call attention to themselves and that flow naturally with the action, dialog, and tone of the scene. The key to creating seamless edits is to make sure each edit is *motivated*. A motivated edit is cued by a line of dialog, a look or gesture from one of the actors, a sound effect, a music cue, or some other element in the film.

The opposite of a seamless edit is the *jump cut*. Jump cuts not only lack motivation, but also break up the basic continuity and linear progression of time. It used to be that jump cuts were to be avoided at all costs. Nowadays, even Hollywood films feature carefully placed jump cuts to jar the viewer, add energy, or create a special effect. In *American Beauty*, jump cuts were used to accentuate the dream sequences, while the rest of the movie was edited seamlessly.

The following are different editing techniques you can use to smooth over a rough edit. All of them will work better if they are motivated in some way.

Cutaways and Reaction Shots

The easiest way to smooth a rough edit is to cover it up with another shot. It's almost like putting a Band-Aid over the cut. *Cutaways* are shots of other things in the scene, outside of the main area of action and dialog: a fly on the wall, a hand moving to the handle of a gun, a foot tapping on the floor.

Reactions are shots of people reacting to the dialog and action of the scene: a passerby looking on as the main characters yell at each other, a crowd cheering at a baseball game, a woman ducking as a gunshot rings out. Used properly, they not only cover rough edits, but also enhance the story. Conversely, there's nothing worse than a random cutaway. In a scene showing a holdup in a bar, a cutaway to one of the bar patrons reacting when the robber pulls out the gun works well, while a cutaway to a static shot of a picture on the wall or a glass on the bar is unintentionally humorous. However, a cutaway to the glass right before the gunman puts a bullet through it can work well. In other words, using a cutaway or reaction shot in the proper context can be powerful and effective; using one that appears random will disrupt the dramatic intensity of a scene.

Avoid Overcutting

Too many unmotivated cutaways can result in the scene looking "cutty." Fast-cutting, as in El Mariachi, *is not the same as overcutting.*

TUTORIAL   ### ADDING CUTAWAYS

Step 1

Open the Richard ring project from the last tutorial. As you probably recall, Anne only has one line in this scene, but she has powerful reactions to Richard's words and actions. In a scene like this, her reactions are more eloquent than words.

Step 2

Watch the scene again and look for a moment that will be intensified by cutting to a reaction shot of Anne. The moment Richard puts the ring on her finger is a good choice.

Step 3

Watch the Anne cu shot and select a look that suits the moment. It's often better to choose a moment when the actor does something—however small—such as a blink or a glance. We humans can read a lot into the smallest facial movement, and a close-up is designed to reveal the most subtle reactions. At about 11 seconds into the shot, Anne looks down at her hands as Richard says, "Look at how this ring encompasses thy finger." Cut this reaction shot into your edited sequence; it should work well at about seven seconds from the beginning of the scene.

Step 4

Think about the content of the scene—is this Richard's scene, Anne's scene, or should it be balanced equally between them? If so, add another reaction shot of Anne to help even out the balance. This will have the effect of giving Anne's reactions equal weight to Richard's words. Save your project. ✂

Matching Action

If your scene involves movement, you might need to *match action* across an edit. Cutting from a wide shot of a man reaching for his gun to a close-up of the gun, from a hand turning a doorknob to the door opening, and from a shot of a man leading a woman dancing the tango to the reverse shot of her as she is dipped, are all examples of edits that need matching action.

Often, if you edit two action shots together as they play out in real-time the cut won't work, especially if you are cutting from a wide shot to a close-up, or vice versa. Because the movement across the screen is small in a wide shot and big in a close-up (Figure 14.6), you might need to show more of the action in the wide shot than in the close-up. Matching action becomes second nature after a while, but it might require some playing around to get the hang of it.

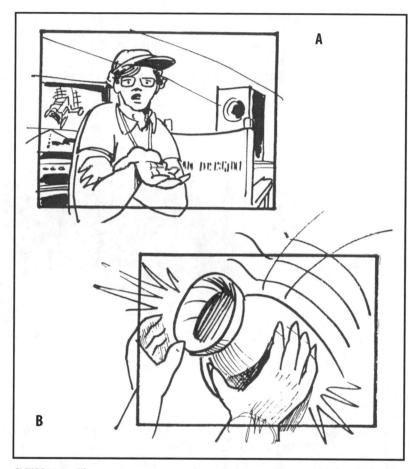

FIGURE 14.6   The movement across the screen is small in a wide shot (a) and big in a close-up (b).

TUTORIAL   **MATCHING ACTION**

Step 1

In this tutorial, you'll finish your cut of the Richard ring sequence. Open the project you saved in the previous tutorial, and drag the shot called Master into the source monitor.

Step 2

Watch for the point where Richard slides the ring on Anne's finger, and edit it into your sequence after Anne's line, "To take is not to give." You might want to try an *insert edit* instead of an overwrite edit.

Step 3

Next load the Ring cu shot into the source monitor. This shot begins as Richard slides the ring on. Cut this into the master shot and play around with it until the two shots feel like a continuous motion. *Trim mode* (Figure 14.7) is a good tool for playing around until the cut feels right. You can adjust the incoming shot, the outgoing shot, or both at the same time.

Last frame of outgoing shot →

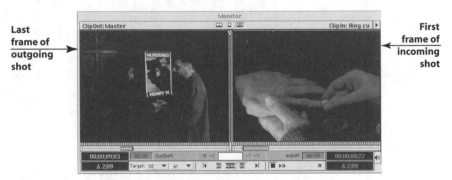

← **First frame of incoming shot**

FIGURE 14.7 Trim mode lets you fine-tune an edit until it feels right.

Step 4

ON THE DVD

At this point, you might have some double lines in your sequence. Use the Razor tool to make some splices, delete the extra dialog, and clean up the scene. Play around with adding more cutaways. Our final version of this scene is in Chapter 14 Tutorials>Final Movies>Richard Ring Sequence.

Matching Screen Position

In a well-composed shot, it's pretty easy to figure out where the viewer's eye will be directed. In a close-up, the eye will be directed at the face of the actor; in an action shot, it will follow the line of action, and if there are no people in the shot, it will be directed at the biggest, most colorful or dynamic thing in the frame. Once you determine where the screen position of the viewer's eye is on your outgoing shot, you can pick a similar screen position on your incoming shot (Figure 14.8a). This is especially helpful when you're trying to match action. You can also intentionally jar and disorient the viewer by mismatching the screen position (Figure 14.8b).

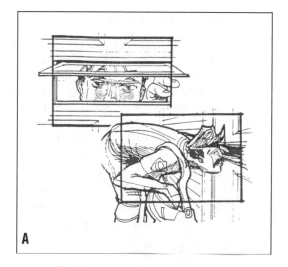

FIGURE 14.8   (a) These two images of the mailman have matching screen positions. (b) These two images do not have matching screen positions.

Overlapping Edits

A common way to refine a dialog scene is to use *overlapping edits*, also called *split edits* or *L-cuts*. If you cut from one actor to the other at the start of each line of dialog, the scene can start to feel like a Ping-Pong match. Overlapping edits help break up this rhythm by extending or shortening the picture while leaving the dialog the same, allowing you to see the reaction of one character as another talks. *Trim mode* and *rolling edits* are useful NLE tools for creating overlapping edits.

Matching Emotion and Tone

It's pretty obvious that you need to match emotion and tone in terms of the actors' performances when you cut from one shot to another. What's a little less obvious is that emotion and tone is carried in other things besides performance—the amount of camera movement in a shot, the amount of movement of the actors in the shot, the composition of the shot (wide, tight, etc.), the lighting and overall look of the shot, and the energy of the background elements are all elements that are capable of implying emotion and tone. If your scene consists of an argument between two characters, it may work well to start out using wide shots and then get tighter and tighter as the scene heats up. However, cutting to a wide shot during the most intense part of the scene will most likely deflate the energy.

Pauses and Pull-Ups

Adding a few seconds of silence can intensify a moment. If one scene shows a man saying "I love you" to a woman, a well-placed pause can completely change the tone of the scene. Putting the pause before he speaks will imply hesitation, put the pause before she answers and you'll have suspense.

Just as pauses in a scene can intensify the moment, shortening, or *pulling-up* the pauses in a scene can help pick up the pace. Whether you're cutting out the "ums" or trimming entire lines of dialog, you can usually find a lot of "fat" in a scene once you start looking for it.

Hard Sound Effects and Music

A hard sound effect is something short, precise, and fairly loud—a knock on a door, a burst of applause, a screech of tires. These sorts of sound effects startle the viewer a little bit and make it easy to hide a rough edit or smooth a jump cut. If your scene has music, it's a good idea to add it early on as you refine the edit. Music can change the pacing, add emotion, intensify action, and tell the viewer how they should be feeling. Many editors have a supply of CDs that they bring to a project as temporary soundtrack elements.

TUTORIAL   **OVERLAPPING EDITS**

Step 1

For this tutorial, you'll need to use Adobe Premiere. You can use the demo version that's included on the DVD. If you haven't already, copy the folder called Chapter 14 Tutorials on the DVD. Inside, there is a sub-

ON THE DVD

folder called 02 Dialog and inside that is an Adobe Premiere project called Richard Dialog. Double-click on it to launch Premiere and automatically open the Richard Dialog project. You can use any of the five files provided for this tutorial.

Step 2

The timeline in the Richard Dialog project contains a long dialog sequence between Richard and Anne that we've already built for you. Right now, it's a Ping-Pong match between Richard and Anne—every time he says a line we cut to him, and every time she says a line we cut to her. Watch the sequence and think about it in terms of technical problems and story. Because this is an intimate dialog sequence, there are only two shots to choose from—the close-up of Anne and the close-up of Richard. You'll have to use overlapping edits to solve any technical problems and to create a pacing that aids the story.

Step 3

Forty seconds into the sequence, there's a technical problem. The actress says "Out of my sight, doest infect mine eyes" when it should actually be "Out of my sight, *thou* doest infect mine eyes." In that shot, Anne cu—take 7, she repeats the line correctly a few seconds later. Load Anne cu—take 7 in the source monitor and find the second line reading, about 26 seconds into the shot. She only says the second half of the line. Set in and out points around that line. In the timeline, use the Razor tool to make a splice after she says "Out of my sight" (Figure 14.9a). Delete the second half of that line in the timeline, and then insert the new line reading (Figure 14.9b and 14.9c). If there's a gap between the end of Anne's line and Richard's next line, close it (14.9d). Next, move the next Richard shot onto Video track 2 (14.9e). Be careful not to move it out of sync with the audio. Select the beginning of the Richard shot and drag it back so that it goes past the edit in Anne's shot (14.9f).

Step 4

Work your way through each edit in the sequence, adding to either the outgoing shot or the incoming shot wherever you see fit. Clean up any extra bits of dialog or double lines. Think about the characters: What are they saying? Is it more important to see the character who delivers the line, or the character who reacts to that delivery? Do some of the moments need a beat before the next line? Let your idea about the story being told help you decide where to overlap edits. When you're done, save your edit. Our version is in Chapter 14 Tutorials>Final Movies>Richard dialog sequence.

ON THE DVD

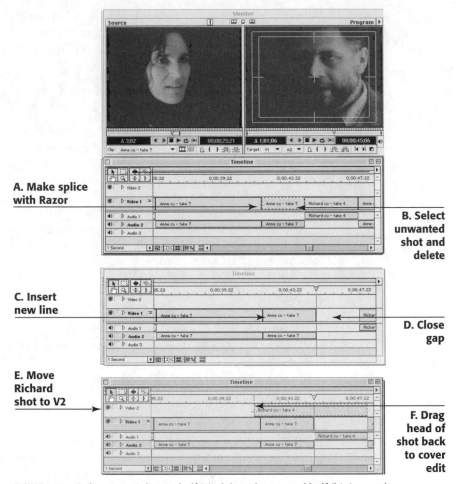

A. Make splice with Razor

B. Select unwanted shot and delete

C. Insert new line

D. Close gap

E. Move Richard shot to V2

F. Drag head of shot back to cover edit

FIGURE 14.9 Splice Anne's line in half (a), delete the second half (b), insert the new second half (c), close the gap (d), move the next Richard shot to Video 2 (e) and pull back the head of the shot to cover the edit in Anne's shot (f).

ON THE DVD

Footage for You to Edit the Entire Richard III *Scene*

So far in this chapter, we've shown you how to edit parts of the scene from Richard III. *The rest of the scene is on the DVD in Chapter 14 Tutorials sub folder "02 Dialog." Because the scene is so long, it's broken into five parts: 01 Opening, 02 Dialog, 03 Knife, 04 Ring, and 05 Ending. Editing this scene together will require most of the skills and techniques discussed in this chapter. A text version of the adapted script, Richard.rtf, is in the Chapter 13 Tutorials folder as well. Our rough cut of the scene is located in Chapter 13 Tutorials>Final Movies>Richard III.*

TRANSITIONS BETWEEN SCENES

There are a number of things that happen "between scenes" in a feature film—a change in location, for example, or a jump forward or back in time, or a jump to an imagined sequence or dream scene. In the early days of filmmaking, each scene began with a fade-in and ended with a fade-out. Later, title cards were added to establish the scene. Both served the function of establishing a new location and a new point in time. Although filmmakers like Jim Jarmusch still use this technique (in films such as *Dead Man*) the typical modern filmmaker relies more on the techniques discussed next.

Hard Cuts

The phrase *hard cut* refers to an edit between two very different shots, without a dissolve or other effect to soften the transition. Hard cuts *within* a scene work best if they are smoothed out with matching action, screen position, and other cues. However, hard cuts can often be used to good comic effect, or to force the audience's imagination in a particular direction. Consider the scene in *Raiders of the Lost Ark* when Indiana Jones and Marion are finally onboard the freighter ship. While he suffers with his bruises, she looks at herself in a mirror. As she flips the mirror over to the clean side, we see the other end swinging up toward Jones's jaw, and then a hard cut to an extreme long shot of the entire ship, and an extremely loud, distant scream.

Hard cuts *between* scenes work best when they are surprising and jarring: a scene of two lovers kissing ends with a hard cut to an extreme close-up of the woman's hand on a gun as she plots to kill her lover. Or, a close-up of a goalie missing the ball hard cuts to a wide shot of the goalie hanging up his uniform, and so on.

Dissolves, Fades, and Wipes

Using a dissolve to transition between scenes can add a feeling of smoothness, and serve to slow the pacing of your story. Dissolves usually imply a period of "reflection" or "introspection" and give the audience a moment to chew on what has just transpired. Dissolves can also indicate the start of a dream sequence or flashback.

Fades and wipes are looking out of date these days, but you never know when a fresh eye can make something old look new. The *Austin Powers* films employed a liberal use of wipes for comic effect, and the hard cuts to black between scenes in *Stranger Than Paradise* added a modern feel to a century-old technique.

Establishing Shots

Carefully placed establishing shots announce that a new scene is about to start, help to orient the audience, and serve to set the location. Without establishing shots, the audience can feel "lost." Often, the establishing shot is built into the first shot of the scene—a crane shot that starts high overhead and ends in a close-up on the main character, a *slow reveal* that pans across a series of objects on a desk and ends on the main character talking on the telephone, and so on. If the director didn't shoot a good establishing shot, then you'll have to find something to "cheat," such as the last few seconds of a wide shot after the cast has cleared frame. You don't need an establishing shot for every single scene in the film, just whenever a significant change in location takes place.

Spending more or less time on your establishing shots is an easy way to change the pacing of your project. A long establishing shot with supporting cutaways will slow things down and give your audience time to "settle in."

To speed things up, you can use a short establishing shot, or economize by combining an establishing shot with a split-audio voice-over. For example, cut to a wide crane-shot of a riverboat while playing audio of your main character saying something like, "The way your mother was driving, I never thought we'd get here." This simple split edit serves to establish the location of your new scene, identify which characters are participating, and provide a little exposition about what they have just done.

Clearing Frame and Natural "Wipes"

An easy way to create a smooth transition between two scenes is to cut out of a shot as the actor clears the frame, and cut into the next shot as she enters frame in another location. This method can become repetitive very quickly if it is overused. When a large object passes through the frame, such as a passing car, a person in the foreground, and so on, it can be used as a natural "wipe" to easily transition to the next scene. In *Rope*, Alfred Hitchcock concealed his few edits in the film by hiding them under natural wipes.

SOLVING TECHNICAL PROBLEMS

Every film has a set of unique technical challenges that often fail to become evident until the editing process actually begins. The following are some of the most common technical issues that get resolved in the editing room.

Missing Elements

The problem you will face most frequently when editing is not having enough material, whether it's because an actor's mic didn't work, the pick-ups don't match the original performance, or there just aren't enough cutaways to allow you to edit the scene the way you want. Most of these types of problems require the on-your-feet, creative thinking that good editors are known for—restructuring the scene so that the bad mic or the pick-ups aren't necessary, or finding an inventive way to recut the scene using jump cuts to make up for the lack of cutaways.

Working with Temporary Elements

When you start editing, it's rare to have all of the elements you need. Whether it's music, pick-ups, or special effects shots, if you don't have all your materials, you'll need some temporary elements in order to create a solid rough cut. Creating a temporary score is a necessity to help "sell" your rough cut, but be sure it's a score that is representative of what you'll be able to use in the final edit.

If you are missing shots because they haven't been shot yet, you can use a placeholder such as a title that describes the missing shot. If you have lots of effects shots and composites, you can use low-resolution proxies imported from your effects software (more about effects in Chapters 16, "Color Correction," 17, "Titling and Simple Compositing," and 18, "Rotoscoping and More Compositing"), or you can create a temporary effects shot or composite in your NLE to use until you get the real thing. Managing lots of temp footage, proxies, and other elements can be an organizational nightmare if you let it get out of control. Be sure to develop some type of naming convention to indicate what's temporary and what's final.

Working with Low-Res Footage

If you're planning to eventually conform your project in an online session, you'll use low-res footage to create your rough cuts. Be aware that some low-res CODECs save space by only compressing one of the two fields in a frame of video. *Single-field resolutions* are fine for rough cuts, but remember that you're only seeing *half* of your footage. If there's a dropout or other problem in the second field, you might not become aware of it until you do the full-resolution online edit. In addition, if you edit up to the last frame of a shot, you have no way of knowing what the other field contains—the end of that shot or the head of the next shot or a field of unstable video. Play it safe by not using the first and last frames of a shot unless your video is uncompressed.

Another way CODECs save space is by compressing the video into a smaller screen size or by cutting the frame rate. You should probably avoid the latter at all costs—if your CODEC drops every third or fourth frame, it limits where you can make an edit. All of these compression techniques make it harder to see your image clearly, and you might find some ugly surprises waiting for you when you see your footage at full resolution.

High-Res Is Unforgiving

If you're editing with low-res offline tapes or a low-res offline CODEC, be aware that when you up-res your project you'll be able to see a lot more than what you saw in low-res. You may find focus problems, sync issues, and objects in the frame that you weren't aware of, such as microphones and cables. If your project is HD or film, this is especially true. And if you "cheated" any dialog or cutaways, you may find they are glaringly apparent on a bigger screen.

MULTI-CAM EDITING

Projects that are unscripted, involve lots of action, or cover a "live" event are often shot with multiple cameras. Sports events, talk shows, reality TV and concert performances are typically shot multi-cam. As long as the cameras are properly synchronized with matching timecode, editing multi-cam footage is a breeze if you have editing software that can handle multi-cam footage.

The first step is to digitize the footage from each camera, breaking it up as needed and maintaining consistency in the clips across the different cameras. For example, if you're editing a boxing match you could create a clip for each round that overlaps by thirty seconds or so. As you log and capture, you would do the same for all the cameras so that if you, say, have four cameras you would then have four clips for round one, four clips for round two, and so on.

The next step is to link the clips from each camera together. The way this is done varies according to your editing software so refer to your user documentation. Each group of camera clips is synched together using matching timecode from the shoot. If the timecode isn't properly synched, you'll have to do the synching yourself, which can be time consuming. You'll have to find a discrete frame—the moment a football flies out of the quarterback's hand, for example—and use that frame to sync all your cameras together.

Now that the clips are locked together, you can start editing. With Avid Media Composer, you load your grouped shot into the source monitor, switch to a multi-cam view (Media Composer allows you to view four or nine sources in a window) select the camera you want, set in and out points, and edit the shot into your sequence. The reference to the grouped shot remains intact so at any time you can match back to the other shots in the grouped clip or use Multicam Mode to switch between cameras or, if you have your keyboard set up for it, use keystrokes to switch cameras on the fly. Apple Final Cut Pro now offers multi-cam editing too.

The biggest issue with multi-cam editing is keeping the right audio in your cut. Traditionally the best audio is linked to the "A camera." (The "A camera" is the primary camera, the next camera is the "B camera," and so on.) If your audio is organized this way, you can often simply use the A camera shot for audio and it will sound great. However, some producers do not follow this convention. You may have to spend a lot of time listening to the various tracks on all the different cameras until you find the audio you need.

Fine Cutting

Now that you have a decent rough cut, it's time to take a harsher look at it: Is it working? Does the story work? Does the dialog make sense? Does it flow naturally? Does it convey the desired mood? Fine cutting is when you will try to make the story and presentation work.

Usually at this point, there's an important editing cliché to remember: the cutting room floor. If your film isn't working, you might need to cut it down. Maybe it's that montage sequence that you love but comes out of nowhere and destroys the natural build of a love story between the main characters. Or, maybe it's part of a secondary storyline that just doesn't fit anymore. Whether it's a scene, a shot, or just a line or two of dialog, cutting out the things that don't work can do wonders for your film.

Woody Allen routinely makes drastic changes between his rough cuts and his fine cuts, often rewriting and reshooting *half* of the movie! This is true for films including *Interiors, The Purple Rose of Cairo, Hannah and Her Sisters, September,* and *Crimes and Misdemeanors.* Such massive reworking is often necessitated because Allen relies on very long master shots. If one line of a five-minute scene is wrong, no amount of editing can save it. In the case of *September,* several actors were no longer available, and were replaced (Sam Shepherd with Sam Waterston, and Maureen O'Sullivan with Elaine Stritch).

After Allen saw the rough cut of *Crimes and Misdemeanors,* he threw out a third of the original story, rewrote it from scratch, and started reshooting. In the process, Mia Farrow's character changed from a geriatric social worker to a television producer; the documentary that Woody

Allen's character was shooting changed from a film about retired vaudeville performers to a film about Allen's TV-producing brother-in-law; and a character played by Sean Young was cut completely.

Although not everyone has the luxury to reshoot as thoroughly as Woody Allen, it's important to recognize that even a director as skilled and experienced as he, still has to feel his way through a project, and make massive changes to reach his goal.

Editing for Style

The editing of feature films today has been strongly influenced by music videos, documentaries, and commercials. Fast cutting, visual effects, and jump cuts are the hallmark of "cool." Movies that fit this model include *Trainspotting*, *The Matrix*, and *Run Lola Run*. However, there's also a counter-trend in independent cinema that involves a no-frills style and lots of long shots where the action plays out with very little manipulation, such as the French documentary film *Trop Tot, Trop Tard* (Too Early, Too Late), or recent movies by Olivier Assayas (*Irma Vep*; *Late August, Early September*). Also popular is the handheld look borrowed from *cinema verité* and reality television, as seen in *The Celebration*. The choice is up to you, but a strong editing style can save an otherwise weak film.

Duration

Although it might sound trivial, one of the biggest jobs in editing is arriving at the proper duration for the project. Some projects have built-in durations: commercials are usually 10, 30, or 60 seconds long, and TV shows are 24 minutes or 48 minutes. Trailers vary from short commercial spots to several minutes long (don't make the mistake of boring viewers with a trailer that tells the entire story). Press kits usually include the full-length trailer(s) from the film, the 30- or 60-second teaser trailer(s), possibly a longer scene or featurette, and some selected takes, such as I.D. shots for each key cast member.

If your project doesn't fit neatly into a predetermined slot, it might be more challenging to arrive at the right duration. If you're editing a short film, keep in mind that it's rare for festivals to accept shorts that are longer than 10 minutes. The average length of the old Warner Brothers cartoons was six minutes and most people seem to expect a short film to be about that length. If yours is a feature film, it will have to be at least 80 minutes long to qualify in most festivals. It used to be that a typical feature film was 90 minutes long, but lately, "serious" films tend to be at least 120 minutes and can often be as long as 180 minutes. Remember, your story should dictate the duration of your film, not an arbitrary number that is the trend of the day.

The Big Picture

Russian filmmaker Andrei Tarkovsky aptly described filmmaking as "sculpting in time," and the longer your film, the more complex the "sculpture." As you try to get a final cut, here are some things to look at in terms of the structure of your film as a whole:

Rhythm and pacing: If you start with a high-energy action scene and try to keep up that level of energy until the end, you'll probably fail. Action seems more intense when it follows a period of calm, and calmness seems more profound when it follows intense action or emotion. Good rhythm and pacing allow intensity to build over time, creating suspense and engaging the audience in the story.

Setups and payoffs: Earlier, we talked about the concepts of setups and pay-offs within a scene or sequence of scenes. However, in a long film, there are also many setups that occur in the early part of the film and don't pay off until much later on. Make sure all the setups that play out over time are paid off later on.

Emotion: Emotion is built into the script and the actors' performances, but editing plays a role as well. If scenes aren't allowed to develop or build, the emotion—whether happy, funny, angry, sad, and so forth—will fall flat. When you look at the film as a whole, make sure all the emotional beats that you intended are there.

Compressing and expanding time: How long is the period of time covered in your story—a day, two weeks, five years? Does the structure of the film seem appropriate for the film's length? Would it benefit from rearranging the order and playing with the timeframe?

EXERCISE

This chapter contains many tutorials that you should work through and become comfortable with. If you didn't try them all, go back and do so now. Once you have worked through the chapter tutorials, try working with some of your own footage.

SUMMARY

Last, but not least, you need to *lock picture*. Locking picture means that you have finished editing for story and will not make any further changes to the content of the film. You might still have some outstanding effects shots that need to be dropped in, but you won't be making any changes that affect the duration. Once picture is locked, it's time to take a more serious pass at editing the sound.

Learn More about Editing from This Shameless Plug

The full art and science of editing is a huge topic that is way beyond the scope of this book. Hopefully, this chapter has given you a good foundation for working on your projects. If you want to learn more about editing, check out Sonja Schenk's book, Digital Non-Linear Desktop Editing, *also published by Charles River Media.*

SOUND EDITING

In This Chapter

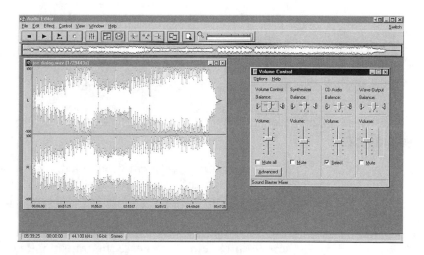

Earlier in this book, we mentioned that many filmmakers consider sound to be 50 percent of a film. If you're not already a believer, once you start editing your project's sound, you'll probably become a convert to this idea. Sound can add emotional depth to a scene, clarify elements of the story, and make special effects and cheated shots pass the viewer's eye without raising any questions. Whether your project is a narrative feature film, a documentary, a corporate video, a commercial, or an animated short, sound editing is one of the most creative parts of the process of finishing a project.

In the course of editing your video, you've already done a lot of sound and dialog editing, but as you probably discovered, things don't always go as planned when shooting. You might have encountered problem areas such as inaudible dialog, unwanted extra sounds, drop-outs, or discontinuities in audio quality. And, of course, you probably didn't add any sound effects or music, unless they were essential to your picture editing (matching action to a particular piece of music or sound effect, for example).

Sound editing is the process of cleaning up all the mistakes and problems in the sound track, adding music, sound effects, and any re-recorded dialog, and mixing and equalizing the whole thing so that it sounds as good as it possibly can.

Like most production processes, post-production sound has been greatly changed by desktop digital editing tools. Your NLE probably has basic sound editing tools, multitrack mixing capabilities, equalization, and a selection of special effects filters for altering the sound of your audio. These features often take the place of what once required huge rooms full of equipment and engineers. However, as with video editing, there are times when you still might need to use a professional audio suite to get higher fidelity sound, output a high-end master, or to enlist the services of a trained professional.

SOUNDING OFF

If your video image is greatly degraded, it's possible that you can pass off such a flaw as an intentional style, but bad-sounding audio will quickly result in a frustrated, bored audience that most likely won't be able to follow your story.

Good sound editing strengthens the effect of each video edit. A few simple sound effects can ease the transition between pieces of audio shot at different times or at different locations.

Sound—whether sound effects, music, or sometimes *silence*—can add to, or completely create, the emotional impact in a scene. Can you imagine the shower scene in *Psycho* without the screeching violins? Or the shark in *Jaws* without the rumbling bass notes? And, of course, just try to imagine a sad scene of emotional confession without a sweet, heart-tugging swell of strings beneath it.

Music is often the most obvious sound effect, and we're all familiar with the experience of music providing important pieces of information. For example: A car drives up, a person we've never seen gets out, and the music suddenly becomes very ominous. Cut circus music into the same scene, and the audience will know this is a very different type of story.

Music is also used to set tone or atmosphere. If you had the opportunity to see one of the early director's cuts of *Blade Runner*, you saw a movie with an orchestral score, rather than Vangelis's synthesized score. As compelling as the visuals in *Blade Runner* are, laying orchestral music beneath them created an atmosphere that was not as effective.

Sometimes, the musical score carries all of the dramatic pacing in a scene. Try watching the last few minutes of *Jurassic Park* with the sound turned down (this works especially well if you've never seen the movie). You might be very surprised to realize the movie doesn't really have a strong ending. If you don't remember the movie, the ending goes something like this: Chased by a giant T-rex, the heroes race to get inside a building. The character played by Sam Neil tosses off a one-liner as they run inside and the film cuts to a sweeping shot of the island as they escape by helicopter across the ocean. There's no giant explosion or climactic death of the T-rex—the actors simply run into a building and close the door. However, at the exact moment that they reach the door, the music swells to a crescendo, making it feel like a satisfying conclusion, and Sam Neil's little joke as icing on the cake.

When you think of sound effects, you often think of special effect types of sounds such as laser blasts or explosions. However, most of the time, your sound effects will be incredibly normal, everyday sounds. As with music, sound effects can often be used to increase the emotional intensity of a scene. Imagine a scene you've probably watched dozens of times: our hero is preoccupied as a villain sneaks into the room, slowly raises a gun, cocks the trigger, and prepares to fire. Next time you watch such a scene, pay attention to just how loud that trigger-cocking sound is. Would the scene carry as much impact without the help of this sound effect?

These types of augmented sounds can add a tremendous amount of drama to a scene, and they're a great way to guide the audience through a quieter, dialog-free scene.

Finally, good sound editing can often be used to "dress" a set to make it more believable. If you cut to a shot like the one shown in Figure 5.10 and throw in echoing ambient sounds of Arabic crowd noise, a faraway steamship horn, and some Middle-Eastern music, your audience will believe that your location really is somewhere in the Middle East.

Like picture editing, the full importance of sound editing can be something that's very easy to overlook. In the rest of this chapter, we'll cover the types of equipment and software you'll need for good sound editing, provide tips for editing sound effects, ambience, dialog, and music, and cover the basics of filters, equalization, and temporary mixes.

SETTING UP

Before you begin any sound editing, you need to determine what types of sounds you'll need. Your sound editing process should begin with a screening of the final locked cut of your project. Ideally, you'll want to have your director, editor, sound editor, and music supervisor present at the screening. Your goal is to determine just what sound edits and effects will need to be created or acquired.

For every scene, you'll need to identify problems, necessary sound effects, and how and where your musical track (if any) will be edited into the scene. This process of watching, assessing, and listing your sound requirements is called *spotting*.

Next, your editor or sound editor will need to prepare your project file—the file you've been editing using your NLE—for sound editing. Presumably, you already have at least two tracks: a stereo left and stereo right track from your original camera audio. You might have some additional tracks if you performed any preliminary audio editing or special effects work when you were editing for picture. You'll want an additional stereo pair for your music, and another track for special effects. Finally, you might want still another track for ambient *rumble* tracks that will be used to smooth the transitions between different sounds and locations. Typically, you'll have a minimum of eight tracks. For projects with simpler audio editing needs, such as those that rely heavily on narration, it's best to stick with eight tracks (or less). This is an easy number to manage and most good NLEs are capable of real-time playback of eight tracks so you can avoid needless rendering.

By the time you're finished, you might have created many, many more tracks. Depending on how you will output your final project, these tracks will be mixed down to just a few tracks, a process we will detail in Chapter 19, "Output."

After the spotting session, you should have a better idea of what type of work lies ahead and you can start thinking about what type of equipment and software you'll need to perform your audio edit.

EDITING SOUND IN YOUR NLE

You will probably be able to perform most edits—audio cuts as well as cross-fades and simple effects—using the sound editing features of your NLE software. Most editing packages provide a waveform display that makes it simple to zoom in on a sound to trim and cut, or to eliminate or replace problem areas (Figure 15.1). As we said earlier, editing packages also usually include most of the audio filters you'll need for creating simple effects, and for sweetening audio.

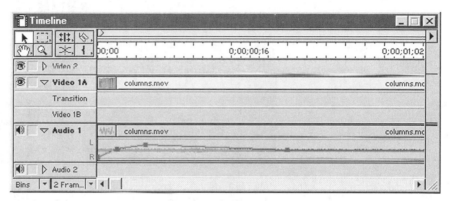

FIGURE 15.1   Waveform editing in Adobe Premiere.

To determine if you'll need any additional sound editing software, you should examine your NLE to see if it has certain audio editing essentials. Consult your manual and do some tests with your software to determine if your NLE provides the following:

Support for the number of tracks you'll need. Most editing packages provide support for dozens of audio tracks. Although your final master might only have four to eight tracks, being able to create extra tracks makes it easier to keep your project organized. If you are using a lower-end editing package that only provides two or four tracks, then you might need to take your audio elsewhere. At the very least, look for editing software that can play back eight tracks of audio in real-time.

Level control for each track. Any respectable, high-end editing package will have this feature, usually in the form of a simple line across the audio track that can be dragged up and down, and edited with control points. Play with your software's controls to see if you feel comfortable with this interface. You might decide you want to take your audio out to a program that provides a more traditional mixing interface. You might even want to take your audio out to a real mixing console. A FireWire mixer, like the one in Figure 15.2, is easy to connect to a computer and provides a good alternative to all that clicking and dragging.

FIGURE 15.2 The Tascam FW-1082 mixing board connects to your computer via FireWire.

Can your NLE scrub audio? For some edits, you absolutely have to be able to scrub through your audio very slowly. Scrubbing means that your audio plays at variable speeds as you drag your mouse through the clip. Ideally, you want an audio scrubber that slows the audio down when scrubbing, just like you'd hear if you played an analog tape at slow speed, as opposed to a scrubber that plays sampled bits at normal speed (the way a CD player does when you search forward or backward). Good scrubbing capabilities can be essential for making precise cuts, or identifying individual words, sounds, and syllables.

Sweetening and correcting filters. There are a number of filters that you'll want to have to improve the quality of your audio, and to correct problem areas. At the very least, you'll want an equalizer filter to adjust the various frequencies in your sound (Figure 15.3). Ideally, you'll want to have a *Notch* filter of some kind, a good selection of *gates* and *compressors*, specialized filters such as *de-essers*, and click and hum removers.

Special effects filters. For added control, special effects filters such as echoes, reverbs, delays, and flangers can be used for everything from creating special sounds to creating ambient tone. Most higher-end NLEs will include a full complement of effects filters (Figure 15.4).

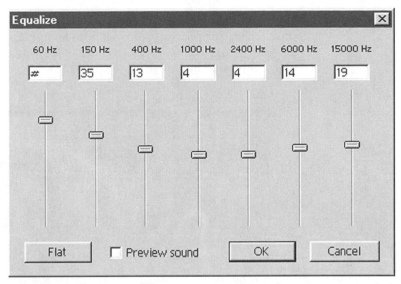

FIGURE 15.3   Premiere's EQ filter.

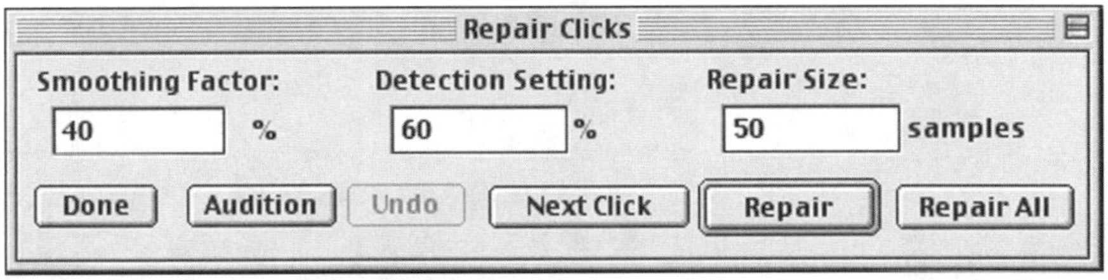

FIGURE 15.4   A simple click-removing plug-in.

DEDICATED SOUND EDITING APPS

If, after looking at your NLE, you decide that you need more audio editing power, then you'll want to consider a dedicated audio editing application. There are several reasons why you might need more sound editing power.

Most NLEs only let you make cuts between individual frames, so if you need to make *very* precise edits, such as an edit at an interval that's smaller than a single frame, or 1/30th of a second, you'll need to move your audio out of your NLE and into a dedicated sound editing app.

As with picture editing, audio editing can be a very tactile process. Feeling where a cut should fall, or "riding" a level or EQ adjustment, are processes where you often want a fine level of hands-on control. If you prefer such controls to a mouse-driven audio editing interface, then you should consider moving your audio to an application that provides better on-screen controls (Figures 15.5 and 15.6), or even hardware consoles that can be attached to your computer.

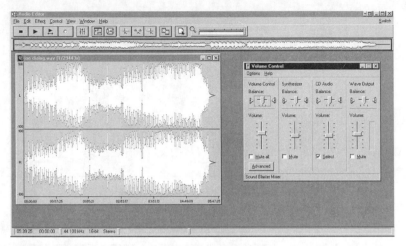

FIGURE 15.5 Ulead Media Studio Pro provides robust audio editing controls.

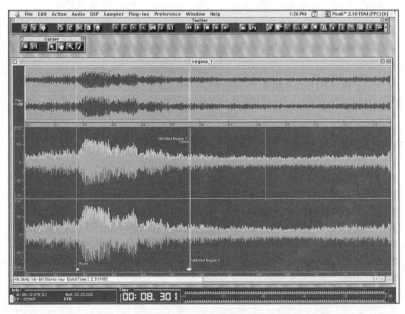

FIGURE 15.6 Bias' Peak provides a full-featured, stand-alone audio editing environment.

Dedicated audio editors provide a number of other powerful features, such as the ability to define and label *regions* in an audio track. Regions allow you to label what each part of an audio waveform is, making it easier to spot locations for additional edits.

To select a digital audio application, you'll want to consider many of the same questions introduced earlier. In addition, look for the following:

- **How does the app play back video?** Many audio editing programs synchronize to videotape; others let you open a QuickTime movie for playback. Some people are willing to spend the time cutting and working with tapes, while others prefer to take the time to capture the video and work with QuickTime. Be aware that the QuickTime resolution that most audio editing applications support is fairly low-res—getting lip-sync with low-res digitized video can be a challenge.

- **Does the app support the timecode you are using?** Although timecode is not essential for performing outboard edits on small pieces of your audio, you'll need it if you want to edit all your sound on a different software app or system (see the sidebar "Moving Your Audio"). Many sound applications use timecode to synchronize their audio timeline to a videotape image during the sound editing process. Video on tape—even VHS—is often of higher quality than low-res QuickTime and therefore more useful for checking sync.

- **Support for OMF?** If you're counting on exporting audio from your video editing app in the OMF format, make sure your sound editing app supports the same version of OMF. (For more about OMFs, see the sidebar "Moving Your Audio.")

- **Are you editing in real-time?** For easier editing, you'll want an application that can apply effects in real-time. When making subtle EQ changes, for example, it's preferable to have your audio editor continuously loop and play the sound so that you can hear changes as you make adjustments. Many applications can perform simple stereo effects in real-time. For other effects, and for real-time processing of additional tracks, you'll need a system with special hardware.

- **Do you have room for more hardware?** If you opt for a system with special hardware, make sure you have enough slots in your computer to support more expansion cards.

- **Do you need surround sound capabilities?** Some sound editing packages make it easy to create a five-channel surround sound mix that takes full advantage of the HD format. If you need surround sound, make sure your software can handle it.

Obviously, if you're not going to be performing your audio edits yourself, then software might not be a concern. If you will be hiring a professional audio house to create your final audio edit, or if your sound editor has his or her own audio hardware, then you will simply need to find out how to deliver your audio. You should also plan to deliver *all* of your original audio material. That is, all of your videotapes if you shot sync sound, and all of your original audio tapes if you shot non-sync sound (actually, for safekeeping, you'll want to deliver clones of your tapes if you can afford it). There's no telling what your sound editor might need in the way of audio. Whether it's re-recording a sound, or building an entirely new sound from other material on your tapes, to do his or her job well, your sound editor will need all of your source material.

Just as there are many video editing applications on the market, there are also many sound editing applications. If you only need basic audio editing capabilities, though, you can stick with the tools in your NLE. However, if you need a more robust toolset, applications like Digidesign ProTools, Apple SoundTrack Pro (Figure 15.7), Steinberg Nuendo, and Bias Peak are of the caliber used by professional sound designers, dialog editors, and mixers. All of them can handle synchronized playback of videotape (with the right hardware components), SMPTE timecode, import and export OMFs, real-time playback and additional capabilities and performance through added hardware such as sound processing PCI cards.

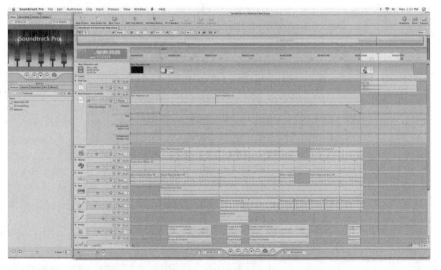

FIGURE 15.7 The audio editing interface in Apple SoundTrack Pro, which lets you import a QuickTime movie for viewing while you score and arrange.

MOVING YOUR AUDIO

If you're going to edit your audio outside of your editing application, you'll need to move your audio—even if you're just moving it from one app to another on the same computer—and moving audio can be tricky.

These days, exporting an *OMF file* is the easiest way to move sounds around. OMF files let you save the tracks in your NLE's edited timeline and can include audio levels settings, dissolves, and the audio media itself. However, OMF files come in a couple of different flavors: OMFs that only contain the timeline information, OMFs that contain the timeline and the level settings, OMFs that contain all of the aforementioned, and so on. Unfortunately, not all editing and sound editing apps are compatible with all the different types of OMFs, so be sure to check your software manufacturer's specs and do a little testing to be certain everything works right. Generally, once you export an OMF file from your editing software, you'll need to convert it to a project file that's compatible with ProTools, Nuendo, or whatever sound app you're using.

If you need to perform a quick fix on a short, isolated piece of sound, then you can simply export your audio from your NLE in whatever format your sound app requires (AIFF, .WAV, SDII, etc.). Be sure to export at full quality so that the sound editor has a high-quality sound signal with which to work. In addition, no matter how you manipulate the piece of audio, you must take care to maintain the *frame rate* (usually 29.97 fps or 24 fps) and the *audio sampling rate* (usually 48 kHz). This ensures that you'll be able to import the new treated audio back into your NLE without losing sync.

If you want to re-edit all of the sound in your entire project, the easiest way to take it out is by using OMF, but you can also output *split audio tracks* to digital tape (DAT, DV, DigiBeta, DA88, etc.). Assuming you have a locked cut of your picture, you'll have several tracks of sound that you edited along with the picture. By outputting each track to a distinct channel on digital tape, and then capturing each track separately in your sound editing app, you'll be able to start polishing the sound with a decent rough cut of the sound already in place. You might need to use more than one tape to get all of your tracks moved, and those tapes will need timecode that matches the timecode of your final locked sequence in your NLE. If the digital tape format you're using isn't capable of recording timecode, then each track will need to have sync marks, or *2-pops* that match the countdown of your locked picture. 2-pops are a single frame of 60 Hz audio reference tone cut into the countdown at the same frame that the two-second counter appears on screen. Timecode and/or 2-pops are absolute necessities for this type of work—losing sync for an entire project is *one of the worst things that can happen in post!*

If you didn't capture high-quality audio in your NLE, or if you just want to start over with clean audio, you can use an OMF or an *EDL* to reconstruct your sequence. You'll need high-end sound editing software and hardware that supports timecode and OMFs or EDLs. Creating an EDL is covered in detail in Chapter 19— if you're creating an EDL for audio only, be sure to talk to your sound editor to make sure you include all the necessary information in the EDL.

High-end sound editing apps such ProTools are designed to work with either a low-res QuickTime video capture or a hardware-synched videotape version of the locked picture cut. Whether you choose split track outputs or an EDL, you'll also need to output a viewing copy of your locked picture sequence with a countdown, including a 2-pop, preferably with visible timecode *and* either address track timecode or audio track timecode for formats that don't support SMPTE timecode, such as DV and VHS. When you're done editing the sound you can reunite the polished audio with the final video master on tape or in your NLE. (More about final mixes and audio outputs in Chapter 19, "Output.") As mentioned earlier, it's crucial that you maintain the same frame rate and audio sampling ratio that you used in your NLE if you want your project to stay in sync.

Audio Editing Hardware

Sound editing applications are powerful tools, but even though you can get away with performing all of your audio edits using software alone, you might want special hardware to augment the process.

Audio Decks

If you want to take your audio out of your computer for editing in a studio, then you'll need some place to put it. Your best option is to record to a DAT or DA88, as most studios will be set up for those formats. You could also, however, dump your audio out to a DV tape, and take your deck and tape to a studio. There, your audio could be bumped to DAT or DA88 for editing.

Mixing Boards

If you're more comfortable with sliders and knobs than with a mouse, then you might want a mixing board for mixing and balancing your tracks. Although you might have used a simple mic mixer or four-track mixing board during your shoot, you'll probably want a beefier mixing board for your post-production editing.

Microphones

Obviously, if you end up needing to re-record dialog, or to record sound effects on location, you'll need microphones. For voice-overs and other dialog recording, your best option will be a good handheld mic. Whether you're choosing to record directly into your computer, or recording into a tape deck, be sure you have the necessary cables and connectors to hook up your mic.

Speakers

It almost goes without saying that all sound editing workstations need a good pair of speakers. See the section on audio hardware in Chapter 12, "Editing Hardware," for more on speakers and other audio related hardware.

Audio PCI Cards

Many dedicated sound editing apps can be paired with special PCI cards designed to process audio in your computer. Check your software manufacturer for details.

TEMP MIXES

It used to be that the "mix" was one of the last steps in the post-production process but nowadays mixing is something that starts during the editing of the video, gets built on during the editing of the sound, and then gets polished at the end in the final mix. The final mix is specific to the type of product you are creating—feature film, TV spot, DVD release, etc.—and we discuss the varieties of final mixes in Chapter 19, "Output." But long before you get to that stage, you'll need to do a temp mix.

Mixing simply means setting the levels of the various sounds in your edited sequence and adding fades and equalization if necessary. Back when films were edited on film, the corresponding sound was edited on synchronized magnetic audio tape, or "mag." Film editing flatbeds typically only had room for two mag tracks and the volume could be controlled separately. Usually one was used for dialog and the other for music and effects. The sounds that accompanied many rough cuts prior to the late 1980s were very limited as a result.

Today, things are very different. Picture editors are expected to do a rough mix using their non-linear editing software in order to make their rough cuts better for screening purposes. They typically arrange the sounds across eight tracks and set the levels, add fades, and even basic equalization if needed. This process is called a "temp mix." By the time the sound editor gets to work on it, the mix should be pretty decent. Since setting the levels for all of the sounds in your piece takes a long time, this saves the sound editor a lot of time. The sound editor continues to adjust levels to new sounds added to the piece as he or she works so that the mix continues to sound good. The goal of a temp mix is that at any time the project can be screened or output as a work-in-progress. By the time you get to the final mix, the mixer usually doesn't need to remix the entire project from scratch—instead he or she will adjust levels on an as-needed basis.

EDITING SOUND

Once your equipment is in place, it's time to start working your way through the list of sound edits that you created during your spotting session. In addition to the obvious sound effects—gunshots, screams, footsteps, howling wind, and so forth—and the questions of mood, atmosphere, and drama that we discussed earlier, there are a number of other sound edits that might be on your list. The following are all things you should look for when spotting and editing.

Unintelligible Dialog

Remember that *you* already know what your actors are saying. Whether you wrote, directed, or edited (or did all three jobs), you've probably heard each line hundreds of times. Consequently, you might be more forgiving of a mumbled or quiet line of dialog. Pay close attention to your character's speech, and make sure that it is clear and intelligible. If it's not, consider using EQ (more on this later), boosting the level, or using a different take (audio, or both audio and video). (Sometimes you can sneak in a word from another take without any visible loss of sync but be careful if you're going to end up projecting on a big screen.) As a last resort, you can always bring the actor in to re-record or "loop" his or her dialog (more on this later, also).

Changes in Tone

Does the overall audio quality change from one edit to another? Changes in tone can result from changes in microphone placement, changes in location, changes in ambient sound, or just weird "acts of God" that you might not be able to explain. Hopefully, you recorded some room tone at your locations.

A change in tone can often be masked by fading from one audio source to the next, to mask the change in sound quality. A bed of room tone, ambient sound, or music can further conceal this "edit" (Figure 15.8).

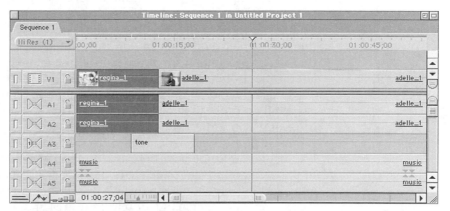

FIGURE 15.8   To improve sounds with mismatched tone, we can apply a bed of room tone. A cross-dissolve between the two bad tracks might further improve things.

Is There Extraneous Noise in the Shot?

When shooting on location, it can often be difficult to keep a quiet, controlled set. If there are extra, distracting noises—a loud conversation or music playing, for example—see if you can mask these sounds by placing sound or music effects that will keep your audience focused on your action.

Remember: The audience will pay attention to the things you lead them to. Just as you can brighten the foreground of your video to draw attention to your subject, you can "brighten" the foreground of your audio to ensure that your audience listens in the right "direction."

Are There Bad Video Edits That Can Be Reinforced with Audio?

Sometimes, a video edit with weak motivation can be reinforced with a good strong sound. The easiest way to reinforce an edit is to place a beat of music at that location. The rhythm of your music track will carry through to the audience's visual sense. If you're using pre-recorded, or "canned," music, consider adjusting the start of the music so that a strong beat falls on your weak edit. If you're working with an original score, perhaps your composer can suggest a change in music.

In addition to music, weak edits can be reinforced with an off-camera sound effect. A breaking window, for example, will provide plenty of motivation for a cut to another shot.

Is There Bad Audio?

There are many technical problems that can corrupt audio, from a boom operator bumping the mic, to a short in a cable, to interference with electrical fields. To eliminate thumps and bumps on the microphone, you can usually just bring the level of the audio down or cut it out. Hopefully, there's no dialog or other important sounds during those moments. If there are, you might need to re-record those audio elements. As we'll see later, other troubles can be corrected through EQ adjustments.

The clicks and pops that can result from a short in a cable are usually easy to fix because they're brief. Even if a click falls over dialog, removing it usually won't affect the quality of your recording. Even if a click is in the middle of a word, sometimes just cutting it out sounds better than leaving it as is. Remember that, as with bumps, when you remove a click or pop you don't want to delete it, or use a "close gap" command, as this will shorten your sound and throw your sound and video out of sync. Instead, use a "lift" command, or select the area and use a silence command to reduce the selected area to nothing, or copy an appropriate length of room tone into the selected area.

If you have a hum in your audio, then your life might have just gotten very complicated. Some hums are easy to fix and can be removed with a simple notch filter. Fluorescent lights and some electrical sources sometimes create a 60 Hz hum in your audio. Setting a notch filter to remove all the sounds at 60 Hz can frequently eliminate or reduce a hum. Note that hums sometimes produce additional harmonic hums that also need to be removed. You can remove these with separate notch filters, or use a special hum remover that automatically notches harmonics.

Some hums might be too "dirty" (that is, they fall over too much of the audio spectrum) to be removed. In most cases, living with it or re-recording your sound track are your only options.

If your hum is slight, you can often reduce or eliminate it with a simple EQ filter.

Are There Vocal Problems You Need to Correct?

While flubbed lines can often be fixed by re-recording, or pulling audio from alternate takes, other vocal problems might require special filtering.

For example, if an actor's dialog has loud, shushing "s" sounds, you can often correct these with a de-*essing* filter or with an EQ adjustment.

DIALOG EDITING

When you edited your picture you, obviously, cut together your dialog as well. However, you'll need to do a fair amount of editing to get your dialog organized so that it can be easily adjusted and corrected, and to prepare it for the final mix.

Checkerboarding is the process of arranging your dialog tracks so that one voice can be easily adjusted and corrected. Your goal is to separate different speakers onto different tracks so that you can manipulate and correct their dialog with as few separate actions as possible. For example, if you've decided that all of your lead actor's dialog needs a slight EQ adjustment, having checkerboarded audio will make it simple to apply a single EQ filter to all of your actor's speech.

It's called "checkerboarding" (or *splitting tracks*) because, as you begin to separate different speakers, your audio tracks will begin to have a "checkerboard" appearance as can be seen in Figure 15.9.

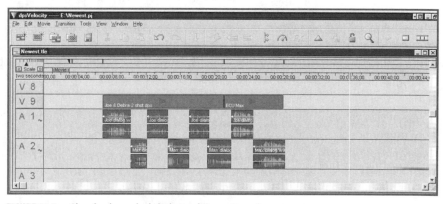

FIGURE 15.9   Checkerboarded dialog editing.

You won't necessarily separate out every single voice or even every occurrence of a particular speaker. Although you might be trying to split out a particular actor, splitting tracks during short lines or overlapping dialog might not be worth the trouble. In addition to splitting up your dialog, you'll also need to move all of the sound effects recorded during your production onto their own track.

In an NLE, the easiest way to split tracks is simply to select the relevant portions of the sound track, and copy and paste them to a new track. Remember not to cut, or you'll throw the remaining audio out of sync. When you've copied all of your data into the appropriate tracks, you can delete your original audio tracks.

This is where the 30 to 60 seconds of *room tone* that you recorded during production will come into play. You'll use room tone to smooth the differences between different speakers, to fill silent areas, and to improve the sense of ambient space in your audio. If you didn't record room tone, then you can try to build up a sample of room tone by cutting and pasting together quiet moments from your original audio track.

ADR

Automatic dialog replacement is used to replace badly recorded sound, fix a muffed line, or insert dialog that could not be recorded on location.

In a professional ADR facility, a projector or deck shows the scene to be re-recorded, and then immediately re-winds and plays the scene again, without audio. The actors then record their lines while watching the scene. Sometimes, a continuous "loop" of the scene is shown; hence the term *looping*.

The actor is usually cued with a series of regular beeps that count down to the start of recording. Their goal is to match their vocal performance to what they just saw on-screen.

Although you might be tempted to rely on re-recording—you might think it easier than trying to get things correct on-set—be warned that getting good ADR is hard work. First, you'll need to try to match the tone and quality of the original recording. Everything from mic selection and mic placement to the qualities of the recording room will affect the tone of your recording. As if getting the actor to match his voice to the lip movements recorded on-screen isn't difficult enough, consider also that the actor's performance will probably be at a somewhat different energy and emotional level than what was originally shot. Outside of the scene, with no actors, build-up, or motivation, it can be difficult for an actor to achieve the same performance quality that he or she delivered on-set.

ADR is most difficult on close-ups because it's easier to see sync problems. An example of a scene that could benefit from ADR is a long shot of two people having a conversation near a freeway. The production sound will be very bad due to the noise from the freeway. Since the actors are far away, it will be difficult for the audience to see if the re-recorded dialog is actually in sync with the actors' mouths. In addition, ADR that appears in sync on the small screen might seem "soft" on the big screen, so use ADR carefully if you're planning on a theatrical projection of your project.

If you have a sound editing product that supports TDM or AudioSuite plug-ins, then you can use Synchro Arts' VocAlign to automatically stretch or compress a re-recorded piece of dialog to match the original production recording. If this sounds impossibly amazing, it is. But it works! If your project requires a lot of accurate ADR, VocAlign is worth the money.

Non-Dialog Voice Recordings

Other voice recording jobs will be simpler. Voice-overs (such as those used in a documentary, or in a flashback scene in a dramatic feature) as well as other vocal sound effects will require special recording sessions but you won't need all the tools required for ADR recording.

For example, if you shot a restaurant scene with a silent background (to better record the voices of your actors), you might record the sound of the other restaurant patrons. (*Walla* is the term for the mumbling, unrecognizable din of a crowd of people.) However, if you can, try to get away with recording walla and other background sounds "wild" instead of paying for a studio recording session.

EQ Is Your Friend

If your home stereo has controls for adjusting bass and treble, then you're already familiar with a very simple form of equalizing (or *EQ*). An equalizer lets you control the loudness of different parts of the sound spectrum, called *frequencies*. For example, if you want to add some resonance to a voice, you might choose to use an EQ adjustment to boost the bass frequencies in the sound. In a sense, an equalizer is just a very refined volume control that allows you to make certain frequencies of sound louder or softer.

A *graphic equalizer* provides sliders for adjusting the volume of specific frequencies, as measured in Hertz (Hz). Move a slider up and the sounds within that frequency will get louder; move it down and they will get softer. It's important to remember that each slider represents a point on a curve. By moving the sliders, you are re-shaping the curve. In other words, frequencies *around* the slider will be affected also (Figure 15.10).

The best way to learn how to use EQ is to experiment, ideally with an editing system or mixing board that provides real-time filtering. Consider using an EQ filter in the following situations:

> **Sweetening or adding richness.** With a simple boost to the low or lower mid-range, you can add presence and richness to a voice. Don't add too much, though, or you'll end up with a muffled sound.

Making speech more intelligible. Raising the mid-range frequencies (2000 Hz, or 2 *kHz*) and reducing frequencies below 100 Hz will frequently make for clearer dialog.

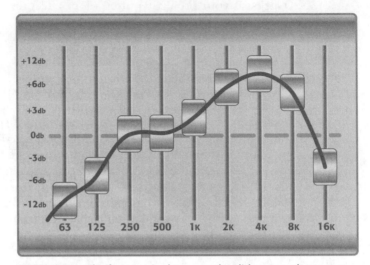

FIGURE 15.10   The frequencies between the slider controls on your equalizer are connected by a curve. Therefore, adjusting one frequency will shift the frequencies in between. Don't expect to be able to adjust *only* the frequencies on each slider.

Too Much of a Good Thing

Because EQ is really just a refined way of adjusting volume, be aware that by increasing some of the frequencies, you can end up increasing the overall volume. Watch your level meter to make sure EQ'd sounds don't peak or distort.

Wind and mic bumps. Wind and microphone noise (such as the low rumble noises caused by poor mic handling) can be minimized by reducing the low frequencies (60 to 120 Hz).

Reducing hiss, and other high-frequency sounds. Just as you can eliminate low-frequency rumbles, you can also eliminate tape hiss and other high-frequency sounds by lowering frequencies above 5 kHz.

Simulating audio sources. You can use EQ to simulate the sound of a voice on a telephone, or music from a car radio by rolling off the appropriate frequencies. For telephone voice, boost everything between 400 and 2000 Hz, and lower everything else. The same effect can be used to simulate a low-quality car radio, by using less extreme values. In other words, keep more of the high and low end than you would for a telephone effect (Figures 15.11 and 15.12).

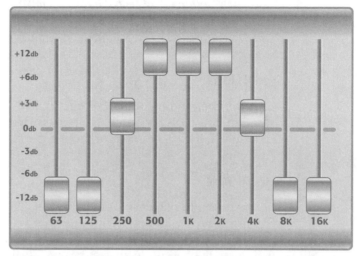

FIGURE 15.11   With some simple EQ adjustments, you can easily simulate the sound of a voice coming through a telephone.

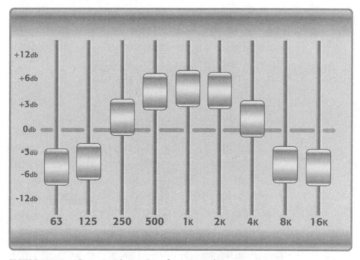

FIGURE 15.12   Or sound coming from a radio or car stereo.

Note that to perform good EQ adjustments, you need to be sure you're listening to your audio on speakers with a wide dynamic range. If you're using speakers with a poor response at one end of the audio spectrum, you'll neither be able to hear or correct troubles.

Mixing Boards

If you're going to do a lot of equalizing, it might be faster to EQ your audio as you capture it by running it through a hardware mixing board, like the ones shown in Figure 15.2. A mixing board is also the easiest way to add an overall EQ or level change to your project when you input or output.

Special Filters

As with video, audio editing has been greatly changed by the advent of digital editing tools. A number of specialized applications and plug-ins can help you fix any number of problems.

Digidesign's DINR

The Digidesign Intelligent Noise Reduction plug-in for TDM or AudioSuite systems can be used for removing any type of noise from a recording. Tape hiss, rumbling air-conditioners, or gnarly hums can all be automatically eliminated. If a bad noise artifact has wrecked some or all of your sound, DINR might be able to save your footage, or prevent an expensive ADR session.

Digidesign's Aural Exciter

Aural Exciter is an excellent tool for increasing the intelligibility of voices in your audio tracks. In addition, Aural Exciter provides powerful features for bringing muddled sounds into the foreground.

Digidesign's Sound Replacer

Sound Replacer does just what it says: it replaces sounds already in a mix. For example, if you mix down your audio and then decide that the door-knob foley isn't quite right, you might be able to use Sound Replacer to reach into your mix and replace the doorknob sound with something else.

Arboretum Ionizer

Similar to DINR, another excellent noise reduction plug-in with extra special effects and pre-set functions for cleaning field recordings and telephone interviews.

Special Effects

For creating new sounds, embellishing old sounds, and creating special effects, there is a huge assortment of plug-ins that do everything from simulating Doppler effect to changing pitch and tone, to simulating the sounds of instruments and machinery.

SOUND EFFECTS

Your choice of what to use for a particular sound effect will weigh greatly on the overall impact of the scene. For example, if a scene needs the sound of a dog barking in the distance, you'll get a very different effect if you choose to use a Chihuahua or a Doberman. Depending on the tone of the scene, one might be a much better choice.

Going with the choice that is less obvious can often have very serendipitous results. Don't hesitate to try a number of different ideas, including ones that might initially sound strange. For example, consider the sound of the tornadoes in the movie *Twister*. Rather than sticking with simple sounds of storm and flying debris, the editors added guttural, snarling, sucking sounds that give the twisters an almost conscious, animal-like menace.

Don't hesitate to create your own sound effects. A good mic and some simple field recording equipment can help you get good source material. In addition to getting sounds that exactly match the pacing and length of your video, you might come up with very original sounds. Consider the laser blasts from *Star Wars*. Originally created by banging on the tail ends of power lines, these sources were masterfully manipulated into high-tech, futuristic effects.

Sometimes one effect isn't enough. Layering two or more effects can add depth and impact to a sound event. The most famous example is the modern movie sound of a gunshot, which was developed by Sam Peckinpah in the early 1970s. Several layers of effects and reverb are combined to create a full, explosive sound, rather than the flat "pop" that's heard from a gunshot in real life.

When adding any type of effect, don't expect it to be perfect as soon as you drop it in. Most likely, you'll have to go through a lot of trial and error. There are no rules or numbers you can follow for these processes; instead, follow your ear.

To improve and blend in a sound effect, remember that you have all of the following with which to work:

> **Levels:** Make sure the level of the sound matches the intensity of what's on the screen—a small handgun shouldn't sound like a cannon.

EQ and effects: You can use EQ to improve the quality of your sound effect and to try to separate the effect from the other sounds in your mix. Other effects can be added to match the sound effect to its surroundings. The sound of dropping a bowling ball in a cathedral, for example, should have a lot more reverb and echo, than the sound of dropping a bowling ball in a convenience store.

The mix: You might be able to improve your sound effect by adjusting other tracks in your mix. Maybe it's not that your airplane sound effect is too quiet; perhaps your dialog is too loud. Play with your entire mix when editing in a sound effect.

Sound Effect Sources

Once you start editing, you'll need a number of different audio sources at your disposal. In addition to your original production audio tapes, you'll probably end up recording extra sounds on your own (called *wild sounds*). You might also want to invest in a sound effects library. Companies such as Sound Ideas provide vast, detailed collections of high-quality pre-recorded sounds. These can be essential tools for adding effects and ambience to your audio tracks. If you're editing in a studio or post-production facility, they might have a sound effects library you can use. More and more of these libraries are available online, as single track downloads, which is a great option if you just need a couple of effects and don't have the time or budget to invest in a full library.

Foley is the process of recording special ambient effects in real-time while watching your picture. Door slams, footsteps, pouring water, clinking dinnerware, and all sorts of other "everyday" sounds that might not have been recorded during your shoot can be added by a *foley artist*. Foley work is usually done on a special stage equipped with props, cars, floor surfaces, and other materials.

Your mic might have picked up many ambient sounds while you were recording. Depending on the nature of your mic, though, these sounds can have varying degrees of quality, tone, and presence. If you used a directional mic to shoot footage of a woman getting out of a car, dropping her keys, picking them up, and closing the car door, some of the sounds might sound too far away or muffled since they were out of the primary field of the microphone. Foley sounds are an easy way to bring these sounds forward to increase the audience's involvement in the scene.

The advantage of adding sound effects with foley work (rather than editing sounds from a sound effects library) is that a good foley artist can often do all of the sounds for a shot (or even a scene) in a single take. In addition to being much faster than editing sounds separately, foley sounds will use fewer tracks in your mix.

With a good mic and a lot of care, you can do simple foley work on your own, although if a scene is very dependent on good foley sounds, you'll probably want to go to a professional foley studio. Experienced foley artists can do a decent pass on a feature film in one day.

MUSIC

As we discussed earlier, music can be used for everything from helping to establish a sense of location, to setting a mood, to embellishing an atmosphere. You'll probably spend a lot of time considering and tweaking the music in your production, and the nature of the tweaking will depend largely on the source of your music.

Typically, there are two types of music used in a feature: the music that *underscores* the action, and the *source* music that is meant to sound like it's coming from a source in your scene (radio, television, singer, etc.).

Most movies use a combination of original music composed specifically for the project, and pre-recorded music that is licensed from an artist and publisher. Determining how much of each to use will depend on your project and the nature of the mood you are trying to create.

An original score can serve to bind themes and characters together throughout your feature. Through the use of repeating motifs and recurring melodies, a well-written score can provide a lot of narrative structure and continuity.

There are a number of reasons why you might choose to use pre-recorded material. Your characters might be listening to a piece of music, for example, or perhaps you've found a song that simply serves the scene better than your original score does. Finally, certain songs, particularly music from a particular period, can do a great job of enhancing the authenticity of your scene.

Such pre-recorded material can also be mixed and layered on *top of* your original score. In addition to creating an interesting "soundscape," pulling a song out of the scene and into the score can be an effective way to move a scene forward, and join one character's action to something else in the movie.

ON THE DVD

For more about music for films, read the interview with a music supervisor on the DVD, in the Chapter 15 folder, "Interview with a MusicSuper.pdf."

Editing Music

Editing music can be a lot of fun, but it's a lot of hard work too, especially if you need your music to sound perfect. Feature films often hire a special music editor to edit all the music in the film. Why would you need a music editor if you already have a composer? Many projects do not have big enough budgets to hire a composer to score a project from start to finish.

Instead, the composer will score key scenes and sequences, and then provide a selection of tracks for the editor to use as needed. Because these tracks are not composed to the timing of the video or film, someone needs to edit them to time. The same goes for pre-recorded or library music.

At the most basic level, editing music means placing the tracks in the edited sequence and deciding where each cut of music needs to start and end. The start is easy—some songs have an introduction, or a "lead-in," to the main part of the song. Often, editors decide to cut out the "lead-in" and start with the main part of the song. Pop songs are usually structured with verses and choruses. Often, you'll decide to jump in with the chorus rather than the first verse. Other songs have musical interludes, or "breaks." Since lyrics can be distracting under dialog, starting with the "break" can be a good choice. No matter where you start the song, you can usually find a spot to make the first edit so that you don't need a dissolve to smooth it out. Each section of a song—the lead-in or intro, the verse, the chorus, the break, and the "outro" or ending—usually has a hard start. You can use the scrub tools in your editing software to find the first frame of that hard sound, whether it's a voice, a drum, or another musical instrument. As long as you avoid clipping the note, you'll be surprised to find that you can often start a piece of music in the middle of a song and the edit will sound good.

Editing the end of a piece of music is a little more challenging. The easiest way is to simply let the song end but usually songs are too long for this to work. The next easiest way out is to put a long dissolve on the end to sneak the music out of your mix. A one-second dissolve is a really long dissolve for other types of sound, but for music it's very short. To successfully sneak a piece of music out so that no one really notices that it's gone you'll need at minimum a three-second dissolve. Last but not least, you can "pull up" the ending of the song by cutting the end of the song onto the middle of the song so that it "ends" where you want it to. This will take a little practice and an ear for music, but once you've done it successfully a few times it will quickly become second nature and is an important skill in every editor's toolbox.

Can't Resolve It, Dissolve It?

This adage refers to the fact that dissolves are used as a bandage to solve every sort of problem in sound editing, from clipped dialog to bad music edits to taking the edge off sound effects. But some people think they have to add a dissolve to every single edit that they make no matter how it sounds. The fact is that if you can't hear a sound edit, it's "seamless," so you don't need to smooth it further by adding a dissolve. And often if an edit sounds bad and you feel it needs a dissolve to improve it, it may simply mean that a small adjustment of the edit—a frame or two—will make it sound good without a dissolve. Dissolves are an extremely useful tool, but they shouldn't become a crutch.

License to Play

When licensing music for use in a film, you'll most likely have to pay a hefty fee. You'll also need to secure the rights, both to the music and to the particular recording that you want to use. Often, the cheapest solution is to acquire the "performing rights," which allow you to hire a band to replicate the song. Whatever your needs, it's really best to consult an entertainment lawyer before you decide to use a copyrighted song. Be sure to do so early on in your production; otherwise, you could very easily end up with a movie that can't be distributed.

Most movies have two people involved in selecting and arranging music. A *composer* writes the original music, while the *music supervisor* selects any pre-recorded material. Often, the music supervisor will select a composer and help guide him or her through the creation of the music.

When you've finished editing your picture, you'll want to sit down and have a screening with your music supervisor or composer to discuss any ideas that you might have about appropriate music. In some cases, you might simply discuss what type of feeling or emotion you're hoping to convey.

You might have already chosen some music to use as "scratch audio" during your editing process. You can use this to suggest music that you feel is appropriate. However, it's often better to simply give your music supervisor some direction and see what he or she can come up with. Your music supervisor might arrive at ideas that you had never considered, but that work perfectly. One problem with using scratch audio is that it's very easy to get attached to it. Be careful not to get too enamored of a piece of music that you can't afford to license!

In addition, don't use scratch music that you would never be able to afford to produce. In other words, if you can't afford to pay for a full orchestra (or to license an orchestral recording), don't use any orchestral music in your scratch audio.

Music Libraries

Just as there is a slew of stock footage houses and sound effects CDs out there, there are many companies that specialize in selling music libraries on CD. With some, you pay a largish sum for the CD itself ($200 or so), and that purchase includes the license to use the tracks on the CD. Others charge per track and per minute. The quality and variety of music available on library collections has improved greatly over the last 10 years and many tracks are available for purchase and download from the Internet.

In addition to ideas about mood and tone, you might need to give your music supervisor or composer a *cue list* showing exactly what pieces of music are needed, and whether or not they have specific timings. If there are musical events that need to happen at particular times (a dramatic organ sting when the villain enters, for example), then these will be listed on your cue sheet.

The Sound of Silence

Don't forget about the power of silence. Not only is silence sometimes more effective than music, it often makes the preceding and following music more powerful. Don't feel pressured to fill every moment with sound and music. Do as much experimenting with no music as with music.

Your music supervisor and composer will usually present you with a number of options for each section of music in your project. You can take these to your editor and see how they work. At this point, your editor or sound designer might have suggestions for how to mix different pieces of music together, or how to mix music with natural sound, or how to apply reverb or other atmospheric effects to better fit the music to the action and mood.

Finding a Composer

ON THE DVD

There are a number of resources for contacting and auditioning composers and music supervisors. You can see a list of these resources in the Chapter 15 folder on the companion DVD called "Finding a mus sup or compos.pdf."

Whoever does the work of choosing a composer might be tempted to select someone simply based on the composer's music. This might not be the best criterion. Certainly, you want to consider a composer's musical tastes and skill, but simply listening to a demo reel gives you no idea of how well the music served as a score. You will also get no idea of how well you can communicate with the composer, or how tuned in he or she might be to the themes and ideas within your piece.

Before you make any decisions, you'll need to show your picture to the composer, discuss ideas, and see how well you can work together.

Today, composers are typically given about six weeks to write a score. While most big-budget films devote 1.5 to 2.5 percent of their budget to a score, low-budget films can often come in much lower. If the composer likes your work, he or she might be willing to work for much less.

In addition to paying your composer, you might need to pay the musicians required to record the piece, although sometimes the cost of musicians is included in the composer's fee. If you were imagining a full orchestral score, remember that you'll have to pay all the people in said orchestra. Many composers can cut production costs by using synthesized instruments, or synthesizers augmented with a few acoustic instruments. You'll need to discuss production costs with your composer, and try to determine what type of music you can afford to record.

Do It Yourself

If you're thinking that you might like to try your hand at composing your own score—or maybe you have some friends who you think could do a good job—remember that composing for the screen is not as simple as just sitting down and writing a song. Not only do you have to compose to achieve a particular narrative or emotional goal, but also, depending on the edits of your scene, you might need to compose with the intent of having certain movements, motifs, or beats occur at a particular time.

In addition, you'll need to compose with the understanding that your music will be competing with other sounds. Remember, your score is meant to complement and assist in the storytelling process. When composing, make sure that you are supporting the other audio in the scene. For example, a scene with many young children talking on a busy playground would not be well served by lyrical, high-pitched violin music, as the violins might be too close to the timbre of children's voices. When mixed with the natural sound, your music would only serve to muddle the sound and make the scene less intelligible.

Halfway between composing and canned music are programs like Apple's GarageBand, which let you string together pre-recorded loops to create original tunes. Far superior to straight canned music, loop editors let you craft songs that exactly match the cuts in your movie. In addition, programs like GarageBand also let you record live vocals or instruments over your sequenced loops.

FIGURE 15.13   Loop editors like GarageBand let you easily create soundtracks that exactly match the timing of your edited picture.

GarageBand is only available for the Mac, but if you're a Windows user, you can get similar functionality from programs such as Sony ACID Pro.

EXERCISES

1. **Prepare to Edit Your Sound:** Before you can edit any of your audio, you'll need to assess the audio capabilities of your NLE. If you haven't already done so, make sure your editing program provides the following:
   - Support for the number of tracks that you need.
   - Adequate sound editing and mixing capabilities.
   - If you have any sound effects needs—echoes, reverb, and so forth—then you'll want to take a moment to ensure that your NLE provides those effects.

   If it turns out that your NLE doesn't offer the audio power you need, you'll need to go shopping for an audio editing program.

2. **Hold a Spotting Session:** Gather your key post-production players—the director, the editor, the composer, the sound designer, etc.—and have a screening of your project where everyone takes notes on different sounds that they think would help. It's usually easier to go one scene at a time. Discuss each other's ideas and make a written list of the sound needs for each scene. Include problems that need fixing—bad audio, soft sync, etc.

3. **Practice Making Music Edits:** Using your non-linear editing software, import several songs from CD. (See Chapter 13, "Preparing to Edit," for instructions.) Most pop songs are three to five minutes in length but most projects will only need 30 seconds to 1.5 minutes of a particular song. Take one of the tracks you imported and cut it down to thirty seconds. Which part of the song will you use? Try adding a long four- or five-second dissolve to end it. Take another song and try to cut the end onto the beginning so that you end up with a minute-long song. Practice with different lengths and different edit points to see what works best. With some songs, you can actually cut the last, sustained note onto another measure to create a new ending. Make more music edits with the remaining songs. Try seamlessly lifting out all the verses or making a mini-song by editing one verse, one chorus and the ending together.

4. **Make a Music Cue Sheet:** Watch your project and make a list of the places where you think it needs music. Use timecode to identify each spot and think about the style, the mix and the tempo. When you're ready, you can pass this music cue sheet on to your music supervisor or composer.

Fix It in the Mix?

As we'll discuss in Chapter 19, "Output," when you perform your final output to tape or film, you will also perform a final, finished mix. Although your final mix will give you the chance to balance your audio levels, and equalize your tracks, don't think that you can just wait and fix any audio problems then. It's best to try to get your audio as polished as possible during your sound editing. This will make it easier to identify any problems with your audio, and will make for a shorter (and possibly less-expensive) mixing session when you create your final output.

16

COLOR CORRECTION

In This Chapter

- To Compress, or Not to Compress
- Color Correction
- Tutorial: Correcting White Balance
- Correcting Color for Film
- Exercise
- Summary

Most of the editing and special effects packages that we've mentioned so far provide tools for correcting and changing the color in your video. Whether you use these tools for artistic reasons—adding more blue to an image to strike a tone—or for more practical concerns such as correcting bad white balance—an understanding of the color correction features of your software is invaluable.

Although we've chosen to discuss this topic *after* the chapters on editing, it's important to understand that color correction—as well as the special effects covered in the next two chapters—will usually be performed *during* your editing process. When working on a digital project, most special effects are not something that you apply to a finished, edited project. Rather, they are created and added during the editing cycle. The only exception to this is a global color correction pass, such as an overall "film look" effect that's applied to your entire project after you've locked picture.

For most color correction tasks, you'll simply use filters and controls inside your editing app. For more complex corrections, and for the type of composites and special effects we'll introduce in Chapters 17, "Titling and Simple Compositing," and 18, "Rotoscoping and More Compositing," you'll use specialized applications such as Adobe After Effects. Consequently, you'll often find yourself switching back and forth between programs, processing and editing a clip in an effects package, and then editing that clip into a sequence using your editing program.

In this chapter, we'll tell you how to use the color correction tools in your editing package to improve the look of your video, as well as to fix problems that might have occurred during shooting.

TO COMPRESS, OR NOT TO COMPRESS

Before we start talking about manipulating the image, it's important to consider some workflow issues that will help you preserve the highest-quality image, and ensure that you make the most efficient use of your disk space.

Think about the following scenario: You're editing a low-budget sci-fi epic about extra-terrestrial book authors who invade Earth and begin boring everyone to death by reading detailed digital video specifications at them. You have a 45-second-long edited sequence of the Grand Canyon. At 10 seconds into this segment, you want to composite an animation of a flying saucer over the edited footage of the Grand Canyon. The saucer will take about 10 seconds to majestically descend into the Grand Canyon and will be out of sight by 20 seconds into the clip (Figure 16.1).

Although you're editing in Adobe Premiere, you plan on performing the composite of the spaceship using Adobe After Effects. Therefore, you'll need to export footage from Premiere, import it into After Effects, perform the composite, and then bring the composited final footage back into Premiere. Simple, right?

  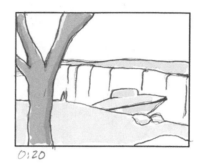

0:00   0:10   0:20

FIGURE 16.1   With good storyboards, we can better determine which parts of a clip are required for an effect.

Not necessarily. Although people often tout digital video's "generationless" editing, the fact is that if you're not careful when moving video files back and forth between programs, you *will* see a loss of quality. Remember that, even when it's fresh out of your camera, digital video has already gone through one round of compression. Like the JPEG compression that is used in graphics files on the Web, DV compression is *lossy;* that is, image quality is lost when the video is compressed. If you pass the footage through any additional compression operations, you'll experience more quality loss. (See Color Plate 11 for examples of overcompression.)

Every time you import a DV clip into an editing or effects program, the clip is decompressed and displayed on your screen. If you perform any functions that alter the image—cropping, applying filters, correcting color, compositing, etc.— then the computer must calculate new pixels and recompress the footage when you go back out to tape or write a DV file to your hard drive. By contrast, when you're performing cuts-only editing with no effects, the computer simply copies the original footage back to tape in the new order that you've specified. No recompression occurs (Figure 16.2).

Therefore, when moving your files between programs, you want to be sure that you don't expose the footage to another round of lossy compression. However, to save disk space, you will want to perform some kind of *lossless* compression on clips that you move between programs. In the interest of storage and processor efficiency, it's important to do a little planning.

Although our Grand Canyon sequence in the preceding example lasts 45 seconds, the section where the spaceship will be seen is only 10 seconds long. Therefore, rather than move the whole 45 seconds into our compositing program, it's better to move only the 10 seconds that matter. In general, most effects shots are very short—a couple of seconds here, a few frames there—so you'll be able to get away with moving very short clips between your effects and editing packages.

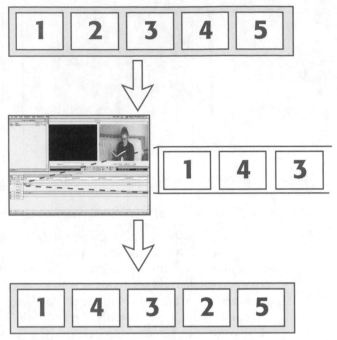

FIGURE 16.2 (a) When editing DV, compressed video is brought into your computer. With your editing software, you might reorder the scenes in your video. When you output to a file or tape, the computer simply rearranges the compressed video into your specified order. (b) However, if you perform an operation that alters the *contents* of the video image, then the computer will have to recompress that footage before outputting. Too much recompression, and your image quality will noticeably degrade.

In the preceding example, our compositing work will proceed as follows:

1. First, we will find the 10 seconds of footage that we need for our composite.
2. This footage will be marked for output. In most editing programs, you do this by setting special in- and out-points in your timeline that denote which section of a sequence will be rendered and output.
3. Next, we will output the selected video. In our output settings, we'll select the QuickTime *Animation* CODEC as our compressor. The Animation CODEC is lossless, but creates substantially larger files than the DV CODEC does. Because the Animation CODEC doesn't compress as much as the DV CODEC, being selective about the footage you work with will save you a lot of disk space (Figure 16.3).

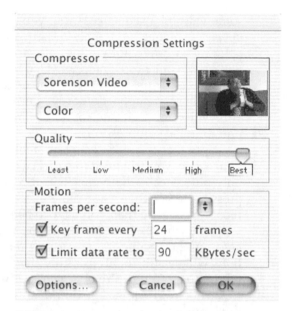

FIGURE 16.3   No matter what application you're exporting video from, at some point you will be given a choice of which QuickTime CODEC to use for compression. When moving between applications, use a lossless CODEC such as Animation.

4. The resulting 10-second clip will be imported into After Effects. There, we will perform our composite.
5. In After Effects, we'll render our finished composite. Again, we'll choose the Animation CODEC when saving, to ensure the highest quality.
6. Now, we'll import the new, composited, animation-compressed clip into Premiere and edit it into our sequence, replacing the footage that was there before. When we create our final output, this new clip will be compressed with our DV CODEC, but as this is just one extra level of compression, we probably won't see a difference.

In the interest of staying organized, when naming new files—such as composites and other effect clips—use the same naming conventions that you used when you digitized your footage, and be sure to back up the new files somehow—on videotape, CD, tape, or another hard drive.

Be aware that even if you are creating effects within your editing package, there is a chance that you could expose the clip to more than one level of compression. Say you have applied a color correction to some video in a sequence. Later, you decide to nest that sequence inside *another* sequence, and apply a sharpening filter to the entire thing. Depending on how your editing software works, there's a chance that this will cause your nested piece of video to be compressed twice. Study your software's manual for a better understanding to determine the order in which filters are applied. Ideally, you want to be sure that you only pass your video through one round of filter application (and, consequently, one round of compression).

Note that if you're using an analog compression system to import your video, you still need to worry about recompression. Remember, the only difference is that your digitizing card is performing the initial compression rather than your camera. As with DV, make certain you don't recompress more than you have to before going back out to tape.

When moving files between apps, you'll also want to be sure that you *always* use the same frame size and frame rate. Note that some applications will default to 30 fps rather than 29.97. The only time you should render to a different size or time base is when you are intentionally trying to shrink your movie for output to the Web or other low-bandwidth medium.

Making Space

If disk space is of critical concern, then it might not be practical to have huge, Animation-compressed files laying around your hard drive. If you find yourself in this situation and need to free up some space, consider converting your animation-compressed files to DV-compressed files by simply printing the animation-compressed footage out to tape. You can then re-import the footage and treat it like any other captured DV footage. However, depending on what you have planned for the rest of your post-production, such a process might not be advisable, as it might introduce an extra round of compression.

COLOR CORRECTION

At its best, a DV camera can shoot beautiful images with nicely saturated, accurate colors. At its worst, a DV camera can shoot horribly ugly images with unflattering casts of green or red. Fortunately, most DV cameras err more toward the beautiful side, but, through operator error, low-light conditions, or plain old bad shooting conditions, at some point you're probably going to need to adjust the color in your footage.

It might not always be bad news that sends you to the color controls of your editing application. Often, you'll want to perform color adjustments for more artistic reasons. Perhaps you want to amp up the reds or blues in an image to strike a certain emotional tone. Or, maybe you simply like certain colors more than others. Whatever the reason, color correction tools will be some of the most-used functions in your editing program.

Although all editing packages include some type of color correction, the controls for these features vary widely. In this section, we're going to discuss when and how to use color correction to solve certain problems. Although some tutorials and examples might center on certain products, we have presented our steps in a generic, conceptual fashion that should make it easy to translate the steps to other products.

Safe Colors

NTSC and PAL video have much smaller color gamuts than your computer monitor does. This means that colors that look fine on your computer screen might not display correctly—in fact, they might look plain awful—when displayed on an NTSC monitor. Very saturated colors will tend to bleed and fringe, with reds suffering the most. (Color Plate 9 and Figure 16.4 show good examples of oversaturated red created in an internal titler.)

Unfortunately, the titling functions of most editing programs will let you choose colors that are not NTSC "legal." This means that you might have to do some experimentation to find colors that are safe for NTSC display. The easiest way to determine if a color is safe is to simply look at it on an NTSC monitor or on a vectorscope.

Both After Effects and Photoshop provide an *NTSC Colors* filter that will convert your graphics to NTSC-safe colors. These tools make it easier to reduce a color to something legal (Figure 16.5).

ON THE DVD

Use That External Video Monitor!

Analog video (whether NTSC or PAL) can't display as many colors as your computer can, so the image on your computer is not a very good reference to use when correcting or adjusting color. Be sure you have an external video monitor connected to your system, and use that as a reference when making any change that alters the video image. Unfortunately, no two monitors are the same, but by calibrating your NTSC monitor with standard color bars, you can at least get it close to an accepted standard. Check out Calibrating Your NTCS mon.pdf in the Chapter 16 folder on the DVD for instructions on how to calibrate a video monitor.

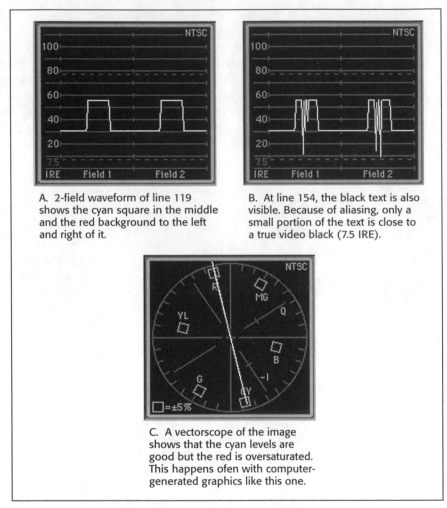

A. 2-field waveform of line 119 shows the cyan square in the middle and the red background to the left and right of it.

B. At line 154, the black text is also visible. Because of aliasing, only a small portion of the text is close to a true video black (7.5 IRE).

C. A vectorscope of the image shows that the cyan levels are good but the red is oversaturated. This happens ofen with computer-generated graphics like this one.

FIGURE 16.4 Waveform and vectorscope of graphic in Color Plate 9. The cyan levels are fine, but the red is oversaturated.

Too Much of a Good Thing: When Color Correction Goes Too Far

If you've ever performed any color correction in an image editing application, then color correcting video will feel very similar. In some cases, you'll even use tools with the same interface and controls. Your color correction tasks will fall into two general categories: color correction and luminance (brightness) correction. Very often, these two tasks are related, because different hues have different brightness colors and, conversely, changing the brightness of an image might make colors appear slightly different.

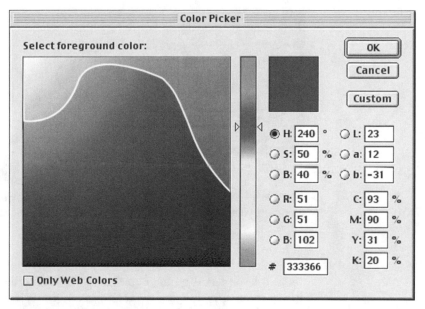

FIGURE 16.5   In the Apple Color Picker, the areas under the striped overlay shown here are probably either too bright or too saturated to be NTSC safe.

We'll take a look at some specific color correction chores later in this chapter. First, though, it's important to recognize that it *is* possible to apply too much color correction.

A digital image is composed of numbers that represent the color of each pixel. Color correction tools simply manipulate these numbers using complex transformations. Unfortunately, a digital image has a finite amount of color data in it. You can manipulate this information, but eventually you'll find that there simply isn't enough data to take a correction as far as you might like. At this point, you'll introduce artifacts and aberrations into your image.

No matter what type of color correction you're doing, it's critical that you keep your eyes peeled for the telltale artifacts that indicate that you've corrected too far.

Consider the grayscale ramp shown in Figure 16.6.

Two hundred fifty-six tones are used to create this smooth gradient from black to white. The small graph next to the image is a *histogram*. It is nothing more than a bar graph of the distribution of tones in the image. As you can see, there is image data from the extreme left end—which represents black—to the extreme right image, which represents white.

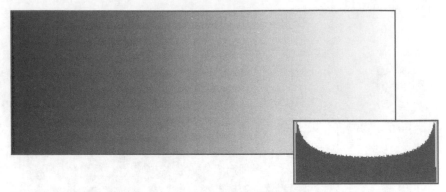

FIGURE 16.6   This image shows a ramp of gray tones that extends from solid black to complete white. Two hundred fifty-six different shades of gray are used to create this ramp.

Now look at the image in Figure 16.7. To create this image, we took the gradient from Figure 16.6 and used Photoshop's Posterize command to reduce the number of tones from 256 to 16.

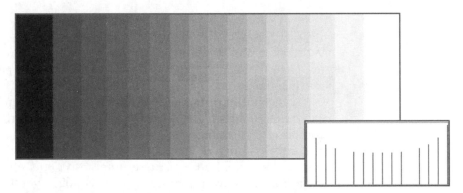

FIGURE 16.7   The gradient ramp from Figure 16.6 posterized to 16 tones.

The ramp is still a gradient from solid black to complete white—in other words, it has the same dynamic range—but it is now composed of far fewer tones. Unfortunately, the human eye is sensitive enough that 16 tones is not enough to create a smooth gradient. Instead, we see a posterized image, one whose smooth details have been flattened into solid colors.

Now look at the histogram that accompanies the image. Note that there is much less data in the image, as evidenced by the tiny number of bars in the graph. The editing operation that we chose required the computer to discard image data, and there's simply no way to get it back.

When you apply color correction operations to a digital image, the computer will often have to discard image data, just as we did in Figure 16.7. The result of these operations will be the same: with less image data, some tones in your image will posterize, resulting in areas of flat color in your picture. These artifacts probably won't be as dramatic as our gray ramp example, but they'll still be there, and they can be very noticeable, particularly in the darker, shadowy areas of your image (Figure 16.8).

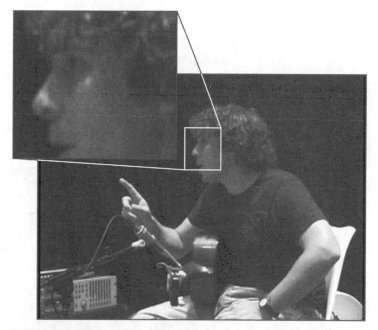

FIGURE 16.8   This image has suffered a little too much correction, resulting in the posterization of some of its tones.

Choosing what type of correction to make is a subjective, aesthetic choice. Knowing when you've corrected too far, though, is a technical skill that separates good correction from bad. In the following examples, practice looking for posterization and reduction of tones as you perform your corrections. This is a habit you will need to develop for all of your personal correction chores.

Correcting Bad White Balance

As we discussed in Chapter 7, "The Camera," properly white balancing your camera before shooting is essential to getting good color. However, there's no guarantee that your camera's white-balance function will always work properly. A bad auto white-balance function can often perform inaccurate—or outright bad—white balancing, and can sometimes change white balance in the middle of a shot. Even if you're manually white balancing, mixed lighting situations—tungsten lights in a sun-filled room, for example—can yield troublesome results.

Bad white balance can lead to everything from a simple green tinge in highlight areas, to an extreme blue cast throughout the entire image. Color Plate 12 shows a *very* poorly white-balanced shot of a woman sitting on a couch. Before we shot this scene, we had been shooting outside on a very cloudy day. Although we had white balanced the camera outside, after quickly moving inside, we forgot to adjust the white-balance settings for the new lighting conditions. As you can see, the bad white balance resulted in an extreme blue cast throughout the image. Color Plate 13 shows the image after it was corrected.

Most NLEs and many effects packages include filters for adjusting the color balance, saturation, and hue of an image (Figure 16.9). In the

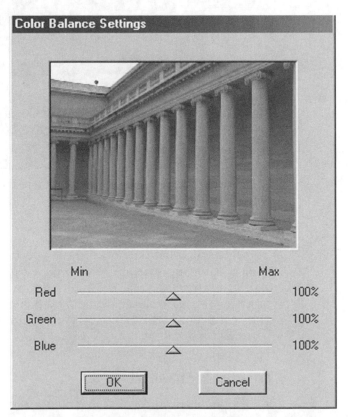

FIGURE 16.9 Most editing programs have a color correction tool similar to this one, Adobe Premiere's Color Balance filter.

following tutorial, we will use combinations of these filters to correct our image. In many programs, you might need to apply multiple copies of the same filter, each with different settings. It's important to note that your program will process these filters in the order in which they are applied. For example, if you apply a filter to change the amount of blue in an image, and then apply *another* filter to change the amount of red, the second filter will operate on the already processed, less-blue image that resulted from the first filter.

When correcting color in any application, follow these general steps:

1. Identify the main color problem (e.g., it's too blue), and apply a filter to correct it.
2. Examine the results, and use additional filters to "touch up" the color correction.

TUTORIAL

CORRECTING WHITE BALANCE

In this tutorial, we are going to use color correction filters inside our editing package to correct the bad white balance shown in Color Plate 12. Our goal will be to achieve an image with the color shown in Color Plate 13. Although the resulting color is not ideal (look at the strange magenta and green tones in the shadows of the adjusted image), it is certainly better than the original. In addition, since we can't afford a reshoot, saving the footage through color correction is our only hope of salvaging the scene!

The colors in an image can be divided into three categories: highlights, mid-tones, and shadows. When trying to decide how to color correct an image, start by identifying problems within these categories. As you adjust the first category, it will become more apparent what corrections need to be made to the other categories. For example, you might find that only highlight colors are out of balance. Adjust these, and then see if the mid-tones or shadows need adjustment.

For this tutorial, we will be correcting the footage using Apple's Final Cut Pro. Final Cut offers many different color correction filters and controls. For this tutorial we will be using the Color Balance filter, partly because it's up to the task, but also because you'll find a similar control in just about any other editing program. Most Color Balance filters, including Final Cut's, let you specify which range of colors—highlights, mid-tones, or shadows—you want to adjust. Because most editing programs include a similar color correction filter, you should be able to follow along with this tutorial using just about any NLE software.

Step 1: Create a Project

Create a new project, import the clip adelle_1.mov from the Corr. White Balance Tutorial subfolder within the Chapter 16 folder, and place it on the timeline.

Step 2: Add the First Filter

Although at first glance it might look like this footage is completely blue, closer examination reveals that the woman's skin tones, and the wood frame behind her, are fairly accurate. It's the white wall, and the white cushion that are particularly blue. Since these fall under the Highlight category of color, adjusting the highlights will be our first step.

Add a *Color Balance* filter to the clip.

In Final Cut, the Color Balance filter provides three radio buttons for targeting the color temperature you want to adjust. Click the Highlights button to target highlights. Because we want to remove the blue cast, begin by sliding the blue slider to the left until it reads approximately –70. If your program doesn't allow you to target a particular range of colors, that's okay, you just might need to make additional adjustments later (Figure 16.10).

Now look at your image—much less blue, but now the highlights are a little too green. No problem, drag the green slider to the left until it reads roughly –50. Better, but still not quite right.

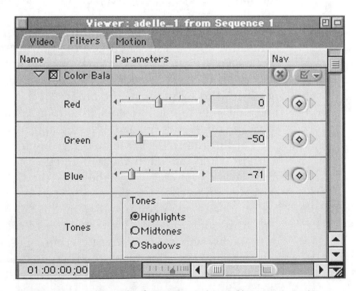

FIGURE 16.10 Adding the first Color Balance filter. Your goal is to address the biggest problem in your image. Don't expect to fix everything all at once.

Step 3: Add Another Filter

Although most of the blue cast was in the highlight areas, there's still a good amount of it in the mid-tones. Add another Color Balance filter to the clip, but set it to target the midtones.

Again, our first step is to reduce the blue. Drag the blue slider to around –60. Look at your image and you'll see that, like before, we now have too much green. Drag the green slider to around –40.

Much better, but now there's a very slight pink tinge. This can be removed by putting the red slider at –10.

Step 4: Add Yet Another Filter

We're almost there, but look at the highlights in the corner of the couch. They're a little green. We could go back and lower the green slider in our first filter to further reduce the green highlights, but this will create other problems. Because the filters are calculated in a certain order, if we go back and change an earlier parameter, the filters and parameters that are calculated later will no longer serve the function we intended. So, add a third Color Balance filter.

Click the Highlights button in the new filter and drag the green slider down to about –30. This should remove most of the green highlight.

Step 5: Now, Add a Filter

Although the color now looks much better, the image has ended up a tad darker because of our adjustments. Add a *Levels* filter to the clip. Drag the Gamma slider to the left to increase the brightness of the midtones (Figure 16.11).

Always Avoid Brightness and Contrast

If your NLE provides Levels or Curves filters, always use these for adjusting the brightness and contrast of an image. Never use Brightness and Contrast filters, as these controls tend to wash out your image. With a Levels or Curves filter, you can control the contrast and brightness, while preserving the white and black tones in your image. (Brightness and Contrast filters tend to change black tones to gray.)

That's it! You've successfully removed the color cast and saved the footage. Now, however, it's important to scrub through the clip and make sure that your settings are accurate for all the sections of your video. In this clip they work fine throughout, but if we had moved the camera or done some other activity that changed the lighting of the scene, then the clip might need different color correction settings for different parts. If

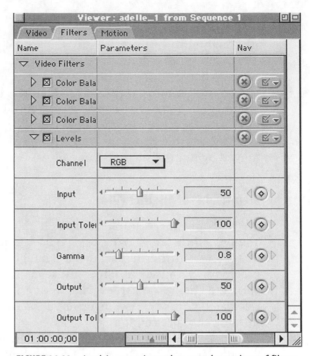

FIGURE 16.11 In this case, it took a good number of filters to deal with every color problem in our shot. Sure, these will slow render times, but they're cheaper and faster than reshooting!

your NLE allows you to animate filters using keyframes, then, with some patience, you can usually get smooth changes in adjustment from point to point within your clip.

This stack of filters will all be calculated and applied when you render and compress your final video. Therefore, by applying all of these filters at once, you'll only have to compress your video at final render time.

Matching Footage from Different Cameras and Shoots

Although tape formats are standardized, different camera vendors take different approaches to processing the data that goes onto a tape. For example, some vendors consistently produce cameras that shoot "warmer" images than cameras from other vendors. If you end up shooting with multiple cameras—either simultaneously, or at different times during your shoot—you could very easily end up with different shots in the same scene that don't have quite the same color quality or sharpness.

Low-budget filmmakers who are borrowing equipment are especially susceptible to this problem, as they might not always be able to borrow the same gear. If your principal shoot is over and you're now trying to get some "pick-up" shots, you might find yourself shooting with a different brand or model of camera, or with the same camera but during a different time of year when the light is slightly different.

Matching footage from different cameras can be difficult because it's often a combination of factors that make footage from one camera look different from another camera. When performing such adjustments, consider the following:

- Use the same approach that we used earlier: identify the main problem, correct it with a filter, and then use additional filters to remove lingering color troubles.
- Note that some cameras have different levels of sharpness and detail. Differences in detail can often be perceived as slight differences in tone or color. Just as a pattern of black-and-white dots in a newspaper photo can appear gray to the eye, more or less detail in an image can make color appear different. Higher sharpness can also increase the level of contrast in an image. Experiment with using lightly applied Unsharp Mask filters to sharpen details from softer cameras. Be very careful, though! When sharpening, you run the risk of increasing aliasing and other artifacts in your image.
- If you determine that there's an easy fix for the color from one camera—maybe it just needs less red, for example—then consider applying the effect by adjusting the chroma levels when you capture. Not all programs provide such a feature, and such tools don't offer fine controls, but if this approach works, it will save you a lot of rendering time.
- Be careful of flesh tones. In the previous example, the blue cast in the image appears mainly in the bright whites of the walls and couch. It's easy to focus on these areas when applying correction. However, it's important to ensure that, while correcting the background of the image, you don't corrupt any skin tones in the foreground. The human eye is very discerning about skin tones and can easily recognize incorrect, or "bad," color.

Correcting Part of an Image

Through the use of masks, stencils, alpha channels, or layers, you can selectively apply color corrections to part of an image, rather than to the entire image. You can even apply different color corrections—one to the foreground, another to the background. We'll discuss this more in Chapter 17, "Titling and Simple Compositing."

Brightening Dark Video

Good lighting is often all it takes to make the difference between bad lighting and good lighting. Unfortunately, good lighting isn't always naturally available, and good artificial lighting is very expensive and requires a skilled crew. For either of these reasons, you will at times find yourself shooting in low light. Whether it's a concert venue, a night shot, or simply a budgetary reality, low-light footage is something you might need to correct for when you start editing.

Fortunately, DV cameras are usually pretty exceptional at shooting in low light. Because digital image sensors are incredibly light sensitive, your camera can capture details that even your eye might not be able to see. However, you might have to coax this detail out of your footage.

Before trying to brighten any footage, prepare yourself for the fact that the resulting image is going to be noisier, grungier, and possibly suffer from a lot of posterization artifacts. How bad these problems will be depends on how dark your source footage is, and how much you're trying to brighten it. In the end, though, noisy grungy footage is usually better than no footage at all. Obviously, it might not cut too well with clean, well-lit footage, but if your entire project is similarly dark, then you'll at least have uniform grunginess throughout your whole piece. One way to work with noisy footage is simply to embrace it. If your footage looks a little grungy, than accept grunge as an aesthetic and maybe consider adding *more* noise!

In image editing, the midpoint between white and black is often referred to as *gamma*. Most editing programs will have a gamma correction tool of some kind. (If your program doesn't have a dedicated gamma correction filter, then look for a Levels filter. A standard Levels control will include a gamma slider.) The great thing about a gamma control is that it lets you brighten the mid-tones of your image without lightening the blacks. This is ideal for dark footage, as it allows you to brighten the image without washing out the shadow tones (Figure 16.12).

Using Tracks and Layers to Adjust Color

If your NLE or effects program provides control over *transfer modes,* then you can perform color adjustments by layering different video tracks on top of each other. Although not so useful for color correction, stacking tracks (or layers in a compositing program) is an easy way to increase contrast, pump up color, and create unique color effects.

Usually, when two video tracks occupy the same space in the timeline, the track that is higher in the stacking order is the only one that's visible—lower tracks are simply covered up. However, if your NLE provides control over the transfer mode of a layer, then you can set upper tracks to mix and blend with lower tracks. (If you've ever changed the transfer mode of a layer in Photoshop, then you've seen such effects in action.)

FIGURE 16.12   Gamma-corrected dark footage.

If you change the transfer mode of a layer, then the pixels in that layer will be mathematically combined with pixels in the lower layer (that layer, in turn, can be combined with the layer below it, and so on and so forth). The pixels that result from the combination can often be very different from either of the original pixels (Figure 16.13).

FIGURE 16.13 In this before and after series, you can see the effects of layer stacking. To create the second image, we stacked three copies of the same footage. The bottom copy was left normal. The copy above that uses a Lighten transfer mode, while the layer above *that* uses a Hard Light transfer mode.

You Say "Track," I Say "Layer"

When we speak of putting a video clip on a layer, this is synonymous with putting a video clip on a track. No matter what terminology your editing or effects package uses, the concept is the same.

Don't Expect Miracles

If you've spent any time editing the color of scanned images or digital photos, then you're probably already used to digital color correction tools. However, you should be aware that video does not have nearly as much dynamic range as a digital still camera or scanned image. A color adjustment that looks great on a still frame can look terrible on a moving image. Consequently, you're not going to be able to pull and push the color as much as you can when editing stills, so don't expect to be able to perform color correction miracles in post-production.

In Chapter 13, "Preparing to Edit," we talked about maintaining image quality and setting video levels when you capture. If your project is destined for video, then all of the rules discussed in that chapter apply to still graphics. The best way to be certain that your graphics are broadcast safe is to look at them on a waveform monitor and vectorscope (hardware or software). Check the tutorials on the DVD for Chapter 13 for more complete instructions.

ON THE DVD

CORRECTING COLOR FOR FILM

If your project will eventually be transferred to film, color correction in the computer will be a bit of a problem. If you've ever tried to print images on a color printer, you've probably discovered that what's on your screen doesn't always correspond to what comes out of your printer. The same is true for transferring images to film. The reasons for the disparity are many, and range from differences in color gamut between video and film, to differences in transfer processes, to differences in how the film is exposed during the transfer.

Professional editing and effects houses try to deal with this problem through expensive, complicated procedures for calibrating monitors and other digital equipment. In the end, such systems still give little assurance of what the final color will look like. If your final destination is film and you want to do a lot of color correction and color effects, it's a good idea to talk to your film transfer house. Tell them you're concerned about color control and ask their advice on how to proceed. You can also give single frames to your film lab and have them shot and tested.

If you're planning on a video-to-film transfer, there's less to worry about. As long as your effects integrate well into the final video output and have acceptable video levels, they should look just fine in your final film print as well.

One More Thing

Finally, we recommend color-correcting your footage before you composite any other elements on top of it. Your composited layers might have color issues of their own, so it's better to separate the color troubles that your layers might have. Once you've corrected each layer, you can composite them together and then apply touch-up corrections to smooth the "seams" of your composites. If you're not sure what we mean about composites, don't worry, a thorough discussion of compositing is coming up next.

EXERCISE

This chapter contains many tutorials, so be sure to work through all the tutorials, and then try working with some of your own footage. In particular, dig in to your software's manual and try to learn about the different color correction tools at your disposal. No matter what the nature of the tool, or the specifics of its controls, you'll still need to be careful not to over-correct, and to stay on the lookout for troublesome artifacts. There is always something new to learn about color, and the more you practice, the better you will become.

SUMMARY

By now you should be comfortable with the basics of color correction using your chosen NLE. If you're still not comfortable using levels, curves, color balance, or the other color correction tools provided in your editing program, then you'll need to get some more practice. The best way to practice is to simply shoot some bad footage (just choose an incorrect white balance setting) and start correcting. Color correction is a staple effect that's well worth learning.

17

TITLING AND SIMPLE COMPOSITING

In This Chapter

Whether it's a simple title, a credit roll, or a complex special effect, you will probably engage in some type of compositing operation at some point during your production. When we say "compositing," we're referring to the process of layering one image on top of another to create a final "composite" image. In the case of titling, you simply layer a piece of text over your image. For more complex effects work, you might layer dozens of images together to create a final shot.

Compositing is one of the most powerful effects tools available to the digital filmmaker, and many of the tools that high-end pros use are readily available for your desktop computer. It's hard to imagine any type of effects shot that doesn't require compositing. Even if your project is heavy on computer-generated imagery, there will be some point where your CGI elements will need to be integrated with live-action shots of your actors or location. This job will fall to your compositor.

Obviously, thorough coverage of complex special effects is way beyond the scope of this book. However, with a thorough understanding of compositing basics, you'll be well on your way to pulling off just about any type of effect that you might ever need to make. As such, in this chapter we're aiming to give you a bedrock compositing lesson that will help you in all of your other effects tasks.

High-end compositing is an art form, and a study all of its own. For every day compositing tasks, though, this chapter should get you up and running fairly quickly.

In most compositing applications you import media—either video, computer generated animations, or still images—into separate layers, which are then stacked on top of each other to create a final image. Your biggest concern when compositing is how to craft the masks and other mechanisms of *transparency* that will allow you to control which parts of each layer are visible in the final composite. Once your composite is built, you'll need all of the color correction techniques we introduced in the last chapter to blend the layers into a seamless, cohesive image.

The simplest, most common compositing task is the creation of titles and credits. Every movie needs opening titles and a final credit roll, and some movies—particularly documentaries—will probably need titles throughout. The creation of titles marks the start of our compositing and special effects discussions, which will continue into Chapter 18, "Rotoscoping and More Compositing."

Titles and Simple Graphics

Although your production might not need fancy special effects such as 3D-rendered dinosaurs, or complicated composites and morphs, it probably will need a title sequence at the beginning and a credit roll at the end. If you're shooting a documentary, you might also need to use titles to identify interviewees and locations. Although your editing software probably includes some titling functions, it might not be up to creating a cool, animated title sequence, or even a simple list of rolling credits.

In this section we'll cover the basics of titling and graphics and, along the way, introduce most of the concepts that you'll need to understand in order to pull off the more complex, sophisticated effects that we'll cover in the next chapter.

Making Titles in Your NLE

Most editing packages include titling functions that let you superimpose simple text titles over your images. Some packages include more advanced functions such as rolls and animated text. Your editing program's manual should cover everything you need to know to use the built-in titler. If your editing program's titler isn't up to snuff, there are many third-party stand-alone and plug-in titlers available. We'll discuss those in more detail later in the "Titling Software" section. No matter what software you use, there arc several things to keep in mind when building your titles.

It is essential that you have a video monitor hooked up to your system when you are creating titles! The only way to determine the legibility of your titles and graphics is to see them on a video screen.

Titles for Film Projects

If you're finishing your project on film, the resolution of titles created in the internal title tool of your NLE will be too low for projection. You'll need to create high-resolution titles using Photoshop or After Effects and have them transferred directly to film.

Safe Titles

In Chapter 7, "The Camera," we discussed the *action safe* area of a shot. As you'll recall, to compensate for the possible differences between different television sets, a video signal actually contains more picture than can be displayed. Your TV or video monitor will crop off a good amount of this *overscanned* area.

Because it's impossible to determine how much a particular TV or monitor will overscan, some lowest-common-denominator averages have been determined. If you stay inside these averages, the odds are good that your titles and essential action will not be cropped outside the edge of the monitor. The *action safe* area is the larger of the two regions, while the *title safe* area is a little smaller. Keep your titles within this area and they should be viewable on any screen.

Most titling functions allow you to display both action- and title-safe guides. If your editing package doesn't provide guides, then try to avoid placing text in the outer 5 percent or so of your screen (Figure 17.1).

Title Safe

Action Safe

FIGURE 17.1 If you want to be sure your titles aren't cropped by the viewer's monitor, be sure to keep them within the "title-safe" area.

TITLE TITLES

As with everything else related to filmmaking, there are a whole bunch of terms related to titling. Whether you use these terms or not is up to you.

Title card: A non-moving title.

Head credits (or opening credits): The typical series of title cards that fade in and out at the beginning of a movie. Typically, head credits follow (roughly) this order: studio or production company, sometimes a producer, main title, lead actors, casting, music, music supervisor, costumes and makeup, designer, director of photography, editor, executive producer(s), producer(s), writer, director.

Tail credits (or end credits): The credits at the end of a movie. Typically, if a movie skipped head credits, it will present the head credit information in reverse order as tail credits, before going on to a normal tail credit roll.

Title roll: A long list of titles that scrolls from the bottom of the screen to the top. Usually used for end credits. A very efficient way of presenting titles, as every name is on-screen for the same duration.

Title crawl: A line of titles that moves horizontally across the screen, usually at the bottom.

Super'ed: Titles that are superimposed over other video.

Lower thirds: Titles that fit into the lower third of the frame. Usually credits identifying a speaker, such as you might use in a documentary. Also called "chyrons."

Pad: A colored background or stripe behind a lower-third title. Pads improve a title's legibility.

Textless version: A print of your feature with no titles. These are almost always necessary for foreign distribution.

Choosing Your Typeface and Size

Remember that analog video is lower resolution and much less sharp than the video on your computer screen. Typefaces with fine lines and swirly details might not read very well on-screen.

When superimposing titles over video, be certain that the typeface you choose is readable throughout the clip. Fast-moving images with lots of clutter will make smaller, finer-lined typefaces more difficult to read. Avoid typefaces that have lines smaller than one pixel in width—they'll flicker when displayed on a TV screen.

When choosing a type size, legibility should be your first concern. At small sizes, some typefaces will be more legible than others, but in general, anything below 20 points will be too small (Figure 17.2).

Ordering Your Titles

If you're working with union actors, their contract might specify where their name must appear in the title sequence. Similarly, credit position might have been stipulated from a "producer" when you talked him or her out of some funding. Be sure to consider all of these agreements and obligations when ordering and creating your titles.

FIGURE 17.2   Be sure to consider both legibility and composition when creating titles.

Start with a Word Processor

If you have a long list of titles, such as lower thirds for a feature-length documentary, subtitles for an entire film (or even just a scene or two), or a long credit list, use a word processing program to create the list of titles, and be sure they are proofread and error-free before you start creating graphic titles. You can easily cut and paste them into your titler when you're ready to create your graphics.

Coloring Your Titles

Text color choice is critical when superimposing your titles over video. First, finding a color that's contrasty enough with your background can be difficult. If the video you're superimposing over is changing a lot, then finding a color will be even more difficult.

Your first impulse will be to go for really saturated colors, but remember that heavily saturated colors might bleed. Remember to stick with an NTSC safe color for broadcast television. If you've got a really busy, or really colorful background, your best way of making your text more visible is to add a drop shadow, or an edge. A drop shadow will place a light border behind the text to separate it from the background, while an edge will simply stroke all of the edges of your text with a specific color. Both of these techniques make text much more readable (Figure 17.2).

Be certain to watch the entire clip that your title is super'ed over, and make certain that the text is legible throughout the entire clip. Although a blue title might look great at the beginning of a clip, make sure there are no blue, title-obscuring objects moving through the frame later in the clip.

Placing Your Titles

If you're planning on superimposing your titles over video, you'll want to give some thought to their placement, not just for the sake of readability, but for good composition as well. Hopefully, you shot the underlying videos with titles in mind. Although titles might sit on top of an image, they should not be thought of as separate. Be sure to consider the composition of the entire image—titles and video—when placing your graphics. If your titles are going to move about the screen, make sure they are readable across all action over which they are superimposed.

Legible titles don't really do any good if the viewer doesn't have time to read them. A good rule of thumb is to leave the title up long enough for you to read it two times aloud. Usually, this means at least four seconds for a fairly short title, not including fades in or out. Even if you read fast, the title will probably be up long enough for most people to read it.

In general, pay close attention to the pacing of your head title sequence. Remember: this is the beginning of your presentation and is a chance for you to set an initial tone for your story. If you have already presented a "prelude" before the credits, your title sequence can function as a dramatic beat to prolong what has come before. Although you don't want to bore the audience with a long title sequence, if the beginning of your story is somewhat somber, a slower title sequence might be just the thing to bring your audience down to a more receptive pace. Titles can serve as another beat in your storytelling process, so give them some thought.

LEARNING FROM OTHER PEOPLE'S TITLES

The next time you're at the movies, consider how the director has used the title sequence. Many action movies, for example, skip titles all together and "cut right to the chase" so to speak. James Bond movies are famous for their elaborate title sequences that occur *after* an initial high-energy sequence. These sequences serve to bring the audience down from the chase-scene high to the typically more sedate "first" scene.

Some movies choose to superimpose their titles over initial, expository action. *Jerry Maguire* is a good example of this technique. Be careful, though. You don't want to distract the audience from your exposition, and you don't want to give short shrift to your titles.

At the opposite extreme from these approaches are the title sequences used by Woody Allen in most of his movies. Simple slates on a black background, these titles sequences are completely separate from the "main" presentation.

Although you might think we're making rather a big deal out of something that can be very simple, don't forget that every frame that you show the audience can—and usually does—carry some type of information about your story.

Titling Software

While all decent editing applications include basic titling functions, they won't necessarily provide all of the titling features that you need. Some basic titling capabilities to look for include:

- The ability to add an edge to title text
- The ability to add a drop-shadow to a title
- A facility for creating a "roll" or a "crawl"

If your software doesn't include these features, then you may want to consider using a third-party titling application or plug-in that's compatible with your editing system. Titling and *motion graphics* applications run the gamut from simple character generators to full-blown animation apps that let you create 3D flying logos with photo-realistic lighting. If you need more titling power, consider one of these options:

Boris FX: Boris makes a number of excellent titling applications and plug-ins. Boris Graffiti and Boris Red are plug-ins that are compatible with over 20 different editing and compositing applications. Both plug-ins provide most of the titling functionality you'll ever need. From simple rolls, to text on a path, to cool shattering effects, Boris' plug-ins provide a tremendous amount of power and can create both 2D and 3D text. Because they plug directly into your editing application, Red and Graffiti are incredibly convenient. However, though perfectly usable, the Boris interface can take a little while to learn.

Adobe After Effects: Listing After Effects as a "titling" application is kind of absurd given that After Effects is a full-blown, exceptional compositing program suitable for feature film effects work.

However, with version 6, Adobe added some excellent type capabilities to After Effects that make it possible to create complex text animations. With 6.5, Adobe made this process even easier by including a large library of canned animations that can be easily applied to any text. Though it can't produce photo-realistic 3D text, for flying 2D text, After Effects is a great option. As a bonus, you get a great compositing tool.

Apple LiveType and Motion: Apple bundles a program called LiveType with Final Cut Pro. It's an excellent titling application, and one that's often forgotten. If you've got Final Cut Pro, take a look at the stand-alone Live Type application. Motion is Apple's exceptional $299 motion graphics package. Offering easy-to-use titling, really cool particle effects, and excellent color correction, Motion is particularly impressive for its ability to perform all of these tasks in real-time, making for a much simpler workflow when it comes time to tweak and refine your titles. Motion is even suitable for simple compositing tasks (Figure 17.3).

FIGURE 17.3   Apple's Motion provides an excellent motion graphics/titling facility that gives you real-time control over your motion graphic.

Creating Titles in Photoshop

Even if your editing package includes a great titler, there might still be times when you want to craft titles in a paint program or image editor. For example, there might be times when you want to create hand-lettered effects, or more illustrative graphics and titles. For these instances, you'll create your title images in your paint program of choice, and then move them into your editing or special effects package to composite them with your video and other graphics.

In the next section, we'll cover everything you need to know to perform these types of simple composites. Even if you don't expect to ever do this kind of titling work, it's worth working through this tutorial for the compositing fundamentals that will be introduced.

COMPOSITING 101

In theory, compositing sounds like a very basic effect: put one layer of video on top of another to create a composite. In practice, though, compositing is one of the most powerful tools at your disposal. At the simplest level, you can use compositing tools to superimpose custom titles and graphics over video, or stack clips on top of each other to create a video collage. More sophisticated compositing tools allow you to do everything from mixing computer-generated elements with live video, to placing your actors inside virtual sets. Although good compositing tools are the foundation of all special effects work, they can also be used for more everyday concerns such as fixing drop-outs and altering the color of an image.

In most non-linear editing packages, you can create a simple composite by creating multiple video tracks, each containing a different clip or image (Figure 17.4). Dedicated compositing programs such as Adobe After Effects provide more compositing power by letting you stack many layers of video and stills, and provide more robust control over how those layers interact. After Effects also lets you animate the properties of layers to create sophisticated, animated effects.

No matter which program you use, the process of compositing is fairly simple. First, you import your video clips and stack them in the appropriate order. Obviously, if you put one piece of video on top of another, the upper clip will simply obscure the lower clip. Therefore, after creating your stack of video, you must define the method by which each layer will reveal the contents of the underlying layers. The method you choose will depend on the type of footage with which you are working.

Compositing methods fall into two categories: *keys* and *mattes*.

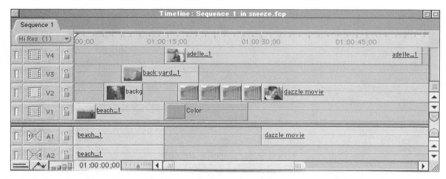

FIGURE 17.4 Composites are made by stacking tracks or layers on top of each other, and then specifying how those layers will combine.

Keys

If you've ever seen a local TV weatherman standing in front of a weather-filled map of the country, then you've seen an example of *keying*. The weatherman is not really standing in front of a map, of course. Rather, he's standing in front of a blue or green screen that is electronically *keyed* out and replaced with the image of the map (Figure 17.5).

Most NLEs provide keying functions that let you superimpose footage shot in front of a colored screen over another video clip, animation, or still image. In these programs, you import both your blue-screen footage and your underlying layers, stack them up, and then tell the program to apply a *chroma key* (sometimes called a *color key*) to the uppermost layer. The chroma key feature will provide controls to let you select which color you wish to key out.

When the image is rendered, the computer will look for every occurrence of the specified key color and make it transparent, allowing the underlying layer to show through.

A *luminance key* functions the same way, but rather than keying out pixels of a certain color, a luma key keys out pixels of a certain brightness. Many programs offer variations of these keys, such as screen, multiply, or difference. Consult your manual for details.

Because you must shoot in front of a specially colored screen, and perform very precise lighting, chroma key effects are not ideal for every compositing task (the screens are blue or green because there is rarely any blue or green in the skin tone of a healthy human). Chroma keys are usually used for situations where you want to superimpose a person in front of another video clip or still. Luminance keys can be used for situations where you can't put a blue screen behind your foreground element. For example, you could use a luma key to key out a bright sky behind a building. Luminance keys can also be used to touch up parts of a chroma key composite that have not keyed out properly.

FIGURE 17.5 The upper image was shot in front of a blue screen, which can easily be "keyed out" and replaced with another image, such as this billowing smoke.

Shooting blue- or green-screen footage requires a great deal of care and expertise.

TUTORIAL   CREATING A LUMINANCE KEY

A luminance key lets you superimpose one layer over another by knocking out either the very bright or very dark parts of a layer to expose underlying layers. In this tutorial, we'll use a luminance key to superimpose a flash of gunfire over another video clip (Figure 17.6).

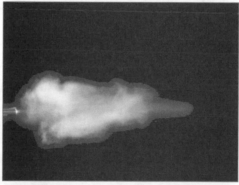

FIGURE 17.6   In this tutorial, we're going to superimpose the footage of a muzzle flash over footage of a hand to create a final composite that will show a hand firing bullets.

For this tutorial, you'll need an editing or effects package that provides luminance keys (e.g., Adobe Premiere, Apple's Final Cut Pro, Adobe After Effects, Sony Vegas, Avid Media Composer). This tutorial assumes that you understand how to add clips to a project, search through them using a "source monitor," add clips to a timeline, and add luminance keys to a clip. If you're unclear on any of these, check your editing software's manual.

Step 1: Set Up Your Project

ON THE DVD

In your editing package, create a project. Import the files hand-gun.mov and GS125.mov from the Luma Key Chapter 17 Tutorial folder. Hand-gun.mov is a short clip showing a hand "firing" bullets. It was shot with a Canon GL-1. GS125.mov is from the ArtBeats Gun Stock Digital Film Library and is a short movie showing a number of muzzle flashes shot in near darkness.

Place the hand-gun.mov clip on the first video track in your timeline. Create a second video track above this one. Place the GS125.mov in the upper video track.

Step 2: Find the First Muzzle Flash

Load the GS125.mov clip in your timeline into your source monitor. Scrub through the clip to find a muzzle flash you like. Position the playback head on the first frame of one of the muzzle flashes, and set an *in*-point. Scrub forward one or two frames to be sure the flash has ended, and set an *out*-point.

Note that most of these flashes are only one frame. Depending on your computer's performance, you might not see each frame during playback. Consequently, you'll probably have to scrub to find the single frames. Look for places in the clip where the hand recoils. This is a good way to zero in on the flash.

Step 3: Position the Flash in the Timeline

In the timeline, scrub through your footage and watch the program monitor to find the frame where the finger seems to fire. This is where you want the muzzle flash to appear (Figure 17.7). Position the GS125.mov clip in a higher track so that it begins at the point in time where the finger fires. Note that the program monitor will now be filled with the muzzle flash on black image of the GS125.mov clip. Your background plate which shows the finger will be completely obscured, but not for long.

Step 4: Define Your Luminance Key

Add a luminance key to the GS125.mov clip. If you're unsure of how to add a key, consult your manual for details. Some luminance keys allow

FIGURE 17.7   Your muzzle flash footage should start right when the finger begins to recoil.

you to choose between keying out light areas or dark areas. Others default to keying out darker areas. If your luma key provides an option, set it to key out darker areas.

Most luminance keys provide at least two sliders for adjusting the key effect: one that specifies which values will be keyed out, and another that controls how transparent those areas will become. Adjust the sliders in your luminance key filter until the black areas are gone and only the flash remains. Your goal is to find a balance of settings that eliminates the background without reducing the luminance of the flash too much. Pay particular attention to the edges of the flash. Even though it's only one frame, a hard edge or a black fringe will be noticeable to the viewer (Figure 17.8).

Step 5: Position the Flash in the Frame

With your key defined, you should be able to see the background beneath the muzzle flash. Unfortunately, the flash is probably over at the left side of the screen. Obviously, we want it to look like it's coming out

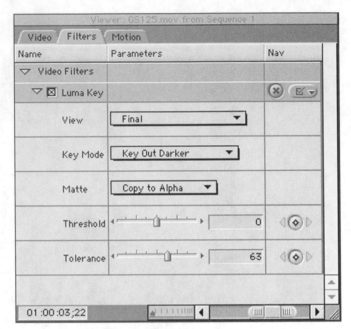

FIGURE 17.8 Experiment to find luminance key settings that eliminate the background, without dulling the intensity of the flash, and without creating a hard, distinct edge on the flash.

of the finger. Using your software's motion controls, reposition the flash so that it sits just off the tip of the finger. You might also want to try scaling it down so that it doesn't overwhelm the composition.

Finally, many of the flashes in the GS125.mov clip have a visible gun barrel on the left side of the frame. Your NLE should provide a motion control tool that allows you to crop the frame so that the barrel is removed from view without affecting the flash (Figure 17.9). (See your user documentation if you don't know how to do this.)

Step 6: Now, Do the Rest

Render your footage and take a look. Pay close attention to the timing of the flash; it might need to be moved forward or backward a frame or two to match the recoil of the finger. You might also see that you need to adjust the settings of your luminance key. When you're satisfied, choose another four muzzle flashes and edit them into the appropriate locations (Figure 17.10).

FIGURE 17.9   Move the muzzle flash to the end of the "barrel" and scale it down to be more appropriate to the "caliber" of this finger.

FIGURE 17.10   When you've placed all of your muzzle flashes, your timeline should have five clips on it.

Filtered Footage

If you don't have, or don't want to use, clip footage of a muzzle flash, consider using a computer-generated one. DigiEffects' Delirium collection of After Effects plug-ins includes an excellent Muzzle Flash filter that can generate muzzle flashes for you.

That's it! With the simple application of some stock footage and a luminance key we've created. . . well . . . a kind of silly special effect. However, you can see that, in a more practical situation, such effects would save you the danger and expense of using a real gun. In the next chapter, we'll increase the realism of the shot through the use of a little rotoscoping, but first, let's see if we hit anything during our little target practice.

TUTORIAL   **USING A CHROMA KEY**

In the last tutorial, we used a luminance key to knock out dark areas of a layer. However, not all footage is suited to luminance keying. With *chroma* keying, we can knock out a specific color to reveal underlying layers.

A chroma key is usually used to knock out a background to superimpose an element over other footage. That's what we're going to do here to create footage of gunshots hitting a door. (The results of this footage can be edited onto the end of our previous tutorial to create a finished shot of a hand firing bullets that hit a door.)

For this tutorial, you'll need an editing or compositing package that supports chroma keying.

Step 1: Set Up Your Project

Create a project and load the following media from the Chroma Key Tutorial folder: door still.psd, bullethole still.psd, bullethole.mov. Place door still.psd in your timeline. If your editing program does not support Photoshop files, you can try the TIFF version of the documents. (Note that, in the interest of saving space on the DVD, we have chosen to use a still of the door, rather than a movie. In practice, it's a better idea to use a video of the door, even though there's no movement in the image. A movie will show changes in noise and grain, while a still will have a slightly different quality that will be recognizable to your viewers.)

ON THE DVD

Step 2: Add a Bullet Hole

Add the bullethole still to a layer or track above the door's layer (this bullet hole is a still from the same ArtBeats Gun Stock collection that provided the muzzle flashes). The door will be completely obscured by the blue surrounding the bullet hole.

Step 3: Add a Chroma Key

Add a chroma key to the bullethole still. Next, you need to specify the color you want to "key out," or eliminate. Many chroma key functions provide an Eyedropper tool that you can use to sample the key color directly from the image in your program monitor. Other programs require you to specify the color numerically, or with a slider.

Don't be surprised if you don't see any changes after selecting the color. Most blue screens have a degree of variation in them, so selecting one single color isn't going to eliminate a entire field of slightly varying hue. Fortunately, most chroma keys also have some type of *tolerance* control that lets you specify a degree of variation from your chosen color. Adjust the tolerance control until your background is removed.

Your chroma key function also probably provides controls for thinning and blurring (or feathering) the edges of the keyed areas. Adjust these to eliminate any remaining blue fringes around the bullet holes, and to soften the edges to better blend them into the door (Figure 17.11).

FIGURE 17.11   By feathering the edge of our chroma key, we can blend the bullet hole into the underlying video.

Step 4: Position and Scale the Bullet Hole

At its normal size, this bullet hole is rather large (after all, it was plainly a small-caliber finger). Scale down the bullet hole to something more appropriate, and then position the hole somewhere on the door. In After Effects, we can scale the bullet hole layer by dragging one of its corners to resize. We can then re-position by dragging the image to another location. Other programs might require the use of a dialog box or special motion command.

Step 5: Tint the Hole

At this point, the bullet hole plainly looks like it's floating over the door layer. But why? What's not quite right? As we've discussed throughout this book, video is composed of luminance and chrominance information (lightness and color). It's good to think in those terms when trying to match two pieces of video, either when editing shots into each other, or compositing them on top of each other. Is there a chrominance difference between the bullet hole and the door? Unfortunately, because the door footage was underlit, it has a very slight greenish hue to it. This is in fairly sharp contrast to the strong reddish tones of the splinters in the bullet hole layer. Using the color correction facilities in your package, apply a slight green tint to the bullet hole.

Next, look at the luminance of the hole. It's a little bright compared to the duller tones of the door. Again, using the color correction tools at your disposal, adjust the luminance to darken the bullet hole a little bit. Because the bullet hole has few highlights, and because its blacks are very black, you can probably concentrate your luminance adjustments to the mid-tones. See Color Plate 14 for before and after examples of this color correction.

Step 6: Still Not Quite Right

It still looks like a decal, doesn't it? Consider the overall image quality of the two layers. Is there any difference? The bullet hole looks sharper and more detailed than the door. This makes sense, since the bullet hole was shot using 35mm film and digitized at high-resolution. Apply a slight blur to the bullet hole layer (Figure 17.12).

Step 7: Add the Rest

When you're satisfied with your first bullet hole, make two more copies of it and stack them on separate layers. Drag each copy to a different location on the door. You should also apply different scale amounts and a little rotation to each bullet hole to hide the fact that they're really all the same image. Separate them by a few frames or seconds in the timeline to corre-

FIGURE 17.12   Our final composite looks good, but as you can see, it takes a good number of filters to get it there.

spond with the timing of the bullet hits. There were four shots fired from our "handgun." For the last one, let's see it actually impact the door.

Step 8: Add the Last Hit

Bullethole.mov actually shows a whole bullet hit. Drag it into yet another layer and apply the same chroma key, color balance, and blur filters that you applied to the still images. Position, scale, and rotate the layer appropriately.

That's it! Now, you can render out a final shot and edit it into your footage of the handgun firing. If you cut to the door shot right before the impact of the last bullet, you'll have a somewhat dynamic little scene.   ✂

NON-SPECIAL SPECIAL EFFECTS

Often, when you think of special effects, you think of giant dinosaurs, or horribly be-weaponed space cruisers. However, you will probably find that most of your special effects needs fall into the simple, non-special realm such as the muzzle flashes and bullet holes we just created. As special effects hardware has grown less expensive, it has become reasonable to create digital effects for many tasks that used to be achieved practically.

Even relatively "simple" practical effects—such as gunfire—can quickly become expensive, even for a high-budget feature. Paul Verhoeven's *Starship Troopers*, for example, used over 300,000 rounds of blank ammunition! With the effects power of the average desktop computer, it's worth spending some time assessing whether some of your "normal" shots and effects might be cheaper to produce using computer generated imagery.

Keying Tips

Getting a good key—no matter what type you're using—has more to do with shooting good footage than post-production tinkering. However, there are some things you can do to get better results from key footage. Consider the following when defining your keys:

It might take more than one. It's okay to apply more than one key to an image. Because it can be difficult to evenly light a blue-screen background—particularly a large one—you'll often find that the blue screen is darker around the edges than in the middle. In other words, the edges are a different shade of blue. Rather than adjusting the tolerance of a single key to include all the blue—a process that will most likely eliminate some of your foreground—use one key for the lighter blue around your subject, and another key to eliminate the darker blue.

Try mixing keys. There are some instances where you can use a chroma key to knock out a background, and a very slight luma key to eliminate some of the leftover fringy weirdness. Because it's easy to overlight the foreground when lighting your blue screen, an additional luma key can help remove halos around your subject.

Use garbage mattes. Don't worry about trying to key out areas that don't contain a foreground element. Instead, mask those areas with a *garbage matte*. Most editing packages include a cropping tool or masking tool that lets you easily crop out unwanted sections of the frame (Figure 17.13). For more complex garbage mattes, consider using an alpha channel (which we'll get to shortly).

FIGURE 17.13   You'll have an easier time keying out the background in this shot, if you first use a "garbage matte" to cut away the unwanted stuff around the edges of the frame.

Use better software. If the keying function in your editing or effects package isn't doing a good enough job, or if your production depends on a lot of key effects, consider investing in some higher-quality keying software such as one of the special plug-ins from Ultimatte. Also take a look at Red Giant Software's Primatte Keyer. Now matter what keying program you use, Red Giant's Composite Wizard provides extraordinary filters for improving your composites. In addition to helping you remove fringes around your foreground elements, Composite Wizard can automatically match the overall color tones of your foreground and background. Composite Wizard can also add light to the edges of your foreground to make it look like your foreground element is affected by the lighting in your background plate.

Some chroma keying plug-ins and apps can use *screen correction* to improve the quality of their mattes. For screen correction to work, you'll need to shoot an additional plate of your blue-screen set with full lighting but no foreground elements. The keying package can use this plate as a reference to pull a cleaner matte.

Mattes

Because it's difficult to get a good composite using a key, and because it's not always possible to hang a colored screen behind something, you can also perform composites using a special type of mask called a *matte*. Akin to a stencil, a matte makes it possible for you to cut areas out of one layer of video (or a still) to reveal the layers below. For example, say you want to create a composite showing a giant tuna flying behind a building. Because you can't hang a giant blue screen behind the building, you'll need to use a matte inside your compositing program to knock out the background behind the building layer to reveal the giant flying tuna in the underlying layer.

In the old-fashioned film world, mattes used to be drawn by hand. Their purpose was to act as a stencil when inserted into a stack of film. For example, if you wanted to composite a shot of a model spaceship into a background that was shot on location, you would photograph film of the model spaceship against a blue background. Matte cutters would then go in and, by hand, black out the background of *each frame* of the model spaceship footage. Through a photographic process, a negative, or inverse, of the matte would be created. Next, the background and inverse matte plates would be stuck into a special machine called an *optical printer*. The optical printer would project the footage of the background onto a new piece of film, but the inverse matte would leave a perfect, spaceship-sized hole in the image. Before developing the piece of film, you would place the spaceship footage and the positive matte into the optical printer, and project that onto the new piece of film. The spaceship would project into the hole left from the previous shot, while the matte would keep the background from being overexposed. Through this sandwich of film clips, you would have your final composite.

If that doesn't sound complicated enough, consider what happens to color when it's diffused through several layers of celluloid. Although that bright-red spaceship model might look great on your original film, after projecting light through it *and* several other pieces of film, its color will definitely change.

As a digital filmmaker, you don't have to worry about such problems and, in most cases, you can have your software create a matte for you automatically. Best of all, your digital mattes can have varying degrees of opacity, rather than the simple stencil-like opacity of a practical matte.

Alpha Channels

Most of the time, color is stored in a digital still image or movie by splitting it into its component red, green, and blue parts, and storing each component in a separate channel (for some print applications, color is stored using four channels: cyan, magenta, yellow, and black). When viewed individually, each channel appears as an 8-bit grayscale image. When combined, these separate channels mix together to create a full-color, 24-bit image.

A fourth 8-bit grayscale channel, the alpha channel, can be added to an image or movie. Each pixel in the alpha channel specifies the level of transparency that will be used when compositing the image or video with something else. In other words, the alpha channel is like a stencil, but with the advantage that some areas can be defined as semitransparent.

In Figure 17.14a, you can see how the different channels combine to create an image. The red, green, and blue channels are mixed together to create a full-color image. In Figure 17.14b, you can see how the alpha channel is then used to determine which parts of this full-color image will be opaque, and which will be transparent. If an area is transparent, underlying video or image layers will show through.

Because each frame of your video includes its own alpha channel information, you can create animated alpha channels (also known as *travelling mattes*) that correspond to the action in your clip. Therefore, in the preceding example, our alpha channel would be animated to follow the movement of the spaceship.

Most of the time, the alpha channel will be stored in your movie document. You won't have to think about where it is, or go through an extra step to import it into your project. However, there might be times when you want to create a separate alpha channel movie for use in more complicated special effects.

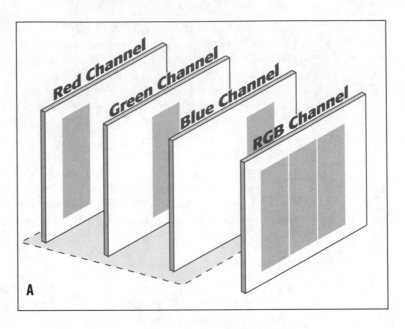

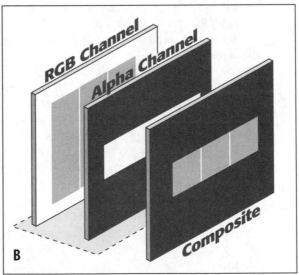

FIGURE 17.14 (a) In a normal color image, the red, green, and blue channels are combined to create a full-color image. (b) If you add a fourth, "alpha" channel, then you can specify which full-color pixels will actually be seen, and how opaque they will be.

There are a number of ways to create an alpha channel. Many programs—such as 3D rendering and animation programs—can create alpha channels automatically when they generate an image. Some editing and effects programs let you generate alpha channels from a key. For example, you could use a chroma key to pull an alpha channel matte from blue-screen footage. For certain effects, working with an alpha channel is easier than working with a key, and alpha channel mattes are fully editable—that is, you can go in and reshape them if you need to—unlike key effects.

Finally, alpha channels can be created by hand. In the next tutorial, we'll show you how to hand-craft an alpha channel for superimposing text over a video clip. In Chapter 18, "Rotoscoping and More Compositing," we'll use special tools to create more complicated, animated mattes. First, though, a brief word about pixel shape.

Pixel Aspect Ratios

As we mentioned in Chapter 3, "Video Technology Basics," although the pixels on your computer screen are square, many digital video formats—including DV—use rectangular pixels. Unfortunately, this means that your images and video can end up stretched and distorted as you move back and forth between different pieces of software.

Because digital video uses rectangular pixels, it will appear wider when displayed on your square-pixel computer monitor. Most editing and effects programs compensate for this by squishing the image horizontally to bring it back to a 4:3 aspect ratio on your computer screen. (If your software doesn't do this, you'll just have to get used to working with stretched footage. *Don't* perform horizontal squishing yourself, or your video will be distorted when it goes back to tape and gets played on a video monitor.)

Today, most video packages let you specify a pixel aspect ratio and let you explicitly configure for DV format when you create a new project. Consult your software's manual for more information on how to set pixel shape (Figure 17.15). If your footage is HD, the pixels are square just like the pixels in the computer monitor.

If you're creating graphics in a paint, image editing, or 3D application, you'll need to do some extra planning if they're destined for videotape.

If you are using a square-pixel analog videotape format such as VHS or Hi-8, you can go ahead and create your graphics at 640 × 480 pixels and import them into your editing application normally. If you're using a square pixel digital videotape format, like HD, create your graphics at the native resolution it was shot at, either 1920 × 1080 or 1280 × 720. If you shot HD with the goal of transferring to film, the 1920 × 1080 resolution is the most popular choice because it is comparable to the resolution of 35mm film. If you're using DV video, then you should create square pixel graphics at 720 × 540 while working in Photoshop, or any other square

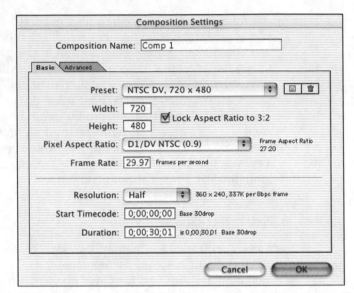

FIGURE 17.15 Most editing and effects packages now let you specify a pixel aspect ratio when creating a project. Shown here is the Composition Setup dialog from Adobe After Effects.

pixel environment. At this aspect ratio, they'll appear the same as they'll eventually look on a video monitor. When you're done with the artwork, save a copy and resize the copies to 720 × 480 before you import them into your editing package (Figures 17.16a, 17.16b, and 17.16c).

In our tutorials, we assume that you are selecting the correct pixel sizes and project settings to compensate for the pixel aspect ratio of your chosen format.

Modifier Keys

Adobe Systems does a great job of creating identical keyboard commands and interfaces for their separate Mac and Windows products. However, to better understand the following tutorials, note that Command on the Mac is synonymous with CTRL on a Windows computer, and Option on the Mac is synonymous with ALT on a Windows computer.

A

B

C

FIGURE 17.16　　(a) When creating images for export to video, start with pixel dimensions of 720 x 540. (b) When imported into a program that supports rectangular pixel aspect ratios, the image will appear too wide. (c) By simply applying a 90-percent horizontal scale, you can return the image to its correct aspect ratio.

All editing packages come with internal title tools these days, but they often leave a lot to be desired. When compared to sophisticated graphics applications such as Photoshop, they appear rudimentary at best. The good news is that you can use a painting or image editing program such as Photoshop to create titles. In your editing program, you can then superimpose your graphics files over your video. (If you don't want to super your graphics, but just want them on a solid background, you can simply import a graphic into your editing package as is.)

Let's say you want to superimpose a simple title graphic over an establishing shot in your video. Although you could go to your favorite paint program, grab the Text tool, type some graphics, and save the file, when you import this graphic into your editing or effects package, the background behind the text will be solid, and thus will obscure any video layered beneath it.

You could try to use a chroma or luminance key as we described earlier, but keys can result in ragged edges around your characters, and require much more time to render. There are some better solutions.

If you will be performing your composite in Adobe Premiere, Apple's Final Cut Pro, or Adobe After Effects, then creating a title with Adobe Photoshop or higher will be fairly simple, because these programs provide direct support for files in Photoshop format:

1. First, create a new document in Photoshop. If your video is in DV format, you'll need to create a document that is 720 × 540 pixels with a resolution of 72 pixels per inch. Other video formats—and some analog digitizing cards—might require different sizes. (See the preceding section, "Pixel Aspect Ratios.") Check your manual for details. In the New Document window, enter the correct dimensions, and check *Transparent* to give the document a transparent background.

2. Now you can simply pick a color, grab the Type tool, and create a title. Your text will be created on a separate *Text* layer. The layer's title will be the first few words of your text. Depending on your editing application, you might have to choose *Layer>Text>Render Text* before you save.

3. Save your document as a Photoshop file, make a backup copy, resize it to 720 × 480 pixels, and import it into Premiere, Final Cut, or After Effects. Upon importing, you'll be given a choice as to which layer you want to import. Select the Text layer, and your text will be imported with full, correct transparency. Place the text in a track that's higher in the stacking order than your video. When previewed, you'll see your text super'ed over your video!

If your editing package doesn't directly support Photoshop files, or if you're using an earlier version of Photoshop, or if you want to perform a more sophisticated composite (such as text that fades from top to bottom), then you'll need to manually create an alpha channel mask for your text.

Step 1: Create a Document in Photoshop

Create a new document with the appropriate dimensions (720 × 540 if you're using DV). In the New Document window, enter your dimensions, and under *Contents,* click *White*. This will create a document with a solid, white background. As an alternative, you can open the document Safe Guides.psd, located on the companion DVD. This Photoshop document measures 720 × 540, has a white background, and includes a separate layer showing action- and title-safe guides. If you choose to use this document, make sure the Background layer is the active layer. You don't want to create content in the Safe Guides layer.

Step 2: Select a Color and Choose Your Tool

Click on the Foreground color swatch to select a color for your text, and then click and hold on the Text tool in the Tool palette to pop out a submenu of other text tools. Select the Horizontal Type Mask tool, the second tool in the menu and the one that looks like a "T" composed of dashed lines (Figure 17.17).

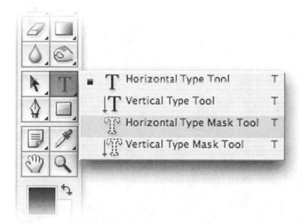

FIGURE 17.17   Photoshop's Horizontal Type Mask.

Step 3: Create Your Type

Click in your document window in a location close to where you want the center of your text to be. Click the Center Justify button on the Photoshop toolbar, then enter your text. Set the typeface, size, leading, and other parameters. You won't be able to correct this text later, so check your work carefully. Click OK when finished.

Step 4: Position Your Type

After clicking OK, you won't actually see any text on your screen. Instead, you'll see a selection, or outline, of your text. You can position this outline by dragging it around with the Move tool (Figure 17.18). (As a shortcut, you can hold down the Command key (Mac) or Control key (Win) to temporarily change your cursor to the Move tool. When you let go, it will revert to the text tool.)

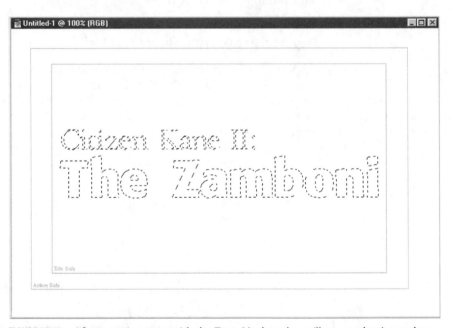

FIGURE 17.18   After creating type with the Type Mask tool, you'll see a selection rather than colored text.

Step 5: Color the Selection

To create your type, select *Fill* from the *Edit* menu and choose to fill using the *Foreground* color. This will fill the selection with your chosen color.

Step 6: Create the Alpha Channel

Now, select *Save Selection* from the Select menu. Accept the defaults in the *Save Selection* dialog and press OK. Open the *Channels* palette. Now, in addition to the normal Red, Green, and Blue channels, you should see an additional channel called *Alpha 1*. Click on this channel in the Channels palette to look at your new alpha channel.

The black areas of the channel will be completely transparent when rendered in your editor. In other words, any video positioned underneath these areas will show through. Just like a stencil, the black areas indicate areas of the text layer that will be masked. The white areas indicate areas of the layer that will be visible. Because the black is masking out the area around our text, we'll see the underlying video. Our colored text will be superimposed (Figure 17.19).

FIGURE 17.19   The black areas in our alpha channel indicate areas of the image that will be masked away to reveal underlying layers. This alpha channel will result in our colored text being visible, but the area around it being transparent.

Step 7: Save Your Document

If you're using the Safe Guides document, switch back to the Layers palette and discard the Guides layer. Make a backup copy and then resize your artwork to 720 × 480. Now, save this document in a format supported by your editing or effects program. Note that you'll need to select a format that supports alpha channels, such as TIFF, PICT, or Photoshop (PSD).

Step 8: Import Your Title and Video into Your Editor

Launch your editing package, and import your source video and the title document you just made. Place both documents in your timeline, with your title document in a higher layer.

Step 9: Define Transparency

Now you need to tell your software to use the alpha channel that is included in your text document. Some applications such as Adobe After Effects automatically treat the alpha channel as a mask and render appropriate transparency. Other applications, such as Avid Media Composer, will ask you to define the alpha channel when you import the image. Still other applications require you to define the alpha channel as transparent, just as you would define a chroma key to knock out a colored background. Consult your manual for details. If you're unsure of where to find such information, check the manual's index for terms such as *Setting Transparency*, or *Alpha Channels*.

That's it! Remember that if you want to change the text, you not only have to recreate the colored text, but the corresponding alpha channel as well. If you're putting multiple titles on the same screen, you might want to consider creating separate title elements in separate documents, and then arranging them on-screen in your compositing program. This will make it easier to keep your titles discreet and editable. ❧

TEXT FRINGING

Depending on the size of your text and the color of your background, you might see a thin white fringe around your text when it is composited. Photoshop smoothes text by slightly blurring the edges of each character into the background, a process known as *anti-aliasing*. Because the background in your document was white, the intermediate hues within the blur contain a lot of white. If the background in your composite is not white, these white pixels might show up.

If your final destination is video, the odds are that this fringe won't be seen. However, if your video is bring prepared for CD, DVD, HD, or online distribution, or if your titles will be scanned directly to film, then it just might be visible. You have a couple of options for removing it:

- Grab a still from the video over which it will be composited, use this as the background layer in Photoshop, and recreate your text over this layer.
- Before exporting, click on the alpha channel in the Channels palette and apply a Minimize filter (Filter>Other>Minimize). Specify a Radius of 1 pixel. If you're using a very thin-stroked typeface, this might cause some of the type's lines to break apart.

Although this might seem like a lot of work just to get a simple title, remember that there will be times when you'll be using these techniques to create titles that can't be made any other way.

Congratulations! Although this example might seem pretty simple (and somewhat boring), you've actually just learned a fundamental, basic task that you will use over and over again for any type of effects work. Alpha channel masking is an essential concept for all types of visual trickery, from advanced color correction to sophisticated effects. In the next section, we'll take your alpha channel understanding a bit further.

More Sophisticated Mattes

In the previous example, you created a simple alpha channel that defined a transparent area within your title, allowing you to "knock out" the background of your title and reveal some underlying video. Now, we're going to take things a little bit further and add some cool effects to your title by creating variations in the transparency of your text.

As you saw earlier, black areas of an alpha channel are completely transparent, while white areas are completely opaque. Alpha channels can also hold gray information, which define areas that are *partially* transparent (or "partially opaque" if you're one of those "glass-half-full" people). In this tutorial, we'll rebuild our alpha channel to create a title that has a smoky transparency that varies in opacity.

TUTORIAL   **VARIABLE TRANSPARENCY**

For this tutorial, you'll need the title document that you created in the previous tutorial. If you don't have that document, you can use the variable title.psd document located in the Variable Transp. Tutorial folder on the companion DVD. Before we begin, there's one more thing you need to know about alpha channels.

In the previous tutorial, you created an alpha channel by defining a selection with the Type Mask tool, and then saving that selection using Photoshop's Save Selection command. In case you hadn't guessed already, it's called *Save Selection* for a reason. Open the Channels palette and drag the Alpha 1 channel down to the leftmost button at the bottom of the Channels palette. You should now see a dotted-line selection of your text. This is the selection that you saved earlier, and you can use it to re-fill your text if you want to change the text's color. You can also use the selection to change your alpha channel.

Step 1: Load Your Selection

If you haven't done it already, open the title document you created earlier in Photoshop. Open the Channels palette and "load" your alpha channel selection by dragging the *Alpha 1* channel down to the leftmost button at the bottom of the Channels palette. (This is the *Load Channels* button, and we'll be using it a lot.) As you probably know, when you've selected an area of a document, any image editing actions—painting, filters, and so forth—will be constrained to the selected area.

Step 2: Modify Your Alpha Channel

Just as you can paint color information into the RGB channels of your document, you can paint transparency information into your alpha channel. For example, if you were to grab the Brush tool, choose a 50% gray foreground color, and paint in your current selection, your text would appear 50% transparent when composited in your editing program. We're going to do something a little more interesting.

Pull down the *Filter* menu, and scroll down to the *Render* submenu. Select *Clouds*. You should now see a smoky, grayscale cloud texture within your selection (Figure 17.20).

Step 3: Look at Your Text

Press Command-D to deselect. Click on the RGB channel in the Channels palette to return to the normal, color view of your document. Your text should look exactly the same, as we've made no changes to the color information; we've only changed the transparency information that sits "beneath" the color.

FIGURE 17.20   By filling the text in our alpha channel with a cloud texture, we can create a turbulent field of varying transparency.

Step 4: Save Your Document

Save your document and return to your editing package. Repeat the compositing steps that were performed in the last tutorial, beginning at Step 8.

When you're finished, you should see a title with variable, smoky transparency.

The ability to vary the transparency of an image lets you do things that traditional, analog matte compositors can't do. We'll get to even more sophisticated alpha channel work in the next chapter, but in the meantime, continue playing with some alpha channel effects to be sure you're comfortable with the concept. For example, try using the Photoshop Gradient tool to create text that fades from full opacity to full transparency (Figure 17.21). ✄

FIGURE 17.21   By using gradients in your alpha channel, you can easily fade one layer into another.

MOVING PICTURES

Today, most editing programs include motion controls that let you move a still image or video clip around the screen. Although great for creating cool video collages composed of lots of moving images, motion features are also ideal for creating animated titles and credit rolls.

Whether or not you think you have a need for such features right now, go ahead and take a look at this section, for in our discussion of motion, we'll introduce several concepts and practices that you'll use to create other types of effects. Because motion features are dependent on a process called *keyframe animation*, reading this section will be a good introduction to the animation effects that we'll create in the next chapter.

Basic Movement

When we speak of the motion features in an effects or editing package, we're not talking about features that let you control the motion of objects *within a shot*. In other words, you're not going to be able to take a video clip of a basketball game and control the motion of the ball. Instead, motion control is limited to specifying the movement of an entire layer. In addition to position, you can control a layer's other properties such as opacity, scale, cropping and rotation.

By combining motion control features with alpha channel masks and multiple layers, you can create some very sophisticated animations.

Keyframes and Interpolating

In traditional hand-drawn cel animation, a director draws certain frames that indicate where a character should be at a particular time. These *keyframes* might occur every 10 frames, or every two minutes, depending on the amount and nature of the action in a scene. Once the keyframes are defined, a group of animators draw all of the intervening frames that are required to get from one keyframe to the next. This process is usually called *in-betweening* or *'tweening*. It can also be referred to as *interpolation*, as the animators must figure out, or interpolate, which frames are required to get from one state to the next.

This same keyframe/in-betweening approach is used in editing and effects programs to animate the properties of a clip or image. By *properties*, we mean the parameters and characteristics that define how a clip looks, such as position, scale, and rotation. Some packages add control over additional properties such as distortion, opacity, cropping, or 3D rotation. Many programs also let you animate the parameters of any filters you might have applied to a layer, letting you change the amount of, say, Gaussian blur or color balance that you've applied to a video clip. The ability to animate all of the properties of a clip is an easy way to create complex effects (Figure 17.22).

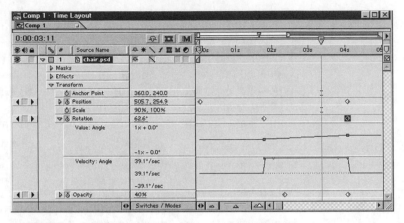

FIGURE 17.22 The Timeline window from Adobe After Effects. Notice the keyframe markers. Also notice that there are many animatable properties ranging from position and opacity to parameters of filters that have been applied to the layers. In addition, you can also adjust the acceleration and velocity of an animated change.

Most keyframe interfaces work roughly the same way:

1. Go to a particular point on the timeline.
2. Adjust the parameter you want to animate.
3. The computer will either automatically set a keyframe at that point, or you'll have to manually tell it to set a keyframe. During playback, the computer will automatically in-between all of the frames between your keyframes.
4. Repeat the preceding steps until your entire animation has been defined.
5. Render and play the video to see the full animation, including all of the in-between frames that the computer has interpolated.

Some programs also give you control over the velocity of an animated element. Such controls let you make an object slowly accelerate and decelerate as it moves, and make it possible to sync the animation of a property to another element in your composition.

A discussion of the specifics of the animation controls is beyond the scope of this book. If you are not familiar with the features of your package, consult your manual. Look for topics such as *animation, keyframes,* and *velocity.*

MAKING TITLES FOR FILM

If your final destination will be a film output, you will need to have your titles recorded from the digital files directly onto film, a process called "film printing," or have them transferred from videotape along with the rest of the project. Until recently, avoiding the intermediary step of video was necessary to produce much sharper titles (particularly at small sizes like end credit rolls) when projected, but now the quality of HD video-to-film transfers is good enough that transferring directly from videotape to film is the norm. It's still true that film printing from digital files can potentially yield a higher quality final image but the resolution of HD-to-film is good enough, even for small type.

You'll need to create your titles at the proper aspect ratio, usually 1920 × 1080. Until the recent advent of 1080 HD, the standard film resolution for digital files was 2 K per frame, or about 2020 × 1092 pixels for 1.85 theatrical release format 35mm. 2020 × 1092 seems bigger than 1920 × 1080 but it includes space for an optical sound track—about 200 pixels of the width—so the image resolution of 2020 × 1092 is actually about 1820 × 1090, a little less than 1920 × 1080. 2 K still exists but its usage is less and less common. There is another standard for film resolution, 4 K, which is double the size of 2 K and almost double the size of 1920 × 1080 HD. 4 K is usually reserved for projects and formats that require a very high resolution, such as the IMAX film format.

Be sure to keep your titles within the TV safe guidelines, even though you'll be creating files with a wider aspect ratio—it's very likely that they'll end up on a Standard Definition TV screen eventually. In some cases, you'll have to create one set of titles for film and another for Standard Definition TV.

TUTORIAL	ADDING CAMERA SHAKE

In Chapter 4, "Choosing Your Camera," we told you to buy a camera with good optical image stabilization. Then we nagged you to use a tripod during your shoot. Now we're going to risk sounding hypocritical and show you how to *add* a shaky camera effect to your footage. Why on Earth would we want to do this?

Next time you see a big action/adventure movie, pay attention to how much the camera shakes when something explodes or when cars crash into each other. Adding a camera shake can greatly increase the sense of impact in a special effect or stunt shot.

Earlier in this chapter we created a video of a finger firing a gunshot. We're going to return to this clip now and add a tiny bit of camera shake to make the image more compelling. We'll do this by animating the position of the clip to make it jitter up and down.

We recommend using Adobe After Effects for these types of effects, as its motion features are much easier to use, as well as more powerful, than many editing programs. A demo version of After Effects is included on the DVD. However, although After Effects is the ideal tool, you can use any editor or effects package that allows you to change and animate the position of a layer (Figure 17.24).

ON THE DVD

Step 1: Create a Project

ON THE DVD

In After Effects, create a project, and import the hand-gun.mov file from the Camera Shake Tutorial folder located on the companion DVD. Create a new composition with the same size and duration as the movie. Place the movie in the composition.

Step 2: Enable Animation of Motion

In many programs, you must specify that you want to animate a particular property before you can set any keyframes for that property. This ensures that you don't accidentally set keyframes for things that you don't want to animate. In the After Effects Time Layout window, open the arrow next to the hand-gun.mov file. Now, open the Transform arrow. Next to each property is a small Stopwatch icon. Click the Stopwatch icon next to the Position property to tell After Effects that we will be setting keyframes for the position of this layer.

Step 3: Set the First Keyframe

In the Time Layout window, scrub forward until you find the frame where the first muzzle flash occurs. When we clicked the Stopwatch icon in Step 2, After Effects automatically set a position keyframe at frame *one*. The current time marker is now at the first frame of muzzle flash. If we reposition the frame here, After Effects will automatically interpolate between the first frame and the current frame, creating a very slow movement of the image between those two frames. That's not what we want. We want a sharp jolt from the first position to a new position.

Back up one frame and set a new keyframe by clicking in the check box at the extreme left of the Time Layout window, in the same row as the Position property. This will set a keyframe at our current position—one frame before the muzzle flash—and serve to "lock down" the position of the image until we want it to move.

FIGURE 17.23 By setting keyframes for the "hand-gun" layer's position, you can make it jitter up and down, resulting in the appearance of a shaky camera.

Step 4: Set the Next Keyframe

Now, move forward one frame. You should be back on the first frame of the first muzzle flash. Click on the image in the Comp window. You should see a bounding box and handles appear over the image. Press the *Up* arrow key three times to move the image up three pixels. Now click the *Left* arrow key twice to move the image two pixels to the left. Notice that After Effects automatically sets a keyframe for you—be sure to thank it.

Step 5: Bring the Image Back Down

Think about how you might shake a camera when you are startled. The initial movement will be sharp and extreme. Going back to your original position will be slower. We don't want a huge shake in this case because the gunfire is not a huge event. However, we still want a slower return to our original position.

Move forward one frame. Press the *Down* arrow twice and the *Right* arrow once. This will move your image most of the way back to its original position.

Now, move forward one more frame. Press the *Down* arrow once and the *Right* arrow once. This will return your image to its original location.

Step 6: Now Do the Rest of the Flashes

Use the same technique to shake the camera during the rest of the flashes. The flashes have different intensities, so not all of the shakes need to be the same. In addition, move the frame in different directions and in different amounts so that each flash doesn't look identical. You might also find that you want to put a second, smaller movement immediately after your first one. This will create a "bounce" as the camera returns to its original position.

When you're done, render your movie and look at it. You might find that some shakes are too quick and need to be slowed down. You can click on a particular keyframe and reposition your image to adjust the degree of shake, and slide the keyframes around to adjust the timing of your camera shakes.

You'll probably also notice that when we moved the frame, we exposed the empty black space that's lying beneath it. If your final destination is video, this is not a problem, as we only moved the frame a few pixels. These black areas are at the far extreme of the action-safe area, so any monitor will crop out these areas.

If you're going out to film, or distributing this movie on the Web, DVD, or film then you'll have a couple of options:

Place another copy of the original footage beneath the shaking copy. When the top copy moves, it will reveal the lower copy. Although the pixels aren't necessarily accurate, they're close enough that no one will notice.

Shrink your image size or enlarge your footage. Instead of the previous option, you can always just crop your frame to eliminate the black areas. If you're going to the Web you're probably going to be reducing the size of your image anyway (usually to something like 320 × 240 or smaller). Therefore, even if you crop your image now, you'll have plenty of pixels left to do a good resizing later. We'll discuss resizing for Web output in detail in Chapter 19, "Output." The other option is to enlarge your footage. For the small screen, you can probably get away with enlarging it 90-95% without noticeably degrading the image. For the big screen, enlarging more than a tiny amount is not recommended. For the

Web, you can get away with enlarging it by 80% or more, depending on your material.

Automatic Camera Shake

If you can afford to spend some extra money, buy the After Effects Professional Edition, which includes a number of powerful extra plug-ins. In addition to superior keying functions, the Professional Edition includes special motion controls such as motion tracking (which lets you match the position of one layer to the movement of an image inside another layer) and The Wiggler, which can automatically insert random, shaky-camera-like motion. DigiEffects Delirium also includes a special Camera Shake plug-in that can greatly ease the creation of camera shake effects (Figure 17.24).

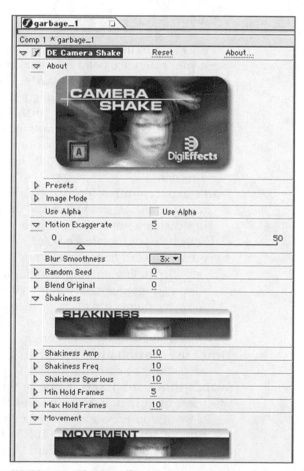

FIGURE 17.24   The DigiEffects Delirium plug-in includes a very good Camera Shake plug-in that can automatically create keyframes to make a layer appear to shake.

Eliminating Camera Shake

Don't worry, we're not going to tell you to take out all of that camera movement that you just put in. However, you can use similar techniques to stabilize footage shot with a shaky camera. *This process is hard, time-consuming work! Don't use it as a substitute for good shooting!*

Just as we animated the movement of an image to make it shake, we can animate the movement of an image to make it stand still. The easiest way to script such an animation is to pick a reference point on your image, and animate the position of your image so as to keep that reference point in the same place. Here are some guidelines:

Work at high magnification. Remember, you're concerned about tracking an individual pixel. So pick an area of high contrast and zoom in close!

Use guides. If your program allows you to set *guides* on an image (as in After Effects), set guides along the top and side of the pixel you are going to use as your reference. This will make it easier to tell if your reference point is in the right position.

Remember to think backwards. Zoomed in close, it can be difficult to remember which direction you need to move. You might have to switch back and forth between frames to figure out which direction the camera is moving (you might also have to stop for a moment to figure out which frame you're looking at). Once you've figured that out, move the camera in the opposite direction.

Don't expect your reference to always look the same. Unfortunately, as the camera moves and the light on the object you're tracking changes, the pixel colors and patterns will change slightly. Although your reference point might have been a nice solid black pixel in the first frame, it might be a 60-percent gray pixel in the second. Depending on your camera, it might even change color as it moves! Consequently, when trying to decide how and where to move the frame, you might need to look at several frames before and after your current location to get an idea of how the pattern you are tracking is changing in appearance.

Don't use motion blur! If your program can blur motion to smooth animation, be sure this feature is off!

Watch those subpixels. Some programs actually calculate movement by using distances smaller than a pixel. When zoomed in close, if you press the arrow key to move the image, you might not see anything happen. This is because the program has performed a subpixel movement. You might have to zoom out to test your footage, or zoom out a few steps and try again. You can probably find a zoom level that will let you move in single pixels.

Aim for a reasonable amount of correction. If your image is moving a lot, you'll have to settle for merely calming it down, as opposed to making it completely static.

Don't bother trying to stabilize blurry footage. If your camera was shaky enough that its motion caused your image to blur slightly, then you're not going to be able to stabilize your footage. The results will be too blurry and weird looking. Image stabilization is really just for evening out slight vibrations and shakes.

As in the previous example, as you move the frame, you'll be exposing the empty space around the edge of the layer. You can fix this problem with the same steps described in the preceding tutorial.

Easier Stabilization

There are two much easier ways to stabilize an image, but they will both cost you some money. The After Effects Professional Edition includes Motion Tracker and Motion Stabilizer features that can stabilize your image. Similarly, compositing systems such as Discreet Combustion and Apple's Shake include excellent stabilization features.

EXERCISE

This chapter contains many tutorials, so be sure to work through all of them, and then try working with some of your own footage.

SUMMARY

You'll most likely find yourself doing some keyframe animation during the course of your project, whether to create animations or simply to create effects that subtly change over time. The most important thing to remember when setting keyframes is that the computer will always interpolate between two keyframes. Therefore, as we saw in our last example, there will be times when you'll need to create a keyframe whose value is the same as its predecessor, to stop the computer from moving something around. Tracking down incorrect keyframes can be tricky, so be sure to save often when you're scripting your animation.

Every movie needs a title, and many movies need effects that can only be created using alpha channels, keys, and keyframe animation. The best effects are those that your audience doesn't notice, that are so real they don't stop to think "how did they do that?" Whether it's simple color correction or complex compositing, honing your skills with these tools and concepts will help you create less intrusive effects. In the next chapter, we'll build on these concepts and practices to create more complex effects.

18

ROTOSCOPING AND MORE COMPOSITING

In This Chapter

- Rotoscoping
- Tutorial: Rotoscoping a Simple Image
- Tutorial: Painting an Alpha Channel by Hand
- Tutorial: Color Correcting Part of an Image
- Tutorial: Exploding Heads
- Special Effects
- Making Your Video Look Like Film
- Tutorial: Creating Film Grain
- Summary

In Chapter 17, "Titling and Simple Compositing," we introduced the concept of compositing, and showed you how you can render part of an image transparent—using a key or an alpha channel matte—to reveal another image lying below. In this chapter, we're going to show you how to create more complex mattes, as well as how to touch up your composites with painting tools, and how to layer your composites to create more sophisticated effects.

Why all this talk about compositing? Compositing features are the workhorse functions of any special effects process. Yes, you might have spent weeks creating maniacally detailed 3D models and animations of a thundering herd of gerbils, and the results might be incredibly detailed and realistic, but unless you can convincingly composite that animation onto your location footage of a plain in Montana, you won't have a shot. No matter where your special effects content is created—painted by hand, shot with a film camera, generated by a computer—in most cases, it will need to be combined with live footage.

Even if your project doesn't require any such special effects, you will need to understand the basics of compositing if you want to perform more complicated color correction, or if you want to fix technical problems such as drop-outs and glitches.

For most of the tutorials in this chapter, we're assuming you own copies of Adobe Photoshop and Adobe After Effects. Although you might be able to achieve some of our compositing and rotoscoping goals using your editing program, if you're serious about any type of effects work, you really need a copy of After Effects. Demo copies of both applications are included on the DVD.

ON THE DVD

Our advanced compositing discussion begins with a digital update of a technique that is as old as cinema.

ROTOSCOPING

Put simply, *rotoscoping* is the process of painting, drawing, or scratching on a piece of film. If you ever shot super-8 footage as a kid and scratched laser beams directly onto the film, then you were rotoscoping. A more impressive example, though, is the epic Disney rotoscopes that can be seen in such productions as *Cinderella*. To achieve some of the extraordinarily realistic, fluid movement, animators painted over footage of live actors dancing and moving.

The digital filmmaker has many applications for rotoscoping. At the simplest level, painting directly onto the frames of your video can be a brute-force solution for achieving certain types of effects. In fact, if you're patient and talented enough, you could simply paint in all the effects you wanted! More practical examples of rotoscoping include removing wires from models or actors, touching up the seams in a composite, adding optical effects such as lighting changes, smoke, fire, or lightning, and performing color correction. In addition, rotoscoping tools let you create complex alpha channels that can be used for fine compositing work.

In the next section, we'll lead you through a number of rotoscoping examples and tutorials and, whenever possible, we'll try to show you these techniques using applications that you already have. However, if your project will require a lot of rotoscoping effects, you'll want to invest in a feature with some dedicated rotoscoping tools, such as Discreet Combustion or Apple's Shake.

As with the other effects topics that we cover in this book, rotoscoping can be a career in itself. Our goal here is to introduce you to some rudiments of the art, so that you can better understand how it might be useful to your production, and how you might personally use it to solve some problems. In addition, having an understanding of the basics will let you speak more intelligently, and interface better with the experts that you might hire for this type of work.

Painting on Frames

Just as Disney used to paint on celluloid, you can open up the frames of a movie and paint directly onto them using your familiar painting and image editing tools. Some programs such as Corel Painter allow you to directly open a QuickTime movie (Figure 18.1). These programs provide a simple interface for painting on a frame, and then moving to the next or previous frame to continue painting. They also offer special *onion-skinning* features that display a semi-opaque copy of one or more previous frames to help you position your paintings on the current frame.

In addition, some programs provide special tools for painting over several frames at one time (for creating real-time, "painted on" effects) and for cloning from one frame to another—an ideal way to create certain types of effects.

If you don't have an app that can open QuickTime files directly, you can always use your favorite image editor or paint program for rotoscoping, by first exporting video from your editing application using a format that your image editor can understand. Most editing and effects programs can export footage in a number of "still" formats. However, you'll need to be careful about managing these images so that you can convert them back into video later.

As we discussed earlier, most effects shots are fairly short, usually just a few seconds, sometimes even just a few frames. Consequently, you usually

FIGURE 18.1 Corel's Painter lets you open a QuickTime movie as a navigable series of individual frames. You can then use Painter's full set of painting tools for your rotoscoping chores.

won't need to move huge amounts of data around. If you'll be rotoscoping in a painting or editing program, you'll need to do the following:

- Isolate the section of video that you want to manipulate.
- Export that section as a series of numbered still images. The file format you choose should be one that can support the full range of color in your video and should, obviously, be one that your painting or image editing app can work with. Most NLEs and effects programs can export PICT, TIFF, or Photoshop format (you don't want to use JPEG, GIF, or any other lossy, compressed format). When exporting, create an empty folder on your drive and point the exported files into that folder. Your editing package will take care of sequentially numbering each image file. As long as you don't change the name of any of these files, you'll be able to easily re-import them later (Figure 18.2).
- Using your image editor, open, paint, and resave each file without changing its name.
- Import your numbered images back into your editing or effects application. Most apps have an option for importing a "numbered sequence." This sequence will usually appear in your project window as a normal movie clip.

Notice that by following this procedure, you will preserve your full image quality since you'll never expose the frames to any compression.

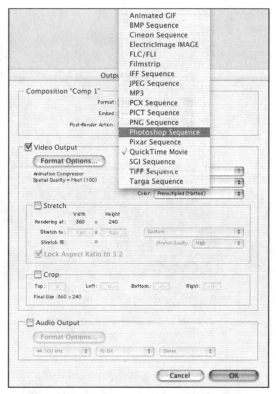

FIGURE 18.2   Adobe After Effects will let you save a movie as a numbered series of still images. You can open each image in a paint program or image editor for rotoscoping.

FILMSTRIP FORMAT

If you're working with Adobe Photoshop and Adobe After Effects, you can use the Filmstrip format to move your video from application to application. (Adobe Premiere also supports this format.) Filmstrip format works just like exporting a series of numbered images, but instead of saving them as separate files, After Effects exports all the frames in one giant tiled image (Figure 18.3). You can open this single image and edit the frames accordingly in Photoshop and then re-save the image. The edited filmstrip file can then be imported back into After Effects or Premiere and used to replace your original video.

FIGURE 18.3   If you're working with Adobe Photoshop and After Effects (or Premiere) you can use Adobe's Filmstrip format for moving your video into Photoshop for rotoscoping.

The nice thing about the Filmstrip format is that it makes for easier file management. However, for long segments, it might tax your computer's RAM more than a series of single frames will. In addition, you don't get the onion-skinning features that you get from an application that can open QuickTime movies, such as Corel Painter.

TUTORIAL

ROTOSCOPING A SIMPLE IMAGE

The easiest way to learn the workflow we just described is simply to try it. For this tutorial, we're going to return to the "hand-gun" movie that we developed in the last chapter. When we left off, we had just added a camera shake to make the firing of the gun more dramatic. Now we're going to use some simple rotoscoping techniques to paint some lighting effects onto the movie.

When the muzzle flashes, it should light up the hand, and possibly some of the shinier objects in the room. We could create a flash effect by applying a Levels filter to brighten the entire image, but this wouldn't look quite right, as everything in the shot would be brightened equally. We want to brighten just the objects that are near the flash; that is, the hand.

As with the "Adding Camera Shake" tutorial, we will be using After Effects and Photoshop for this example.

Step 1: Open Your Project and Prepare Your Media

Open the Camera Shake project that you created at the end of Chapter 17, "Titling and Simple Compositing." Our plan is to rotoscope each frame where there is a muzzle flash. We don't want to use the frame in our current composition, because it has been moved to create our shake effect. Instead, we want to manipulate the original image. Therefore, create a new composition and place the hand-gun.mov file into it.

Step 2: Export Your Single Frames

In your new composition, place the current time marker on the frame containing the first muzzle flash, and then select Composition>Save Frame As>File. Enter the name muzzle flash 1.psd and save the file. This will save the current image as a Photoshop file.

Step 3: Paint It

Open muzzle flash 1.psd in Photoshop. As we explained earlier, our goal is to add highlights to areas that would be flashed by the muzzle fire. Select the Dodge tool and paint the inside of the thumb, the front of the forefinger, and the tops of the other fingers that would be illuminated by the flash. You might also want to remove the shadow around the ring on the ring finger. You'll need a small brush, and you might need to use several strokes.

Now is also a good time to correct any weirdness in the muzzle flash itself. When we cropped the image, we ended up cropping a little too much off the left, resulting in a hard edge on the flash. Using the Smear and Clone tools, we can easily correct and reshape the flash.

There are some dull specular highlights on some of the objects in the background, particularly the molding on the doorway frame, and the bright white rolls of paper. Brighten these highlights using the Dodge tool. When you're done, save the image in Photoshop format (Figure 18.4).

Step 4: Import the Modified Image

Back in After Effects, import your now-modified muzzle flash 1.psd image and place it into your camera shake composition. Place it in a layer above the hand-gun.mov layer, and position it so that it begins on the exact frame as the muzzle flash in the original movie. Shorten the layer's duration to one frame (Figure 18.5).

In the previous tutorial, you repositioned the movie to make the camera appear to shake. Set the muzzle flash 1.psd layer to the same position as the movie.

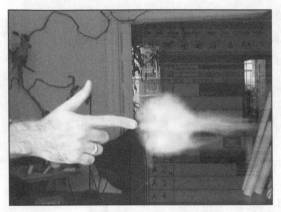 

FIGURE 18.4 You can use Photoshop's Dodge and Burn tools to paint in a flash on the frame of video where the "gun" fires.

FIGURE 18.5 Position your still image in a layer above your video.

After Effects does not perform pixel aspect ratio compensation when it imports a Photoshop image. In other words, the imported image will be too wide because of the difference in DV's rectangular pixels and the Mac's square pixels. You can compensate for this by specifying DV pixel ratio in the comp. settings dialog.

That's it! You've effectively replaced the original frame with the new, modified one. Now you can perform the same procedure with the other muzzle flashes, and then export your rendered shot to your editing program.

Whether working with single or still frames, the process just described is the basic workflow for rotoscoping. In the following tutorials, we'll be using these same techniques to move video between compositing, painting, and rotoscoping applications.

RENDERING FOR DV OUTPUT

If you will ultimately be putting your project back out to DV tape, it's important to set the proper rendering settings when exporting clips from a compositing or effects package, especially if the clip you're rendering incorporates video captured from DV.

Because DV is interlaced, you should export your final renderings as interlaced output. DV is *lower field dominant*, so you'll need to specify this at render time.

Figure 18.6 shows the proper After Effects settings for DV rendering. These are the settings you should be using for the tutorials in this chapter. Note that if you ultimately plan on distributing via the Web, email, or CD, you don't need to worry about interlacing.

FIGURE 18.6   Render settings in After Effects.

Better Rotoscoping through Filters

As we saw in Chapter 16, "Color Correction," most editing programs provide special effects filters such as the Color Balance and Levels filters that we used for color correction. Adobe After Effects-compatible filters have become something of a standard for effects plug-ins, and if your app supports them (or if you're using Adobe After Effects), you can buy filters that do a lot of special effects tasks that have traditionally fallen into the realm of the rotoscoping artist.

Often referred to as *opticals,* there are many effects that, until the advent of computers, were painstakingly rotoscoped by hand. Lightning bolts, sparks and flashes, laser blasts, and special color adjustments are all effects that can now be achieved automatically through filters. Although these filters don't always provide exactly the effect you're looking for, they often serve as an excellent starting point and can sometimes be combined with other filters and effects to get the desired look.

As a reference, here are some of the packages we recommend for creating a variety of "optical" effects:

- **DigiEffects Delirium** is probably the most useful single collection of plug-ins that we've seen. Providing excellent Fire and Smoke filters, along with very impressive Rain, Snow, and Fairy Dust filters, Delirium provides an excellent balance of practical effects with fun, "trippy" effects (Figure 18.7).

FIGURE 18.7 DigiEffects Delirium collection includes a number of excellent After Effects filters, including this very realistic Snowstorm filter.

- **Alien Skin Eye Candy** provides a number of improvements over After Effect's built-in filters, including a Gaussian Blur filter that can extend beyond the boundaries of a layer, and an HSB Noise filter. Eye Candy also provides excellent filters for beveling, chiseling, and carving shapes out of a layer, as well as a nice filter for making a layer glow.

- **Red Giant Software's Image Lounge** packs a variety of plug-ins. In addition to very stylized text, texture, and distortion filters, Image Lounge includes high-quality fire, clouds, and smoke effects, and unique to this package, special camera effects such as rack focus (Figure 18.8).

FIGURE 18.8   Red Giant Software's Image Lounge collection is one of many packages that includes a fire filter.

STOCK FOOTAGE OR FILTERS?

In Chapter 17, you saw how a number of effects can be achieved by compositing stock film footage with your video. Fire, smoke, lightning, gunshots, weather, and many other effects can be achieved by purchasing high-quality stock footage from companies such as ArtBeats. Alternatively, If you're really resourceful, you can always create your own footage for compositing.

However, as you can see from the list of special effects filters, there are a number of plug-ins that will also create fire, smoke, lightning, and even rain and snow. Therefore, which is the better choice?

If realism is your primary concern, stock footage wins out over current plug-in technology. In addition, compositing stock footage with other video—even when using complex luma and chroma keys—will be faster than rendering effects with plug-in filters.

On the other hand, special effects plug-ins offer a degree of control and scriptability that you'll never get from stock footage. If you need flame, for example, that flickers and flares at precise moments, or lightning that travels between two very specific points, then plug-in effects will be the better choice. In addition, plug-ins don't take up additional storage on your drive the way stock footage can. Finally, filters can often interact automatically with other CG elements, such as the falling snow and logo shown in Figure 18.7.

Ideally, of course, you want both, frequently mixed together—for good fire effects, for example, several layers of composited fire for realism mixed with plug-in fire effects for more control.

Rotoscoping an Alpha Channel

As we saw in the last chapter, an alpha channel matte is essential for compositing elements and layers that don't have a background that can be easily cropped or keyed out. If your foreground element is computer generated—a 3D animation, for example—then your 3D animation package will probably render an alpha channel for you. However, if your foreground element was shot on video or film, then you'll need to create an alpha channel by hand.

Just as you can use rotoscoping techniques to paint into the image part of a piece of video, you can also use rotoscoping techniques to paint into the alpha channel of a piece of video to create complex, "hand-painted" mattes. As you'll see in the following tutorials, you'll often use a number of different tools and applications to rotoscope an alpha channel. (See Color Plate 15 for before and after shots of our intended effect.)

TUTORIAL | **PAINTING AN ALPHA CHANNEL BY HAND**

Painting an alpha channel by hand is often the only way to create a matte for a complex foreground. If your foreground plate contains a variably hued background that can't be keyed, or a complex foreground with more detail than you can easily crop, then hand-painting your alpha channel might be your only option. If this sounds tedious, don't worry, there are a number of tips and shortcuts that make hand-cutting an alpha channel matte much simpler.

ON THE DVD

Open the Backyard Tutorial folder on the companion DVD and look at the Backyard raw.mov file. You should see a 1.5-second establishing shot of a house (sorry, we'd love to have longer, more meaningful clips, but we felt it was more important to deliver a few full-res DV than lots of lower-res, smaller clips). Although the shot of the house is nice, we were originally envisioning a more dramatic sky. Our goal in this tutorial is to knock out the existing sky and replace it with something more dramatic. To do this, we'll need to create a custom alpha channel matte to define transparency in our backyard raw layer. This layer, along with a more dramatic sky layer, will be placed in After Effects to produce a final composite.

Step 1: Stabilize the Footage

Unfortunately, our backyard source plate has a tiny bit of movement to it. Therefore, our first step is to stabilize the image. If the image is perfectly still, then we can create a single frame of alpha channel that can be used throughout the entire movie. If the image jitters or moves, then our alpha channel has to move in the same way. In the end, it's easier to stabilize the shot than to create a jittery alpha channel.

As we discussed in Chapter 17, stabilizing an image by hand is possible, but very difficult. Consequently, we've chosen to use Adobe After Effects Professional Edition to stabilize the image. The After Effects Professional Edition has an a very good motion-tracking feature that can stabilize an image with the push of a button (well, two or three buttons, but it's still very easy) as you can see in Figure 18.9. Note that the Standard Edition of After Effects lacks the motion tracking feature that is required for image stabilization.

If you don't have a copy of the After Effects Pro edition (or another compositor with a motion tracker such as Discreet Combustion), don't worry, we've included a copy of the stabilized footage, called backyard stabilized.mov.

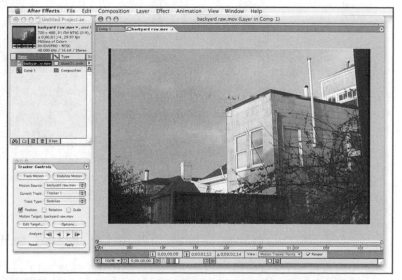

FIGURE 18.9   Stabilizing footage using Commotion's Motion Tracker and Stabilize feature.

Step 2: Create Your Project

Load the backyard stabilized.mov file into After Effects and place it in a new composition. Since this footage is a stabilized shot, we don't need to create an alpha channel for each frame in the movie. Remember, our goal is simply to eliminate the sky. The waving tree branches in front of the house don't cross into the sky, so we can simply create an alpha channel for the first frame and trust that it will work for the entire movie. Save the document as backyard.ae.

Step 3: Export the First Frame

We will be creating our alpha channel in Adobe Photoshop, so our first task is to get the first frame of our movie into a form that will be usable in Photoshop. With the current time marker on the first frame of the movie, select Composition>Save Frame As>File to export this frame as a Photoshop file (Figure 18.10).

FIGURE 18.10 We can export the first frame of this movie as a Photoshop file, and then hand-cut a matte in Photoshop.

Step 4: Open the Image in Photoshop and Start the Mask

Take a look at the image and consider what will be required to cut a good mask. Fortunately, this image is pretty simple. The houses and chimneys all have a good, strong border. The only potentially troublesome area is the bush to the left side of the image. As we saw in Chapter 16, "Color Correction,"an alpha channel can be created in Photoshop by defining a selection, and Photoshop has a number of tools for creating selections.

You could try to use the Magic Wand tool to select the sky, but since the sky is slightly cloudy, the Magic Wand won't be able to zero in on a single color. Similarly, the sky is a little too mottled for Photoshop's Color Range tool. If you're using Photoshop 5.5 or later, you might be wondering why we aren't just using the Magic Erase or the Extract command, both of which were designed to eliminate backgrounds. The problem with these tools is that they simply erase the background; they don't define a selection or provide any way of translating the masking information that they generate into an alpha channel.

No, the easiest way out of this one is to paint the mask by hand. Fortunately, Photoshop is well equipped for this type of work. Click on the Photoshop QuickMask tool located at the bottom of the Tool palette. When in this mode, we can simply paint the areas that we want to mask. Masked areas will appear red. Grab a big brush and fill in the large, empty portions of the sky. Don't worry about getting in close around the houses or foliage; just mask out as much of the sky as you can using a large brush.

 ### *Change Your Cursor*

The rest of this lesson will go much easier if you go to File>Preferences>Display and Cursors, and set Painting Cursors to Brush Size.

Step 5: Outline the Houses

Now, grab a smaller brush and zoom in to the right side of the image. Our goal here is to create a tight mask around the houses. Fortunately, the houses are mostly made of straight lines. Click at the right edge of the image where the doorway meets the top of the frame. Position the edge of your brush against the line of the roof, and click. Follow the roofline and you'll see that that edge goes for a short distance and then turns 90° to the left. The corner of that angle is the end of the first straight "segment." Hold down the Shift key and click once at this corner. Photoshop will automatically connect your first click to this second click and create a straight line between. Continue outlining the houses using this manner until you reach the shrub.

Step 6: Prepare for the Shrub

Obviously, trying to paint around the shrub will be a frustrating exercise. Instead of painting around the shrub, make a couple of broad strokes around it to close it off from the rest of the image. Your painted areas should now look like Figure 18.11. Click on the Selection button at the bottom of the Tool palette (the button to the left of the QuickMask button). This will convert your painted areas into a selection. Save the selection into an alpha channel. We won't be using this channel, but we're going to save it anyway, just in case something goes wrong in the next step.

FIGURE 18.11 With the QuickMask tool, we painted around each house and up to, but not including, the complicated shrubbery. We'll add that selection later using a different tool.

Step 7: Select the Shrub

With your selection still selected, pick the Magic Wand tool. Hold down the Shift key and click on the sky-filled areas in the bush. With the Shift key held down, each Magic Wand selection will be added to your hand-painted selection (although the alpha channel you saved earlier isn't being altered). Continue Magic-Wand-selecting the areas around the bush until you feel like you've selected all of the most conspicuous areas. Don't expect to get rid of all of the varying hues of sky visible in the bush; don't worry, we're going to correct for those problems later. If you make a mistake that you can't undo, press command-D to deselect, and then reload your selection from your alpha channel and start over with the Magic Wand.

Step 8: Save Your Alpha Channel

When you're satisfied with your Magic Wand work, save the selection. Now, open the Channels palette and you'll see you have two alpha channels. You can delete the first one, as it was our safety copy. Click on the second one to view it. The Magic Wand tool does not always create a smooth selection, so select the Blur tool and paint over the "bush" areas to smooth out, or feather, the Magic Wand selections that you made in Step 7. Remember, the blurry, gray areas of the mask will be semi-opaque when composited and will serve to smooth and blur the fuzzy bush shape into the background (Figure 18.12).

FIGURE 18.12 Our completed matte for the backyard footage.

Save 9: Save Your Document

Now we want to do something new. We want to apply this single alpha channel to each frame in our movie, so we need to export the alpha channel from this document, and then attach it to our movie in After Effects.

From the Channels palette menu (the triangle thing in the upper right-hand corner of the Channels palette), select Duplicate Channel. For Destination, select New. Press OK, and a new document will be created that contains only our alpha channel. Before you save this document, however, you need to change its Mode to Grayscale. Select Image>Mode>Grayscale.

Save the document in Photoshop format as backyard matte.psd.

Step 10: Create Some Clouds

Before we leave Photoshop, we're going to create some clouds to place in the background. Although we could use stock footage of clouds, or render animated clouds in a 3D program, we're going to stick with a simple still of some wispy clouds. Create a new RGB document measuring 720 by 640 pixels at 72 dpi. Click the foreground color swatch and select a slightly undersaturated, reddish-orange. Make sure the background color swatch is white. Choose Filter>Render>Clouds. Voilà! Instant clouds. Save this document as a Photoshop document and call it clouds.psd.

Step 11: Back to After Effects

Open the backyard.ae file that you created earlier. Import the backyard matte.psd document and the clouds.psd document. Place the clouds in your composition beneath the backyard stabilized.mov layer. You won't see the clouds at all, since the backyard plate is obscuring them. Place the backyard matte document into your composition, and layer it above the backyard stabilized file. It should completely obscure the backyard stabilized layer. In the Timeline window, click the Eyeball icon in the backyard matte layer. This should make the matte layer invisible (Figure 18.13).

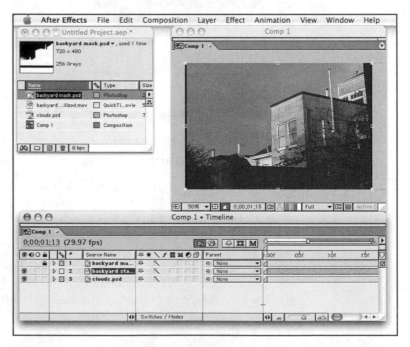

FIGURE 18.13 Our AE project before activating our alpha channel. Note that the backyard matte layer has its visibility turned off. We don't need to see it, we just need access to its luminance information.

Step 12: Define the Alpha Channel

Now we want to tell After Effects to use the backyard matte layer as the alpha channel of the backyard stabilized layer. Click on the backyard stabilized layer in the Time Layout window and choose Effect>Channels> Set Channels. Set Channels lets you redefine the source of each channel in the current layer. We want to use our backyard matte document as the alpha channel for the backyard stabilized layer. In the Set Channels dialog, change the Set Alpha to Source pop-up menu to Luminance. In the field above that, set Source Layer 4 to backyard mask.psd. This tells After Effects to use the luminance information of the backyard matte layer as the alpha channel in the backyard stabilized layer. Because the backyard matte layer is all luminance (it's black and white, no chrominance), it will correctly interpret our alpha channel.

You should now see the clouds composited behind the houses!

If there is slight fringing or other artifacts between the foreground and background, you can always go back to Photoshop and try to correct them. Before you go to that much trouble, though, render the file out (using the Animation compressor, of course) and import it into your editing program. Then, look at the footage on your video monitor. You might find that any slight fringes are invisible.

For a little extra drama, consider adding a slight movement to the clouds layer to make the clouds slowly drift behind the houses. ✄

Creating Animated Alpha Channels (or "You, Too, Can Make Traveling Mattes")

In the film world, when you cut a separate matte of each frame of film to follow the action of an element, you are creating a *travelling matte*. You can create the same effect in your DV files by creating an animated alpha channel. Using the same techniques described in the previous tutorial, you could create a separate matte for each frame of your video. If you think hand-cutting a separate mask for each frame of your movie sounds like a tedious chore, you're right! Fortunately, there are some techniques and tools that can greatly simplify the process.

TUTORIAL

COLOR CORRECTING PART OF AN IMAGE

In Chapter 16 we showed you how to use color correction filters to change the color in your image. When a color correction filter was attached to a layer, the filter's effect was applied to every frame of the clip. In this tutorial, we're going to show you how to color correct *part* of your image—not just some frames, but a specific element *within* a frame.

ON THE DVD

Open the Animated Alphas folder and watch the jose.mov file. You should see a brief clip of a big green parrot sitting on a perch. To make a more stylized image, and to bring more attention to the bird, we want to convert the background of the image to black and white.

Converting a movie to black and white is easy; we simply use a Saturation filter to desaturate the movie, effectively stripping away all the color information. However, if you desaturate the jose.mov file, everything, including the bird, will be desaturated. We need a way to mask the image so that the effect is only applied to the background. In other words, we need an alpha channel.

However, unlike our previous example, the area we want to mask in this movie (the parrot in the foreground) is moving. If we use a simple, single-frame matte like we used in the previous tutorial, as the bird moves, parts of him will move outside of the mask and be subject to the same desaturation as the background. Therefore, we must create an animated mask.

Again, we assume that you will be using Adobe Photoshop and Adobe After Effects for this tutorial.

Step 1: Move Your Video into Photoshop

Photoshop can't open QuickTime movies, so you'll need to convert the jose.mov file into something that Photoshop can open, either a sequence of still images, or a Filmstrip file. Create a project in After Effects and import the jose.mov file. Create a composite of the same size, frame rate, and dimensions as the movie. Place the movie into the composite and choose Composition>Make Movie.

Create a new folder on your hard drive called jose stills. Title your movie jose stills and save it in your new folder. In the Render Queue dialog, click on the Current Settings text next to Render Settings. Set Quality to Best, and click OK. Now, click on the Current Settings text next to Output Module. Click on the pop-up menu next to Format and select Photoshop Sequence (Figure 18.2).

Click OK, and then press Render. After Effects will write out your movie as a series of Photoshop documents, numbered in sequential order. You will modify each of these documents, and then bring the modified documents back into After Effects.

Don't worry about saving this After Effects project; you don't need it for anything else.

Step 2: Open the First Frame in Photoshop

In Photoshop, open the first of your stills. Look at the image to assess what will need to be done for this effect to work (Figure 18.14). First, the good news: the background behind the parrot is composed of glass bricks that are mostly shades of gray. This means that our matte doesn't have to be perfect. If there's some extra space around the bird, it probably won't matter, as those areas will look mostly gray anyway.

FIGURE 18.14   This is the image we'll be masking. We'll need to create a matte that changes with the movement of the parrot.

If you go back and watch the movie again, you'll see that the parrot's movements are mostly confined to a horizontal axis and that his overall shape doesn't change too much when he moves. His feet and tail are firmly planted, and even his back and wings stay fairly stationary. His movement is confined to his head, neck, and beak. This makes our job easier.

At this point, there are two ways to proceed. You can paint a mask using the QuickMask tool, as we did in the last tutorial. After painting the mask and saving it as an alpha channel, you can copy that channel into the next frame. If the mask needs to be altered, you can correct it, and then copy that new mask to the next frame, and so on and so forth.

A more flexible alternative is to use Photoshop's Pen tool to define a path around the bird. You can use this path to create an alpha channel, then copy the path to the next frame, adjust it, create an alpha channel, and move on to the next frame.

Because they are easier to modify, we're going to use paths.

Step 3: Create a Path

Open the Paths palette and click on the New Path icon at the bottom of the palette. Select the Pen tool and begin tracing around the parrot starting on the left side where his foot touches the perch. Work all the way around, including his toes (don't worry about the toenails, they're already black—we're worried about protecting areas of color) and the section of green visible between the wood perch and the metal perch support. Finally, work your way back to where you started, and close the path.

After completing your outline of the bird, you'll need to outline the section of tail that hangs below the perch (Figure 18.15).

FIGURE 18.15   We can use Photoshop's Pen tool to outline the bird, and then convert this path to a selection. Because paths are easily modified, it will be easier to change this selection for later frames.

Step 4: Convert the Path to an Alpha Channel

When you're satisfied with your paths, hold down Command and Shift and click on each path to select them all. From the Paths palette menu, choose Make Selection. Make sure Anti-aliased is checked and set a Feather value of 1. Click OK and a selection will be made, based on your path.

Step 5: Save Your Selection and Your Document

Choose Save Selection from the Select menu and accept the defaults. A new alpha channel will be created. Now save your document (Figure 18.16).

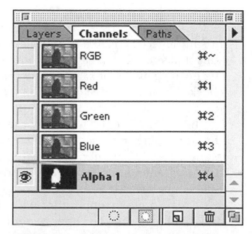

FIGURE 18.16   As in the previous tutorial, your Channels palette will show the red, green, blue, and your new alpha channel.

Step 6: Move Your Paths

Press Command-D to deselect your selection. Make sure that all your paths are still selected (if not, Command-Shift click on each one to select them all), and press Command-C to copy them. Open the next still in the sequence and press Command-V to paste your paths into this document. If your paths need to be moved, you can drag them to the proper position while they're still selected. If they need to be adjusted, drag individual control points until the path fits the bird in the new frame.

Step 7: Repeat Steps 4 through 6 for Each Frame

Now, convert the paths to an alpha channel, save it, then save your document, and copy the paths to the next frame. Continue in this manner until all of your frames have been given an alpha channel. Many of the frames will be fine as is—you won't need to adjust the paths. It's only when the parrot starts moving that you'll have to make a lot of adjustments, but adjusting paths goes very quickly. When you've processed each frame, quit Photoshop and return to After Effects.

Let Us Work for You

If you don't want to go to the trouble of cutting each matte, we've included a movie called jose with matte.mov *within Folders Chapter 18/Animated Alphas Tutorial that already has an alpha channel. You can use it for the remainder of this tutorial. However, to save space on the DVD, this movie has been reduced to pixel dimensions of 360 × 240. You'll need to adjust the size of your other media accordingly.*

ON THE DVD

Step 8: Create a New AE Project

In After Effects, create a new project. If you are going to use the modified stills that you created earlier, choose File>Import>Import File Footage. In the ensuing dialog box, select the first frame of the sequence. Be sure to check the Photoshop Sequence box, and then click OK. If you're going to use the jose with matte.mov file, just import it as normal.

In the Interpret Footage dialog, accept the default of Treat as Straight. If you're using the jose with matte.mov file, be sure to check the Invert Matte check box (when we created the alpha channel, we masked out the foreground instead of the background—this is no big deal since After Effects can invert it on import).

Create a new composition with the same size, duration, frame rate, and pixel shape as your imported movie (Figure 18.17).

FIGURE 18.17 When you import the jose with matte.mov, be sure to select Treat as Straight in the Interpret Footage dialog. (See your After Effects manual for details.)

Step 9: Add Your Media

Place the movie in the composition. You should immediately see black in place of the background. This is because After Effects is already interpreting the alpha channel in your movie, and rendering those areas transparent. Because there's nothing beneath the movie, the masked areas appear as black.

Now, import the original jose.mov file and place it in your composition. In the Timeline window, drag the jose.mov layer down so that it sits below your masked layer.

Now your composition should look normal. Since the masked foreground layer is sitting on top of the original background layer, and the two layers are in perfect sync, you can't tell that any modifications have been made. In reality, you now have one layer for the background, and another layer for the foreground.

Step 10: Add Your Filters

Click once on the lower layer in the Timeline window to select it. From the Effects menu, select Adjust>Hue/Saturation. In the Hue Saturation controls, slide the Master Saturation slider down to –100. Close the Effects window.

That's it. Your background should now be grayscale, while your foreground is still color! Of course, for added effect, you can also modify the foreground layer or apply additional filters and effects to either layer.

Building Effects with Multiple Layers

In the last tutorial, you built a complicated effect by stacking slightly modified versions of the same video clip. Although it might seem simple, this is an important concept, and an approach that many beginning compositors often miss. It can be tempting to try to create a lot of effects inside of one layer by applying filters and masks. However, most of the time, you'll need to break an effect down into a number of different processes, and use a separate copy of your video for each process. For many effects, you'll create several duplicates of a video clip and spend a lot of time cutting a different alpha channel for each clip. These clips will be filtered and manipulated separately, and then stacked on top of each other.

In the next tutorial, we will combine layer stacking with rotoscoping to create a complicated effects shot of a person literally sneezing his head off.

TUTORIAL

EXPLODING HEADS

In this tutorial, we're going to create a complex composite using several instances of the same video clip. By combining several hand-cut mattes, a lot of hand-painting, and an After Effects filter called Shatter, (which is part of the standard After Effects package), we will create a movie showing a person's head shattering into fragments after an over-strenuous sneeze. (In the industry, this type of film is known as "high concept.")

When planning an effect such as this, you might not be able to imagine exactly what post-production manipulations the shot will require. Most likely, you'll have to feel your way through the process and add new layers and filters as necessary. However, you can make some informed decisions about how to begin.

ON THE DVD

The Sneeze tutorial folder contains a video clip called sneeze orig.mov. This is our source footage that shows a person sneezing, and then stumbling out of frame. To see how the shatter plug-in works, load the sneeze orig.mov footage into After Effects and apply the Shatter effect. You'll see that the entire image shatters, and in a form that doesn't really look like a shattery explosion (Figure 18.18).

FIGURE 18.18   The Shatter filter is nice, but we want to change its
shatter settings to create more of an explosion effect, and we
want the plug-in to only affect the actor's head.

We can easily adjust the plug-in's settings to create a more appropriate type of shatter. (Figure 18.19). However, since we want just the head
to shatter, we need to mask out the rest of the frame using an alpha
channel. This will be our starting point.

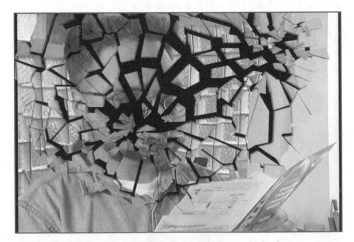

FIGURE 18.19   The Shatter filter can easily be modified to create a
more appropriate explosion-type effect, but we still need to find
a way of constraining the effect to just the actor's head.

Step 1: Create an Alpha Channel of the Head

The Shatter filter works by taking the image of a single frame, shattering it into pieces, and then animating those pieces so that they fly across the subsequent frames of the movie. Therefore, our first step is to decide when in the movie we want the shatter to occur. That frame will be shattered by the Shatter plug-in. However, as we've already seen, we don't want to shatter the entire frame. Instead, we want to create an alpha channel to limit the shatter effect to just the head. Because the shatter effect only operates on one frame, we only have to create an alpha channel for that single frame. We chose 00:00:03:10 (or frame 101) since there's a nice, slight head jerk that will add to the feeling of impact.

Choosing Time Display in After Effects

You can change the time display in After Effects so that it displays frame numbers instead of hours:minutes:seconds:frames. For this tutorial, we opted for frame number display, which you can activate by going to File>Project Settings, and selecting Frames. (In some older versions of After Effects, this setting is kept under File>Preferences>Time.)

For this tutorial, we will be creating masks as separate files, rather than as alpha channels embedded in our movie files. This will allow for more flexibility to correct and change the mattes. As we did in the last tutorial, we're going to create our alpha channel using Photoshop. In After Effects, export a still of frame 101 from the sneeze orig.mov movie. To do this, load the sneeze orig.mov movie into a composition, select its layer in the Time Layout window, and then choose Composition>Save Frame As.

Rather than create a selection as we did in previous tutorials, you can simply paint over the background areas with black paint, and the foreground areas with white paint. Because you probably won't need to re-edit this image, go ahead and use Photoshop's Image Size command to perform a 90% horizontal scale. Scaling your image here will save you a tiny bit of rendering time later. Save this image as a Photoshop file called head matte.psd (Figure 18.20).

Step 2: Set Up Your Project

Now, go back to After Effects, create a project, and import the sneeze orig.mov movie and the head matte.psd file that you just created. Make a new composition with the appropriate size and duration to hold the movie. Name this comp Main.

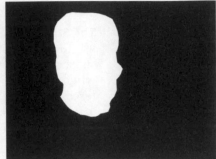

FIGURE 18.20 Still frame, and accompanying matte.

In a moment, we will use our new matte to confine the effects of the Shatter plug-in to the actor's head. Since this matte will eliminate the rest of the frame, we will see *only* a shattering head. Therefore, as we did in our previous tutorial, we will need to layer two copies of the same movie on top of each other. The top one will have the matte and the Shatter effect applied, and the bottom will serve to keep our "background" visible.

Place the sneeze orig.mov file into your composition. This layer will be our background.

Step 3: Prepare the Second Layer

At this point, we could start heaping more layers on top of the first one. In the interest of housekeeping, though, we're going to isolate some effects and layers by putting them in their own compositions. These compositions can then be nested inside our main composition to ease organization of our project.

Create another composition with the same settings as the first, but name this one Exploding Head.

Add the sneeze orig.mov clip to the Exploding Head composition, and double-click on it in the Time Layout window. This will open the movie in its own layer and allow you to easily set the in-point. Drag the current time marker to frame 100, and click the In-Point button. Close the window.

With the in-point set here, the movie in this comp now starts one frame before we want our explosion to begin (the Shatter effect doesn't become visible until the second frame of a clip).

Now, import the head matte.psd image you created earlier. Add it to your Exploding Head comp and disable the matte's visibility by clicking its Eye icon in the Time Layout window. Click on the sneeze orig.mov file in the Exploding Head Timeline window to select it. Earlier in this chapter, we used the Set Channels filter to define a separate file as an alpha channel for our current layer. Now we're going to use the Set Matte filter. With the sneeze.org layer selected, choose Effect>Channel>Set Matte. Set the Take Matte From Layer popup to Head Matte.psd, to indicate that we will be using that layer as the source for our matte. In the Use for Matte popup select Luminance to indicate that we will build our alpha channel from the luminance information in the Head Matte layer (Figure 18.21).

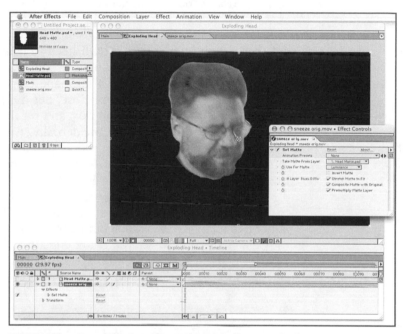

FIGURE 18.21   Our second composition, Exploding Head, after the footage and matte layers have been added. Note the Set Channel filter, which is used to activate the matte.

Step 4: Add the Shatter

Now, put the Exploding Head comp inside the Main comp. The easiest way to do this is inside the Project window—just drag the Exploding Head comp on top of the Main comp.

The Main comp should now have two layers, the sneeze orig.mov clip and the Exploding Head comp. Notice that the Exploding Head comp acts just like any other layer. You can move it, change its in- and out-points, and relayer it. If you want to go back and change its contents you can, and those changes will automatically filter up to the Main comp.

Re-position the Exploding Head comp so that it begins on frame 100 (Figure 18.22).

You can also add filters to a nested comp. Do that now by selecting the Exploding Head layer and choosing Effect>Simulation>Shatter. To

FIGURE 18.22 With the Exploding Head comp properly positioned, the explosion will occur right after the actor has sneezed.

get the best-looking shatter, you'll need to change some settings in the Shatter filter dialog. Open the Shape property and set Pattern to Glass.

Click on the crosshairs next to Shape Origin, and click in the comp window, just below the person's nose. Set the Shape Repetitions to 20. Set the shape direction to about 60°, and set the Force 1 position to just above the person's right eye. (Incidentally, there's no science to determining these settings. These are simply parameters that we came up with after much trial and error. As you work through creating the shot, you might want to create a different-looking shatter.)

In the Effects palette, change the View parameters for the Shatter filter to Rendered so that you can see the actual rendered effect. Step forward about five frames to see the beginning of the effect, then render a small test movie so that you can see the entire effect (or, if you have enough RAM, you can do a RAM preview within After Effects) (Figure 18.23).

FIGURE 18.23 The shattering head layer composited on top of our original background footage. Though our original, unshattered version is showing through, at least the shatterered layer is constrained to just the actor's head.

Something's very wrong, isn't it? The shattering effect looks nice, but there's still a head left behind. Obviously, the shatter effect can't calculate what's supposed to be behind the head in our original footage, so we're going to need to create that information ourselves through some very tedious rotoscoping.

Step 5: Start Rotoscoping

In our Main comp, we have our original video layer, and a shattering copy of that same video layered on top of it. If our bottom layer was footage of a headless body, then when the top layer shattered, it would reveal the underlying headless footage and our effect would work.

Unfortunately, we didn't shoot footage of a headless body (we had cast a headless body, but he turned out to be a real prima donna and so we fired him), but we can create some headless body footage through rotoscoping.

How to rotoscope is up to you. You could export the movie as a set of still files and repaint them in Photoshop. Alternatively, as we chose to do, you could open the movie file in After Effects and rotoscope it there.

Your goal is to paint out the head, and build a collar and hole to go where the head used to be. After Effects has a Clone tool that works just like the Clone (or Rubber Stamp) tool in Photoshop. But, After Effects clone tool has the added benefit of being able to use *other frames* as a source for cloning. At the end of the original clip are a few frames of footage *without* the actor. We can use these as source frames to clone the background over the actor's head in the earlier frames (Figure 18.24).

FIGURE 18.24   In After Effects, we used the Clone tool to clone background from an empty frame at the end of the movie into the frames where we want to erase the head.

In the Timeline, double-click the sneeze orig.mov to open it up in layer view. Here you can begin cloning. Select the Clone tool in the Tool palette. In the Paint palette, make sure that both Aligned and Lock Source Time are checked. Normally, to clone, you would option-click on the area you want to clone from and then paint into the area you want to clone to. This procedure will work the same way, but first we want to select a frame to clone from. Scrub to the end of the click and find a frame that includes a clean shot of the wall behind the actor. Option click in any area of the frame, taking careful note of the X,Y coordinates in the Info palette.

Now return to the frame you want to clone into (frame 100). Position your mouse at the same X,Y coordinates that you option-clicked in on the source frame, and click. You have now set up your cloning relationship. Now, you can brush in paint from the source frame into the current frame, effectively erasing the head to reveal the background.

Carefully paint out the entire head, making sure to leave as much of the collar and shirt as possible.

After Effects' painting and cloning tools don't actually change the pixels in the original image. Rather, the location of your paint strokes is stored in the After Effect project file. These paint strokes are composited onto the original media, providing you with a non-destructive form of editing. More importantly, though, because After Effects is remembering your actual strokes, it can composite them with all of the other frames in your movie, saving you a lot of painting time.

In the Time Controls palette, click the Next Frame button to go forward one frame. You should see that this frame also has the head cloned out. In fact, all of the subsequent frames have been similarly cloned! However, though this is a great time-saver, it's not perfect.

Play the movie and you'll see that, as the body moves around, it falls "behind" the paint strokes that you've created. Though After Effects has saved you a lot of time, you now have to go in and touch up some of your strokes.

Return to frame 101. As you can see, the paint strokes that you originally made have erased part of the collar. You need to restore the collar by *erasing* the clone stroke that you painted here. Grab the Eraser tool, and select Paint Only from the Erase pop-up menu in the Paint palette. Brush over the collar with the erase tool to erase the clone strokes that are obscuring it. If you "erase" some of the head back into view, then use the Clone tool to brush it back out (Figure 18.25).

As you can see, there's no free ride with this kind of rotoscoping. Though After Effects has done a lot of the work for you by replicating your clone strokes onto every frame, you still have to perform some touch-up.

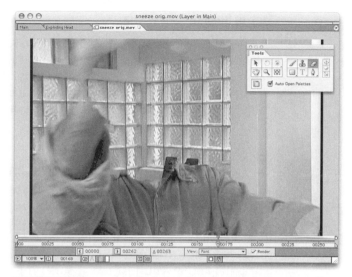

FIGURE 18.25   Because our original clone strokes are inappropriate for this frame, we have to go in and erase some of those strokes using After Effects' Eraser tool.

You could perform the same rotoscoping task in any number of ways. Another example:

- Export the frames you want to roto as numbered files into a folder.
- Open the last file in Photoshop, one of the ones that is a shot of the empty, after the actor has wandered off.
- Open the first frame that you want to roto, select all and choose copy to copy the entire frame.
- Switch to the "empty room" frame that you opened first, and choose paste. This will paste the frame you want to roto into a separate layer above the "empty room" frame.
- Using Photoshop's erase tool, simply erase the head from the upper layer to reveal the room layer beneath.
- Flatten and save and then repeat with the next frame you want to edit. (To save some time, build a Photoshop Action that automatically performs the copy and pasting of layers.)

Alternatively, you could save the movie as Filmstrip format and use Photoshop's clone tool to clone from one of the empty frames into your roto frame.

As always, there's no "right" way, and there's no way around the fact that this type of roto work takes a lot of time. There's a reason big budget effects movies are so expensive!

Step 6: Build the Shirt Collar

Once you've erased the head, you'll need to build the back of the shirt collar, and fill in the hole where the head used to be. All of this can be painted in with black or dark tones of gray. As always, there are a lot of ways to do this. You can step through each frame in After Effects, and paint in the collar and hole, or you can export the frames to Photoshop or Painter and perform your edits there.

However, probably the easiest way is to use After Effects Pen tool to create an animated mask.

Begin by selecting Layer>New Solid to create a solid layer of black in your composition. Position this layer just above the sneez orig.mov layer. The sneeze movie will be completely obscured by the black plate. Double-click on the color layer to open it in layer mode and use After Effects Pen tool to create a rough collar shape somewhere in the middle of the frame. Now click back to the Main comp to view it. You should see the rough black shape that you just drew, superimposed over the sneeze movie. This is the masked black layer that you created.

Edit and reposition the mask to the appropriate shape, as shown in Figure 18.26. What's great about this technique is that you can now tweak the collar mask's control points on subsequent frames, and After Effects will automatically animate the shape and position of the mask for the intervening frames (Figure 18.27).

FIGURE 18.26 Edit and reposition the animated mask for the collar using After Effect's pen tool.

FIGURE 18.27   By clicking the stopwatch icon next to the Mask Shape property of the mask on our color layer, we can now edit the shape and the position of the mask at each frame where the headless body changes position. In this way, we can make the mask automatically follow and reshape the collar. In addition, note that we've added a slight feather to the mask's edge so that it blends into the video.

ON THE DVD

However you choose to do it, the process will take you a while. To save you some time, we have included on the companion DVD a rough, first pass of our rotoscoped movie, a file called sneeze roto.mov. Although a good place to start, this file still needs work to clean up some cloning artifacts, and to retouch and improve the collar and neck. For now, it will work fine.

Step 7: Add the Rotoscoped Movie

Back in After Effects, replace the sneeze orig.mov movie in your Main comp with your new rotoscoped version. Render the movie (Figure 18.28).

Now things are looking better! When the head explodes, you should see a headless body that staggers off-screen.

However, the effect could still be better. The explosion looks like an animated explosion stuck on the front of a piece of video. It would be more realistic if the explosion had a sense of depth. Is there a way we could get some of the explosion parts to fly *behind* the body? Of course!

What if we added another copy of the headless body, but this one with a matte, so that the explosion pieces are obscured by the matte? Obviously, we don't want all of the explosion to fall behind the body, so we'll create a second instance of the exploding head layer. This addition will also add drama to the shot by adding even more shattering debris.

FIGURE 18.28 The same After Effects project, but now with the rotoscoped, headless version of our original footage.

Step 8: Mask the Body

Unlike our head matte, the body matte that we'll use to mask our second shatter effect will actually need to be a travelling matte. Using whatever technique you prefer, create a travelling matte of the relevant frames of the headless body movie. Obviously, you don't need to worry about anything before frame 101. Take a look at your previously rendered movie to determine how long the explosion lasts. You don't need to worry about masking any frames after this point.

Again, we chose to use After Effects and created a simple, animated mask to follow the outlines of the body. We rendered the matte as a separate file, which is stored on the companion DVD as body matte.mov.

ON THE DVD

Step 9: Add the New Explosion

Back in After Effects, create a new comp called *body w/matte*. Put the *sneeze orig.mov* and body matte.mov files into the new composition. As before, set up body matte.mov to serve as the matte.

Now, add the body w/matte comp to your Main comp. Put the current time marker at frame 106. As you can see, the body w/matte layer now obscures part of the explosion, making it look as if the shattered pieces are falling behind the body (Figure 18.29).

FIGURE 18.29   The shatter fragments now fly behind the body.

Now we need to get pieces falling in front. In the Time Layout window, duplicate the exploding head comp. Drag the copy so that it is the topmost layer. Now you should see some pieces in front of the body as well. Note that, with the same settings, both copies will produce identical shatter patterns. Change the Shatter settings on one of the Exploding Head layers to create a different-looking explosion. We chose to change the lower layer to create the effect of pieces flying backward (Figure 18.30).

FIGURE 18.30   We managed to get shattering pieces to fly both in front of, and behind the body, by stacking several copies of the same layer.

Now, render the movie.

Looks better, but there's still a problem. The shards of the top explosion fly in front of the actor's right hand. Since the hand serves to indicate a lot of depth in the image, we should create yet another masked layer—this time of the hand—to put in front of everything else.

Step 10: Matte the Hand

Again, using your method of choice, create a matte for the relevant frames of the hand. As before, watch the original footage to try to determine which frames will interact with head fragments. You don't want to worry about masking frames that don't matter.

Step 11: Add the Final Layer

Back in After Effects, create another comp called Hand. Add another copy of the sneeze roto.mov as well as a copy of the hand matte. Use Set Channels to set up your alpha channel. Add this comp to the Main comp and put it at the very top.

Render the movie.

Much better! Head parts are flying everywhere—in front of the body, behind the body, and behind the hand! However, we want to make one more small adjustment.

The Shatter plug-in renders its fragments with very sharp, defined edges. The amount of sharpness doesn't really match the quality of our original video, so we need to soften the explosion images up a bit to better match our source footage.

Apply a Gaussian Blur filter to both of the Exploding Head layers. Set a Blurriness of 2.0. You can experiment with more blur, but you don't want to blur the images too much, or they'll be blurrier than the source footage (Figure 18.31).

Render the final movie, put it in your editing package, and look at it on your NTSC monitor. There you can better see how to fix the collar and neck rotoscoping, as well as look for any leftover clone artifacts.

 After Effects and Echo Fire

The latest version of After Effects lets you preview movies on an external video monitor via a FireWire cable and deck, just like in an editing package. This can save you a trip back to your editing program for NTSC previewing.

To touch up the movie you can choose to re-paint your final movie, or go back and correct the sneeze roto.mov file, and then re-render your

FIGURE 18.31   The completed composite.

movie. Because we used multiple copies of that same movie, you can simply correct the original file and your changes will filter throughout your entire After Effects project.

Performing your touch-ups on your final rendered movie might be the best choice, as you won't waste time touching up areas that are obscured by falling debris. In addition, you can use the opportunity to smear the falling artifacts so that their motion quality better matches the footage of the actor.

If you perform your touch-up in the original rotoscoped file, then you can always make other changes and improvements in After Effects, and re-render the file.

You might also play with animating the values of the blur filters that you applied to the Exploding Head layers. By setting keyframes for the blurriness, you can make the fragments get more and less blurry as they speed up and slow down throughout the course of the explosion.

As you can see, with just a single clip of video and some clever layering, you can create very complex effects. Ideally, you'll need to do some planning before you shoot your initial footage. For the exploding head shot, for example, you might have been able to ease your rotoscoping work by shooting some additional photographic plates. In the end, you'll want to weigh the time and money spent rotoscoping against the time and money needed to shoot multiple plates.

SPECIAL EFFECTS

With the procedures and concepts we've covered in the last three chapters, you now have all of the basic tools that you'll need to create almost any effect. Of course, there are many other tools and programs you can learn for creating the content that you will composite into your video—3D modeling and animation programs, for example—but your compositing process will always involve the concepts we've covered here.

Often the difference between the effects you've been creating here and a more complex effect is simply scale. Many complex effects will involve the same techniques but use many more layers, composites, and custom-generated mattes, each serving to add a little more to the shot. As we saw in the last tutorial, good effects work is often a process of patient trial and error. It might take you a while to find the right combination of layers, filters, hand-painting, and custom settings to achieve the effect you're looking for.

In the rest of this chapter, we're going to present a number of effects that use and build upon the skills we've already discussed. These effects cover everything from fixing drop-outs to making your video look more like film. Hopefully, these examples will help you better understand the concepts we've already covered, as well as help you to recognize how those concepts can be combined and altered to create more effects.

We will not be presenting step-by-step tutorials for these discussions. Rather, we'll simply outline the steps required to achieve each effect. We will present no new concepts, so if you find yourself confused, look back over the previous chapters.

Fixing a Drop-Out

If you've ever worked with analog video footage, you've probably developed a healthy fear of drop-outs, those brief moments of static and jittery footage that can ruin otherwise perfect video. Fortunately, with digital video, drop-outs are a little more manageable and there are a number of ways to repair them.

As we discussed in Chapter 3, "Video Technology Basics," some tape formats are more resistant to drop-outs, but in the end, all digital formats are susceptible. A drop-out occurs when the magnetic particles in a particular part of the tape get scrambled. This can occur because of magnetic damage to the tape, and can even be caused over time by the effects of gravity.

In digital video, a drop-out appears in your image as a box of gray, usually 32 pixels wide. You can often get rid of a drop-out by simply rewinding the tape and playing it again. If the drop-out was caused by some type of debris, rewinding will often shake it loose and clear your image (Figure 18.32).

FIGURE 18.32   Drop-outs in digital video are different from analog drop-outs. Although no less annoying, they can be easier to fix.

If that doesn't work, try playing the tape on a different deck or camera. Sometimes, you'll find that drop-outs appear on one deck but not on another. If the tape plays properly on another deck, you can try capturing your clip from that deck, or you can try making a digital copy from the good deck to the bad.

If the drop-out persists, your best course of action is to repair the problem digitally. Fortunately, most drop-outs only last for one or two frames, so digital fixes are fairly simple. There are several approaches to take.

Edit the previous frame over the frame with the drop-out. This is the least favorable alternative, as it will create a brief, possibly perceptible stutter in your motion. If you're in a hurry, though, this will be the quickest fix.

Rotoscope the drop-out. Take the individual frames into an image editor and fix the bad areas with a Paint Brush or Clone tool. If you have a copy of After Effects, use the Clone tool to clone the same area from a good frame.

Mask and composite over the drop-out. Take a still of a frame that isn't bad and composite it over the bad frame. Using Cropping or Masking tools, matte the upper layer to create a small patch that covers the drop-out in the lower layer.

Fixing Lost Video

In a really messed-up analog tape, you might find places where the audio plays fine, but the video loses sync. This is usually a sign of a corrupted control track. If you have dubbed analog footage to DV with the idea of capturing it, your editing program might not be able to handle the break in timecode caused by the corruption. You can sometimes fix this problem by doing an additional dub from your analog tape. Try the following:

1. First, do a straight dub from your analog tape to DV (you might have already done this).
2. Next, do another dub from your analog tape to DV, but this time, take only the video. For the audio, take the output from *another* source, such as a CD player, another tape deck, or a DVD player. This external audio source might help you get a cleaner control track on your dub.
3. In your NLE, sync up the audio from your first dub with the video from your second dub. There might still be a glitch, but at least your NLE will be able to work with the footage.

Compositing Elements from a 3D Animation Package

For the ultimate control when creating special effects, you might want to consider rendering some elements using a 3D animation program. This is an entire art and science unto itself, of course, but 3D rendering is how the most complex, most realistic effects are created. Whether you need to create rampaging dinosaurs, marauding tornadoes, or even a more pedestrian effect such as adding extra cars to a street scene, 3D animation tools will give you far more control than practical models or photography will.

Unless you're very skilled and experienced in 3D modeling, rendering, and animation, you'll probably need to enlist someone else to do your 3D work. As a digital filmmaker, though, you'll want to be sure to consider the following:

Storyboard! Although easier than practical shooting, 3D animation still requires a lot of time and effort. Don't waste your money or your animators' time. Prepare and storyboard everything before you have someone generate animation.

Use your entire crew. Be sure your 3D animators are in contact with your cinematographer and designers. Good communication between your crewmembers will ensure that your computer-generated elements will match your live action.

Make sure your 3D animations have what you need to perform your compositing. Do your animations need alpha channels? Do others need luma keys? These concerns have to be considered ahead of time. In addition, make sure your animations are created with pixel dimensions that will allow for any necessary resizing. In other words, be sure to plan for differences in rectangular and square pixels.

Don't get fancy unless you can afford it. Many things can complicate a 3D effects shot. If you shoot video of a background using a moving camera, for example, you'll have a very difficult time matching the movements of your virtual 3D camera to the motions of your real camera. Unless you can afford a lot of skilled, expensive animators, keep your 3D shots simple.

MAKING YOUR VIDEO LOOK LIKE FILM

No matter how great your video looks, many videographers still envy the look of film. With its softer contrast and focus, different color gamut, grain, and slower frame rate, images shot on film look very different from what you can shoot on video.

Before you get dead set on a "film" look, though, spend some time and look at what you already have. Film might be pretty, and it's certainly what we're all used to watching, but a good three-chip DV camera is nothing to sneeze at either. Rather than trying to force it to be something it's not, consider what DV can do that film can't, and try playing to those strengths.

If you're dead set on a film look, though, there are a number of things you can do. Some things (progressive scan, 16:9 aspect ratio, special filtering, etc.) involve shooting and were covered in Chapter 8, "Shooting Digital Video." Other options are digital processes that can be applied in post-production.

Before you go filtering all of your video, though, be aware that there are different concerns for different types of output. If your final output will be film, then you don't need to worry about most of what is covered here. The transfer to film will be all you need to make your video look like film. Don't add extra grain, gamut enhancement, temporal changes, or special filters. (We cover film transfers in detail in Chapter 19, "Output.")

Film look is really for people who are mastering to video for distribution on video. Your goal is to make your footage look as it if were shot on film and transferred to video. When creating a film look, there are three characteristics that you'll need to modify: texture, color, and temporal quality.

Creating Film Texture

A piece of motion picture film consists of a layer of photo-sensitive silver halide particles suspended in an emulsion that is bonded to a strip of celluloid. The texture of these particles results in what's known as *film grain*.

The more light sensitive the film stock, the bigger the silver halide particles, and the more visible the grain. Instead of grain, video has electronic *noise* that looks very different—it's bigger, moves around more, and is more colorful.

To get a film-like texture out of a piece of video, it's a good idea to start with a relatively noise-free signal. Ultimatte's Grain Killer is a plug-in that is used to get rid of video noise when creating blue-screen mattes. Once you've reduced the video noise, you need to add grain. The easiest way to do this is to use one of the plug-ins listed later in the chapter, or you can create your own grain using a simple compositing technique in your editing program.

TUTORIAL CREATING FILM GRAIN

You can easily add a layer of grain to your final movie by using some simple compositing techniques in your editing program. Alternatively, you can import your finished video into a compositing program such as After Effects, and add the grain there. Although you can add film grain to your effects on a shot-by-shot basis, it's usually easiest to apply the effect to your finished edit. Note that for this effect to work, your editing program must be able to create solid color layers, have a noise filter of some kind, and be able to change the blending or transfer mode of a layer.

Step 1: Add a Color Layer

In your editing program, add a layer of 50% gray above all of the other layers in your project. Most editing programs have a facility for creating solid color layers. If yours doesn't, then you'll have to move to a compositing program. With the layer in place, your video should be completely obscured.

Step 2: Create the Grain

Now we want to make this gray solid into a noisy gray solid. We'll then composite this over our footage. Your editing program should include some kind of Noise filter, use it to add some monochrome noise. If it offers a Gaussian noise option, select this. How much noise is up to you, but grain is a very subtle effect, so don't go crazy with it.

To keep the effect from being too strong, you'll want to reduce the contrast of the noise. Use your editing program's Levels or Contrast control to lower the contrast of the noisy solid.

Step 3: Change the Blending Mode

Now set the blending mode of your noise layer to Hard Light. Some programs call this the "Transfer" mode and not all will have a Hard Light option. If yours doesn't, try the other transfer modes until you find one that looks good. You will probably also want to adjust the opacity of the noise layer to control the amount of grain (Figure 18.33).

FIGURE 18.33   With a slight opacity adjustment, you can reduce the intensity of your virtual film grain.

That's it! Instant grain. What's more, it's instant, adjustable grain. You can alter the opacity of your Grain layer to make the grain more or less pronounced. Try adding a Gaussian Blur filter to your Grain comp to make the granule size larger or smaller. (Use really small blur amounts— .3 to 1—to make the grain "chunkier.")

Add Grain

If you have After Effects, you can use its Add Grain filter to produce very realistic-looking grain, with a tremendous amount of control.

Creating Film Color

Film typically has a very different color quality than video does. What's more, different types of film yield very different types of color. We've all seen the bright, Technicolor pastels of 1950s cinema, and we've also seen the hip, overexposed grunge colors of modern music videos. Using the color correction techniques presented in Chapter 16, "Color Correction," you can often push or pull the colors in your video to appear more like film color. We say "often" because if your video was underlit, or suffers from other color artifacts, you're going to have less latitude to play with when shifting your color.

Film typically has a lower contrast ratio than video. Keep this in mind when making color adjustments. As we mentioned in Chapter 8, "Shooting Digital Video," you can shoot with special ProMist filters to reduce the contrast in your video image, to soften colors, and to create blooming highlights.

You can also create a simple ProMist-like effect in After Effects. Just create a new comp and add *two* copies of the comp to which you want to add the ProMist effect. Apply a Gaussian Blur (20 to 40%) to the upper copy, and set its opacity to around 20% and its transfer mode to Lighten.

You can adjust the amount of the effect by experimenting with the opacity and blur amounts. If you have a lot of hot spots that you really want to see bloom, try switching to a much smaller blur amount, and use the Luminance transfer mode (Figure 18.34).

Higher Contrast

In a similar manner, you can *increase* the contrast of a clip by layering two identical copies and applying an Unsharp Mask filter to the upper one. Set an Unsharp Amount between 50 and 70, a radius between 25 and 40, and a Threshold of 0. Keep the upper layer's opacity at 100%, but change its transfer mode to Darken.

Changing Video Time

With its frame rate of 60 fields per second, video effectively has more than twice the frame rate of film's 24 frames per second. While you might think that more frames must be better, in the case of moving images, it seems that less frequently is more. Film's slower frame rate tends to engage the viewer more than video's perfect, higher-frame-rate motion

FIGURE 18.34   Applying virtual ProMist filters in After Effects.

does. Since film presents the viewer with less information, it effectively asks them to do more, and thus brings them "into" the scene in a way that video can't.

As we discussed in Chapter 8, "Shooting Digital Video," if you shoot progressive scan video, you have a good head start on a more film-like motion. If you shot normal, interlaced, 60-field motion, you'll need to do some post-production processing to change the temporal quality of your video.

De-Interlacing

The easiest first step is to de-interlace your video. De-interlacing will throw out one field of video, and duplicate the remaining field to fill in the missing lines. This means that every pair of fields (that is, every 60th of a second of displayed video) is identical, effectively reducing your frame rate to 30 fps. This will immediately give your video a more film-like motion. Unfortunately, it will also lower the detail in your image and can worsen any existing aliasing troubles.

You can try to soften the aliasing problems with a localized blur, and improve detail with some strategic sharpening. Obviously, these processes will take time, so you'll want to do some experiments before you commit to de-interlacing. Try some short clips and make sure that the de-interlacing effect gives you results that you like.

Blurring

Film also has a very characteristic motion blur that results in images that are a little softer and blurrier than the sharp contrast of video. Hopefully, when shooting, you kept your shutter speed to something reasonable like 1/60th of a second, so you've already got some motion blur in your image. You can try to create more blur through post-production manipulation, but be warned that less is definitely more when adding such effects.

Although it won't produce the most accurate results, adding just a little blur to a single color channel (red, green, or blue) in your video can serve to soften the image just enough so as to imply a slurry film look. Blurring different channels will yield very different results, so do some experimenting with each channel.

Plug-Ins

There are a number of good plug-ins that can create a film look for you. If you're serious about matching particular film stocks, creating a complicated effect such as old film, or having a high degree of control, the extra expense of these filters might be worth it.

> **Red Giant Software Magic Bullet:** The current state-of-the-art in software film look is Red Giant's Magic Bullet. Available for a variety of editing and effects programs, Magic Bullet handles all of the issues we've discussed here including texture, temporal changes, and color shifts. Magic Bullet ships with a very good collection of pre-sets that allow you single-button access to a range of complex, stylized and traditional film looks (Figure 18.35).

FIGURE 18.35   Red Giant Software's Magic Bullet provides a state-of-the-art film look solution with excellent pre-sets that provide quick access to traditional, as well as highly stylized film looks.

DigiEffects Cinelook/Cinemotion: Cinelook provides very good controls for modifying the color of your video (you can actually pick film stocks by name from a list of standard film types) and the latest version includes built-in temporal controls as well as excellent 3:2 pulldown simulation for the exacting producer.

DigiEffects Delirium, Aurorix, and AgedFilm: Some of DigiEffects other plug-in collections include film simulators. Delirium provides a FilmFlash plug-in for simulating the flicker of a film camera, while Aurorix provides an AgedFilm filter for adding debris. Windows users can buy the stand-alone AgedFilm plug-in for adding debris, scratches, and color shift.

ArtBeats libraries: ArtBeats, the company that sells the muzzle flashes and impacts that you used in earlier tutorials, also sells a nice collection of Film Clutter. These scratches, countdowns, hairs, and dirt can be luma or chroma keyed over your video to create a very convincing old film look.

SUMMARY

Whether or not you're creating your own effects, an understanding the fundamental compositing concepts covered in this chapter—rotoscoping and layered compositing—will help you more effectively plan your shoot and post-production workflows. In addition, knowing the concepts here will make for more effective communication with your effects crew.

Perhaps the most important thing to know about effects work is that there's rarely ever a "best" way to do something. Every effects shot is a puzzle with many different solutions. In the end, if you get the look you want, then it doesn't really matter how you pulled it off. Don't be afraid to experiment and explore, and be prepared to try different approaches to your effects troubles. As long as you keep your original files backed up, are diligent about not compressing video through your workflow, then there's nothing to risk by experimenting.

19

OUTPUT

In This Chapter

- Mastering Your Outputs
- Videotape Masters
- The Final Audio Mix
- DVD Output
- Outputting for the Web
- Getting your 35mm Film Release Print
- Archiving and Backups
- Summary

MASTERING YOUR OUTPUTS

There seem to be two attitudes about the task of outputting final masters: nonchalance or terror. Some people think "it's no big deal—just stick a tape in the deck and press Record," while others envision their budget spinning out of control while words such as *online, streaming media,* and *film recording* send them into a panic. Both reactions are based on ignorance—creating a high-quality final output is a process that takes a lot of care, research and attention to detail, but if you're properly prepared, you should have no trouble getting the results you want. Whether you're doing it yourself or with the help of professionals at a post-production facility or film laboratory, knowing how the process works will help you master the art of the output.

The Best-Case Scenario

First the good news: in the five years since we wrote the first edition of *The Digital Filmmaking Handbook,* finishing film and video projects has gotten a lot easier. However, if your project is a feature film, you still need to know about all the different types of outputs covered in this chapter because you will probably create more than one master, as well as many supplemental materials.

A film that gets theatrical distribution usually needs all of the types of outputs described in this chapter (Figure 19.1). You'll need DVD viewing copies to send to film festivals and distributors (page 540). You'll need Web-ready output to post trailers and promos of your film on the Web (page 546). If your film is accepted to a festival, you'll either need a film print or a high-quality videotape master for screening. You'll need a videotape produced in an online editing session to get a good videotape master (page 526). You'll need to have mixed stereo audio tracks on your videotape master (page 537). You'll need a backup of your NLE project files, just in case you need access to them again. You'll back up uncompressed copies of your video and audio on optical tapes or digital videotape (page 558), and also keep an edit decision list (EDL) of your project. In addition, you'll make an eight-track output of your audio so that you can easily remix it at a later date if necessary (page 538), and you'll possibly take your master videotape to a film recordist who will create a negative (page 555). You might need to create digital files of your titles and special effects shots and have them transferred to film separately.

Say you screen the resulting release print at Sundance, and find a distributor who wants to release the film in theaters and, later, broadcast the film on the Independent Film Channel and on European TV. You'll have to decide whether to broadcast from your videotape online master or, more likely, create a new master from the film print by having it telecined back to videotape (page 536). You'll take the eight-track audio-only output you created and remix according to the different broadcast specifications of the Independent Film Channel, European broadcasters, and others. For Europe, you'll need a split-track dialog, music and effect (DM&E) mix, in addition to a stereo mix so that they can dub your film into other languages (page 537). If you hate dubbed films, you'll probably have to add subtitles yourself, with the help of a post-production facility that specializes in subtitling. Finally, the new telecined videotape master will be used to create the DVD for home video distribution and the DVD press kit (page 540).

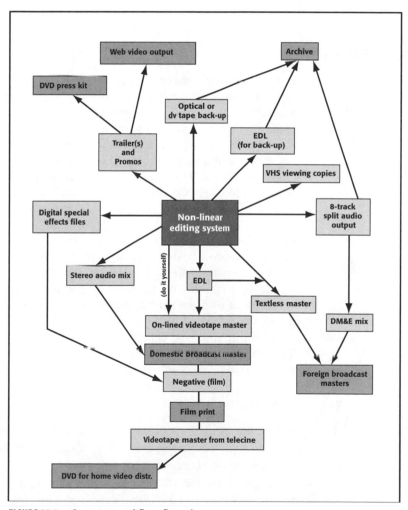

FIGURE 19.1   Outputs workflow flowchart.

The Big Decision

Most likely, you have no idea what will happen to your film once you've finished post-production. Will you need a film print or simply a videotape master? The most cautious choice is to start small but keep your options open: create a "do-it-yourself" videotape master and audio mix; put your trailer or clips up on the Web; and make some VHS and DVD outputs as viewing copies to pass around. Be sure to back up your media and your project in case you want to go back and re-edit or re-master and eventually finish on film. We recommend that you read this entire chapter before proceeding.

VIDEOTAPE MASTERS

If you're ready to make a videotape master, you need to decide whether you want to do it yourself using your NLE, or go to a post-production facility for a high-end digital online master. You'll need to take into consideration the format you shot on, the format you wish to master onto, and whether or not you want to eventually make a film print.

If you shot on a digital format, you can save a lot of money by creating a master yourself. The quality of your master is entirely dependent on how well your footage was shot and how much care you took with your video levels when you originally captured your footage (see the section "Capturing Quality" in Chapter 13, "Preparing to Edit"). Professional online editors will know how to get the highest quality from your original tapes, and will probably create a better-looking master than you can make on your own.

If you shot on an analog format, like BetaSP, your decision of how to master will depend on your final product. If you're going to film, you should do a professional tape-to-tape online session. If your final goal is broadcast, you can create a master yourself. If you can't afford a professional online but are bent on going to film, you should recapture your video in an uncompressed format. Even if this means renting extra equipment, it will save money in the long run.

Counting Down

Any output you make should have a 10-second countdown and a title card before the actual sequence. Your timecode after that countdown should start at hour 01:00:00:00. To be safe, the countdown should have a 2-pop at the 2-second mark of the countdown to guarantee sync. The title card, also called a head slate, should list the name of the project, the name of the producer/director, the name of the editor, the production company, the date of the output, the type of output (master, rough cut, audio-only, textless, etc.), the total run time (TRT), and, possibly, contact and copyright information. It's also a good idea to put this same title card up as the tail slate at the end.

Preparing for a Professional Online Edit

Having your project online edited by a professional editor adds a level of polish that is difficult to replicate yourself, but that quality comes at a price. Most online sessions start at around $500 an hour. Depending on the number of edits in your project, an online session for a 90-minute feature could take four or five days, maybe more if you have lots of effects. If you're new to the world of high-end video, the expense and the atmosphere might be a bit daunting. As with any part of the filmmaking process, don't be afraid to ask questions. Remember that only the inexperienced refrain from asking questions. The more experienced you are, the more questions you'll have.

Making the Calls

First, you need to find a facility that's right for you. If your project is DV, DVCAM, or DVCPro, make sure that your facility can online directly from that format. A surprising number of post houses do not yet have DV equipment. Instead, they will probably offer to "bump up" your DV tapes to BetaSP (just say no!) or Digital Betacam (expensive and unnecessary). Instead, go with a house that's DV-friendly.

You also want to determine how many source decks are dedicated to your session. The more source decks you have at your disposal (you should have a minimum of two), the faster you can finish—one deck can be cueing up a tape while the other is in use. Next, you need to determine what your mastering format will be. If you're spending the money for an online session, you should make it worth your while and master to a high-quality digital format such as Digital Betacam or D1. You should also arrange for a clone of your master—also known as a *protection copy*—once it is completed. If something goes wrong to your master, or if you sell your project, you'll still have a high-quality copy for yourself.

Stripping Down Your Sequence

You'll have to take an EDL to your online session, and to output a good EDL, you'll need to prepare your edited project. Make a copy of the project and remove all of the elements that don't need to be there for the online session—temporary titles and effects, music, voice-overs, and so forth—from the copy (Figure 19.2). All that should remain is the video and audio that came from your timecoded source tapes, including special effects shots that you created and mastered onto videotape. You should make sure that all of your video is on a single track.

These days, you'll probably never need a linear on-line editing session, but if you do, you can learn more from the Preparing For a Linear Online PDF located in the Chapter 19 folder of the DVD.

ON THE DVD

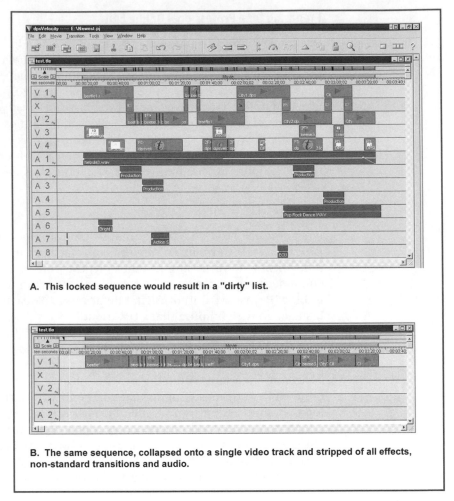

A. This locked sequence would result in a "dirty" list.

B. The same sequence, collapsed onto a single video track and stripped of all effects, non-standard transitions and audio.

FIGURE 19.2 A timeline view of a locked edited sequence (a), and the same edit, stripped of all temporary and/or unnecessary elements (b).

Hour 01:00:00:00

Make sure that the first frame of your edited sequence starts at 01:00:00:00. Although it isn't crucial, it's standard for video masters and outputs to start at hour one. Things will go smoother (i.e., faster) at the post facility if you follow the norm. If your project is broken down into film reels, it's customary to start Reel 1 at hour one, Reel 2 at hour two, and so on.

Your goal in an online session is to get your video laid down correctly. You'll polish and correct the audio later, when you mix your sound. That said, you don't need to put any audio in your EDL if the DigiBeta or D1 master isn't going to be the source for the sync audio in your mix (Read the section "The Final Audio Mix" later in this chapter if you're not sure how you'll be mixing your audio.) If you want to add the sync audio during your online session, *checkerboard* it across three tracks. The fourth audio track should be left empty to save room for a *guide track* (see "Guide Tracks," later in this chapter). Professional videotape formats have four channels of audio, so even if you don't want a guide track, you'll have to make sure your audio is limited to four tracks (Figure 19.2).

The List

After you've stripped your project down to its online essentials, you'll be ready to create an edit decision list, or EDL. You'll create the EDL in your editing application and take it to the online facility along with your source tapes. Before you make your EDL, it's important to talk to the post facility to find out exactly how they need the EDL formatted. Here's a list of things to ask about:

EDL type: Different types of linear editing hardware need different EDLs. The most common format is CMX 3600, which is considered the default nowadays. If your editing software doesn't offer any options for EDL formats, it's probably generating a CMX 3600 EDL. Other popular formats include Sony, GVG, and Axial. Ask your post house what type they need.

Disk type: Most linear editing systems cannot read PC or Mac formatted disks; instead, they use another format, called RT11. To format an RT11 disk on a PC or a Mac, you'll need an *unformatted* 3.5″ floppy and a software utility that can format RT11 disks, such as Avid's EDL Manager. If you can't create an RT11 disk on your system, make sure the online facility knows you'll be bringing a disk in another format and that you'll need transfer time before your $500+/hr online session starts.

Sort mode: The edits in your list can be sorted in several different ways, depending on the needs of your project, and the requirements of the online facility. *A-mode* is the most common and easiest to understand. A-mode EDLs are sorted in terms of master record-in. In other words, your edits will be performed in a linear manner, from start to finish. This is the simplest and most intuitive way to go, but often *C-mode* is a better choice. C-mode EDLs are sorted by source tape number, and then by master record-in. With C-mode, the online editor starts with the lowest tape number and sets the video levels for that source tape. Then, all the shots from that reel are edited onto the master. The same procedure is followed for the next source tape, and so on. Say you have 20 source reels and 650 video edits in your list. With A-mode, the online editor will have to set the video levels up to 650 times; with C-mode, he'll need to set up as little as 20 times. Other sort modes include B-, D-, and E-modes, which are rarely used for long-format projects. Figure 19.3 shows a short EDL sorted in A-mode and C-mode.

Sample EDL

Event #	Tape #			Source T.C. In	Source T.C. Out	Master T.C. In	Master T.C. Out
001	005285	V	C	17:09:22:20	17:09:23:14	01:05:11:10	01:05:12:04
002	005287	V	C	19:22:55:18	19:23:00:29	01:05:12:04	01:05:17:13
003	005286	V	C	18:23:50:17	18:23:58:17	01:05:17:13	01:05:25:13
004	005285	V	C	17:28:50:16	17:28:51:15	01:05:25:13	01:05:25:12

Tracks selected (in this case video only)

FIGURE 19.3 A short CMX format A-mode EDL (a), and a C-mode EDL (b).

Number of events: Depending on your EDL type, you might be limited to 800 or 1000 lines of text per EDL. Since each edit, also known as an *event*, takes up at least one line of text in an EDL, if your project has more than 800 edits, it's best to break it into two EDLs. Make this cut at a hard edit somewhere in the middle of your project.

Track selection: You'll need to decide which tracks to include in your EDL. Usually, this will be one track of video and the sync audio that goes with it. Remember that videotapes can only have four tracks of audio and one track of video.

Optimizing your EDL: Usually, this is done by the post facility. They'll go through your EDL and make sure there aren't any unnecessary edits in the list, a process known as *list cleaning*. Unless you thoroughly understand the EDL process and the equipment involved, this is best left to the experts.

Comments: Most NLEs allow you to add comments to your EDL—you can add notes to the online editor, tape names, clip names, and other information. Usually, the list you give to the post house should not have any more text than is absolutely necessary, due to the aforementioned number-of-events limitation. Instead, you should create a secondary EDL with comments that you print out for yourself and other human readers.

Pre-reading and b-reels: If you want to dissolve between two shots on the same source tape, this will be accomplished using pre-read edits or a b-reel. To create a dissolve, linear editing systems need to be able to play the a-side of the dissolve and the b-side of the dissolve simultaneously. A linear editing system with pre-read capability is able to store the frames contained in the b-side of the dissolve in memory. If this option isn't available, you'll need to create a "b-reel"—a new source tape with all the b-sides of dissolves that occur on the same source tapes. You can do this yourself ($), or have the post facility do it for you ($$).

Digital Video Effects (DVEs): Unless you have very deep pockets, an online session is not the place to deal with complicated special effects. However, if you do plan to do anything more than a simple dissolve in your online session, you'll need to order special DVE equipment for your session.

EDLS AND EFFECTS

EDLs can be rather limited when it comes to information about digital video effects. While motion effects, dissolves, color effects, and resizing are commonly included in an EDL, you should check with your post-production facility before assuming that their equipment can *automatically* recreate these effects. Typically, you will be limited to dissolves, 20 standard wipes (all of which you'll probably hate), and one static superimposition track (think "1980s news graphics"). Anything more complicated will have to be recreated by the online editor. In addition, if you have motion effects in your sequence, you need to make sure that you've used a frame rate that the linear-editing hardware supports. Ask the post house to send you a list of acceptable frame rates and/or percentages.

Guide Tracks

To avoid confusion during the online session, it's a good idea to create an *audio guide track* that will serve as a guide while you are editing. If you place a copy of the audio from your final edit onto one of the audio tracks on the tape you will be onlining onto, you will have an audible reference that will help ensure that your edits are correct, and in-sync. Audio guide tracks are especially useful if you're doing a C-mode online, or editing video only.

Before your online session, do an output of your final edit (not the stripped-down version!) with mixed audio onto a timecoded video source, preferably BetaSP or a DV format. Have the post facility record a track from your mixed audio output onto one of the four audio tracks on your DigiBeta or D1 master. Remember that this is usually a real-time process, so you'll want them to do it overnight to have it ready for your session.

Some people also like to have a visual guide, which can be created by recording the video from your output onto the DigiBeta or D1 master. During the online session, the guide video is covered up by the high-quality online video. Usually, the quality difference is large enough that it's easy to determine what's old and what's new. However, tracking down a missed shot or a flash frame is much harder with guide video than with a black master tape. We recommend that you use an audio guide only. Whatever your preference, be sure to let the post facility know what you want in advance—some will automatically create a video and audio guide, others won't.

Supervising the Online Session

As a director or editor supervising an online session, your goal is to make sure your final master looks as you intended it to look. For example, you might have a scene that was intentionally shot with unnaturally blue levels. Unless you are there to tell them otherwise, the online editor will probably try to correct this "problem" by taking down the blue. Most projects will include situations such as this so it's important that you sit in on the session.

You should arrive at the session with a printed version of your EDL containing comments, source names, and clip names. If you find the EDL confusing to read, spend some time at your NLE learning to interpret and understand where each scene begins and ends on the printout. You should also "spot" your film for scenes that have technical problems such as bad color or drop-outs. All of these things should be noted on your printed EDL. Make a photocopy of your EDL and notes for the online editor.

Your secondary goal when supervising an online session is to make sure it doesn't take too long. Two heads might be better than one, but they can also waste a lot of time chatting, discussing the merits of leaving the scene blue or correcting it, and so on. Let the online editor stay focused, and avoid talking and interrupting too much. Just because you're sitting there doing nothing doesn't mean they aren't busy setting video levels and managing your list. On the other hand, you are not expected to pay for "downtime." If there are technical problems (that aren't *your* fault), or if the online editor makes an error, pay attention to how much time it took and make a note of it. These things are inevitable, and most online editors will be taking notes of such things themselves. At the end of each day, they'll have you sign a type of invoice—be prepared to negotiate over lost time and technical problems.

Semi-Supervised Online Sessions

Save time and money by doing an overnight, unsupervised, C-mode online edit, and then spend the next day or two going over your project in a supervised session to fix any errors, or drop-outs, and to add special effects.

Color Correction and Titling Sessions

After you have your online master, it's common to spend half a day doing an additional color correction pass. High-end digital color correction systems, like Avid Symphony, offer a level of control that isn't available to the online editor. Usually, the color correctionist aims to make skin tones look their best. Nowadays, it's also common to add a "film look" effect to the entire piece.

If you haven't already had titles created by a motion graphics artist, you'll spend a few hours creating titles at the end of your online session. It's always a good idea to have a clone made of your color-corrected master before you add titles. This *textless master* will be the master for foreign dubbed and subtitled versions. Moreover, if you're transferring to 35mm, it's better to transfer the textless master to negative and have film resolution titles added later, separately. Typically, the titles you'll do at this point will consist simply of the end credit roll. Be prepared to provide a proofread text file of your credit list on a floppy. If your film is a documentary, you might need to add some *lower thirds* (see Chapter 17, "Titling and Simple Compositing"). If you need a subtitled master, you'll have a clone made of your master and provide a text file with all your subtitles on it. Usually, you'll want to go to a facility that specializes in su-titling.

Now you're ready to finish the audio. Audio outputs and mixes are covered in "The Final Audio Mix" section of this chapter.

The Do-It-Yourself Digital Online

We're going to make a big leap of faith and assume you have computer hardware with enough processing power (Chapter 10, "Building a Workstation") and editing software (Chapter 11, "Non-linear Editing Software") to play back full-size, full-motion video. If you didn't capture your video carefully the first time, you'll need to recapture to get the best quality video into your project (Chapter 13, "Preparing to Edit"). If your editing software doesn't offer control of video levels, you should rent a hardware waveform monitor and vectorscope for a day to help you recapture your footage.

If your source tapes were analog and you're planning to transfer to film, you should redigitize the tapes uncompressed to get the best quality possible. Whether you're working on digital or analog video, be sure that all of your digital effects shots are in place and rendered at the best quality possible. Finally, you should rent a DVCAM, DVCPro, or Digital Betacam VTR for a day to record your master videotape. This will set you back about $200 to $900. Refer to Chapter 12, "Editing Hardware," if you have more hardware questions, and Chapter 13, "Preparing to Edit," for detailed instructions on capturing online quality video.

Presentation Values

If you do your own online and dubs, be sure to create professional–looking tape labels for tapes that you are sending out. 3M and Avery create blank laser printable tape labels for all sizes of videotapes. For VHS, get plain cardboard or plastic boxes. Tape labels should include the following information: production company, producer/director's name and contact info, project title, date, total run time (TRT), and format.

Preparing Your Sequence for Output

Before you output your video, you need to prepare your sequence. Make sure you've replaced all temporary footage and proxies with the real thing. If your project is longer than the available master tapes for your videotape format, you'll need to break your sequence into two parts. Be sure to make these breaks at a hard cut, not at a dissolve. You also need to determine whether you'll be outputting your audio or doing it as a separate pass. See the section "The Final Audio Mix" later in this chapter for more about preparing and mixing audio for outputs.

Head Room

Avoid using the first minute or two of the videotape for your project. This is the part of the tape that is most prone to physical damage. Instead, cover the head of the tape with bars and tone followed by a head slate and a countdown. Most videotapes are a minute or two longer than their stated length, so don't worry about wasting a little tape.

Insert versus Assemble Edits

There are two different ways to make an edit onto videotape: *assemble* edits and *insert* edits. A typical piece of videotape consists of several tracks: the video track, two to four audio tracks, an address track for timecode, and a control track. The control track contains sync pulses that indicate where each frame starts and ends.

An assemble mode edit records over all the tracks on the tape including the control track. When you stop recording in assemble mode, a short break results in the control track (see Figure 19.4). In this break or hole there is no video signal, no audio signal, no timecode, and no control track. The result is an image that we've all come to know as "snow" on our television sets. Assemble edits tend to be frame accurate at the in-point, but not at the out-point. If you are planning to lay off your entire sequence to tape in one pass, there's nothing wrong with using an assemble edit. In fact, if you're going out to a DV format, you won't have a choice, as DV decks provide only assemble editing and aren't capable of frame accuracy unless you're using RS-422 deck control (see Chapter 12). However, if you need to lay off your project in more than one pass, you need to be certain that you set the in-point of your second edit *before* the hole in the control track. In addition, be aware that you have to lay off your passes sequentially. When assemble editing, you cannot go back and insert one piece of video *before* another without damaging your control track.

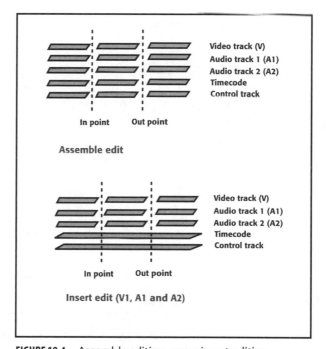

FIGURE 19.4   Assemble editing versus insert editing.

Black and Coding

Before you output using an insert edit, you should start with a tape that's been "blacked and coded." Set the timecode start at 00:58:30:00 and send a black signal from your black burst generator into your VTR. Press Record and let the VTR record timecode and black video onto the duration of the tape. This process ensures a stable video signal and timecode starting at 1:00:00:00 a minute and a half into the tape.

Insert edits offer much more control than assemble edits do. With insert edits, you can record over any track except the address track and control track. To make an insert edit, you need to start with a tape that's already striped with a control track and timecode (*black and coded* tape). Naturally, you need a VTR that's capable of making insert edits as well. Make a three-point edit by setting an in and out on your edited sequence and an in-point on the record deck. You can choose to output just the video track, just the audio tracks, or all three. If you plan to make lots of short edits onto tape, insert editing is the way to go. You won't have to worry about breaks in the control track, and you can easily make changes to things you've already output to tape.

Watch Your Output!

It might sound silly, but many people don't watch their output as they're recording. By the time you get to the point of outputting your master, you've probably watched your project hundreds of times. This time, forget about story, pacing, and other concerns, and just watch the video images. Look for drop-outs, glitches, and other inconsistencies.

Protection Copies

In addition to creating a textless master, it's a good idea to make more than one copy of your final master. Either you can do two outputs from your computer, or, if your master is digital, have it cloned at a post-production facility.

VIDEOTAPE MASTERS FROM TELECINE

To make a videotape master from a film print, you need to do a film-to-videotape transfer or *telecine*. Your film negative will be put on a machine, typically a Rank Cinetel, and as it plays, the image will be recorded onto videotape. The telecine operator can do some color correction during this process, but if your film is already color-timed, it's unlikely that it will benefit from any serious tweaking.

If your film was shot on video, then transferred to film, then telecined *back* to video, you might find that you don't like the results. Wim Wenders' film *The Buena Vista Social Club* was shot on several different videotape formats, primarily Digital Betacam and DV, and then transferred to 35mm film. The producers decided that a telecined video master of the film print wouldn't look good, so they went back to their original videotape sources and created a new videotape master using a combination of effects on a Sony DME 3000 to get a "film look" effect.

THE FINAL AUDIO MIX

Your final cut might have 20 or more tracks of sound if it's a complicated feature. To do an output, you'll need to mix those tracks into a more manageable number, usually between two and eight tracks. High-end professional videotape formats usually only have four tracks of audio, while low-end professional and consumer videotape formats usually only have two tracks. Audio for films often has five or more tracks to accommodate the surround sound that's used in theatres. Films that have been transferred to DVD for home video release offer both a stereo mix and a surround sound mix so that viewers can choose according to their hardware setup.

Mixing the audio consists of setting the levels for each piece of sound in the project, and then combining the tracks into a final mix. There are several standard types of mixes:

Mono: Mixing all your audio down to one track is called a *mono mix*. While mono mixes are sufficient for VHS viewing copies and radio broadcasts, for any other final output, you should at least do a stereo mix.

Stereo: Stereo mixes are what we're all most familiar with. The tracks in your project are mixed down to two channels, left (track 1) and right (track 2). For true stereo, these tracks should be slightly panned to the left and right, respectively, but often, only the music is true stereo. Some stereo mixes feature specific sounds that move from the left to the right channel, much like those old Led Zepplin guitar riffs. For broadcast and film, a stereo mix is standard.

Dialog, music, and effects (DM&E): In a four-channel DM&E mix, the sync dialog is mixed down to one channel, while the stereo music is placed on the second and third channels. The fourth channel is used for sound effects. By keeping these three elements separate, a DM&E mix allows you to keep your remixing options open. For example, you can easily replace the dialog for foreign language dubbing.

Surround sound: Surround sound might seem out of the league of the independent filmmaker, but with the advent of the "home theater" and HDTV, surround sound is becoming the standard, even for low-budget movies. Dolby Digital (or AC-3), DTS (Digital Theater System), and SDDS (Sony Dynamic Digital Sound) are the currently available digital surround sound formats. Dolby Digital and DTS use 5.1 channels: left, center, and right speakers in the front of the theater, left and right surround speakers in the rear, and an LFE (Low Frequency Effects) subwoofer channel. (The subwoofer only uses a tenth of the dynamic range of a normal channel; hence, you get a total of 5.1 channels.)

SDDS uses 7.1 channels, adding center-left and center-right speakers in the front. In addition to theatrical support, Dolby Digital is also supported by DVD players and digital televisions using the DTV format. Surround mixes are generally balanced toward the front channels, with the rear channels used for occasional effects or ambience. Overuse of the rear channels tends to distract the viewers from the screen.

Preparing for a Professional Audio Mix

The quality of the digital audio in most NLEs (44.1 or 48 kHz) is sufficient to merit using the tracks directly from your NLE as sources for your mix. To do this, you'll need to create a split-track output from your NLE. How many tracks you choose to output can vary depending on your project, but it's somewhat impractical to output more than eight tracks. The video decks you're likely to have in your editing room will only be capable of recording two audio channels. If you rented a Digital Betacam or high-end Betacam SP deck, you'll be able to record four channels. If you need to output more channels than that, you'll have to use additional video-tape stock with matching timecode. One popular solution is the Tascam DA88, which records eight channels of digital audio plus timecode onto a blacked and coded Hi8 tape (Figure 19.5).

FIGURE 19.5   Tascam's DA98 records up to eight digital audio tracks with SMPTE timecode using Hi8 tapes.

As with video onlines, it's important to arrive at the audio mix prepared. Before you go to the mix, you should have a sound spotting session to make notes of things you'd like to fix or change. A basic professional mix starts with a short *sweetening*, or sound editing, session. If you know of special effects you want to add, it's a good idea to let the sound effects editor know about them in advance so that he'll have some options loaded up and ready to work with at the beginning of your sweetening session.

Your sound effects editor will probably be working on a ProTools or other high-end sound editing system. Unless you have lots of time and money, the amount of sound editing you do in the sweetening session will be limited to things you couldn't do on your NLE, such as edits smaller than a frame of video.

After you've tweaked your sound, it's time to mix. Your tracks will be sent through a large mixing board and out to a high-quality sound recording format such as DA88 or DAT. The mixer will set the levels as your video master plays and the resulting audio will be recorded. Once you've gone all the way through your entire project, the tracks from the 24-track will be recorded back onto your videotape master, a process known as the *lay back*. If you want more than one type of mix—for example, a stereo mix and a DM&E mix—you'll have to lay back onto two videotape masters. If you're creating a Dolby surround sound mix for a film print, a technician from Dolby will record the mix on a special magneto-optical (MO) disk.

Do-It-Yourself Final Mixes

Doing the audio mix yourself using your NLE gives you the luxury of time, but it's unlikely that you'll be able to do anything more complicated than a stereo or DM&E mix. Since you won't be paying expensive hourly fees, you'll have the freedom to get your mix exactly right. Most likely, you were mixing your tracks as you worked, so you'll probably only need a final pass to set the levels across the entire project.

When it comes to mixing, dialog is usually king. Watch the meters on your video or audio deck as you mix; they're more reliable than the digital meters in your NLE. The dialog should tend toward a consistent dB range throughout your project. Music and effects should fall at a significantly lower dB except in special circumstances when they need to be intentionally louder. Mixing is a very subjective art, and many people think their way of mixing is the only way to do it right. If you're not confident about your "ear," get a professional sound editor to come in for a day and do a mixing pass on your film.

But Will It Play in Peoria?

Many sound editors have a secondary set of speakers in their editing rooms. These speakers are designed to sound like a low-quality TV speaker. Silly as it might sound, listening to your mix through lousy speakers can help you determine whether your mix is working under the worst possible conditions.

Conversely, if high fidelity is of primary concern, don't depend on the small "multimedia" speakers hooked up to your computer. Either invest in better-quality speakers, or, if you have a nice stereo system, string a cable from your computer to your stereo and use it to monitor your audio.

No matter how many audio tracks you have, you'll want to start by mixing them down to eight tracks. A typical eight-track configuration includes two to four tracks of checkerboarded sync production dialog, including a track of voice-over if applicable, two tracks of sound effects and ambiences, a track of stereo left music, and a track of stereo right music. Remember to work on copies of your sequence as you mix down your tracks, in case you need to go back and remix. Refer to your NLE software documentation for directions on how to mix down tracks of audio. At this point, you might want to make a digital audio tape backup of your eight tracks. If you're working with a DV format, you can also consider outputting your eight-track audio mix back to a DV tape.

Make a copy of your eight-channel split track sequence for each different type of mix you want to create. To create a DM&E mix, mix the sync production sound and voice-over down to one track, and the effects and ambience tracks down to another track. Leave the music as is on the last two tracks. If you are recording your mix onto videotape that only has two channels, you'll need to make two outputs with matching timecode. *Be sure to send each channel to the VTR separately.* You can output the video at the same time, or do it in a separate pass if your system is capable of frame-accurate insert editing. Either way, it's good to have video on both tapes. To create a stereo mix, you need to mix the dialog, effects, and stereo music left to channel one, and the dialog, effects, and stereo music right to channel two. Be sure to balance your levels, since this different configuration can easily result in the dialog and effects overpowering the music. Again, be sure to separately send each channel to the VTR.

DVD Output

As DVD players rapidly overtake VCRs in popularity, and with DVD burners and media down to the same price as recordable CDs, DVD-Video has rapidly become the most popular and convenient form of full-res delivery. The fact that its quality is substantially higher than VHS tape is a nice bonus.

DVD-V

While most people use the term "DVD" to refer to a DVD disk containing video, it's important to remember that there are different DVD specifications. There are the DVD-ROM formats that your computer can read data from (these, in turn, break down into subcategories by format and operating system) and there's DVD-Video (or, DVD-V) which is a complex specification for presenting standard definition video onto a DVD disk. You'll use DVD-ROMs for backing up your project, and possibly for delivering QuickTime versions of your video. You'll use DVD-V when you want to give someone copy of your video that can be played in a normal DVD player. For this discussion, we'll be concerning ourselves with DVD-V.

DVD output falls into two categories: the small batches that you can make at home using your computer's DVD burner, and larger batches that you can have created by a professional duplication house. No matter how your final disks will be made, you'll still need to prepare the content that will go onto them.

While outputting to videotape is fairly simple—just hit record on your deck and send it a video signal—DVD-V output is a little more complicated. In addition to having to compress your final video into the MPEG-2 format that DVD-Video demands, you'll need to author the menuing system of the disk. If you've ever watched a commercial DVD video, you know that DVDs can have complex interactive menus that allow the viewer to select specific scenes, configure special audio options such as commentary tracks, activate and deactivate subtitles, and view slide shows of still images.

Even if you don't want a menu, if you want a disk that simply plays your movie when you hit play, then you'll need to do a tiny bit of authoring to set up the disk so that it works this way. All of these tasks are accomplished using a DVD authoring program.

The commercial DVDs that you rent in the movie story come in several different formats. Though they all conform to the DVD-V specification, they might have very different capacities depending on whether or not they have information on both sides, or on separate layers within the disk. Table 19.1 shows standard DVD-V formats:

TABLE 19.1   Standard DVD-V formats

NAME	TYPE	CAPACITY
DVD-5	Single-sided, single-layer	4.7 GB
DVD-9	Single-sided, dual layer	8.54 GB
DVD-10	Dual-sided, both sides single-layer	9.4 GB
DVD-14	Dual-sided, one side dual-layer	13.24 GB
DVD-18	Dual-sided, both sides dual-layer	17.08 GB

(Note that in terms of actual storage capacity, these formats all have slightly less capacity than what's listed here. A DVD-5 disk only holds 4.37 GB, as far as your computer is concerned. This is because computer manufacturers consider a GB to be 1,024 MB while DVD manufacturers consider a GB to be 1,000 MB. The figures listed here are the numbers you'll see proferred by DVD manufacturers. They're the numbers you'll most commonly see.)

Most computer-based DVD burners write in the DVD-5 format. Though this is the lowest capacity, it's still enough room to easily hold a two-hour movie while maintaining very good image quality. At the time of this writing, DVD-9 recordable drives are available, and have dropped to very reasonable prices. However, the media is still very expensive. By the time you read this, dual-layer recordables might be as common as single-layers are now.

What format you need depends largely on your project. If you simply want to create viewable DVDs as a way to give copies of your movie to people, then a single-layer DVD burner will be fine. Similarly, if you're creating a final master for delivering to a DVD duplication facility, and you've authored some simple menus and added a couple of audio commentary tracks, then a single-layer DVD will still probably be plenty of capacity. (We'll talk more about preparing for mastering at a duplication facility later in this chapter.)

If you've got a more complex project that requires more storage—a movie with lots of menus, lots of extra video, several commentary tracks or different audio mixes—then you may not be able to fit all of that into a 4.7 GB disk, and will need to consider moving to a higher capacity.

You probably won't ever need to worry about DVD-14 and 18. These are generally used for distributing entire seasons of TV shows, or extremely long documentary productions.

Your first step in outputting to DVD begins with compressing your final video.

DVD Compression

Video for DVDs is compressed using MPEG-2 compression, yet another variant of the MPEG compressor that you might use for web distribution. (MP3 audio files are simply the audio component of the MPEG-3 specification. MPEG-4 is yet another variation that we'll discuss in more detail later in this chapter.) After your video is completely finished and you've locked picture and audio, you can consider your MPEG compression options.

There are several different ways to go about MPEG encoding:

- Most DVD authoring packages include built-in MPEG encoders. In most cases, you can simply export your final movie as a QuickTime file, import it into your DVD authoring program, and it will perform the MPEG-2 encoding for you. For your initial export, you'll want to choose an appropriate CODEC. If you've been working with a DV format, you can export using the DV CODEC.
- If your DVD authoring package doesn't include its own software MPEG encoder, you can install a software-based encoder and compress the video yourself. In addition to stand-alone software encoders, you can also get QuickTime CODECs that allow you to export MPEG-2 video directly from your editing program.
- Because software encoding can be very slow, a hardware encoder might be the best choice, if you have a lot of video. Offering real-time or better performance, hardware encoders usually produce higher-quality results than software encoders. The downside is that they can also be very expensive. For a regular DVD production workflow, though, the expense might be worth it. An alternative to a hardware encoder is to buy an ad-

ditional computer and use it as a dedicated MPEG encoding machine using a software encoder. It won't be any speedier, but it will free up your current computer for continued work.

LaCie FastCoder

If you're a Macintosh user, be sure to take a look at the LaCie fast coder. This tiny box plugs into your computer's FireWire port and delivers real-time hardware MPEG-1 or MPEG-2 encoding. Faster than a software encoder, and yielding excellent quality, the most impressive thing about the FastCoder is its price: $249 at the time of this writing (Figure 19.6).

FIGURE 19.6   The LaCie FastCoder provides a tiny, portable, real-time MPEG-2 encoder at an extremely affordable price.

Whether you're using a hardware or software compressor, you'll need to give careful consideration to your compression settings. Choosing MPEG-2 settings is a process of balancing disk capacity, image quality, and the throughput capability of the DVD specification. If you're trying to cram a lot of extra material onto a disk, you might have to sacrifice some image quality. Similarly, if you want your movie to contain lots of alternate camera angles, then you may have to endure some quality loss, not only for space considerations, but because DVD players can only deal with a limited amount of parallel video information at one time.

DVD audio comes in five flavors: PCM, Dolby AC-3, MPEG, DTS, and SDDS. *PCM* audio is the same as the audio that's recorded on audio CDs and you can use any WAV or AIFF file as the source for PCM audio in a DVD project. *Dolby AC-3* is 5.1 channel Dolby Digital Surround Sound that has been compressed using a special CODEC. Typically, the 5.1 channels are designed to create a surround environment in a movie theater, so the channels are laid out as left, center, right, left surround, right surround. The .1 channel is an optional subwoofer track for low-frequency sounds. However, if surround sound is out of your league, don't worry. Dolby AC-3 doesn't require that your sound tracks be arranged this way—you can also have just a normal stereo mix. *MPEG* audio is not used in North America. *DTS* and *SDDS* audio are other forms of surround sound used for feature films—we discussed them a little in the section on audio mixes earlier in this chapter. You'll need a professional mixer to get DTS or SDDS sound, and they will be able to give you the mix in the properly encoded format for inclusion on a DVD. DVDs can also have multiple streams of sound, each containing a full mix for different language versions or extras such as director commentaries. Though you might often err on the side of PCM audio, since it's uncompressed, if you have a lot of audio or alternate audio tracks, then you might need to compress some or all of them using Dolby AC-3, simply to fit them all onto your disk.

Finally, DVDs have up to 32 special built-in subtitle tracks, again for distribution in many languages.

All of these details and concerns will be further explained in the documentation for your DVD authoring package.

Content Is King

The biggest selling point for DVDs is proving to be the supplemental content beyond the feature film itself. Outtakes, gag reels, featurettes, original storyboards, rough special effects shots, director commentaries, and interviews with cast and crewmembers are all part of what makes a DVD better than a VHS tape. The latest trends include Web links and hidden bonus tracks. The production of some of these materials will require time during your regular production schedule—on-the-set interviews, making-of segments, etc. Other features, such as audio commentaries, can be produced after you've finished your final cut.

DVD Authoring

Once you've compressed your files, you're ready to author the menus and interactivity that will form the interface for your DVD. Through special DVD authoring software, you'll use still images and short video clips to create the menus and interface for your DVD, as well as establish how the user will navigate using their DVD remote.

Many packages such as Apple's DVD Studio Pro include software MPEG-2 encoders, allowing you to buy a complete DVD authoring system for under $500. If you're a Windows user, Adobe's Encore is an excellent professional-level authoring tool (Figure 19.7).

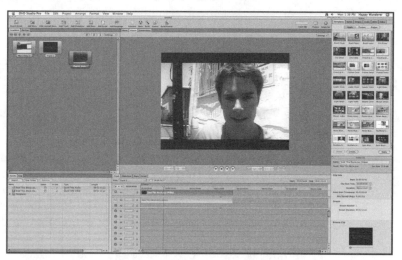

FIGURE 19.7   Apple's DVD Studio Pro lets you author professional-quality DVD videos, complete with menus and interactivity.

When creating your DVD, here are some technical tips to keep in mind:

- DVDs are designed to play on both video and computer monitors. This means that they are susceptible to all the limitations of video. Unless you're absolutely certain that your DVD will only play on a computer monitor (perhaps because it's a corporate or industrial presentation that will be shown under controlled conditions), you'll need to make sure your DVD interface uses only NTSC-safe colors, and that the buttons and text all fall within the standard title-safe area. Test your DVD on a video monitor before you publish it.
- Pretty much all DVD players have a handheld remote control device, while computer-based DVD players include an equivalent virtual remote—don't forget to program interactivity for the remote as well as the on-screen menus.
- Whatever the size of your DVD, you'll need to double that in computer storage space in order to create the DVD. If your DVD is 4 GB, you'll need 4 GB for the source materials for your compressed MPEG-2 video, and 4 GB for the rendered DVD files.
- DVD graphics should be created at 72 dpi, with a pixel resolution of 720 × 480 (for NTSC video). Remember that if you create menus and buttons in

a square-pixel environment, like Photoshop, you should work with files that are 720 × 540, and then resize them to 720 × 480 when you're ready to import them into your DVD authoring application.

If you plan on burning the disk yourself using a recordable DVD drive, then you'll want to be sure that you buy the right type of media. Recordable DVDs come in several flavors. First, there's DVD-R and DVD+R. These days, most DVD players can read and write both formats, but if your burner is older, you should double-check its compatibility and choose your media accordingly. Also, recordable DVDs are broken down into two flavors, DVD for General, and DVD for Authoring. Both types can be played back on DVD consoles or DVD-ROM drives, but your recorder probably only supports one. The main difference between the two formats is that DVD for General allows for special copy protection encryption that makes it more difficult to copy the disk.

If you plan to have your DVD mass produced by a professional replication house, then you should consult with them about the different capacities (and prices) that are available. If your final DVD will be a higher-capacity disk and you only have a single-layer burner (or no burner at all), you can still author the disk yourself; you'll just have to write the final files to your hard drive, and move the resulting files to the replication house when you're ready to make the disk. Most authoring programs allow you to output to DLT tape, or to a hard drive. Check with your replicator to find out what media they can accept.

Pass the Buck

If all of this sounds too complicated, there are companies that will take your final video master and create a DVD for you. Services provided by these companies vary from simple MPEG compression to full mastering, including interface authoring.

OUTPUTTING FOR THE WEB

Although presenting video on the Web was kind of a silly idea a few years ago, it's now a feasible means of video distribution. With the proliferation of cable and DSL modems, more users are capable of high-speed downloads of large video files. In addition to faster connections, running the latest compression and streaming technologies on today's faster desktop computers makes it possible to get video of very good quality.

A lot of your Web output decisions are dependent upon how you will host your file. Different web hosting services provide support for different video formats. If you have a preference for a very particular video technology, then you'll want to find a host that supports that. If you already have a host, then you might need to determine what technologies they're capable of serving before you commit to a particular approach.

The good news is that basic movie delivery is something that pretty much every Web host is capable of. Things only get trickier if you are interested in streaming.

Streaming or Nonstreaming?

Streaming is kind of like on-demand broadcasting. When a user decides to view a streaming movie, the host server begins sending a data stream to their computer. That stream is decompressed by the user's computer and displayed, but no copy of the movie is kept on the user's machine. When the stream is over, the user has to re-stream if they want to view the stream again.

Streaming is ideal for live events and for content that you don't want the user to be able to save a copy of (although, this is not foolproof, as there are ways for the user to capture the stream and save it in a reusable format).

If you want to use a streaming technology, you first have to ensure that your host supports your chosen streaming server. Most services charge money for hosting streaming media, so you'll probably have to pay an extra fee for streaming hosting. In addition, you'll need to compress your final movie using special software provided by the makers of your chosen streaming system.

RealPlayer is the most popular streaming format, at the time of this writing.

Most users will simply want to make a movie file available on demand, without the hassles of streaming, and without concern for whether or not the user can save it at the other end. Just as you can create a link to a graphic or a file in an HTML page, you can create a link to a movie. When a user clicks that link, their computer will automatically download and play that movie, assuming their computer is outfitted with the appropriate playback software, usually either QuickTime, Video for Windows, or Windows Media Player.

These days, most video architectures and web browsers are smart enough to not download the entire movie before starting playback. Instead, they employ a *progressive download* scheme. The downloading begins and the computer calculates how long the entire download will take, based on the current download throughput. When enough content has download that the computer can play back the entire movie without outrunning the download speed, then the movie will start playing. This greatly reduces the delay that the user experiences before the movie begins playback. (Nearly instant playback startup is another advantage of streaming video. Progressive downloads, though, can be very quick to start, depending on the user's connection speed, your hosting speed, and the duration of your movie.)

Compressing for the Web

As you've probably already guessed, your final video must be compressed before it can be served from the Web. In fact, it has to be compressed *a lot*. Fortunately, there are a number of high-quality compressors now that allow you deliver first-rate quality from a Web download. Your choice of compressor depends largely on the video architecture that you're using. QuickTime and Video for Windows offer different compression options.

Compressing

No matter what CODEC you choose, compressing can take a long time. You'll want to make sure that you have everything right before you start compressing, and you'll probably want to perform your compression overnight.

Ultimately, you might want to compress your video using several different options to support the greatest number of users.

Though it's a close race, QuickTime is still the most popular architecture for online video. With a free player available for both Mac and Windows, you can be pretty assured that just about anyone will have the capability to play back your movie if you post it in QuickTime format. If you decide to do a multi-format posting, then you'll need to recompress your video using the appropriate software for each format that you want. Converting from one compressed format to another is not always possible, and when it is, will always produce severely degraded video.

The standard QuickTime export box provides access to all of the standard QuickTime CODECs. Anyone who has installed the latest version of QuickTime will have these CODECs, so feel free to select any one.

For Web delivery, your best CODEC choices are MPEG-4, H.264, or Sorenson 3. These CODECs all yield exceptional results and produce very small files. For an example of the quality that can be achieved using Quick-Time compression, check out *www.apple.com/trailers*. You can see samples of Sorenson compression on the DVD that accompanies this book—the media in the Chapter 14 tutorials was all compressed with the Sorenson CODEC.

ON THE DVD

Some compressors provide lots of settings and customization options, allowing you to finely balance final movie size with image quality. Knowing how to optimize these settings can make for dramatically better-looking footage. Often, the best way to determine good settings is just through trial and error. Because compression can take a long time, perform your tests on a small clip of your final movie, ideally one with representative lighting and color.

In addition to setting compression options, you'll also need to resize your movie. In general, Web-based QuickTime movies max out at around 320 × 240 pixels, though if you know your server and intended audience

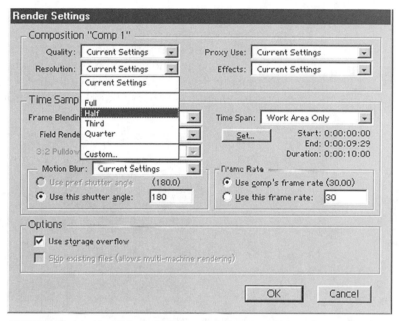

FIGURE 19.8   In most NLEs and effects packages, you can set the output size when you render your4 final movie. After Effects lets you easily define half-, and quarter-size renderings from its Render Settings dialog box.

can handle it, you can go bigger. This resizing step is also where you'll correct for the change from rectangular pixels to square. For example if your project is DV-based, it will appear horizontally stretched if you output it at its native resolution. When you select a size for your Web output, such as 320 × 240, you'll be squishing the movie back down to 4:3 aspect ratio.

Online Movie Theaters

There are a number of different "movie theater" sites that screen independent shorts and features. These are not only great venues for watching indie films (and great venues to which you can submit your own work), they're also good showcases for different compression technologies.

Note that there is no overscanning when exporting for the Web—in other words, the viewer will see the entire frame. If you want to conceal action outside of the action-safe area of your screen, you'll need to crop your frame before exporting. With others, you'll need to crop your video, save it in a lossless format, and then perform another rendering pass to resize and compress (Figure 19.8).

Also note that some video formats, such as VHS, typically have an area of jittery garbage at the bottom of the frame. This garbage is usually obscured by your monitor's overscan, but it will be visible in your Web outputs, so it's a good idea to crop the image a little to eliminate this area.

Similarly, some cameras produce a black edge or border within the overscan boundary. You'll definitely want to crop this out.

FIGURE 19.9 Movies are partially compressed by storing only the pixels in the intermediary frames between key frames.

Choosing a Data Rate

Some CODECs let you limit your movies to a specific data rate. Choosing a data rate is one of the ways that you can choose to balance file size and image quality. A higher data rate will yield better image quality, but much larger files. Though you will usually want to strike a balance of these, to deliver good-looking video in a reasonable file size, there might be times when you need to opt for a larger, higher-quality file—perhaps to post a file for a "private" screening by an investor—or a very small file for users with slow connections.

Choosing a Keyframe Interval

One of the techniques that a CODEC employs to compress video is to only store pixels that change from one frame to another. In compression terms, a *keyframe* is an entire frame that has been compressed *spatially*; that is, its color information has undergone some compression (Figure 19.19). The next frame is called an *intermediary frame*, or *i-frame* and contains only the pixels that have changed since the previous frame. (They're called intermediary frames, because they're the frames that come between keyframes.) Each successive i-frame contains only the pixels that have changed from the previous i-frame. The next *keyframe* contains a complete frame, which corrects for any errors or artifacts introduced in the intermediary frames.

Obviously, the more keyframes you have in a movie, the higher the quality will be, but the lower your compression ratio will be. Video with a lot of action will benefit from more keyframes, while clips that are more static can get away with very few keyframes.

Creating a Video CD

Although not very well known in North America, in Europe and Asia the VCD format has quickly becomes as popular and prolific as VHS tapes. Introduced by Philips and Sony in 1993, VCD was a predecessor to DVD. VCD uses MPEG-1 compression to store up to approximately 70 minutes of full-screen, full-motion video on a 650 MB CD or CDR.

VCDs can be played on special console VCD players (which are widely available in Europe and Asia), on some DVD video players, and on most current Mac and Windows-based computers. VCDs have all the advantages of CD-ROM delivery, but with the extra advantage of full-screen video, and more playback options. (Note that some console DVD players have a difficult time reading CDRs, whether audio or VCD. Therefore, even if your DVD player says it supports VCD, it might not support the reading of recordable CDs, meaning it will be limited to playback of commercial VCDs only.)

Creating a VCD is pretty simple. As with CD-ROM and Web delivery, you might want to do some test MPEG renderings to determine if your video needs any color correction. You might also want to experiment with de-interlacing your video, and you might need to crop the edges. After finishing your final edit and polish, you'll need to compress your video with an MPEG-1 compressor. Since QuickTime doesn't ship with a built-in MPEG-1 CODEC, you'll need to purchase one separately. If speed is of the essence, and you still have some money in your budget, consider buying a hardware MPEG-1 encoder for faster compression.

Once your video is compressed, you can write it to a CDR using a standard CD recorder. You'll need software that can write VCD format such as Roxio's Toast for Macintosh or Easy CD Creator for Windows.

GETTING YOUR 35MM FILM RELEASE PRINT

High-quality video footage is the key to a successful tape-to-film transfer. Everything that looks bad on video is going to look worse on film, especially when projected. The resolution of 35mm film is much, much greater than that of video, and any overexposed whites will read as large expanses of white nothingness, without the detail you would normally expect to see in film. In addition, any artifacts, noise, focus problems, and other image flaws will be enlarged as much as 25 times. If you shot your video properly—that is, if you took the time to light it like film, and set your video black and white levels properly when you created your videotape master—then you'll be giving your film recordist the best possible image, containing the most information. Avoid any type of image processing that removes information, such as de-interlacing. In addition, avoid any image processing that adds artifacts or noise, like boosting the video gain. The company that does your video-to-film transfer will take care of these things. If you're careful, well-shot DV footage transferred to film can look surprisingly good.

Keep Your Crew Involved

Your director of photography and your editor probably know a lot more about film and video image quality than you do. Keep them involved throughout the entire process, from digital image enhancement, to onlining your videotape, to film transfer.

There are two ways to deliver your footage to the film recordist: digital files or videotape. We've already discussed how to best create a textless videotape master via a professional online session, or by doing it yourself. This is the easiest and most practical way to deliver your film to the film recordist. The other option is to deliver digital video files, usually Quick-Time, Targa, or sequential PICT formats on a hard drive or high-capacity tape backup format. Talk to your film recordist before assuming that they can work with digital files.

The primary reason to deliver digital files is if you've done some effects work such as color correcting or compositing and do not want to recompress those shots by going back out to tape. Titles should also be delivered digitally as high-resolution 2 K files, or else they should originate on film via optical printing. (See the section on titles for film in Chapter 17, "Titling and Simple Compositing.") Ask your film recordist how they prefer to have titles and effects shots delivered.

Reel Changes

If you're heading for a film transfer, you'll most likely have to break your project into 20-minute segments to accommodate reel changes. Talk to your film recordist about this as early as possible. Be sure to make these breaks at a hard cut, not at a dissolve. In addition, make sure they're at a natural lull in the soundtrack, not in the middle of a line of dialog or music—the transition from one reel to another might not be seamless. As a rule, make sure there isn't any important dialog in the one to two seconds leading up to and following a reel change.

Film Editing and Cut Lists

Projects shot and finished on film but edited on videotape have a different workflow than projects shot on video or finished on video

After film is shot and sent to the lab for processing, the film is transferred to video through a process called *telecine*. Each frame of the film negative has a number on it, called the *keycode*. These keycode numbers are recorded onto the videotape image along with the picture itself. Since the frame rate of film is 24 frames per second and NTSC video is 29.97 fps, the telecine machine uses a process called *3:2 pulldown* as it transfers the film to videotape. (For PAL editing, there is usually no pulldown process; each frame is transferred one to one, since PAL's frame rate of 25 fps is so close to that of film.)

The video worktapes that result from the telecine transfer are then edited on a film non-linear editing system that can handle the frame rate issues involved in film editing—Avid's Film Composer, for example, or Apple Final Cut Pro with Cinematools.

Once the film is edited and "locked," the editing system generates a *cut list* to give to the negative cutter. A cut list is the film equivalent of an edit decision list (EDL), and lists each edit by film roll and keycode numbers. The process of generating the cut list is also called *film matchback*.

The negative cutter (yes, this is a person) then takes the computer-generated cut list and conforms the camera-original negative to match the final edit created on the non-linear editing system.

Before generating a cut list, you need to make sure your edited sequence is ready:

- Strip the sequence down to a single track of video.
- All temp effects should have been replaced with film-printed effects (with the exception of dissolves).
- Use your film editing software's *dupe detection* feature to make sure you haven't used any frames more than once. (Remember, there's only one negative, so you can't use a film frame twice unless you have a second negative made from an *interpositive*.)
- Make a guide output of your final video edit for the negative cutter as a reference. This guide should have window burn with keycode numbers on it from the telecine transfers.
- After you generate the cut list, spot check your list for accuracy by comparing the keycodes at an edit point in the cut list with the keycodes shown as window burn in the videotape image that you've been editing with.

The Film Printing Process

If you're planning to make a film print of your video, it's important to understand the traditional film printing process (see Figure 19.10). 16mm and 35mm motion picture films are very similar to 35mm still film: the negative is exposed in the camera, and the film is taken to a lab where it is processed, resulting in a print of the film. If you've ever compared a bad "one-hour photo" print to a professional print of the same image, then you know how different two prints from the same negative can look. Good film printing is all about controlling the look of the final film print. Some film transfer companies have their own labs, others work closely with a nearby lab, or others will work with the lab of your choice. Once you have a negative, you'll follow the same process as traditional film printing.

One-Light Prints

When a print is made from a film negative, the print is exposed using three lights—red, green, and blue—to create a full-color image. The lab takes the negative and determines the best RGB light settings for the entire film. The film is then printed using that setting, and the resulting print is called a *one-light print*, since the settings—the light—stay the same for the entire print.

Color Timing

With color timing, a specialist at the lab watches the one-light print and determines the light settings on a scene-by-scene basis. Often, the director and DP are present during this process. The negative is then reprinted

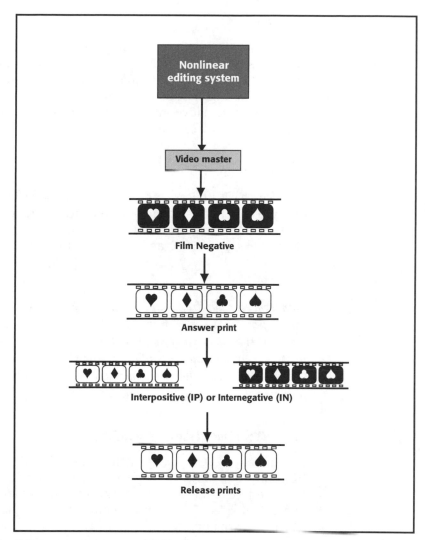

FIGURE 19.10   Achieving a final 35mm print from your DV files is a complex process involving several stages.

using these special light settings. The result is a timed color print. In traditional filmmaking, several trial prints are made at this stage. The final, successful print is called the *answer print*.

Most labs that do video-to-film transfers include a videotape color correction session as part of the package. Because these color adjustments have already been made before the video is transferred to film, you might spend little or no time dealing with color timing as compared to a film-original project. In addition, your film recordist will have a special formula for getting the best possible film print from your video.

Release Print

Once an answer print is made, an intermediate is created using the answer print. The intermediate will either be a color *internegative* (IN) or an *interpositive* (IP). The IN or IP is then used to strike the release prints. Because these intermediate prints are used to strike release prints, you can store your original negative away for safekeeping. If your intermediate print gets damaged, you can create a new one from your original negative.

Optical Soundtracks

Once you have a release print, a stripe of photoactive chemicals is added to the print next to the picture. A sound facility specializing in optical soundtracks will then take your audio master, either an MO (magneto-optical disk), videotape or DAT, and record it onto the optical stripe on the film.

Film Math

Film is measured in frames and feet (hence the term footage). 35mm film shot at 24 frames per second has 16 frames per foot. Typical film lengths are 50' (about 30 seconds), 100' (about a minute), 400' (about 4.5 minutes), 1000' (about 11 minutes), and 2000' (around 22 minutes). 16mm film shot at 24 frames per second has 40 frames per foot. When companies quote prices for film, they might quote by the frame, by the foot, or by the minute.

Getting Your Video Transferred to Film

At Sundance 2002, many of the "video films" were indistinguishable from the "film films." They were listed separately in the catalogue, but, once projected, it was often hard to tell the difference between 16mm and digital video. The improvements in image quality from a few years ago are astounding.

It's important to choose a lab for your video-to-film transfer fairly early in the editing process. Each lab has a different, usually proprietary, method for transferring video to film, and they will have specific instructions for you—how long each reel should be, how the white levels and black levels should be set, how to deal with text on-screen, and so on.

They might suggest that you use their facility to do a digital online of your project before the transfer to film, rather than a do-it-yourself DV output from your own system. This will cost more money, but the resulting quality might be worth it. However, if you're really on a shoestring budget, you should shop around for a lab that thinks they can work with your straight-to-DV output. Technically, this shouldn't result in any significant image problems if you have good video levels.

Once you've created a master, your transfer facility will consider color correction. By color correcting the videotape, it's less likely that a lot of color timing will be required later. During this stage, the video is also de-interlaced, and sometimes a special, secret film-look effect is added. Bear in mind that the "film-look effect" that the lab adds is designed to look ideal once recorded onto film. It's not the same as a "film-look effect" that's destined for video. Once the video image is color corrected and prepared, it is recorded onto film. Usually, the image is filmed off a very high-quality CRT monitor.

At this point, you now have a film negative, which will be used to strike answer prints and the final print, the same way it would be for a film-original project.

Wedges

You can select representative frames from each scene, called wedges, and have them test-printed before you do the full transfer. This will usually cost anywhere from $200 to $500.

ARCHIVING AND BACKUPS

The final step in the entire digital filmmaking process is to archive your project. Usually, you won't be able to back up captured media—it takes up way too much disk space. Moreover, if you've cloned your original tapes, you already have a backup of them. You can, of course, back up your project files and edited sequences, and you can always use these to recapture your media if you need to change or re-create your project. For the final exercise in this book, be sure to archive your project using one of the following methods:

The bare minimum: Back up your project files and shot logs to a another hard drive, Zip disk, CD, or floppy. If you lose anything, you'll have to redigitize, but at least you won't have to start from scratch.

DVDs: A single-layer DVD burner can only write 4.3 GB of data to a disk, while a dual layer drive can store around 9. Unfortunately, that isn't much in the digital video world—about an hour's worth of DV footage. However, DVD-Rs are a good choice for backing up non-timecoded media, such as digital special effects shots, VHS footage, and audio that's been recorded on-the-fly.

Optical tape backup systems: Optical tape backup systems such as Exabyte, DTS, and DLT are expensive to purchase, but relatively cheap to rent for a day (around $200). For about $50 a tape, you'll be able to back up 40 GB of uncompressed video and audio—enough space to store an entire DV feature. If you're going to put your project on the shelf for a while, this will save you the time of redigitizing. It's also a good safety net if you have lots of special effects footage that you created on your computer. Other tape backup systems use DAT tapes and DV tapes, but do not hold quite as much media. Note that, technically, these tapes are not recommended for long-term archival storage.

Backing up to digital videotape: If you shot on a digital video format, you can output your footage back to that format without losing any quality. Be careful though, if any extra compression or transcoding is involved, you may see some artifacts in your image. Backing up to tape is also a good idea if you're creating composites and other special effects shots on your computer.

EDLs and batch lists: EDLs are a very efficient way of backing up an edited sequence. Since an EDL represents your final edit, you can use it later to recapture and reconstruct if necessary. EDL files are simply text files, so they fit on a standard floppy disk. Saving the final EDL is *always* a good idea at the end of a project. You can also export text-based logs, a.k.a. batch lists, of the bins in your project.

Dubs and clones: If you need to back up your tapes themselves, you'll need to make *dubs,* or duplicates, of your tapes. If your tapes are analog, you will lose a generation in the process. If you have digital source tapes, you can have them *cloned,* which avoids any risk of generation loss.

EXERCISES

Though we've put this output discussion at the end of the book, output is often something you need to think about earlier in your production process. Keeping an eye on your output will affect decisions ranging from equipment choice to shooting and audio recording techniques. If you're just starting your production, make a list of all of the different forms of output that you think you'll need to make (for example: web, DVD, VHS work copies, 35mm transfer, etc.) Once you've listed all of your outputs, take note of the requirements of the format that has the highest quality. You'll need to maintain these specs throughout your production workflow.

For example, if you're only going to output to the web at 320 × 240 with compressed video and audio, then you know that you don't need super high resolution. Now you can double-check your equipment choices to ensure that you have what you need.

You can also review your shooting plans, production design, effects pipeline and all of the other aspects of your production with an eye towards evaluating whether you've got the requisite level of quality for your intended output. You might not need to worry about super-refined design and effects work if your final output is going to be very small. On the other hand, if your final output will be 35mm projection, then you'll need to keep a close eye on even the smallest details in your frame.

SUMMARY

Believe it or not, over these last 19 chapters, we've been covering the *easy* part of film production. Now the hard part begins: selling your product. Hopefully, you have some idea of who might be interested in your final product. Or perhaps you have backers who are already committed to moving your project forward.

Odds are, though, that you have no idea what will become of your piece. Now is the time to make something happen. With new delivery technologies such as the Web, CD-ROM, and inexpensive DVD production, there are any number of avenues you can pursue to sell your feature or documentary.

If you don't already have an "in," or know someone "in the business," then the best place to start is the film festival circuit. These days, *everyone* is hosting a film festival. Find out the entry requirements, raise the entry fees, and submit your finished product. If everything works well, you'll catch the eye of a distributor who will want to release your feature.

However, even if you don't get distribution, getting feedback from a live audience, other directors, and actors can be an invaluable, and fun, experience for improving your current project, or starting your next one.

ABOUT THE DVD

This DVD contains all of the sample media and support files that you need to complete the tutorials in The Digital Filmmaking Handbook, 3rd Edition. All files are grouped into folders by chapter.

In addition, many chapter folder contains PDF files that include additional essays and articles on topics related to that chapter. To read these files, you will need a PDF viewer such as Adobe's free Acrobat Reader, which can be downloaded from *http://www.adobe.com/acrobat*.

Finally, the DVD also contains demo versions of the Macintosh and Windows versions of Adobe After Effects, and Adobe Photoshop, as well as the Windows version of Adobe Premiere Pro, Adobe Audition and Adobe Encore Pro DVD. For best results, copy these installers to your computer's hard drive before attempting to run them.

SYSTEM REQUIREMENTS

Mac

- 300 MHz G3 or better
- 128MB of RAM
- 650MB+ of available hard disk space
- 24-bit or greater video display card (recommended)
- QuickTime 5.0 or higher

Windows

- Intel Pentium processor, Pentium II, Pentium II or multiprocessor system recommended
- Win 98 (32MB RAM), or WIN NT 4.0 or later (65MB RAM)
- 650+MB of available hard disk space
- 24-bit or greater video display card (recommended)
- QuickTime 5

GLOSSARY

2-pop   In a traditional eight-second countdown before a film starts, there is a short pop that occurs at the first frame of the "2" (as in "8, 7, 6, 5, 4, 3, 2"); the last two seconds before the first frame of the film are black. The "2-pop" makes it easier to tell that the film is in sync before it starts.

3:2 pulldown   A method for transferring 24-fps film to 29.97-fps NTSC video. The film is slowed by .1% and the first film frame is recorded on the first two fields of video, the second frame is recorded on the next three fields of video, and so on.

3-point editing   See **three-point editing**.

A/B rolling   See **checkerboard**.

acccelerator cards   Custom hardware that can accelerate (or even provide real-time display of) certain features such as 3D rendering, rendering of plug-in filters, or compositing.

action safe   The area of your image that will most likely be visible on any video monitor. Essential action should be kept within the actionsafe area, as action that falls outside this area might be lost due to overscan.

address   A frame of video, as identified by timecode information.

AES/EBU   An acronym for the Audio Engineering Society and the European Broadcaster's Union; also a standard for professional digital audio that specifies the transmission of audio data in a stream that encodes stereo audio signals along with optional information.

aliasing   The "jaggies," those stair-stepping patterns that occur on a diagonal or curved line on a computer or video display. Can be smoothed or corrected through anti-aliasing processes.

alpha channel   An 8-bit color channel (see **channels**) that is used to specify the transparency of each pixel in an image. An alpha channel works like a sophisticated stencil, and is the digital equivalent of a matte (see **matte**).

alternate data rates   When streaming QuickTime files from a Web site, it is possible to specify several copies of the same movie, each optimized for a different data rate. The server can then decide which movie is best for the speed of the user's connection.

A-mode EDL   An EDL sorted in order of master record in timecode.

amp   Short for ampere, a unit that measures the voltage of an electrical source.

analog   Information represented electronically as a continuous, varying signal. (See also **digital**.)

anamorphic lenses   Special lenses that shoot a wide-screen 16:9 image, but optically compress the image to a normal 4:3 aspect ratio for storage on 4:3 film or video. The widescreen image can be uncompressed by a projector fitted with a similar anamorphic lens, by a monitor that displays 16:9 video, or by software that knows to stretch the image.

Animation compressor   A lossless QuickTime CODEC.

answer print   The final print of a film after color-timing.

anti-aliasing   The process of eliminating "jagged" edges on computergenerated text and graphics. Anti-aliased graphics have their edges slightly blurred and mixed with background colors to eliminate the jagged, stair-stepping patterns that can occur on diagonal or curved lines.

aperture   In any type of camera, light is focused by the lens, through an aperture and onto the focal plane. The size of the aperture controls how much light passes through to the focal plane. In addition to controlling the brightness of the exposure, the aperture controls the depth of field in the image. By balancing the size of the aperture (as measured in f-stops) with the shutter speed, you can trade off between varying depth of field, and/or the ability to better resolve fast motion.

array   See **RAID**.

art director   The person in charge of the execution of the production designer's vision. The art director manages set construction, set dressing, props, and scenic painting.

aspect ratio   The ratio of the width of an image to its height. Aspect ratios can be expressed as ratios, such as 4:3, or as numbers, such as 1.33.

assemble edit   When editing onto videotape, an edit that records over the entire tape, including the video track, the audio tracks, and the control track.

ATA   A type of hard drive interface. Not as fast as SCSI, but fast enough for DV.

ATSC   Advanced Television Systems Committee—established to set the technical standards for DTV, including HDTV.

attenuator   A circuit that lowers the strength of an electronic signal.

audio compressor   A filter (or piece of hardware) that reduces the dynamic range of a sound to accommodate loud peaks.

audio guide track   A mixed audio track generated from the final cut. The guide track is placed onto one of the audio tracks of the online master for reference during the online editing session.

audio mixer   A piece of hardware that takes several audio signals and mixes them together, allowing for the combining of different sources. Mixers usually include some type of equalization control.

audio sampling rate   The number of samples per second that are used to digitize a particular sound. Most DV cameras can record at several audio sampling rates. Higher rates yield better results. Measured in kilohertz, 44.1 kHz is considered audio CD quality, and 48 kHz is considered DAT quality.

AVR   Avid Video Resolution, a series of low and high-resolution CODECs included with the Avid family of editing systems.

Axial   One of several linear hardware-based online editing systems.

balanced audio   A type of microphone connector that provides extra power. Sometimes needed if you want to have microphone cable lengths of 25 feet or longer.

balancing light sources   In a lighting setup with several different light sources, the process of making the color temperature of all the lights the same, either to match daylight or tungsten light. Usually, this is done with CTO or CTB lighting gels.

bandwidth   The amount of digital information that can be passed through a connection at a given time. High bandwidth is needed for high-quality images.

barndoors   A set of hinged door-like flaps that attach to the front of a light and serve to control where the light falls.

bars and tone   A combination of color bars and 60 Hz audio reference tone, usually recorded onto the head of each videotape. Used for calibrating video and audio levels.

bin   A film-editing term that refers to the place where the shots for a scene are stored. In software editing systems, bins can also be referred to as *folders*, *galleries*, or *libraries*.

binary   A system for encoding digital information using two components: 0 and 1.

black and coded tape A "blank" tape that has been striped with a combination of a black video signal and timecode.

black burst A composite video signal with a totally black picture. Used to synchronize professional video equipment. Black burst supplies video equipment with vertical sync, horizontal sync, and chroma burst timing.

black burst generator A piece of video hardware that generates a black composite video signal, or *black burst*. Used to sync professional video equipment, and to black and code tapes.

black level The black level defines how dark a video image is allowed to get. Improperly set black levels can result in dull, grayish blacks.

black wrap A heavy-duty aluminum foil with a matte black coating on one side used to block light. Can also be wrapped around light sources to make them more directional.

blue spill In blue-screen shooting, a bluish light that is cast onto the back of a foreground subject due to reflection from the blue screen.

blue screen A special screen, usually composed of blue cloth or backdrops painted with special blue paint, that is placed behind a foreground element. Blue-screen shots are those shots that you intend to later composite with other elements through the use of a chroma key function. Sometimes, blue elements are used in the foreground to facilitate later compositing.

BNC connector A connector used to carry composite video, component video, timecode, and AES/EBU audio signals.

boom A long (sometimes up to 100) pole with a microphone at the end. Technically, a boom is a large, sometimes hydraulically controlled device, as opposed to a fishpole, a smaller, handheld pole. Increasingly, the term *boom* is used to refer to any stick with a mic on the end.

bounce card A piece of white material, like foam core, used to create soft, indirect lighting.

break-out box A box that has connectors and ports for attaching video and audio peripherals. The box can be fitted to some video cards to provide easier access to the input and outputs provided by the card.

broadcast colors Your computer monitor can display many more colors than can NTSC or PAL video. Broadcast colors are those colors that are safe—that is, they will display properly—on a television set. Many programs, such as Adobe Photoshop and Adobe After Effects, include special filters that will convert the colors in an image to their nearest broadcast safe equivalent. (See also **NTSC legal**).

broadcast quality A somewhat vague term, referring to the minimum quality considered acceptable for broadcast television. Until the 1980s, 3/4" Umatic tape was considered broadcast quality, then Betacam SP was introduced and became the standard for broadcast quality. Today, DV is often considered broadcast quality.

BT. 601 A document that defines the specifications for professional, interlaced video standards as the following: 720 × 480 (59.94 Hz), 960 × 480 (59.94 Hz), 720 × 576 (50 Hz), and 960 × 576 (50 Hz) 4:2:2 YCbCr. Also called *CCIR 601* and *ITU-R 601*.

bumping up The process of transferring a videotape from a lowerquality format to a higher-quality format; for example, bumping up DV tapes to DVCPro.

byte A unit of computer storage. How much one byte equates to depends on what you are storing. If you're just storing text, then a single byte can hold one character. For video or audio, what a byte holds depends on how your video is compressed and stored.

camera negative After film stock is exposed in the camera and is processed, the result is the negative, also called the *camera negative*, which is usually transferred to video using a telecine process and then, after editing, is used to strike the final print.

candelas A measurement of the intensity of light.

capturing The process of moving video data from a camera or deck into a computer.

cardioid The roughly heart-shaped pattern that certain mics can "hear."

CCD See **charge-coupled device**.

CCIR 601 See **BT. 601**.

CDR CD Recordable. A special type of compact disc that can be recorded by the end user using a special drive. Standard audio or data formats are supported by most recording programs, along with Video CD, a special format that can store 70 minutes of full-screen, full-motion MPEG1-compressed video, and the DVD video format, which can store about 18 minutes of full-screen, full-motion MPEG2-compressed video.

Century stand See **C-stand**.

CG Character generator. A special machine for creating titles and other text characters for inclusion in a video. Most editing packages include CG features.

CGI Computer generated imagery. Used to refer to any effect that is created digitally, be it a composite, or a fully digital image such as a walking dinosaur. CGI is often used as a noun: "we'll fill that spot with some CGI of a duck."

channel The color in an RGB image is divided into channels, one each for the red, green, and blue information in the image. When these channels are combined, a full-color image results. Certain effects are easier to achieve by manipulating individual color channels. Additional alpha channels can also be added for specifying transparency and selections (see **alpha channel**).

charge-coupled device (CCD) A special type of chip that can convert light into electronic signals. A modern video camera focuses light through a lens and onto a CCD where it is converted into electronic signals that can be stored on tape.

checkerboard A way to arrange each piece of sound across a group of audio tracks so that no piece of sound is directly "touching" any other piece of sound, resulting in a checkerboard-like appearance. Also called *A/B rolling*.

chroma key A function that will render a specific color in a layer transparent. For example, if you shoot someone in front of an evenly lit blue screen, you can use a chroma key function to render the blue completely transparent, thus revealing underlying video layers.**chroma** The part of the video signal that contains the color information.

chromatic aberration Color shifts and color artifacts in an image caused by faults in a lens, or by the camera's inability to register all three channels of color information. Single-chip video cameras are especially prone to chromatic aberration.

chrominance The saturation and hue of a video signal. Although slightly different in meaning, this term is often used interchangeably with the term *chroma* to refer to color.

Chyron A title identifying a speaker in a documentary that runs along the bottom of the screen. The name derives from the Chyron character-generator once popular in many post facilities. These I.D. titles are also known as *lower thirds*.

cinematographer See **director of photography**.

Cinepak A QuickTime CODEC. Very lossy, but good for delivery mediums with low data rates such as CD-ROM or the Web.

clipping In digital media, an electronic limit that is imposed on the audio and/or video portion of the signal in order to avoid audio that is too loud and video that is too bright, too saturated or too dark. Clipped blacks are any blacks in an image that are darker than the set black level, or 7.5 IRE. Clipped whites are any whites that are brighter than the set white level, or 100 IRE. Clipped audio is any sound that goes into the red area on an audio level meter. Clipped media is indicated by a flat line in a waveform view of the signal.

close-up   A shot where the subject fills the majority of the frame. If the subject is a person, the shot will consist primarily of the person's head and shoulders.

C-mode EDL   An EDL sorted nonsequentially by source tape number and ascending source timecode.

CMX   A hardware-based linear online editing system. CMX-3600-format EDLs are the default for many other editing systems.

CODEC   COmpressor/DECompressor, an algorithm for compressing and decompressing video and audio.

color bars   A test pattern used to check whether a video system is calibrated correctly. A waveform monitor and vectorscope are used, in conjunction with color bars, to check the brightness, hue, and saturation.

color depth   The number of colors that a given video system can display. The more bits-per-pixel that are used to store color, the higher the color depth.

color sampling ratio   In component digital video, the ratio of luminance (Y) to each color difference component (Cb and Cr). 4:2:2 means that for every four samples of luminance, there are two samples of chroma minus blue and chroma minus red. 4:2:2:4 indicates an additional four samples of the alpha channel or keying information.

color spectrum   The range of visible light that extends from violet to red.

Color Temperature Blue (CTB)   A special color of lighting gel or camera lens filter that changes tungsten light to daylight.

color temperature   Light sources have different color temperatures, which are measured in degrees Kelvin. The color temperature of tungsten light is 3200°K, and the color temperature of daylight is about 5500°K.

Color Temperature Orange (CTO)   A special color of lighting gel or camera lens filter that changes daylight to tungsten light.

color timing   The process of setting the red, green, and blue lights when creating a film print. Usually, the color settings are timed to change with each significant scene or lighting change in the film.

color correction   A post-production process to correct the overall color of a videotape master in order to get the best quality image, with an emphasis on enhancing skin tones.

component video   A video signal consisting of three separate color signals (or components), usually RGB (red, green, blue), YCbCr (Luminance, Chroma minus Blue, and Chroma minus Red), or Y, R-Y, B-Y (Luminance, Red minus Luminance, Blue minus Luminance.)

composite video   A video signal that contains all the luminance, chroma, and timing (or sync) information in one composite signal.

compositing   The process of layering media on top of each other to create collages or special effects.

condensor   A type of mic that records sounds through a "capacitance" mechanism. Condensor mics require a power supply (usually in the form of a small battery). Because of the nature of their pickup mechanism, condensor mics can be made very small.

conforming   The process of meticulously recreating an off-line edit using, usually, higher quality footage with the aid of an EDL or cut list.

continuity   During a shoot, the process of keeping track of dialog changes, actors' positions, wardrobe, and props so that the footage from shot to shot, and day to day, will cut together. Usually, the person in charge of continuity—the script supervisor—makes notes on a copy of the script and takes photos of the set.

control track   A part of the video signal that contains the timing, or synchronization, information, used to regulate the motion of the tape itself as it plays through a VTR.

co-processors Extra processors that are used to speed up a computer, or to perform special functions. See **accelerator cards**.

coverage Shooting all of the footage that will be needed to properly cover an event or scene.

CPU Central processing unit. In a computer system, the box that contains the motherboard, peripheral cards, and some storage drives. Also used to refer to the main processing chip that the system uses.

cross-platform Programs or hardware that come in different versions for different platforms. Ideally, the program's interface and features are identical from one platform to the next.

CRT monitor The monitor attached to your computer. Short for *cathode ray tube*.

C-stand A rolling metal stand designed to hold lighting accessories, such as flags and nets.

CTB See **Color Temperature Blue**.

CTO See **Color Temperature Orange**.

cutaway n a scene, a shot of something other than the main action or dialog. Used to build the story and smooth rough edits.

D.P. See **director of photography**.

daisy chain A group of storage devices that have been chained together. Although cabled in series, each can be accessed independently.

DAT Digital Audio Tape, an audio tape format developed by Sony that records audio using a sampling rate of 48 kHz and is capable of recording SMPTE timecode information.

data rate The amount of data that a particular connection can sustain over time. Usually measured in bytes per second.

DaVinci A professional digital color-correction system.

daylight Daylight is the combination of sunlight and skylight.

dBm See **decibel milliwatt**.

dBSPL See **decibel sound pressure loudness**.

decibel milliwatt A unit for measuring sound as electrical power.

decibel sound pressure loudness A measure of the acoustic power of a sound.

decibel The standard unit for measuring sound. A subjective scale where one unit equals one increment of "loudness."

degauss To completely erase all the information on a magnetic video or audio tape, using a demagnetizing device.

depth of field A measure of how much, and what depth, of the image is in focus.

destination monitor The monitor or window that displays an edited sequence as it plays, as opposed to the source monitor, which plays unedited source footage. Also called the *record monitor*.

destructive editing Any form of editing (either video or audio) that physically alters your original source material.

device control The ability of a piece of hardware, such as an edit controller or a CPU, to control a peripheral device, such as a VTR, via a remote control cable.

diffuse light Light from a soft, undirected source, such as a typical household light bulb.

diffusion gel A semi-transparent piece of white plastic used to make a light softer.

digital Information recorded electronically as a series of discrete pulses, or samples, usually encoded using a binary system.

digital zoom A "fake" zoom that creates a zooming effect by enlarging the image digitally. Unfortunately, the process of enlarging usually severely degrades the image.

digitizing   The process of taking analog video or audio information from a camera or deck and turning it into digital information that can be used by a computer.

diopter   An adjustment on the eyepiece of a camera that allows you to correct the focus of the eyepiece to match your vision.

director of photography   The film lighting and camera specialist responsible for the look of the photography, and the person in charge of the camera and lighting crews.

dissolve   A transition in which the first shot is partially or completely replaced by a gradual superimposition of the next shot.

distressing   A process of making objects on a set look aged or weathered.

DLT   An optical tape backup system, DLT tapes typically hold about 40GB of media.

DM&E   Acronym for *dialog, music, and effects*, a four-channel, split audio mix that allows for easy remixing in case the audio needs to be dubbed in a foreign language.

drag-and-drop editing   A two-step editing method where the user selects a shot and drags it from one position and drops it in another position; for example, from a bin to the timeline or from one position in the timeline to another.

drive chassis   A box, mount, or rack for holding hard drives. Usually separate from the CPU.

drop-outs   A weak portion of the video signal that results in a problem in playback. Hits are small drop-outs that are only one or two horizontal lines in size, glitches are larger, where 5 percent or more of the image drops out. Large analog drop-outs can result in a few rolling video frames, and large digital drop-outs can result in random "holes" across the screen for several frames.

DTV   Acronym for *Digital Television*, the new digital television broadcast standard that will be adopted in the United States by 2006. DTV is an umbrella term that includes several subgroups, including HDTV and SDTV.

dual-stream processing   The ability to handle up to two video signals at a time.

dub   A copy of a videotape, also known as a *dupe*.

Duvetine   A black felt-like cloth used to block unwanted light sources, such as windows.

DVD   Digital video disc (sometimes called "digital versatile disc." An optical storage medium that is the same physical size as a compact disc. There are several different DVD standards and formats ranging from DVD-R (a rewritable format) and DVD-ROM (a read-only format) to DVD-video (the format that is used for video releases).

DVD-R   Recordable DVD. Similar to CD-R, recordable DVDs can store 4.7GB of data on an inexpensive DVD disk, using a special drive attached to a computer. DVD-Rs can also be used for creating DVDvideos.

DVD-RAM   A re-writable DVD format that uses special DVD cartridges for storage.

DVD-RW   Re-writable DVD. DVD-RWs work just like a DVD-R, but you can erase them and re-use them later. Note that most DVD-Rs can only be read using the same drive that created them.

DVE   An acronym for *digital video effects*. The term comes from the professional linear video editing world and applies to what has become a fairly standard set of effects: wipes, dissolves, picture-in-picture, barn doors, and split screen, to name a few. Based on a trade name for a system sold by NEC.

dynamic microphone   A mic that derives its power from the pressure of the sound that is being recorded. Handheld mics are usually dynamic.

edit controller   A piece of hardware used in linear editing systems to control and synchronize multiple video decks.

Edit Decision List   A list of all of the edits in a project, identified by a chronological event number, source name, source in-point, source out-point, master in-point, and master-out point.

EDL   See **Edit Decision List**.

egg crate   A sectioned metal frame that attaches to soft light sources to make them more directional.

EIDE   A type of hard drive interface. Not as fast as SCSI, but fast enough for DV.

EIS   See **electronic image stabilization**.

EISA slots   A type of expansion slot used in Windows-based computers.

electret condensor   A cheaper, lower-quality version of the condensor mechanism.

electronic image stabilization   Special circuitry in a camera that attempts to eliminate or reduce camera shake by electronically shifting the image. Electronic image stabilization frequently results in a slightly blurred image.

electronic zoom   Electronic controls that are used to zoom the lens in and out. These are the only zoom controls found on most prosumer camcorders.

EQ   See **equalization**.

equalization   The process of adjusting the volume of individual frequency ranges within a sound. Equalization can be used to correct problems in a sound, or to "sweeten" or enhance the sound to bring out particular qualities.

Ethernet   A standard networking protocol for connecting computers together through one of several types of networking cable.

Exabyte   A digital, optical tape-based storage system, used for backing up projects with large amounts of data.

exposure   The process of allowing light to enter the camera and expose the film or video stock to produce a recorded image.

fade out   A dissolve from full video to black video or from audio to silence.

field dominance   The order in which the two fields in a frame of interlaced video are displayed. Hardware and software that play the field of video containing the odd-numbered scan lines first are known as *upper field dominant*. Those that play the field of video containing the even-numbered scan lines first are known as *lower field dominant*. See **field**.

field   Each frame of interlaced video consists of two fields: one field contains the odd-numbered scan lines, and the other field contains the even-numbered scan lines. In NTSC video, each field has 262.5 horizontal lines.

film grain   Images are recorded on film by exposing the film's lightsensitive emulsion. Composed of chemical particles, the film's emulsion has a visible grain when projected. Many video producers try to mimic this grainy look to produce an image that appears more filmlike.

film recorder   See **film recordist**.

film recordist   The person responsible for transferring (or recording) video to film.

filters   Special glass attachments that can be added to a camera lens to change the optical properties of the lens. Or, special pieces of software that can be added to a host application to perform image processing functions.

FireWire   Apple's name for the IEEE-1394 specification.

flag   A black cloth held by a metal frame, used to block light.

flats   Large wooden "walls," used on a soundstage to construct the set.

fluid head tripod   A special type of tripod head that is filled with hydraulic fluid that smoothes the motion of the camera head.

focal length   The size of the angle of view of the lens, measured in millimeters. The smaller the number, the wider the lens. Zoom lenses have a range of focal lengths.

focal plane   The area in a camera onto which light is focused. In a film camera, the film rests on the focal plane; in a digital video camera, the CCD rests on the focal plane.

focus ring   A rotatable ring on the lens of a camera that allows for manual focusing. Ideally, a focus ring should have distance markings so that you can perform more complicated manual focus effects such as pulling or racking focus.

foley   The process of creating and recording ambient sound effects in real-time while the video or film plays. Foley work is usually performed by two or more foley artists on a foley stage equipped with special surfaces and props. Named for Jack Foley, the originator of the technique.

footcandles   A measurement of the amount of illumination falling on a subject, using the English measuring system. (See also **lux**.)

fps   Fps, or frames per second, is used to describe the speed at which film and video play. Film plays at 24 fps, PAL video at 25 fps, and NTSC video at 29.97 fps.

frame accuracy   The ability of a device, particularly a VTR, to accurately perform edits on a specific frame. Non-frame accurate VTRs might miss the mark by one or more frames.

frame   One complete film or video image. Moving images need at least 18 frames per second to appear as full-motion, and 24 fps to allow for sync sound. NTSC video plays at 29.97 fps and PAL video at 25 fps.

frame rate   When speaking of video or film recording, the number of frames per second that are recorded (and then played back).

frequency   An audio signal is made up of different frequencies, or wavelengths, that yield the high (or treble), mid, and low (or bass) tones. The human voice resides mostly in the mid-tones. Light is also composed of different frequencies, which appear to the human eye as different colors.

fresnel lens   A lens attached to a light that allows for focusing the beam of light.

f-stop   A measure of the size of a camera's aperture. The higher the fstop, the smaller the aperture.

gain boost   A method of electronically increasing the strength, or amplitude, of an audio or video signal. In video, the image gets brighter but has more visible noise.

gain   The strength (or amplitude) of an audio or video signal.

garbage matte   A special matte used to knock out extraneous objects in a compositing shot. Garbage mattes are usually applied to a bluescreen shot before chromakeying. They can be used to eliminate props, mic booms, and other objects that can't be eliminated through keying.

gate   A special type of audio filter that only allows a specific range of frequencies to pass. Also, the mechanism that holds a frame of film in place behind the camera or projector's lens.

gel frame   A metal frame that holds lighting gels in front of the light.

Glidecam   A camera-stabilizing mechanism similar to a Steadicam.

globes   The professional term for *light bulb*.

green spill   The same as blue spill, except that it occurs with a green screen as a backdrop, rather than a blue screen.

green screen   Same as blue screen, but used for those occasions where you need to have blue elements in your foreground.

handheld microphone   The typical handheld mic used by rock stars, comedians, and wandering talk show hosts. Usually an omnidirectional, dynamic microphone.

handles   Extra footage at the head and tail of each shot that allow the editor room to add dissolves and manipulate the pacing of a scene.

hard cut   An edit from one shot to another without any type of transition in between, such as a dissolve.

hard light   Light from a direct, focused light source.

HDTV   High-definition television, a subgroup of the new DTV digital television broadcast standard that has a 16:9 aspect ratio, a resolution of either 1280 x 720 or 1920 x 1080, a frame rate of 23.96, 24, 29.97, 30, 59.95, or 60 fps and either interlaced or progressive scanning.

HDV   A video format that can record high-definition video on standard DV tapes. HDV was designed as an affordable interim format for producers who are trying to make the transition from SD to HD. At the time of this writing, several excellent HDV cameras in various form factors are available. All of the most popular desktop editing packages now support HDV. HDV uses MPEG-2 compression making it more prone to artifacting than regular DV, but its HD specs give it much higher resolution.

HMI lights   High-powered arc lights used to simulate daylight. The lights at a baseball stadium are HMI lights.

horizontal blanking interval   The part of the composite video signal between the end of the image information on one horizontal scan line and the start of the image information on the next horizontal scan line.

horizontal delay   A display feature available on professional video monitors that shows the video signal offset horizontally, so as to allow the editor to see and analyze the horizontal sync pulses. (See also **vertical delay**.)

horizontal line resolution   The number of lines in the visible portion of the video signal.

horizontal sync   The sync pulses in the video signal that regulate the movement and position of the electron beam as it draws each horizontal scan line across the video monitor.

hot-swapping   Replacing a peripheral without shutting off the computer's power. Note: Not all peripherals are hot-swappable!

HSB   Just as colors can be defined by specifying RGB (red, green, and blue) values, colors can also be defined by specifying hue, saturation, and brightness. Many color pickers allow you to switch to an HSB mode. For some operations, selecting a color is easier in one mode than in another.

hue   The shade of a color.

IDE drives   Hard drives that adhere to the IDE interface specification.

IE1394   See **FireWire**.

IEEE-1394   A high-speed serial interface that can be used to attach DV cameras, storage devices, printers, or networks to a computer.

I-frame   A video compression term. An intermediate frame between two keyframes. I-frames store only the data that has changed from the previous frame.

iLink   Sony's name for the IEEE-1394 specification.

illumination   The amount of light cast on a subject.

inbetweening   The process of calculation (or interpolation) that is required to generate all of the frames between two keyframes in an animation.

incidental light   Light that comes from a direct source, such as the sun, a light, and so forth.

infrared   The area beyond red, outside of the visible part of the color spectrum.

in-point   The starting point of an edit.

insert edit   An edit onto videotape that does not replace the control track and allows for the separate editing of video, audio, and timecode. (See also **assemble edit**.)

insert mode   In most NLEs, a method of editing in the timeline that allows the placement of a shot between two shots without covering up what's already there. Instead, the second shot (and all the shots following it) are pushed down the timeline to accommodate the new clip. (See also **overwrite mode**.)

intensity (of light)   The strength of a light source, measured in candelas.

interface   The controls and windows that you use to operate a program.

interlace scan   The process of scanning a frame of video in which one field containing half the horizontal lines is scanned, followed by another field that contains the other half of the horizontal lines, adding up to a complete frame of video.

interlaced   See **interlace scan**.

interleaving   The process of alternating data across multiple discs, as in an array.

Internegative   An intermediary step sometimes necessary in film processing. The camera negative is printed and a new negative, the internegative, is made (or struck) from that print. The internegative (or IN) is then used to create more prints.

interpositive   An intermediary step sometimes necessary in film processing. The camera negative is printed and this print, called the *interpositive* (IP), is used to create a new negative. The release prints are then struck from that negative.

iris   Synonymous with *aperture*. The iris is the physical mechanism that can be opened or closed to change the size of the aperture. "Irising down," for example, means to close down the iris (go to a higher fstop).

IRQ   Special addressing information used by peripherals attached to a Windows-based computer. Each peripheral must have its own IRQ.

ISA slot   A type of expansion slot used in Windows-based computers.

ISO-9660   A format for writing CD-ROMs. Can be read by either Mac or Windows-based computers.

ITU-R 601   See **BT. 601**.

JKL   A way of editing using the J, K, and L keys on the computer keyboard. Allows for fast shuttling through clips in an NLE.

Kelvin scale   A temperature scale used by scientists. The color temperature of light is described in degrees Kelvin.

key effect   Different types of "keys" can be used to render parts of a video clip transparent, thus exposing any underlying video. See **chroma key** and **luminance key**.

keyframe interval   When compressing video, the frequency at which a keyframe will occur.

keyframe   In animation, keyframes allow you to explicitly define the parameters of each property of each element in the animation (motion, position, transparency, etc.). The computer will automatically calculate the changes that occur between each keyframe (see **inbetweening**). In video compression, a keyframe is a non-interpolated, spatially compressed frame.

kinescope   A method of making a film copy of a videotape by recording the image off a video monitor.

Kino-Flo tubes   Color-corrected fluorescent light tubes used to replace normal fluorescent light tubes when shooting at a location that will have fluorescent lights visible in the shot.

LANC (or Control-L)   A device control protocol most commonly found on consumer equipment and incapable of frame accuracy. (See also **RS-422** and **RS-232**).

latitude   The size of the gray scale ranging from darkest black to brightest white. The human eye sees more latitude than can be recorded on film or video.

lavalier   A small, clip-on mic. Usually an omnidirectional, condensor microphone.

layback   The process of recording the finished audio back onto the master videotape after sweetening.

LCD   Liquid crystal display. The type of display used as a viewfinder on most cameras. In terms of cameras, LCD usually refers to a small, flipout screen, as opposed to the optical viewfinder.

lens   Usually a series of separate glass lenses, the lens on a camera focuses light onto the focal plane to create an image.

letterboxing   The process of putting black bars at the top and bottom of the screen to change a 4:3 aspect ratio image to a wider aspect ratio image.

light kit   A set of professional lights, light stands, and lighting accessories, usually contained in a heavy-duty carrying case.

light meter   A small, handheld device used to measure the illumination at a particular location. Usually measured in footcandles or lux, which can then be translated to f-stops.

lighting gel   Translucent pieces of special colored plastic used to change the brightness and color of a light source.

linear editing   Editing using linear media—tape to tape—as opposed to using random access media stored on a computer hard drive. All tape is linear, so linear media can be either digital or analog.

locking picture   The process of formally finalizing the editing of a film for story, so that the sound editors can start working without have to deal with any changes in timing.

logging   The process of recording the contents of each field tape using timecode, shot names, and descriptions. The first step in the editing process.

long shot   A shot that plays out over a long period of time.

looping   The process of re-recording dialog in a studio. Called "looping" because the actor sometimes watches a continuous loop of the scene that is being re-recorded. Also known as *ADR*, for automatic dialog replacement.

lossless   Used to denote a form of compression that does not degrade the quality of the image being compressed.

lossy   Used to denote a form of compression that degrades the quality of the image being compressed.

lower thirds   See **Chryon**.

LTC   An acronym for *longitudinal timecode*, a type of timecode that is recorded onto the audio track of a videotape.

luma clamping   See **luminance clamping**.

luma key   See **luminance key**.

luminance clamping   The process of clamping (or clipping, or scaling) the luminance value in a video signal. In video that has been luma clamped, luminance values over 235 are eliminated, frequently resulting in video with bright areas that look like solid blobs of white.

luminance key   A special key function that will use the luminance values in a layer to determine the transparency of that layer. For example, a luminance key could be set to render the darkest areas of the layer transparent.

luminance   The strength (or amplitude) of the gray scale (or brightness) portion of a video signal.

lux   A metric measurement of the amount of illumination on a subject. (See also **footcandles**.)

Master shot   A wide shot that contains all of the action in particular scene. Used as the basis for building the scene.

M-JPEG   See **MJPEG**.

MJPEG   A lossy, high-quality CODEC that can deliver full-motion, fullframe video. Almost always requires special compression hardware.

montage   In editing, the process of juxtaposing two shots against each other to arrive at an effect different from what each shot would imply on its own.

motherboard   The main circuit board inside a computer.

motion blur   When an object moves quickly, it will be look blurrier. Individual frames of video or film should show a certain amount of blur around moving objects. Motion blur is usually the result of average shutter speeds (1/60th to 1/125th of a second). Faster shutter speeds will result in less motion blur; slower shutter speeds will result in more. A lack of motion blur will result in stuttery, stroboscopic motion.

MPEG   A lossy, high-quality CODEC. Comes in several flavors. MPEG1 is used for the VCD format, MPEG2 is used for DVD format video. Both flavors are suitable for distribution of full-motion, full-frame video.

ND   See **neutral density**.

negative cutter   The person who physically cuts the film negative to conform to the final cut.

neon light   A light consisting of a glass tube filled with neon gas, which varies in color.

net   A large screen used to decrease the strength of the light falling on the subject, usually used for exterior shoots.

neutral density   A lens filter or lighting gel that tones down brightness without changing the color temperature.

NLE   See **non-linear editing system**.

non-destructive editing   Any form of editing (either video or audio) that leaves your original source material unaltered.

non-linear editing system   A digital editing system that uses a software interface and digitized audio and video stored on a hard drive. An NLE allows for random access, non-linearity, and non-destructive editing.

notch   A special type of audio filter that can eliminate a specific, defined frequency of sound.

NTSC   An acronym for *National Television Standards Committee*, NTSC is the broadcast video standard for North America and Japan, with a frame rate of 29.97 fps and 525 horizontal scan lines.

NTSC legal   Refers to colors that fit within the NTSC guidelines for broadcast television. A vectorscope is used to determine if an image is within the NTSC legal color boundaries.

NTSC Monitor   See **NTSC/PAL monitor**.

NTSC/PAL monitor   The monitor attached to your camera, video deck, or NTSC outputs of your video digitizing system. Used to display the video you are editing.

omnidirectional microphone   A mic that picks up sounds from all directions.

off-line clip   An off-line clip is one that has been logged but does not have any audio or video media attached to it, whether that is because it hasn't been captured yet or because the media has been deleted.

off-line editing   Off-line editing means working in a draft mode with the intention of eventually taking the project to a better resolution and possibly better videotape format in order to do a final pass that will improve its look, quality, and polish.

OIS   See **optical image stabilization**.

one-light print   A one-light print is a film print created from the film negative. A single, constant, optimized light setting (i.e., one light) is used for the red, green, and blue lights used to create the print.

onion-skinning Some animation programs can display semi-opaque overlays of previous frames. These "onion-skin" frames can be used as a reference for drawing or retouching the current frame.

online editing Creation of the final master videotape, whatever the means or format involved, usually conformed from the original production footage using an EDL.

operating system The low-level program that controls the communication between all of the subsystems (storage, memory, video, peripherals, etc.) in your computer.

optical image stabilization A special optical apparatus in a camera that attempts to compensate for shaking and vibrating by altering the camera's optical properties on-the-fly to compensate for camera movement. Because OIS doesn't alter your image data, there is no image degradation.

optical viewfinder On a camera, the eyepiece that you look through to frame a shot, as opposed to the flip-out LCD viewfinder present on some cameras.

opticals Special effects that are traditionally added by an "optical" department. Usually, these are effects that are added through a separate optical printing pass. Lightning bolts, light flares, glows, and halos are all traditional optical effects that can now be performed through rotoscoping, or with the application of custom filters.

out-point The end point of an edit.

overexposure Refers to video or film that was shot with too much light, or the wrong camera settings, resulting in a whitish, washedout, faded-looking image.

overlapping edit An edit where the picture ends before or after the sound ends. Also called an *L-cut* or a *split-edit*.

overscan All video formats scan more image than they need to compensate for the fact that not all monitors and televisions display images at exactly the same size. To keep your action and titles within the visible area, you'll want to pay attention to the action- and titlesafe areas of the screen.

overwrite mode In most NLEs, a method of editing that allows the placement of a shot that covers up anything that was previously occupying that space in the timeline. (See also **insert mode**.)

PAL An acronym for *Phase Alternate by Line*, a television standard used in most of Europe and Asia, with a frame rate of 25 fps and 625 horizontal scan lines, resulting in somewhat higher quality video than NTSC.

PAL Monitor See **NTSC/PAL monitor**.

pan To rotate the camera left and right around the camera's vertical axis.

parabolic A special type of mic that can be used to record sounds from great distances.

patch bay A rack of video and audio input and output connectors that makes it easier to re-configure the hardware in an editing system.

pedestal To raise the camera up or down.

phono connector A medium-sized single-prong connector used primarily for analog audio, especially headphones. Also known as *1/4" connector*.

pistol grip tripod A tripod with a head that is controlled by a single pistol-grip mechanism. Such heads can be freely rotated around all axes simultaneously, making it very difficult to perform a smooth motion along a single axis.

pixel Short for *picture element*. A single point on your screen.

platform The computer hardware/OS combination that you have chosen to work on.

plug-ins Special effects and add-ons that can be added to a host application. (See **filters**.)

polarizer A lens filter that polarizes the light coming into the lens. Can be used to increase saturation and to eliminate reflections in glass or water.

post house See **post-production facility**.

post-production facility   A service bureau that provides editing and other post-production facilities and services.

practical light   A light source that is both part of the scenery and a source of light for the camera.

preroll   The process of rewinding the videotape to a cue point several seconds prior to the in-point, so that playback of the tape is stabilized and up to full speed when the tape reaches the in-point.

prime lens   A lens with fixed focal length.

prism   A special optical construct (usually a single piece of glass) that can split light into its component parts.

production board   A hardbacked set of spreadsheets designed specifically for organizing film production.

production designer   The designer who is responsible for the look of the entire production. Supervises the set decorators, costumes, and other visual artists.

production strip   A removable color-coded paper strip that fits into the spreadsheet layout of the production board and allows for easy re-organization.

progressive scan   A type of video display where each horizontal line is scanned consecutively from top to bottom, resulting in a full frame of video without the need for fields. (Compare to **interlaced scan**.)

prop   Short for *property*, a prop is any object on the set that is used by the actors, such as a knife, as opposed to set dressing and scenery, which provide a backdrop for the action.

proxy   A placeholder. Usually used in editing programs to take the place of video that has yet to be shot, or that has yet to be digitized at the highest quality.

pull focus   Pull (or pulling) focus is a technique used to change focal lengths during a large camera or subject move, such as a dolly. The camera assistant literally moves the lens to compensate for the camera/subject movement so that the subject remains in focus throughout the shot.

QuickTime   A software architecture for displaying and manipulating time-based data (such as video and audio) on a computer.

rack focus   A shot where the focus is set on an object in the background, then the focus is pulled, or racked, to an object in the foreground (or vice versa).

radio cut   An edit of a scene based on dialog only, disregarding whether the picture works or not. The idea being that the result should play like an old-fashioned radio show.

RAID   Redundant Array of Independent Discs. A group of hard drives that have been arranged to act like a single, very fast storage device.

RAM   Random access memory. The electronic memory inside your computer used to hold programs and data when working.

RCA connector   A small, single-prong connector most commonly used to carry composite video and unbalanced audio signals.

reaction   A shot of a person reacting to the dialog or action in the scene.

Real Media   A special streaming video and audio architecture created by Real, Inc.

real-time   A function, such as playback or recording, that occurs immediately without the need for rendering and without any speeding up of the process, such as 4x (quadruple speed) recording.

real-time editing   Editing that can happen in real-time. That is, effects and edits do not have to be calculated or rendered before they can be seen.

reflective light   Light that comes from an indirect source, such as a bounce card, the sky (but not the sun), and so forth. (See *also* **incident light**.)

reflector   A shiny board or fabric used to redirect a bright light source, such as the sun.

RGB color space   The range of colors that can be displayed and recorded by your computer.

room tone   The sound of the room in which a scene was recorded. During a shoot, the sound recorder will record roughly one minute's worth of the quieted location to create an "empty" sound with the right atmosphere. This sound will be used by the dialog editor to fill spaces between edits.

rotoscoping   The process of painting over existing frames of video or film. Used for everything from painting in special effects, to painting custom-made mattes for compositing.

rough cut   An early edit of a project, as opposed to the final cut.

route   An electronic patching system for audio and video equipment.

RS-232   A serial device control protocol that allows for computers to control video decks and other hardware. RS-232 is most commonly used for low-end professional and consumer equipment.

RS-422   A serial device control protocol that allows for computers to control video decks and other hardware. RS-422 is the standard for professional equipment. It carries the SMPTE timecode signal and is capable of frame accuracy.

RT11   A floppy disk format used by high-end linear online editing equipment to store EDLs.

SAG   Acronym for the *Screen Actors' Guild*.

saturated colors   The technical term for bright, bold colors is *saturated*. For example, a pure red is saturated, while pink and maroon are desaturated reds.

saturation   The amount of color in the video signal.

screen correction shot   A shot of a blue-screen or green-screen stage that has no actors in it. Screen correction shots are used by compositing software to help create a more accurate key effect.

scrim   A lighting accessory used to tone down the brightness of a light. Single scrims dim the light by 1/2 f-stop, and double scrims dim the light by a full f-stop. Half scrims are a half-moon shape, to allow for further manipulation of the light.

SCSI IDs   When using SCSI devices, each device on the SCSI chain must have its own, unique SCSI ID. A SCSI port can support up to seven devices.

SCSI   Small Computer Systems Interface. An interface standard for connecting hard drives and other peripherals. Comes in many different flavors, including SCSI-2, Ultra-SCSI, and Ultrawide-SCSI.

SDI   An acronym for *Serial Digital Interface*, SDI is the professional digital video standard I/O protocol with a data rate of either 270 Mbps or 360 Mbps. (See also **FireWire**.)

SDTV   An acronym for *Standard Definition Television*, a subgroup of the DTV broadcast standard designed as a digital update of the current NTSC standard.

seamless edit   A style of editing where the edits appear natural and do not call attention to themselves. A traditional Hollywood movie dialog scene is usually seamlessly edited.

SECAM   An acronym for *Sequence Colour à Memoire*, SECAM is the broadcast television standard for France, Russia, and much of eastern Europe.

sequence   An assembly of shots edited together.

sharpening   In a video camera, a special algorithm that is applied to the video image to make it sharper.

shooting ratio   The ratio of the length of footage shot to the length of the final film. For example, a project with a 5:1 ratio would have shot five hours of footage for a one-hour long final project.

shot list   A list of the shots a director plans to shoot on a particular day of filming or taping. Usually, a shot list is derived by carefully going over the script, the storyboard, and blocking the scene with the actors in rehearsals.

shotgun   A very directional mic that is often affixed to the front of the camera or to a boom or fishpole.

shutter speed   The speed of the rotation of the shutter inside the lens, measured in rotations per second.

shutter   In a camera, a rotating plate that opens and closes to control how long the focal plane is exposed to light. There is no physical shutter in a digital video camera; instead, the camera's CCD samples light for an appropriate length of time, and then shuts off.

sides   A dialog-only version of a script, used to make readings easier for actors.

signal   Electronic information (video or audio) that is passed from one device to another.

single-chip   A camera that uses a single CCD to gather all three (red, green, and blue) of the signals that will be used to create a full-color image.

single-field resolution   Some low-resolution CODECs cut down the size of the captured video files by discarding one field for each frame of video. The resulting single-field video plays fairly well, but contains half the information of two-field video.

sixty-cycle tone   (60 Hz) Sixty-cycle tone, or 60 Hz tone, is used as an audio reference to calibrate the audio levels on editing equipment and speakers. Typically, the 60 Hz tone should fall at 0dB on a VU meter.

skylight   The ambient light from the sky, which consists of the reflected light of the sun. On a cloudy day, there is no sunlight, but there is still skylight.

slating   When recording the sound separately from the video or film, the process of holding a slate in front of the camera. On the slate are written the scene and take numbers. The top of the slate can be clapped to produce a distinct sound that will be used for syncing the audio and video.

slow reveal   A moving shot, often a pan or dolly, that reveals something slowly, such as a slow pan of a bathroom that reveals a dead person in the bathtub.

slow-motion   A shot that plays at a slower speed than full-motion film or video. Usually described as a percentage of full motion.

SLR camera   A single lens reflex camera. Unlike a camera with a separate viewfinder, in an SLR camera, you actually look through the lens at your subject. A 35mm still camera with removable lenses is typically an SLR.

slugline   In a screenplay, the first line of a scene. Identifies whether the scene is interior or exterior, the location, and the time of day, all in uppercase letters.

SMPTE   The Society of Motion Picture and Television Engineers, an organization that has developed many of the technical standards for film and video in the United States, including the specifications for timecode, SMPTE timecode.

snow   The image that results from a video signal that lacks a control track. Also known as *noise*.

soft light   Light from a diffuse, often indirect light source.

Sorenson compressor   A lossy but very high quality QuickTime CODEC.

source monitor   The monitor or window that displays the unedited source footage, as opposed to the destination (or record) monitor, which plays the edited sequence.

SP-DIF   Short for *Sony/Phillips Digital Interface*, a digital audio format used for consumer equipment.

spin rate   Measured in revolutions per minute, the speed at which a hard drive spins.

split-track dialog   Dialog that is spread across several separate tracks, rather than mixed onto a single track. Usually, split track dialog has one track dedicated to each actor, or if the dialog is checkerboarded, two tracks dedicated to each actor.

spot meter   A type of light meter that measures reflective light rather than incident light.

spotting   Watching a locked-picture edit of your project with the intent of identifying all of the sound effect and music cues that will be needed.

Steadicam   A special camera mount that provides hydraulic, gimbaled support for a camera. Allows steady, fluid motion of the camera.

storage   Non-volatile storage that is used for long-term holding of programs and data. Usually magnetic or optical.

streaming video   Video that is downloaded, on-demand, interactively, to the viewer's computer.

striped drives   Hard drives that have been indexed with special information so that they can be used as an array.

strobing   The odd, stuttery motion caused by fast shutter speeds. Strobing appears because of a lack of motion blur.

sunlight   The light from the sun.

super   To superimpose. Usually used to refer to the process of superimposing a title over an image.

supercardioid   A very narrow cardioid pattern that indicates that a mic is very directional.

S-video   See **Y/C video**.

S-video connector   A proprietary cable that used to carry the Y/C video signal.

sweetening   The process of polishing the audio on a project by adding effects, equalizing and fine-tuning edits.

switcher   See **router**.

sync   Short for *synchronization*, the electronic pulses used to coordinate the operation of several interconnected pieces of video hardware. Also, the electronic pulses used to regulate the playback of the videotape in the VTR. (See also **sync sound**.)

sync sound   Recorded sound and video that are synchronized together, whether onto the same tape or by two or more separate recording devices.

TBC   Acronym for *time base corrector*, an electronic device used to correct video signal instability during videotape playback. Most modern professional VTRs have internal TBCs.

telecine   The process of transferring film to videotape.

telephoto lens   A lens with a very narrow field of view (and, therefore, a long focal length). Telephoto lenses magnify objects in their field of view. Typically, lenses with focal lengths greater than 70 mm (equivalent to a 35mm film camera) are considered wide angle.

termination   A connector used at the end of a SCSI chain. The last device in a SCSI chain must have a terminator. Bad termination can result in the entire SCSI chain malfunctioning.

textless master   A videotape master that has no titles or any other text in it. Used for foreign language versions.

three-chip   A camera that uses three separate CCDs to gather separate red, green, and blue data.

three-point editing   A method of editing where each edit is performed using an in- and an out-point on both the source footage and the edited sequence. Once the editor enters three of the four in- and out-points, the NLE or edit controller will automatically calculate the fourth in- and out-point.

three-point lighting   The standard way to light a person using a strong directed key light, a diffuse, less intense fill light, and a strong backlight.

throughput   A measure of the speed at which data can be moved through a computer or storage system.

tilt   To rotate the camera up and down around its horizontal axis.

timecode   Timecode is a numbering system encoded in the video tape itself. It measures time in the following format: hh:mm:ss:ff, where h= hours, m=minutes, s=seconds, and f=frames.

timeline   A chronological display of an edited sequence in a non-linear editing system.

title safe   Another guide similar to the action-safe area, the title-safe area is slightly smaller. To ensure that your titles are visible on any monitor, always make certain that they fall within the title-safe area.

transcoder   A device that changes the video signal from one format to another, such as from component to composite or from analog to digital.

transfer mode   The type of calculation that will be used to determine how layers that are stacked on top of one another will combine.

travelling matte   A matte (see **matte**) that changes over time to follow the action of a moving element. Travelling mattes are used to composite a moving element into a scene. In the digital world, an animated alpha channel serves the same function as a travelling matte.

trim mode   The process of adjusting, or fine-tuning an existing edit in an NLE.

tungsten light   Light from an incandescent source, such as a household light bulb. Tungsten light is weaker than daylight, and tends to have a warm cast.

turnkey system   A video editing system that is preconfigured and assembled.

tweening See **inbetweening**.

UltraATA   A type of hard drive interface. Not as fast as SCSI, but fast enough for DV.

ultraviolet   The area beyond violet on the color spectrum, beyond the range of visible light.

uncompressed video   Video that has not had any compression applied to it, either by the camera or by a computer.

underscan   A display feature available on professional video monitors that allows the viewer to see the complete video signal, including the sync pulses.

unidirectional   A mic that picks up sounds from a particular direction.

USB   Universal Serial Bus. A standard for attaching serial devices such as keyboards, disk drives, and some types of storage. USB devices can also be used to digitize Web-resolution video clips.

UV filter   A filter that can be attached to the front of the lens. Filters out excess ultraviolet light and serves to protect the lens from scratching and breaking.

vacuum tubes   Before the invention of the CCD, video cameras used vacuum tubes to convert light into electronic signals.

VCD   Video compact disc. A format for storing 70 minutes of full-frame, full-motion, MPEG1 compressed video on a normal compact disc or recordable compact disc.

vectorscope   A special monitor for calibrating the hue, or color information, in a video signal.

vertical banding   Bright vertical smears that can occur in some video cameras when the camera is pointed at a very bright source.

vertical blanking interval   The period during which the video image goes blank as the electron beam returns from scanning one field of interlaced video to start scanning the next field. This "empty" space in the video signal is sometimes used to store VITC timecode, closedcaptioning, and other information.

vertical delay   A display feature available on professional video monitors that shows the video signal offset vertically so as to allow the editor to see and analyze the vertical sync pulses. (See also **horizontal delay**.)

vertical line resolution   The number of horizontal lines in a frame of video.

vertical sync The sync pulses in the video signal that control the fieldby-field scanning of each frame of interlaced video.

VGA monitor The monitor attached to your computer.

Video for Windows A software architecture for displaying and manipulating time-based data (such as video and audio) on a computer.

virtual memory A process by which disk space can be used as a substitute for RAM.

VITC Vertical Interleave Timecode, timecode that is encoded in the vertical blanking interval of the video signal.

VTR Video tape recorder, the professional term for VCR.

VU meter Volume unit meter. The volume meters on a sound recording device. VU meters help you gauge whether you are recording acceptable audio levels.

wattage A measurement of the amount of electrical power used by a light, which determines the light's intensity.

waveform monitor A special monitor for calibrating the brightness, or luminance, of a video signal. Waveform monitors are used to set the proper white and black levels.

white balance When a camera has been calibrated to correctly display white, then the camera is white balanced. Once it is calibrated for white, other colors should display properly.

white level The peak level of the luminance (or gray scale) of the video signal; in other words, the brightest part of the image, usually set at 100 IRE.

wide angle lens A lens with a very wide field of view (and, therefore, a short focal length). Typically, the smaller the focal length of the lens (measured in millimeters), the wider the angle.

widescreen Footage that's shot with a special anamorphic lens that squeezes a 16:9 image onto a regular frame of video. Requires a special monitor to play back the image at full size and correct aspect ratio. Most film features are shot in a widescreen aspect ratio.

wild sounds Non-sync sounds recorded by hand "in the wild" using a portable recording system.

wipe A type of transition where one image is wiped over another.

XLR cable See **XLR connector**.

XLR connectors Three-pronged, balanced audio connectors for connecting mics and other recording equipment.

INDEX